PENGUIN BOOKS

PUSHCART PRIZE, XII

The Pushcart Prize series has been awarded *Publishers Weekly's* Carey-Thomas Award for distinguished publishing and editions have been named Outstanding Book of the Year by *The New York Times Book Review*.

Abby Taylor

THE PUSHCART PRIZE XII:

BEST OF THE SMALL PRESSES

BEST OF THE SMALL PRESSES

. . . WITH AN INDEX TO THE FIRST TWELVE VOLUMES

An annual small press reader

EDITED BY BILL HENDERSON

with The Pushcart Prize editors

Introduction by Frank Conroy

Poetry Editors: Jorie Graham, Robert Hass

PENGUIN BOOKS

THE PUSHCART PRIZE, XII:

PENGUIN BOOKS
Published by the Penguin Group
Viking Penguin Inc., 40 West 23rd Street,
New York, New York 10010, U.S.A.
Penguin Books Ltd, 27 Wrights Lane,
London W8 5TZ, England
Penguin Books Australia Ltd, Ringwood,
Victoria, Australia
Penguin Books Canada Ltd, 2801 John Street,
Markham, Ontario, Canada L3R 1B4
Penguin Books (N.Z.) Ltd, 182–190 Wairau Road,
Auckland 10, New Zealand

Penguin Books Ltd, Registered Offices:
Harmondsworth, Middlesex, England

First published in the United States of America by
Pushcart Press 1987
Published in Penguin Books 1988

Note: nominations for this series are invited from any small, independent,
literary book press or magazine in the world. Up to six nominations—tear
sheets or copies selected from work published in the calendar year—are
accepted by our October 15 deadline each year. Write to Pushcart Press, P.O.
Box 380, Wainscott, N.Y. 11975 if you need more information.

Pushcart Press sends special thanks to The Helen Foundation of Salt Lake
City for its generous awards to the authors of our lead short story, poem, and
essay.

(CIP data available)
ISBN 0 14 00.9470 9
ISSN 0149-7863

Printed in the United States of America by
R. R. Donnelley & Sons Company, Harrisonburg, Virginia
Set in Caledonia

Acknowledgments

The following works are reprinted by permission of the author and publisher.

"The Ghost of Sandburg's Phizzog" © 1986 Ellis Press, StoryQuarterly
"Mr. Goldbaum" © 1986 Raritan: A Quarterly Review
"Duppy Get Her" © 1986 Kelsey Street Press
"My Father's Moon" © 1986 Grand Street
"Beautiful" © 1986 Ploughshares
"One of Two" © 1986 New Letters
"Shamsky and Other Casualties" © 1986 Iowa Review
"The Place In Flowers Where Pollen Rests" © 1986 Conjunctions
"On The Meaning of Life" © 1986 Hermitage Press and © 1986 Irina Ratushinskaia
"An Embarrassment of Ordinary Riches" © 1986 New England Review/Bread Loaf Quarterly
"A Red Sweater" © 1986 The American Voice
"Persian Lamb" © 1986 Curbstone Press
"The Lover of Horses" © 1986 Zyzzyva, Harper and Row Inc.
"Yukon" © 1986 TriQuarterly
"The Birthing" © 1986 Graywolf Press
"Jack of Diamonds" © 1986 Kenyon Review
"Paper Tigers" © 1986 Sulfur
"Against Nature" © 1986 Antaeus
"Some Snapshots from The Soviet Union" © 1986 Kenyon Review
"The Secret Sharer" © 1986 Ploughshares
"Her Secrets" © 1986 Threepenny Review
"Against Joie de Vivre" © 1986 Ploughshares
"A Tree, A Streamlined Fish, and A Self-Squared Dragon: Science As A Form of Culture" © 1986 The Georgia Review
"The Impact of Translation" © 1986 Yale Review
"Poland of Death" © 1986 New Directions
"that they were at the beach: aeolotropic series" © 1986 American Poetry Review
"Le Petit Salvié" © 1986 Paris Review
"A Crowded Table" © 1986 Zyzzyva
"Simple Questions" © 1986 Shenandoah
"Querencia" © 1986 Poetry
"A Sketch of the Great Dejection" © 1986 Threepenny Review
"World With A Hard K" © 1986 Temblor
"Unattainable Earth" © 1986 Ecco Press
"Oyster Bar on the Road to Mururua" © 1986 Ploughshares
"Four from the Baudelaire series" © 1986 Acts
"from The Person" © 1986 Sulfur
"Walking In The 15th Century" © 1986 Threepenny Review
"Bela" © 1986 American Poetry Review
"At P. C. Sergeant's House" © 1986 Laughing Waters Press
"Short Day" © 1986 American Poetry Review
"The Promise of Light" © 1986 Georgia Review
"Psalm and Lament © 1986 The New Criterion
"Viewing the Coast" © 1986 Grand Street
"The Alias: A Survey" © 1986 Indiana Review
"His Funny Valentine" © 1986 Hudson Review
"Shrubs Burned Away" © 1986 Kenyon Review
"The Underground" © 1986 Another Chicago Magazine
"Unwritten Laws" © 1986 BOA Editions Ltd.
"The Imagination of Flowers" © 1986 Field
"Lament for the Makers" © 1986 Paris Review
"Eve" © 1986 American Poetry Review
"Heliopathy" © 1986 Temblor

This book is for
Meg Charlton

THE
PEOPLE WHO HELPED

FOUNDING EDITORS—*Anaïs Nin (1903-1977), Buckminster Fuller (1895-1983), Charles Newman, Daniel Halpern, Gordon Lish, Harry Smith, Hugh Fox, Ishmael Reed, Joyce Carol Oates, Len Fulton, Leonard Randolph, Leslie Fiedler, Nona Balakian, Paul Bowles, Paul Engle, Ralph Ellison, Reynolds Price, Rhoda Schwartz, Richard Morris, Ted Wilentz, Tom Montag, William Phillips. Poetry editor: H. L. Van Brunt.*

EDITORS—*Walter Abish, Ai, Elliott Anderson, John Ashbery, Russell Banks, Robert Bly, Robert Boyers, Harold Brodkey, Joseph Brodsky, Wesley Brown, Hayden Carruth, Raymond Carver, Frank Conroy, Malcolm Cowley, Paula Deitz, Steve Dixon, Andre Dubus, M. D. Elevitch, Loris Essary, Ellen Ferber, Carolyn Forché, Stuart Freibert, Jon Galassi, Tess Gallagher, Louis Gallo, George Garrett, Jack Gilbert, Reginald Gibbons, Louise Glück, David Godine, Jorie Graham, Linda Gregg, Barbara Grossman, Donald Hall, Michael Harper, Robert Hass, DeWitt Henry, J. R. Humphreys, David Ignatow, John Irving, June Jordan, Edmund Keeley, Karen Kennerly, Galway Kinnell, Carolyn Kizer, Jerzy Kosinski, Richard Kostelanetz, Seymour Krim, Maxine Kumin, Stanley Kunitz, James Laughlin, Seymour Lawrence, Naomi Lazard, Herb Leibowitz, Denise Levertov, Philip Levine, Stanley Lindberg, Thomas Lux, Mary MacArthur, Thomas McGrath, Daniel Menaker, Frederick Morgan, Howard Moss, Cynthia Ozick, Jayne Anne Phillips, Robert Phillips, George Plimpton, Stanley Plumly, Eugene Redmond, Ed Sanders, Teo Savory, Grace Schulman, Harvey Shapiro, Leslie Silko, Charles Simic, Dave Smith, William Stafford, Gerald Stern, David St. John, Bill and Pat Strachan, Ron Sukenick, Anne Tyler, John Updike, Sam Vaughan, David Wagoner, Derek Walcott, Ellen Wilbur, David Wilk, David Wojahn, Bill Zavatsky.*

CONTRIBUTING EDITORS FOR THIS EDITION—*Lee K. Abbott, John Allman, Philip Appleman, James Atlas, Bo Ball, Jim Barnes, Bar-*

bara Bedway, Linda Bierds, Michael Blumenthal, Philip Booth, Christopher Buckley, Frederick Busch, Michael Dennis Browne, Henry Carlile, Kelly Cherry, Naomi Clark, Peter Cooley, Douglas Crase, Philip Dacey, John Daniel, Susan Strayer Deal, Terrence Des Pres, Mark Doty, Rita Dove, John Drury, Stuart Dybek, Louise Erdrich, Jane Flanders, Michael Finley, Richard Ford, H. E. Francis, Ken Gangemi, Gary Gildner, Patricia Goedicke, Barry Goldensohn, Patrick Worth Gray, John Haines, James Baker Hall, Don Hendrie Jr., Amy Hempel, Brenda Hillman, Edward Hirsch, Linda Hogan, Garrett Kaoru Hongo, Mary Hood, Andrew Hudgins, Lynda Hull, Colette Inez, Elizabeth Inness-Brown, Josephine Jacobsen, Laura Jensen, August Kleinzahler, Dorianne Laux, Li-Young Lee, Gerry Locklin, D. R. MacDonald, David Madden, Dan Masterson, Cleopatra Mathis, William Matthews, Robert McBrearty, Joe-Anne McLaughlin, Wesley McNair, Sandra McPherson, Barbara Milton, Susan Mitchell, Mary Morris, Lisel Mueller, Joan Murray, Naomi Shihab Nye, Jonathan Penner, Lucia Perillo, Mary Peterson, Joe Ashby Porter, Tony Quagliano, Bin Ramke, Donald Revell, William Pitt Root, Pattiann Rogers, Vern Rutsala, Michael Ryan, Sherod Santos, Lynne Sharon Schwartz, Bob Shacochis, Jim Simmerman, Mona Simpson, Tom Sleigh, Arthur Smith, Ted Solotaroff, Elizabeth Spires, Ann Stanford, Maura Stanton, Pamela Stewart, Mary Tallmountain, Eleanor Ross Taylor, Barbara Thompson, Sara Vogan, Marilyn Waniek, Michael Waters, Gordon Weaver, Bruce Weigl, Eliot Weinberger, Harold Witt, Christine Zawadiwsky, Pat Zelver.

DESIGN AND PRODUCTION—*Ray Freiman*

EUROPEAN EDITORS—*Kirby and Liz Williams, Lily Frances*

MANAGING EDITOR—*Hannah Turner*

ROVING EDITOR—*Helen Handley*

ASSOCIATE EDITOR—*Timothy Clark*

FICTION EDITOR—*Genie D. Chipps*

ESSAYS EDITOR—*Anthony Brandt*

POETRY EDITORS—*Jorie Graham, Robert Hass*

EDITOR AND PUBLISHER—*Bill Henderson*

PRESSES FEATURED IN THE PUSHCART PRIZE EDITIONS

Acts
Agni Review
Ahsahta Press
Ailanthus Press
Alcheringa/Ethnopoetics
Alice James Books
Amelia
American Literature
American PEN
American Poetry Review
The American Voice
Amnesty International
Anaesthesia Review
Another Chicago Magazine
Antaeus
Antioch Review
Apalachee Quarterly
Aphra
The Ark
Ascent
Aspen Leaves
Aspen Poetry Anthology
Assembling
Barlenmir House
Barnwood Press
The Bellingham Review
Beloit Poetry Journal

Bennington Review
Bilingual Review
Black American Literature Forum
Black Rooster
Black Scholar
Black Sparrow
Black Warrior Review
Blackwells Press
Bloomsbury Review
Blue Cloud Quarterly
Blue Wind Press
Bluefish
BOA Editions
Bookslinger Editions
Boxspring
Brown Journal of the Arts
Burning Deck Press
Caliban
California Quarterly
Calliopea Press
Canto
Capra Press
Cedar Rock
Center
Chariton Review
Charnel House
Chelsea

Chicago Review
Chouteau Review
Chowder Review
Cimarron Review
Cincinnati Poetry Review
City Lights Books
Clown War
CoEvolution Quarterly
Cold Mountain Press
Columbia: A Magazine of Poetry
    and Prose
Confluence Press
Confrontation
Conjunctions
Copper Canyon Press
Cosmic Information Agency
Crawl Out Your Window
Crazy Horse
Crescent Review
Cross Cultural Communications
Cross Currents
Cumberland Poetry Review
Curbstone Press
Cutbank
Dacotah Territory
Daedalus
Decatur House
December
Dragon Gate Inc.
Domestic Crude
Dreamworks
Dryad Press
Duck Down Press
Durak
East River Anthology
Ellis Press
Empty Bowl
Epoch
Fiction
Fiction Collective
Fiction International
Field
Firelands Art Review

Five Fingers Review
Five Trees Press
Frontiers: A Journal of Women
    Studies
Gallimaufry
Genre
The Georgia Review
Ghost Dance
Goddard Journal
David Godine, Publisher
Graham House Press
Grand Street
Granta
Graywolf Press
Greenfield Review
Greensboro Review
Guardian Press
Hard Pressed
Hermitage Press
Hills
Holmgangers Press
Holy Cow!
Home Planet News
Hudson Review
Icarus
Iguana Press
Indiana Review
Indiana Writes
Intermedia
Intro
Invisible City
Inwood Press
Iowa Review
Ironwood
Jam To-day
The Kanchenjuga Press
Kansas Quarterly
Kayak
Kelsey Street Press
Kenyon Review
Latitudes Press
Laughing Waters Press
L'Epervier Press

Liberation
Linquis
The Little Magazine
Living Hand Press
Living Poets Press
Logbridge-Rhodes
Lowlands Review
Lucille
Lynx House Press
Magic Circle Press
Malahat Review
Manroot
Massachusetts Review
Mho & Mho Works
Micah Publications
Michigan Quarterly
Milk Quarterly
The Minnesota Review
Mississippi Review
Missouri Review
Montana Gothic
Montana Review
Montemora
Mr. Cogito Press
MSS
Mulch Press
Nada Press
New America
The New Criterion
New Directions
New England Review and Bread
    Loaf Quarterly
New Letters
North American Review
North Atlantic Books
North Point Press
Northwest Review
O. ARS
Obsidian
Oconee Review
October
Ohio Review
Ontario Review

Open Places
Orca Press
Oyez Press
Painted Bride Quarterly
Paris Review
Parnassus: Poetry In Review
Partisan Review
Penca Books
Pentagram
Penumbra Press
Pequod
Persea: An International Review
Pipedream Press
Pitcairn Press
Ploughshares
Poet and Critic
Poetry
Poetry Northwest
Poetry Now
Prairie Schooner
Prescott Street Press
Promise of Learnings
Quarry West
Quarterly West
Rainbow Press
Raritan: A Quarterly Review
Red Cedar Review
Red Clay Books
Red Dust Press
Red Earth Press
Release Press
Revista Chicano-Riquena
River Styx
Rowan Tree Press
Russian *Samizdat*
Salmagundi
San Marcos Press
Sea Pen Press and Paper Mill
Seal Press
Seamark Press
Seattle Review
Second Coming Press
The Seventies Press

Sewanee Review
Shankpainter
Shantih
Shenandoah
A Shout In The Street
Sibyl-Child Press
Small Moon
The Smith
Some
The Sonora Review
Southern Poetry Review
Southern Review
Southwestern Review
Spectrum
The Spirit That Moves Us
St. Andrews Press
Story Quarterly
Stuart Wright, Publisher
Sulfur
Sun & Moon Press
Sun Press
Sunstone
Tar River Poetry
Telephone Books
Telescope
Temblor
Tendril
Texas Slough
13th Moon
THIS
Thorp Springs Press
Three Rivers Press

Threepenny Review
Thunder City Press
Thunder's Mouth Press
Toothpaste Press
Transatlantic Review
TriQuarterly
Truck Press
Tuumba Press
Undine
Unicorn Press
University of Pittsburgh Press
Unmuzzled Ox
Unspeakable Visions of the
    Individual
Vagabond
Virginia Quarterly
Wampeter Press
Washington Writers Workshop
Water Table
Western Humanities Review
Westigan Review
Wickwire Press
Wilmore City
Word Beat Press
Word-Smith
Wormwood Review
Writers Forum
Xanadu
Yale Review
Yardbird Reader
Y'Bird
ZYZZYVA

CONTENTS

INTRODUCTION

by FRANK CONROY

DURING THE twelve years that the Pushcart Prize series has been in existence, many observers have noted a narrowing down of literary activity in the commercial arena, and an opening up in the small presses and lit mags. This has happened despite the best efforts of many good people in the commercial world to hold up their end. After almost five years of observing the scene from my former post at the Literature Program of the National Endowment for the Arts, I can offer only the not very surprising theory that the narrowing down has occurred because of changing economic forces far too large to be controlled by even the major players in publishing. The opening up is a movement into an under-served market as well as an act of faith carried out, for the most part, by dedicated people who believe in literature and its future. Of course, the independent presses have always been an important part of American literary life, (see Cynthia Ozick's intro to Pushcart XI), but it seems they are destined to play a progressively larger role, culturally speaking.

While Pushcart Press has survived without grants, most of the publications who initially printed the work which appears in Pushcart are, or have been, grantees of the NEA. Quite a few of them would have a hard time operating without these modest grants, and it is precisely that, in combination with the implications of the greater responsibility which lies before them, which moves me to sound a modest note of warning. Gains made under present relatively favorable conditions must be consolidated in such a way as to reduce future dependency on the NEA, if not to escape it altogether. This will not be possible for everybody, but the stronger organizations should make contingency plans.

Why? Do I anticipate an end to the category of support for Literary Publication? No, I do not. That seems to me an extremely remote possibility, and no one is calling for it. But there are signs that increasing pressure will be brought to bear, from a few members of the National Council on the Arts, the NEA's advisory board, to "do something" about the Literature Program, by which I understand them to mean a general shift towards conservative values.

Remember that the NEA is primarily concerned with the performing arts, and that literature is a small program of no particular interest to most of the people on the Council. In the past the program had been left more or less to its own devices. Toni Morrison, while a member of the Council, kept a steady, independent, and basically protective watch, but her term has expired. Buddy Jacobs, another friend to literature and protector of independence for all programs, is also gone. The active members in matters literary at the moment are relatively recent appointees— Allan Drury, who has consistently supported the program, albeit quietly, and Samuel Lipman and Joseph Epstein, voluble conservatives with such a marked animus to contemporary American literature (don't take my word for it; read them!) that it would appear their agenda is not to support it, but to change it. They are genuinely and deeply distressed by what they perceive to be the situation in American letters, and seem to be intent on a cure without benefit of a consensus on the nature of the disease. Their legal power is of course limited to advice to the Chairman of the NEA, but Mr. Lipman in particular is an extremely energetic and tenacious man who routinely takes up almost as much speaking time in any given Council meeting as all the other members put together, and who is, as well, highly active behind the scenes. On at least one occasion, he personally interviewed a new Program Director before appointment—which may well have been a characteristically intelligent political move on the part of the Chairman, but remains an indicator of Lippman's activist posture.

Remember also that the Literature Program, by the very nature of the art forms it supports, is particularly vulnerable to attack. In his delicious intro to *Pushcart Prize X*, George Plimpton described the famous Allen Ginsberg Vaseline Jar flap. During my time at the NEA a down-home Congressman from Texas, hot on the trail of degeneracy, sent some clean-cut (and actually quite pleasant) young people from his staff to my office to go through the files of poetry fellowship winners. "This stuff don't rhyme", one of them remarked to me. When I asked what their instructions were, another one answered "We're supposed to find dirty words. Sex words, and like that." Despite days of reading, and many pages carried back for the Congressman's perusal, they apparently couldn't find anything horrendous enough. The Congressman changed his tactics. Using a flashy, trashy article from a right-wing magazine as his source, he picked some controversial names from past winners of poetry fellowships, took lines and sections out of context from work done over their whole careers, (none of which work was ever part of a fellowship application, or was written during the period of support) and waved his peculiar anthology around in the air during the vote on the NEA budget in the House of Representatives, claiming the taxpayer's money was going to support "filth". We can laugh, certainly, but the fact is this crude, dishonest tactic resulted in a substantial cut in the budget of the entire agency. Thousands of artists in many different genres were affected. (A pyrrhic victory for the Congressman, however, who went home to read the startling news in the local paper that the state of Texas had for years gotten much more money back from the NEA than it had contributed to it through taxes, and what on earth did he think he was doing, etc.) Literature will almost always be the first target of the ignorant. In their minds, nude ballet, for example, although suspicious, might possibly be art, whatever art is, but a poem with the word fuck in it is self-evident filth. In order to hold the line against bozos from all quarters the Chairman needs the enthusiastic support and prestige of the presidentially appointed Council. With regard to literature, because of Lipman and Epstein's animus towards current writing, (entirely unrelated to the animus of the bozos, by the way—rather springing from intellectual conviction), it remains to be seen whether he'll get it.

As well, beyond the question of the players of the moment lies the possibility that the Endowment, more or less as a function of its age, will continue to move towards large institutional grants and away from the kinds of small grants which most benefit the small presses. There are political pressures to be considered, and it is a fact that younger agencies tend to be considerably more volatile in terms of policy than older ones. It is both heartening and amazing to consider the very wide range of literary publishing that has been supported by the NEA in the past, and we can hope that this happy arrangement will continue. Perhaps it will, but it would be foolhardy to count on it.

The *Pushcart Prize* Series is fed by, and attests to, the vigor and excellence of independent literary publishing in this country. Particularly in the area of variety, the small presses have become indispensable. It is there that we come across the fresh essay on an unexpected topic, or the short story the author felt compelled to write for his or her own aesthetic reasons, or the poem that experiments with language itself. Bill Henderson has been accused of publishing well-known writers, (as if there were some special sin in that), but the fact is that even well-known writers often find it difficult to publish some of their most interesting work in the commercial arena. More and more, they go to the lit mags and small presses. In this issue of *The Pushcart Prize*, for instance, we find important work by Rosellen Brown (*New Letters*), Joyce Carol Oates (*Antaeus*), William Gass (*Kenyon Review*) and Paul West (*Conjunctions*).

It is also a truism that most of our new writers first publish in small presses. You will find a host of arriving writers in PPXII: Martha Bergland, Norbert Blei, Patricia Henley, Fae Myenne Ng and Opal Palmer Adisa to name but a few. As in past years, many of the presses are reprinted here for the first time also. The preceding list of more than 275 presses that have appeared in this series attests to the continuing democracy in Pushcart's selection.

Known writers, new writers, presses both established and obscure, Henderson prints them all, which is as it should be.

Pushcart Prize XII contains a wide, rich selection and I invite you to join the celebration by turning the page.

THE
PUSHCART PRIZE XII:
BEST OF THE
SMALL PRESSES

SHAMSKY AND OTHER CASUALTIES

fiction by ROBERT COHEN

from THE IOWA REVIEW

AFTER THE EVENING NEWS, I have a long talk with my seven year old boy. He wishes to understand why I, or any adult person for that matter, would willingly subject myself to half an hour of something which provokes in me the sort of behavior one normally associates with middle linebackers and the criminally insane. He is a cheerful, sharp-nosed little boy, with the olive skin and dark forceful eyes of a Mediterranean prince. These he gets from his mother. From me he gets his curiosity, his temper, and what pass for his values. "Why are you so mad at the President, Jack?" he asks in a reasonable tone. "What'd he do that was so bad?"

And so I explain to my son, with carefully chosen phrases and emphatic gestures, all about unemployment and militarism and humorless fanatical moralists running roughshod over a vacuous electorate. "*Really?* He did all those things? Somebody should shoot him!" (He has also inherited from me a melodramatic naiveté much more suited to his age than mine.) "But how come they can do all that stuff? Can't someone stop it?"

"I don't know, sport. Maybe in time *you* will." I kiss him on the forehead. His face brightens. "Now, get out of here, go play with your friends."

"Right, Jack." He rushes off, pulling on a grey sweatshirt.

"Wait a minute, sport. What *aren't* you going to do this evening?" I ask this in a school-marmish tone that makes even me wince.

His sweatshirt tangled thickly around his neck, my son responds matter-of-factly. "Kill birds with rocks." Several months ago, encouraged by his pals, he threw a small rock at one of the local bluejays, which consequently died.

"Why won't you?"

"Because I'm not a fash-hist!" he declares, racing out the door. I am satisfied with him, with myself, and even—now that the news is over—with the world at large. I am thirty-eight years old. I live in the hills of Oakland and work in the private sector. I am trying to be a good provider. I undertake minor chores around the house— fix appliances, tighten bolts, replace worn washers, fight innumerable small battles against domestic decay. It is not such a bad life. I have adjusted, seven o'clock rages notwithstanding, to the times.

And yet, maybe I haven't. For often, on summer nights like this, as I gaze off into a sunset already half-obscured by the eastward-creeping Pacific fog, my thoughts jerk restlessly backwards—or perhaps only sideways—and I find myself eulogizing, to no one in particular, the fallen Shamsky, the finest canvasser ever to ring a stranger's doorbell.

The first I heard about it was back near the beginning of March. It was evening, dishes were rattling in the kitchen, and I was going over some reports for a client I didn't like. Sylvie appeared at the door of the study, twisting the dishtowel in her hands into a tight knot. She cleared her throat. "Telephone," she said.

"Well, who is it?" I asked this even as I picked up the receiver, which, to tell you the truth, I hadn't noticed ringing. I'm a fairly intense concentrator, or so Sylvie—who hadn't moved from the doorway—likes to tell me. "Yeah?"

"Jack, it's me." The familiar absurdity of this understatement pinched me right in the heart. I glanced quickly towards the doorway.

"Hello, Girlfriend," I said, my voice shaking just a little. "What can I do you?"

"Listen Jack, I think maybe you should come over here." Her firm tone belied the 'maybe.' "Something's wrong with Shamsky. *Very* wrong—I mean he's like a corpse or something. That's why I'm calling."

4

"What does she want?" Sylvie asked.

I put my hand over the receiver. Just for the hell of it, I told her the truth.

"I'll *bet* she wants you to come over!"

"Jack? Are you there? Have you heard me?"

"I heard you. Listen, he's probably just hung over or something. Probably nothing to it."

"Jack, don't be stupid. He doesn't drink."

This was true, in fact. Shamsky wasn't a drinker. Never even *tasted* the stuff, not even during this past spring, when everything got so bleak. Not that I didn't urge him to. In my opinion, which used to be worth something around here, it would have helped matters somewhat. "Well then, maybe he's sick. What are his symptoms?"

Girlfriend snorted impatiently. "Symptoms? Symptoms! How about total inertia. How about not saying a word to me or anybody else for three weeks. How about cancelling all the magazine subscriptions. You want to read hate mail? You should see what they're writing him, Jack."

"What who writes him?"

"You know, *Nation, Partisan, Mother Jones.* Also *Commentary, National Review, Dissent;* you name it, everybody up to and including *Sports Illustrated.* The Right is more conscientious, of course, but the Left can be very nasty. *The Militant* threatens reprisals. And it doesn't even faze him. All of a sudden he's too busy watching the Flintstones to take notice. Jack," she said, her voice pitched high with emotion, "I wouldn't call you if it wasn't serious. Come on over, okay? He listens to you."

"But Girlfriend," I protested, watching Sylvie squeeze the life out of the dishtowel, "he *hates* me. We haven't said two words since Saigon fell. Besides, I've got work to do. My boss thinks I'm a goof-off as it is."

Sylvie nodded soberly, adding to the consensus. She smiled without warmth. I could hear the distant cries of boys down the street as robins, woodpeckers and bluejays ducked for cover.

"Jack, I'm not going to beg for christ's sake," she said, hanging up.

"Hmmm," I said, to fill the ensuing silence.

Sylvie, a pretty intelligent woman, said nothing, eyeing me carefully. She holds an inconsistent belief in avoiding unpleasant

5

subjects. I say inconsistent because she herself doesn't really practice it, though she urges it on others. Me for instance.

But at work the next morning, instead of settling down to client files, I pushed back from my desk and reflected on what might be wrong with Shamsky. Health? He had the figure of a Michelangelo statue, no vices, a vegetarian diet, and a jogging regimen like an Olympic runner. No, not health. And not money, either. Girlfriend had some inheritance, and the two of them lived like monks.

Girlfriend. She hadn't always been an unpleasant subject. It was the night of Nixon's resignation, the Sebastiani flowed freely, and we, the staff of United Citizens in Action (UCA), had given ourselves over to boisterous singing, drunken boasting, and, in the spirit of shackles newly-broken, erotic byplay. In the outer office, Perlmutter danced a lewd tango with Fat Maxine. Bando had Rhonda backed against the filing cabinet and was running through his Elmer Fudd impression. Levine walked around in one of his party depressions, acting surly and quoting Mao. The Sony was belting out some Santana, and a lot of people were coming in off the street, attracted by the noise, the high spirits, and the prospect of a free drink or two. Hickey, who had just announced his *own* resignation (he was leaving to farm melons, or it may have been scallions, in Arcata) led us all in a number of mock-formal toasts: to Sam Ervin, to the Plumbers (this conducted in Spanish), to the L.A. Rams. Bando countered with toasts to Grace Slick, Jerry Lewis, and the Oakland Raiders. Several of the crashers ventured their own tributes, most of them well to the left of coherent. By midnight we had thanked both houses of Congress, most of the National Football League, assorted celebrities, and the closest relatives of practically everyone in the room, and even Levine was beginning to smile. Girlfriend, chipper in her green fatigues and peasant blouse, cheeks flushed and glasses steamed with our victory, came up from behind and hugged me around the waist. "Where's our boy?" I asked, leaning back against the warm comfort of her upper body. But I knew where. Convinced that it was, as he called it, "the best, the consummate night for a canvass," Shamsky was hoofing it door-to-door a half-mile away—striking while the iron was hot, as I'd taught him. Behind me Girlfriend swayed to the music, her hands resting knowledgably around my stomach. "Y'know, I miss you sometimes, Jack," she said like a purr. Before I

6

could reply, Levine skulked by, nibbling a brownie. "Be aggressive, not retiring," he lectured. "Prepare the way to Heaven." Alice passed around a pipe full of Lebanese hash. Girlfriend and I both took a little, then stood looking at each other almost sheepishly.

The result was a glorious night in the Emeryville Holiday Inn. You can read about it in Girlfriend's article, "Adultery and the Left: The Dialectics of Liberation," published in *Seven Days* a few years back. That's where Sylvie read it. I'm not sure *when* Shamsky heard, or from whom, but the day before Saigon fell he charged into the office with two Saturday Night Specials from the corner pawn shop and challenged me to—that's right—a duel. "We'll have to hunt up some bullets," he said apologetically. "They were out of them down there."

Of course I talked him out of it. I wasn't his mentor for nothing. But it was our last conversation.

I finally put Girlfriend's distressed phone call out of my mind and busied myself with small distractions, attending parties, playing tennis. It was a new era, and my backhand was getting to be an embarrassment. So I concentrated. Only, a few weeks later, Levine showed up at the door wearing one of his wretched flea market sport jackets and a face like Ed Muskie. "Jack, I'm interrupting, maybe? Say the word and I'm gone."

"Don't be silly, Levine. Sylvie's at jazzercise, the kid's in bed. Come in already."

"You sure I'm not interrupting."

"I'm sure, dammit." He was, and he looked terrible, to boot. "You look terrible. What's the matter, you lose at the track again?"

"Who can afford the track anymore? I'm lucky I can dress myself."

"You call that dressing yourself?"

Levine's brown eyes flashed. "Excuse *me*, Mister Impeccable-Taste-with-the-Fat-Salary. You used to dress like this yourself, before the big turnaround."

"*Again*, Levine? Again with the resentment and name-calling? Again with the simple-minded labeling? Again wi—"

"All right, all right, don't get so defensive," he grumbled. "Never mind about all that. Methinks he doth protest too much, but . . ." He watched my fists begin to clench, then clucked his tongue. "Never mind. How about a drink for the civil servant?"

He had been a good canvasser, in his day. Five years on the streets, and if he hadn't ruptured that Achilles tendon in a touch-football game, who knows how far he could have gone? A moody, driven man. Now he worked for Unemployment, in Records, and spent most of his free time either gambling recklessly or filling out applications for any number of exotic research grants he wasn't qualified for. I brought out some scotch, poured a couple stiff ones, and went into the study with Levine, who seemed even more depressed than usual.

"So guess who I run into at Lucky's the other day, Jack." He sighed heavily, taking off his shoes. I let a moment pass. "Slottman. Mark Slottman. Remember?"

"Slottman?"

"You know. He was with us in FSM. Played the banjo. Owned his own bullhorn."

"That guy who tried to feel up Angela Davis during a rally?"

Levine was pounding his upper thigh. "That's him! Sure. Another Jewish boy with a fantasy, eh? He's got a couple brats now, lives in Hayward. A dentist. He tells me in Lucky's that his father was a dentist, his grandfather was a dentist, and it was probably in the back of his mind all that time we were running around with Mario that *he'd* turn into a dentist. So much for free will, Jack, eh? Anyway, we talked old times for awhile. Christ it felt good."

"Why so sentimental, Levine? Drink your Chivas."

"I'm turning into an unhappy person, Jack, I think."

I shrugged and said nothing. He had *always* been an unhappy person, but never mind. I'd have liked to do something for him, but I wouldn't have known where to start.

"Guess who else I ran into, Jack." He paused. That slow pitch used to work well with housewives and cops, but it cost him in the welfare neighborhoods. "Girlfriend. She tells me there's som—"

"Something wrong with Shamsky," I said impatiently. "I know all about it, she called a while ago."

"Sounds pretty serious, you ask me. The magazines and everything. Missed all those shifts at work, and you know him—with the flu, he worked; when we flew east for the Moratorium, he worked. Hell, he worked the night Nixon resigned." I shot him a look, but he ignored it. "I'm a little worried about that kid, Jack. I don't like it."

The implication, of course, was that I *did* like it. "Whattaya want me to *do*, Levine?" It came out of me like an explosion. "You want me to play nursey to Shamsky, just cause he's feeling down? Since when am *I* responsible for him? Besides, I've got a lot of work—"

Levine snickered. "Work? This is work? This—"

I cut him off before he could get rolling. "There's work, there's this house to maintain. Plus a wife to keep happy, and a kid who kills birds in the backyard. Him I'm supposed to teach morals. You think it's all so easy? You think I'm a bastard?"

Levine drained his glass. "Yeah." Then he got up, pulled his shirtsleeves down under that mothy coat, and made for the door.

"Levine! Wait a minute, dammit!"

But he wouldn't. "Prepare the way to heaven, Jack," he tossed over his shoulder, disappearing into the darkness outside.

I switched on the television and went toe-to-toe with the eleven o'clock news.

He had been a great one, Shamsky. A pheenom. When he showed up at the UCA office that December morning in '68—a lean, broad-shouldered kid fresh off the Santa Cruz jitney, cheeks smooth, hair cropped short, on his back a faded red nylon rucksack full of Marx, Weber, Marcuse and the rest; this large, almost feminine mouth pursed into a smile so rich with good intentions it made your eyes water—I figured he'd last about two weeks. Canvassing is hard work, Marx or no Marx. Still, there was something winning in his manner, a kind of halting charm, and as I walked him around the office to meet the staff—Perlmutter, Hickey, Rhonda, Fat Maxine, Bando, Levine, and some others, now forgotten—I was struck by how courteous everyone seemed to be around him. None of the sarcastic quips, or the outright condescension that usually went along with meeting a new man. With one exception. "And this is our publicist, Ruthie. Sweetheart, this is Harold Shamsky. He's training with us today."

Ruthie, crumpling an empty pack of Benson and Hedges, gave him the once-over as he stammered something to the effect that he preferred to be called Shamsky, just Shamsky. His words tumbled out gently and a bit tentatively, as if they were reluctant to exit that stunning mouth of his too quickly. "Okay, Shamsky-just-Shamsky. I'm Ruthie-just-Ruthie, and welcome to the good fight."

He nodded, started to say something, then thought better of it. I led him over to the TOTALS board and chalked in 'Shamsky' on the bottom line. "Okay, kid, for tonight I don't want you to worry about an amount. Normally you should aim for fifty a night, minimum. You don't average at least that much, you won't be asked to stick around. Understand?"

He nodded some more, fumbling with his rucksack. He withdrew a small blue notebook, the price tag still on the cover.

"Commission's thirty per cent. It's not much, but it'll keep you alive, if you live cheaply, until the revolution comes."

More nods. I should mention that I was at least partially aware of how much I sounded like a grade-B drill sergeant at the time. According to Ruthie, "if Trotsky was as much of a hard-ass as you, Jack, they'd have done him in much earlier." But we did see it as warfare, of a kind—we were the people's army; Nixon, Mitchell, General Motors, landlords, and industrial polluters were the Czars; and the streets were our battlefield. Erring on the side of toughness, who could blame me? Didn't history have different yardsticks for our toughness and theirs?

I plunged ahead. "The important thing, Shamsky, is to deliver a good pitch, hard and sincere, then step back and be able to gauge your effect. If it's no go, then don't waste time arguing politics, just move on. But if you've got them hooked, or you think you might, then for christ's sake don't let up. Pour it on thick. Jimmy yourself right up next to them and talk. Smell them, taste them, crawl inside their clothes to show you know what their concerns are, you know how badly they want to do what's right . . . and then pitch again, this time as if the future of the universe as we know it is hanging in the balance. Because Shamsky, it *is*. And then, before they have time to think it over, or to stall, or pack up and move to Bakersfield—tell them that we prefer checks, if possible, so they'll have receipts."

Shamsky—who had been writing all this down in that blue notebook, nodding away in obedient rhythm to my words—looked up with a querulous expression. "Is . . . is that really why?"

I softened my tone a bit. "No, that's not really why. Really why is because when they're writing the check, they make the numbers rounder than when they're paying cash. Still, this country loves receipts, it runs on them. An American with a receipt is a happy American, and Citizens in Action aims to please." I laughed, trying to relax him a little. "Okay, so put down the notebook." He did, but with great reluctance. "Your shift goes out in fifteen minutes. You'll be in Levine's car. You feel ready?"

Shamsky nodded, straightened his collar, walked into the bathroom, and threw up.

"Dammit, Jack, I wish you wouldn't make them so nervous," Ruthie snapped. Perlmutter giggled into his clipboard. "Get fucked, Perlmutter."

I ignored them and turned to Levine. "Listen, spend about an hour with him, then let him go off on his own. But keep an eye out, okay?" I was privately revising my estimate of Shamsky. He might not even last the whole shift, I thought.

He went out that night, canvassed four blocks in Walnut Creek, and raised a hundred-twelve for the Mobilization. Levine came back gurgling like a fountain. "Jack, such a *pitch* this kid's got! It's like music, the way he delivers. It's, it's . . . *elegant.*" He leaned heavily over my desk, scattering papers. "He doubled me, Jack. *Doubled* me!"

Well, we all made a big fuss over him, particularly Levine ("A Nobel Prize before he's thirty, I predict!") and Ruthie, who couldn't seem to congratulate him enough. For my part, I was going to reserve judgment. I'd seen one-night sensations before, guys wired on adrenaline, idealism and *chutzpah* who rake it in as if by magic, only to fall on their faces later in the week.

As if he sensed my train of thought, Shamsky approached my desk cautiously, handed over a pile of checks, a fat wad of bills, and—this killed me—enough quarters to keep every laundromat in Oakland busy for a week, then mumbled into his shirt, "Just a lucky night, I guess."

"All this change, Shamsky. Where'd it come from?"

He seemed embarrassed. "I ran into some kids at a playground. They didn't *have* checking accounts, Jack. You don't mind, do you?"

He pitched to a bunch of kids playing ball? And they *went* for it? If it had been anyone else, or stated in any other way, I'd never have believed it. "Nah. Good work. Good night, Shamsky."

"Night, Jack." He gathered up the rucksack and ambled towards the stairs. I watched him go. Let's see how he does in San Leandro, I thought.

In San Leandro he did one-forty-three and Levine's smug grin was beginning to cloud with envy. "Don't tell me," I said, when they came in at ten that evening. "He doubled you again." Levine nodded, pulling off a checkered jacket a dead man wouldn't wear. "How about the others? Perlmutter, Bando."

"You know Bando. Sixty-five, the usual. And Perlmutter's on the rag about some girl, didn't even make quota."

"And the kid?"

He shook his head wearily. "I don't know how he does it, I tell you. And *strip*-mining, yet!"

"What're you talking about strip-mining? We're still supposed to be doing Mobilization out there. Didn't you tell him?"

Ruthie came over and sat down on the corner of my desk, wiping her glasses on the bottom of her shirt. I caught a glimpse of her smooth, tanned stomach over the waistband of her jeans. There was more to life, it occurred to me, than fighting Richard Nixon.

"That's what I'm trying to tell you," Levine went on. "This kid's pitching two things at once! I heard him do it: he snared this old rural guy with some wilderness pitch, brings up strip-mining, they get to talking, and then Shamsky hits him with the war, don't ask me how. I mean, this guy's sen*sational!* An artist!"

Ruthie lit a joint and squinted at me through the smoke. "There's something about the way he looks at a person, you know. Even I've noticed it."

Yes, I thought, I've noticed you noticing it. "Let's just hope it lasts."

I went into the back office to find Shamsky moving his lips slightly as he totalled his checks. When he'd finished, I asked him to do his pitch for me, role-playing as if I were a vaguely-interested homeowner. And Levine was right, it *was* like music—the intonation, principally, though he made certain gestures of expression which didn't hurt him any. He'd hook you with the soft, hesitant tremor in the voice, the damp eyes that weren't quite wet, the head cocked to one side (he had a bad ear, he explained later) almost inquisitively, as if even while his mouth was moving his ears were straining to listen, to comprehend, to receive. And then he'd smile this grand, slow smile, and his twin rows of high ivory-like teeth would glow like a harvest moon. Yes, he had style, that Shamsky. I made him pitch again, and this time I stopped him at odd points, throwing him off, but he never failed to recover. Sometimes I felt like he'd forgotten I was there, for once he got rolling he seemed entirely without self-consciousness, without tentativeness, without any fear of failure whatsoever. Afterwards I gave him a few pointers—certain tricks of emphasis, inflections, a relevant joke or two (which he didn't seem to get—Shamsky had no discernible sense of humor). We sat there for a couple of hours

12

until everybody but Ruthie had gone home, until I'd told him almost everything I'd ever known about canvassing, which I'd been doing since I was ten, and Shamsky wrote every word down in that notebook of his, nodding along furiously. I was very taken with his enthusiasm. He was never quite still, though I detected a kind of rigidity in him, too, some vague formality that made me wonder what he was really like inside—what music he listened to, what teams he rooted for, what kind of birthday cards he sent his mother.

Still, he had talent, and he was a quick learner, and it might have just been that bad ear that made him seem a little off. After he'd gone, I went up to record the evening's figures on the big board, humming to myself. The office overlooked a particularly seamy stretch of Telegraph Avenue. I stood at the window, chalk in hand, staring off into the jagged lines of neon that criss-crossed the night, listening to the traffic of two and a half million souls. I felt tired and strangely proud, as if I'd just passed the baton in an important relay. The radio was full of anti-war news: someone was burning draft records back east. My pulse jumped. With kids like this in action, who knew? History was on our side, after all. Maybe our train was finally pulling into the Finland Station! Ruthie walked in, and I said, "Hey, babe? Let's get married."

She turned out the office lights and tossed me my keys. "I'm not the wife type," she said, with much affection. "I'm the girlfriend type."

Hence, Girlfriend. A couple of months later, she moved in with Shamsky.

And so it went. With Cambodia, Kent State, Attica, McGovern, UFW boycotts, UMW strikes, AIM demonstrations, nursing home corruption, abortion reform, and environmental misdeeds to be addressed, we managed to keep ourselves occupied. Thanks to a fortunate convergence of our enthusiasm, public sympathy, and world events, things began to take off: I hired half a dozen more canvassers, we took on three extra lobbyists in Sacramento, and my picture began to appear regularly in the local papers beside the press releases Girlfriend and I co-wrote while Shamsky and the others walked the neighborhoods. Even as I was taking a good deal of the credit, I was fully aware that it was Shamsky who provided our guiding force. True, I made the decisions. But the drive, the single-minded determination, came from Shamsky.

This became abundantly clear after the '72 elections, a bitter time for us all. I personally couldn't drag myself out of bed for a week. Hickey ran off to Mexico on a bender, Rhonda went into therapy, and even Levine (who'd voted socialist as always) admitted that his dread had localized into utter loathing for America, for himself, and for most of the rest of us. But not, I'd bet, for Shamsky, who appeared thoroughly undaunted. He kept going, five nights a week, working an extra hour to pick up everyone else's slack. The amount he brought in varied somewhat, but rarely dipped below a hundred—a fact he was careful not to flaunt on the drive home from a shift, so as not to discourage his less-successful co-workers. They knew, though, and this knowledge, instead of embittering them, had the opposite effect—they came to love him, to emulate him. And soon his model was inspiring everybody in the office—even some of the more jaded veterans—and we kept the fight going, plugging ahead on several fronts at once (state propositions, mayoral races, even—ironically—gun control) and having enough success that, by the time Watergate began to unfold, we'd already bought a couple of new typewriters from Bando's brother-in-law and made a few more contacts in the statehouse. Thus with Nixon, hated Nixon, on the ropes, we were able to launch a superb petition drive and move in high gear towards the knockout punch.

Amidst all this turbulence, I'm happy to say that my personal life had finally stabilized. Within six months of McGovern's defeat, I married a woman I had met selecting graphics at the typesetter. Sylvie (who, like Girlfriend, was a publicist) immediately became pregnant, and for the first time in my adult life I began, perhaps infected by Levine's despair, to consider another line of work.

Besides, it was getting more and more difficult to share an office with the two of them. I mean Girlfriend, who, when Shamsky was out on a shift, would putter about the office with a disconsolate inattention to most of the details that made up her job (and to me, I might add; though Sylvie's phone calls usually prompted her to one or another ironic comment) until Shamsky's nightly six o'clock call. This she would receive breathlessly, with a lot of unnecessary cooing and murmuring. To his habitual question, "How's Jack?" she'd toss off carelessly, "Jack? Oh, Jack's Jack, as always," and merely wave her wrist in my direction. Upon hanging up she'd sigh deeply, as if made pregnant by the noble sound of his voice, and then, duly inspired, she'd sharpen some number 2 pencils, roll

14

up her sleeves, and settle down to write about three or four of the finest press releases it has ever been my pleasure to read.

"Shamsky *idolizes* you, Jack. He really does," she liked to tell me. Well, maybe. But as time went on the little things about him that unnerved me seemed to multiply: the humble manner, the cocking of the head, the abstracted gaze he often wore, the nightly phone calls, and the relentless diligence—bordering on fanaticism—he brought to his craft. And all perfectly genuine, too. After a shift he'd come over to the desk and, in that shy way of his, attempt a little small talk while I went over his checks. "Just a lucky night, I guess," he'd say, as he'd said that first night.

Equally amused and annoyed, I'd laugh shortly. "Lucky? Kid, you're the best. As Levine would say, you're an artist."

"Hell, I just try to remember what you told me. People want to think they're good people, after all. I just help them out. They don't care about the politics of it so much."

Yes, he was genuinely modest. And the two of them would retreat to their little brown-shingled cottage in the Berkeley flatlands, with books all over the floor and something like two dozen cats and dogs howling away in the yard. They planted a nice garden, I remember, in a small plot next to the foundation, and were forever pressing on me their anemic carrots and dirty lettuce. But we weren't really social. I had a baby, for openers, and Sylvie had already made it clear that she could live without "that self-satisfied harlot" and her "vacant, downright creepy" boyfriend. The two of them were into a Thoreau phase, anyway, making organic goodies on the weekends and reading by the fireplace. Shamsky, a prodigal reader, gobbled political theory like popcorn. Michelet, Burke, Mills, Hegel, Fanon—he'd already left me far behind, but around the office he liked to ask my opinion about them anyway. "Tell me something, Jack," he might say, "when Engels talks about motive and will, you think he means the same thing Feuerbach meant by them?"

"I'm a little rusty on my Feuerbach, Shamsky. What do *you* think?"

"Well, if you remember, Feuerbach posited a certain correlation between . . ." and he'd be off on a long summary which, if it had been designed to impress (and I'm sure it wasn't), certainly did its job. But the curious thing was—though I didn't realize it at the time—he never, in the end, really *gave* me his opinion. In fact, for all the information he had at his disposal, with his perceptive

15

reading eye and finely-tuned memory, he didn't really seem to *have* an opinion, on Engels or, come to think of it, on much else either. Perhaps that is what put Sylvie off Shamsky, for she believes strongly that opinions are fundamentally religious—expressions of the essence, if you will—and, the two of us coming from Jewish homes full of outspoken-to-the-point-of-pathological hardheads, it's easy to see why I agree with her.

So I watched with interest when Shamsky bent over a book in the office, or when he flipped through one of the dozens of magazines that began flooding in addressed to "Shamsky, c/o UCA." "Girlfriend says they're cluttering up the house," he explained, cocking his head, when I raised the issue. "She said you didn't mind. You don't, do you?"

I made a gesture of dismissal. "But why some of these right-wing rags, kid? It's bad for our image."

He rubbed his smooth chin mildly. "Well, I just want to keep up with all sides, Jack, so when I talk to people, I know other sides of things. I don't want to sound *dogmatic,* after all. Besides, Girlfriend says when you used to canvass, you'd carry around three or four newspapers with you, to point things out to people. I thought that was a good idea. I want to be the best, you see."

"You *are* the best. Believe me."

"Yeah, but," and he grinned at me winningly, "to *stay* the best. To scale the heights. That's what this is about, Jack." And with that he buried his nose in the latest *New Republic*, lips moving silently as his eyes ran along the columns, absorbing everything he could on Beirut, or the Supreme Court, or the auto workers, for the remainder of the half-hour before his shift.

This is the Shamsky I'd prefer to remain fixed in my memory, the dedicated boy wonder—not the temporarily berserk cuckold who stormed into my office on a windy spring afternoon in 1975, or the lost shadow he's become these past months. As a matter of fact, if not for the visit I made to his cottage at the end of April, I'd still be able to think of him without sadness; he'd be a fond, if eccentric, object of where-is-he-now speculation, someone for Levine and me to make nostalgic jokes about over scotches at the track. Yes, on the bloated ledger of regrets I carry inside my head, that visit is circled in red ink. And (because I am a competent anticipator of such things) I had no intention of making it in the first place. To Levine I was a bastard, to Girlfriend a rat. Even my old friend Bando, calling (collect) from New Orleans, where he runs the census these days, thought I was being, as he put it, "an unconscionable shmuck." But I held firm for a long while. More than anything, I was afraid to become implicated in Shamsky's malaise, which (like Levine's despair) I suspected might be contagious.

But, to paraphrase the Chartists, if political power was our means, social happiness was our end.

In short, Sylvie thought it was the right thing to do. "Maybe he really does need you, Jack. You *were* his mentor, after all. I don't see why you won't even talk to him, if he's in trouble. Everybody seems to want you to." This said as we waited in line to see yet another interminable movie about divorce.

"Honey," I said, "it'd be useless. I don't understand Shamsky, not even a little. Why does everyone persist in thinking it's up to *me* to straighten him out?"

"Are you kidding? If he looked at *me* the way he used to look at you, if he wrote down every word *I* said, *I* would certainly conclude I had some influence over him."

"That was before he tried to kill me, remember?"

"He didn't try to kill you, don't be so melodramatic. You said yourself they weren't even loaded."

"An oversight for which I'm grateful."

We went into the theater and found seats behind two basketball players, which did wonders for my mood. "Now you're being silly."

"Fine. That's the nicest thing I've been called this month." Just then the movie started, and the top half of the screen, at any rate, was so relentlessly depressing that I began nervously rubbing the fine, translucent hair on Sylvie's forearm, as if attempting to free some captive genie. She left him to find herself; he had to raise the kid on his own. And why? Presumably because he wasn't sensitive enough to her needs, or to anyone else's. I hated him.

We walked slowly, arm in arm, towards the car. "I'll go see Shamsky tomorrow," I said.

Sylvie, still teary and blowing her nose, didn't hear me.

To my relief, there didn't seem to be anybody home. It was the middle of the afternoon, the retrievers were barking away like mad in the yard, and the garden looked like the Cambodian jungle. Nobody answered my knock on the door. Maybe he's gone back to work, I thought. I tried the knob. It yielded under my hand, and I slipped inside. "Hey," I called out, "anybody home?"

The shades were drawn, newspapers blanketed the floor, and the air was heavy and stale. The television blared away some sort of cretinous game show, the volume loud enough to ruin his *other* ear. And there—lying on the sofa, his feet propped high on a couple of throw-pillows, an open jar of Planter's Peanuts resting between the legs of his checkered pajama trousers—there was Shamsky. Six years since our aborted shoot-out, and I swear he still looked the same: smooth chin, apple cheeks, short groomed hair, study-bent shoulders. "Hey, Jack," he said dully, eyes not straying from the television.

I tossed a two-week-old editorial page to the floor, clearing a space for myself on their patched La-Z-Boy. "Mind if I sit down? My arches are collapsing."

He didn't say anything, just watched the screen. I sat anyway. A woman from Riverside impugned her husband's masculinity, and was rewarded with a set of patio furniture. Shamsky, despite himself, chuckled softly. He stretched his arm over the three feet of distance between us, proffering the Planter's jar. "Peanuts, Jack?" "Sure." Bathed in the blue light from the television, we nibbled peanuts. I was tempted to ask for a drink, but I forced myself to proceed with the business at hand. "So . . ." I said, open-endedly. There was a pause. "Girlfriend tells me you've gone mahoola."

He grunted. I was immediately furious with myself for mentioning Girlfriend. What if he *hadn't* returned those pistols?

"What's going on, kid? How come you're not working? Sick?"

"Not sick, Jack. Dead."

"Dead men watch game shows in the afternoon?"

"I'm serious. It's all over. I cancelled the magazines and everything."

"I hear they're not taking it so well."

He grunted again. "Sure, they're boiling. Two letters last week—one from Buckley, the other from, what's his name, the guy at *Harper's* . . ."

"Lapham."

"Right. Blames everything on me, says he's going to have to sell, nobody wants to be informed anymore. Ah, Jack, what's the difference, it's all for shit anyway."

"You're just burnt-out," I said, though it was a guess. "Listen, you have something to drink, maybe? I'm parched."

He sat up with an effort. "Check the refrigerator."

Calistoga water, apple juice, nonfat milk, some cooking sherry. I stood there considering. Meanwhile, he began to talk.

"We were in Hayward, Jack. Southeast district. Neighborhood's mostly middle and lower-middle, a couple retirees, some GM people from the Fremont plant, you know?"

Of course I knew. I'd canvassed there myself—for Bobby, I think.

"So I was going along great guns, giving a twin pitch: first nursing homes, then the whales. Hell, it only takes an extra second or two, and I get bored doing just one or the other. It might be seven, seven-thirty, and I've already made quota and then some."

"Naturally."

He ignored me, sinking further into himself, looking up at me as if from a great distance. "I come to the next to last house on the block. At first there's no answer, so I knock on the screen one more time, figure nobody's home, and take a minute to get my clippings in order for the next house. I'm standing there and the door opens, and this woman looks at me—doesn't open the screen, doesn't say anything, just kind of hovers there—and I go into my pitch. She's maybe forty, forty-five, pleasant face. What I can see of the living room behind her looks very tasteful. A nice framed Picasso, redwood furniture. I figure she'll go for at least a twenty-dollar check.

"First I show her this clipping from the *Mercury*, with the old people lying around the game room naked and—"

"But that picture," I interrupted, "that picture's been around since *my* day. It must be ten years old!"

"It's a good picture, Jack. Dramatic. They *bleed* when they see that one."

I poured myself some milk and remained where I was. I wouldn't argue ethics; it was a whole new administration over there at UCA (Girlfriend having left in '79 to write editorials for the *Trib*). The milk smelled sour. "Go ahead, what happened?"

"She doesn't look at the picture, Jack. She looks at *me*. Right into my eyes, mumbles something I couldn't catch, and then just stares at me from behind the screen with a peculiar expression on her face. It was almost as if I *horrified* her or something. Well, at this point I'm about willing to give up and take my chances on the last house. But when I start to turn to go, I hear a little moan come out of her throat, as if she doesn't want me to leave, as if she'll *scream*, in fact, if I tried to leave. So I don't leave. Maybe I sold her on

19

nursing homes after all, I think. So I say, "we prefer checks, ma'am, so you have a receipt for the contribution."

"And then she changes her expression for the first time. Now it looks like *pity*, Jack. She takes a little step sideways and I see something on the floor behind her. 'Young man,' she says, and Jack, if you could've heard this voice—it was this low monotone, very disembodied, like from the other side of a cave—'Young man,' she says to me, 'that's my husband. He's stopped *breath*ing,' she says. And then she just stands there *looking* at me."

His voice broke, and I looked over at the television for a moment, thinking that I wasn't really up for any more of this. But Shamsky rose from the couch, put his hands in his pajama pockets, and looked at me expectantly. The smooth skin on his cheeks looked slack. "Jesus Christ," I said. "What'd you do?"

"That's the pathetic part, Jack," he said, and the tears began to flow down his face. "*I started to pitch!* I just freaked—I couldn't help it. I have this armful of magazine articles, my clipboard, and a pocketful of checks and cash, and I can't stop myself, I start to pitch—I did San Quentin, nuclear power, the bottle bill, SALT II . . . God, I think towards the end I was running down old stuff like the Mobilization and McGovern, for god's sake, that's how crazy I was. So I can't shut up, and she can't stop listening to me, and her husband meanwhile is behind that screen door on the floor somewhere and I'm riffing through my clippings, showing her this and that, and her eyes are on me the whole time, the *entire* time . . . Man it was horrible! It was the way I imagine Hell must be . . .

". . . anyway, after about ten more minutes of this the ambulance finally came to take her husband away. When it pulled into the driveway she said something I didn't catch. Maybe it was a thank you, huh, Jack?"

Asking my opinion, like the old days. "Maybe it was."

"Maybe it was," he repeated, though his expression remained dark. "Then I went on to the next house on the block. The last house."

"And?"

"And nothing. They didn't bite. Neither did anybody else for the rest of the night. Even Perlmutter brought in more than I did. Perlmutter!" From his gesture of disgust, I realized that even his modesty had deserted him. "The whole next week it continued. I couldn't get the words out, or, if I did, couldn't sound like I meant them. With all the magazines, all the books, all the years of doing

20

it—with all that, I couldn't answer a single goddamn question. Jack, it's over. That should've been me lying on that floor in Hayward."

His despair was so comprehensive, so heartfelt, and so thoroughly alien to everything I'd ever associated with Shamsky that I was reluctant to say anything, for fear I'd make things even worse. But there was a terrible quality to the silence which engulfed us, and I was there for a reason, after all. "Maybe it's for the best," I offered. "Times have changed. Look around—the G. O. P.'s got the Senate, money's tight, Kissinger and Ehrlichman write bestsellers, and nobody gives a damn. You've been on the front lines for nearly twelve years, Shamsky. I'd say you deserve a break."

It was, I realized sadly, exactly what he wanted to hear. "You're probably right, Jack," he said quickly. "I'm thirty-one years old, you know. Jack, you—you think there might be a place for me in the private sector?"

"What about Girlfriend? How would *she* feel about this?"

He swallowed hard. "The truth is, Girlfriend's gone."

"Gone? Work gone, or gone gone?"

"Gone gone. Gone gone gone." And as his eyes swept back towards the television—where happy couples maneuvered about in the simple choreography of life-in-the-present which comes naturally, it seems, to everyone but those people I know personally—I anticipated his next words and swore under my breath as he said them aloud: "I asked her to marry me."

"That was an incredibly stupid thing to do, wasn't it?"

He snapped off the television. The picture shrank into a pale spot. "I don't know. I thought it might be a good idea. And don't patronize me, Jack. I still haven't forgiven you, you know. *You*, who I always looked up to."

"It was a long time ago," I said simply.

"A long time ago?" Shamsky looked doubtful; his head dipped somewhat so that his right ear was held higher than his left. It was a familiar enough motion, the old cocking of the head, but this time it struck me with a great deal of force, for in it I thought I saw the key to Shamsky's rise, and the key to his descent.

He was literally deaf to history.

And I stood there thinking—at how many doors had that bad ear of his screened out the sounds—apathy, pain, ignorance, rage—made by those who lived their lives within? And for how many years, I wondered, could he possibly have gone on like that, pitching without interference from the cries of hungry babies, the barking of angry dogs, the thunder of a thousand petty demands? No wonder they'd all believed in him so, emptied their pockets to him, given themselves over with gratitude to the perfect and obstinate hope he embodied. Yes, they—*we*—had all spoiled him, spoiled him terribly. And now, looking at Shamsky in his pajamas, I thought of Lenin's statement to Gorky: "When history retaliates, it stops at nothing."

But that's not what I said. What I said was, "You poor bastard."

He didn't seem to hear me. He asked me again whether there was anything I could do for him, and the tremor in his voice and the dampness in his eyes were affectingly genuine as always. Only his manner no longer struck me as proudly elegant, and I detected no artistry—just a raw and throbbing innocence, the victim of a wayward injury.

nominated by DeWitt Henry and Mona Simpson

PAPER TIGERS

by ELIOT WEINBERGER

from SULFUR

T.

The Maharajah of Rewa, according to his English Adviser, had his own method of hunting tiger:

> He found the easiest way to bag tigers was to take with him a book and a monkey on a long string. When seated in the *machan* [a platform in the trees] he would release the monkey, who immediately climbed into the top branches. He would then give the signal for the beat to start and settle down to read. As soon as the tiger approached the monkey would spot him and give the cough with which all monkeys warn the jungle folk that "Sher Khan" the tiger is on the prowl. His Highness would then quickly put down his book and pick up the rifle.

At the turning of a page, the apparition of a tiger:

Y.

Berggasse 19, March 10, 1933: H. D., one of the last patients of Freud, records her sessions with the Professor:

> Curiously in fantasy I think of a tiger. Myself as a tiger? This tiger may pounce out. Suppose it should

attack the frail and delicate old Professor? Do I fear my own terrors of the present situation, the lurking "beast" may or may not destroy him? I mention this tiger as a past nursery fantasy. Suppose it should actually materialize? The Professor says, "I have my protector."

He indicates Yofi, the little lioness curled at his feet.

And a few days later:

I spoke again of our toy animals and he reminded me of my tiger fantasy. Wasn't there a story, "the woman and the tiger," he asked. I remembered "The Lady or the Tiger."

G.

A King invents a peculiar system of justice: The accused is placed in a large arena before the entire populace and must open one of two identical doors. Behind one, a tiger, which will leap out and tear the man into pieces, establishing his guilt. Behind the other, a lady "most suitable to his years and station," whom he must immediately marry as a reward for his innocence. ("It mattered not that he might already possess a wife and family, or that his affections might be engaged upon an object of his own selection. The King allowed no such subordinate arrangements to interfere with his great scheme of retribution and reward.") The accused, then, must "open either [door] he pleased, without having the slightest idea whether, in the next instant, he was to be devoured or married."

As might be expected, the King has a daughter, and she falls in love with a handsome commoner. Learning of this transgression, the King declares that the boy must be sent to the arena. For one door, the most ferocious tiger in the land is found; for the other, the most beautiful maiden—more beautiful, in fact, than the King's own daughter.

Before the trial, the wily daughter discovers the secret of the doors, and as the boy enters the arena she signals him with her right hand. He immediately opens the right door . . . But which would be worse for this "hot-blooded semi-barbaric princess": to see her beloved ripped to shreds, or happily married to a woman

24

more lovely than she? What was the meaning of her sign? Or, as the story ends: "Which came out of the opened door—the lady, or the tiger?"

E.

Frank Stockton's "The Lady, or the Tiger?," first published in *The Century Magazine* in 1882, quickly became an international obsession. At the time inconclusive endings were vexatious, not modern, and for the twenty years until his death Stockton was besieged with solutions, sequels, and threats. Among the latter, Rudyard Kipling subjected Stockton to a bit of impeccable Raj ragging, as reported by the San Francisco *Wave* in 1896:

> Stockton and Kipling met at an author's reception, and after some preliminary talk, the former remarked: "By the way, Kipling, I'm thinking of going over to India some day myself." "Do so, my dear fellow," replied Mr. Kipling, with suspicious warmth of cordiality. "Come as soon as ever you can! And, by the way, do you know what we'll do when we get you out there, away from your friends and family? Well, the first thing will be to lure you out into the jungle and have you seized and bound by our trusty wallahs. Then we'll lay you on your back and have one of our very biggest elephants stand over you and poise his ample forefoot directly over your head. Then I'll say in my most insinuating tones, 'Come now, Stockton, which was it—The Lady or the Tiger?' . . ."

And Mrs. Stockton recorded this ludicrous scene in her diary:

> Miss Evans, our niece, wrote to us that a missionary who was visiting her mission station among the Karens [a tribe in northeast Burma], told her she had just come from a distant wild tribe of Karens occasionally visited by missionaries and to her surprise was immediately asked by them if she knew who came out the door, The Lady or the Tiger? Her explanation of it was that some former visitor had read to them this story as suited to their

fancy; and as she had just come from the outside world they supposed she could tell the end of it.

Men generally favored the lady, women the tiger. An exception was Robert Browning, who declared he had "no hesitation in supposing that such a princess, under such circumstances, would direct her lover to the tiger's door." In fact, Freud's slip was to the point: it is an *and,* not an *or,* proposition. The choice between lady or tiger, "devoured or married," was to its readers hardly a choice at all. As one W. S. Hopson of San Francisco wrote in 1895:

> When my wife flies into a passion,
> And her anger waxes wroth,
> I think of the Lady and the Tiger,
> And sigh that I chose them both.

R.

A few years after Stockton's death, Elinor Glyn's *Three Weeks* (1907) was the steamy bestseller of its day, its success due largely to its famous seduction scene on a tiger-skin rug:

> Paul entered from the terrace. And the loveliest sight of all, in front of the fire, stretched at full length, was his tiger and on him—also at full length—reclined the lady . . .
> "No! You mustn't come near me, Paul . . . Not yet. You bought me the tiger. Ah that was good! My beautiful tiger!" And she gave a movement like a snake, of joy to feel its fur under her, while she stretched out her hands and caressed the creature where the hair turned white and black at the side, and was deep and soft.
> "Beautiful one! Beautiful one!" she purred. "And I know all your feelings and your passions, and now I have got your skin—for the joy of my skin." And she quivered again with a movement of a snake.

Alas, tiger's fur is short and coarse, and would make for an itchy tryst. But Glyn's book effectively played on the fusion of lady and tiger in the popular imagination. It also inspired this piece of anonymous doggerel (and mnemonic guide to proper pronunciation):

> Would you like to sin
> with Elinor Glyn
> on a tiger skin?
> Or would you prefer
> to err
> with her
> on some other fur?

T.

Tiger, woman, passion. Glyn's sin comes out of ancient tradition, for the tiger has always been first female, and later male.

The earliest recorded tigers in the West were those presented to Seleucus I (d. 280 B.C.). (Alexander of course had seen tigers in Persia.) In Latin poetry *tigris* is always feminine (the word means "arrow," and was applied to the swiftness of the animal and the river); in Roman art tigresses are nearly always portrayed. Female tiger is often paired with male lion, much as Freud's "lioness" Yofi checks H. D.'s tiger. Bacchus' chariot was drawn by such a pair. It is a distinction Keats articulates in "Hyperion" as "tiger-passioned, lion-thoughted." (Similarly, the Brontës' cats were named "Tiger" and "Keeper.") As late as the eighteenth century it was believed that the way to capture a tiger cub—the only way to get a tiger for one's menagerie—was the procedure first described by Claudian nearly two thousand years before: steal the cub and, with the tiger in pursuit, scatter mirrors in her path; her female vanity is such that she will gaze fondly in the mirror and forget about the baby.

In China the tiger was originally *yin:* associated with the underworld, and with the West (where the sun enters the underworld). In the *feng-shui* system of geomancy, it is paired with the *yang* green dragon. (The Buddhists would later reverse the genders of the tiger/green dragon pair—stressing the tiger's *yang* nobility, and pointing out, quite correctly, that tigers wear the character for "king," *wang* 王, on their foreheads). Wordsworth's description (in *The Prelude*) of Jacobin Paris as "Defenceless as a wood where tigers roam" may owe something to Virgil's characterization of Rome as "a wilderness of tigers." But both are identical to the stock

27

Chinese metaphor for a corrupt and sick society: a tiger *(yin)* in a bamboo grove *(yang)*, the dark within the light.

Most important is the Chinese tiger-monster, the *tao tie* ("the glutton") which is prominent as early as the Shang dynasty. The *tao tie* is a devourer, and almost always appears in funerary art; sometimes the burial urn itself is in the shape of a tiger. It is the earth eating the dead to provide nourishment for the living—much as the Greek word *sarcophagus* means "to eat flesh." (In the pre-Columbian Americas where there were no tigers, the jaguar was its exact equivalent: an earth-image paired in Mesoamerica with the sky-symbol of the feathered serpent, in South America commonly portrayed in burial urns. The whole city of Cuzco was originally laid out in the form of a jaguar—a kind of living necropolis, *polis* as affirmation of death and life.)

Although frequent in the early Harappan art of the Indus Valley, the tiger is rarely visible as an icon in India until its masculinization in Mughal times—quite strange, considering that Hinduism tended to find metaphysical uses for nearly every indigenous thing. In Hindu iconography it appears only occasionally as the vehicle for the Durga, the terrifying destroyer-goddess. There are, for example, no tigers in Vidyakara's *Treasury,* the great Sanskrit poetry anthology, where so much of Indian life is represented. But among the jungle tribes the tiger was an active presence as devouring mother, fecund mother. "In Akola," writes William Crooke in 1894, "the gardeners are unwilling to inform the sportsmen of the whereabouts of a tiger which may have taken up quarters in their plantation, for they have a superstition that a garden plot loses its fertility from the moment one of these animals is killed." And among the Gonds, wedding ceremonies were marked by the appearance of "two demoniacs possessed by Bagheswar, the tiger god" who "fell ravenously on a bleating kid, and gnawed it with their teeth till it expired."

Y.

Rachel Blau DuPlessis, explicating one of her own poems, writes:

> In "Crowbar," the whole argument comes to the poised
> end in the doubling of two words: *hungry* and *angry*

which grasp towards the odd *-ngry* ending they hold in common. *Hungry* meant complicit with the psychic cultural construction of beautiful, seductive and seduced women; *angry* meant critical of the same.

Hungry woman, angry woman: destroyer, devourer, nurturer: tiger images all. It is curious in this context to read Emily Dickinson's two enigmatic poems on tigers:

566

A Dying Tiger—moaned for Drink—
I hunted all the Sand—
I caught the Dripping of a Rock
And bore it in my Hand—

His Mighty Balls—in death were thick—
But searching—I could see
A Vision on the Retina
Of Water—and of me—

'Twas not my blame—who sped too slow—
'Twas not his blame—who died
While I was reaching him—
But 'twas—the fact that he was dead—

872

As the Starved Maelstrom laps the Navies
As the Vultures teased
Forces the Broods in lonely Valleys
As the Tiger eased

By but a Crumb of Blood, fasts Scarlet
Till he meet a Man
Dainty adorned with Veins and Tissues
And partakes—his Tongue

Cooled by the Morsel for a moment
Growns a fiercer thing
Till he esteem his Dates and Cocoa
A Nutrition mean

I, of a finer Famine
Deem my Supper dry
For but a berry of Domingo
And a Torrid Eye.

G.

There are no tigers in the Bible, and there were no tigers in medieval Europe—the bestiaries tended to classify them as birds or snakes. For nearly a thousand years, there were no tigers that look like tigers in Western art. So, when they began to be imported again into Europe from the animal market of Constantinople at the end of the fifteenth century, they were among the only creatures with no metaphysical meaning. In the absence of a fixed iconography, the West had to invent its allegorical tiger.

Shakespeare compares the murderous Queen Margaret (in *Henry VI Part 3*) to a tiger, and has Romeo express his rage in *yin* imagery:

The time and my intents are savage-wild,
More fierce and more inexorable far
Than empty tigers or the roaring sea.

But he also uses the tiger in its now-familiar masculine role: symbol of military valor. (Almost all the armies of the world are decked with tiger images.) Henry the Fifth, in his "Once more unto the breach, dear friends" speech:

But when the blast of war blows in our ears,
Then imitate the action of the tiger:
Stiffen the sinews, summon up the blood,
Disguise fair nature with hard-favored rage;
Then lend the eye a terrible aspect . . .
Now set the teeth and stretch the nostril wide,

30

Hold hard the breath and bend up every spirit
To his full height! On, on you noble English . . .

E.

The Western image of the tiger was permanently altered in the
eighteenth century by the reign of the Mughal prince Tipu Sultan
(1750–99), the self-styled Tiger of Mysore and a perfect incarnation
of the perennial Orientalist nightmare of the Eastern despot.

A stern moralist, Tipu abolished polyandry and instituted his
version of Koranic law. He changed the calendar and all weights
and measures; he renamed all the cities and towns. He sponsored
the arts and commercial enterprises, reformed every detail of daily
existence from the way the markets ran to the way crops were
planted and gathered. He kept a book of his dreams. At night he
slept on the floor on a coarse piece of canvas, and each morning he
ate the brains of male sparrows for breakfast.

He commanded an army of 140,000, sworn to wipe out the
British. Prisoners were subjected to particularly grotesque torture:
boiling oil, special devices for removing noses and upper lips. In
his most brilliantly insidious punishment the enemy was turned
into the Other: British soldiers were forced to cut off their foreskins
and eat them.

He was also, in his mind, a tiger. His throne was mounted on a
full-size gilded tiger with rock-crystal eyes and teeth; its finials
were tiger heads set with rubies and diamonds; its canopy was
tiger-striped with hammered gold. His soldiers dressed in tiger-
patterned ("bubberee") jackets and kept their prisoners in tiger
cages until it was time for them to be thrown to the tigers. Their
cannons had tiger breech-blocks, their mortars were in the shape
of crouching tigers, their rifles had tiger-headed stocks and hammers, their swords were engraved with tigers or forged in a striped
blend of metals. Live tigers were chained to the palace doors.
Tipu's handkerchiefs were striped; his banner read "The Tiger is
God."

All this, to put it mildly, made quite an impression in the West.
The newspapers were full of Tipu: if an elderly servant was
murdered in a siege, she was immediately transformed into four
hundred beautiful British virgins throwing themselves on swords
rather than face the ravishment of Tipu's troops. In London, Tipu

plays were a permanent attraction for thirty years. (The first, *Tippoo Sahib, or British Valour in India,* began running at Covent Garden on June 1, 1791. It was followed the next year by *Tippoo Sultan, or the Siege of Bangalore.*) When Tipu was finally slain and his capital, Seringpatam, captured by the British in 1798, it was cause for national celebration. Robert Ker Porter's 120-foot-long painting, "The Storming of Seringpatam," was mounted on the stage of the Lyceum, and the crowds paid a shilling each to view the great scene. Wilkie Collins in 1868 added an aura to his *Moonstone* by having it come from the plunder of Seringpatam, and as late as 1898 Sir Henry Newbolt had a popular schlock epic poem on Tipu's defeat.

The tiger, then, took on a fearful androgyny: a masculine military ferocity within a dark Eastern feminine otherness. The tiger was, in the words of Capt. Williamson's *Oriental Field Sports* (1807), "the mottled object of detestation": an obstacle to progress; everything that was not white, Western, male, good. Its literal and metaphorical vanquishing became a British obsession. For a century boys' stories were full of man-eating tigers. With a short leap, the word "man-eater" was soon applied to women.

R.

Blake's "tyger," according to the exegetes, stands for wrath, revolution, untamed energy and beauty, the romantic revolt of imagination against reason. Its direction is East—contrary to the Chinese, but obvious for a Westerner. It is associated with fire and smoke: "burning bright," roaming "in the redounding smoke in forests of affliction," "blinded by the smoke" issuing from "the wild furies" of its own brain. Numerous critics have pointed out that "The Tyger" of *Songs of Experience* was written in 1793, during the French Revolution. But it was also a time when the papers and theaters were crazy with tales of Tipu.

Did Blake ever see a real tiger? The Tower of London menagerie had been opened to the public in the middle of the century (price of admission: three ha'pennies or one dead dog or cat), and it frequently featured tigers. A new specimen was acquired in 1791, the year the first Tipu play opened. And when Blake lived at Fountain Court, the Strand, he could have strolled over to Pidcock's Exhibition of Wild Beasts, where tigers were often on display.

Pidcock and Blake form two sides of a tiger triangle: the third is George Stubbs, the first English painter of tigers. His *The Tyger*, as Kathleen Raine points out in *Blake and the Tradition*, was first exhibited at the Society of Artists of Great Britain in 1769, at the same time and in the same building where the twelve-year-old William Blake was studying drawing at Pars' school. (It was, by the way, Pidcock who sold Stubbs the dead tiger which the artist used for his last work, which bore the matchless title *The Comparative Anatomy of Humans, Chickens & Tigers*.)

Raine remarks on the effect that the painted tiger must have had on the boy Blake. She does not consider, however, the painting itself: Stubbs' "tyger," like all tigers he painted, is not an icon of untamed energy, but rather a recumbent, noble but cuddly, large cat. (In contrast, his lions are always portrayed committing acts of terror in a storm-tossed landscape—as in the famous *Horse Attacked by a Lion*, now at Yale; a motif Stubbs copied from Roman statuary, which was itself a copy from Scythian art.) And when Blake came to illustrate his "The Tyger" the animal was so oddly passive and sweet, almost smiling, that some friends complained. Shakespeare's hard-favored rage had been disguised by fair nature.

There is no doubt that Blake associated tigers with wrath and revolution, but it is interesting that Blake drew his physical image from Stubbs' painting and the half-dead animals in the local cages—surely he could have imagined it otherwise. (Consider the terror of his flea.) Or is Blake's (and Stubbs') tyger meant to demonstrate the possibilities latent beneath a passive exterior, as yogis traditionally sat immobile on tiger-skin mats, as the men of the industrialized West saw women: a dormant volcano? Is the tyger's blank smile its most fearful symmetry?

T.

It is quite probable that Blake had heard of the death of Sir Hector Munro's son, the most famous tiger-kills-Englishman story of the century. This account appeared in *The Gentleman's Magazine* in July 1793, the year "The Tyger" was composed:

> To describe the aweful, horrid and lamentable accident I have been an eye witness of, is impossible. Yesterday morning Mr Downey, of the [East India] Company's troops, Lieut. Pyefinch, poor Mr Munro and myself

went onshore on Saugor Island to shoot deer. We saw innumerable tracks of tigers and deer, but still we were induced to pursue our sport, and did the whole day. At about halfpast three we sat down on the edge of the jungle, to eat some cold meat sent us from the ship, and had just commenced our meal, when Mr Pyefinch and a black servant told us there was a fine deer within six yards of us. Mr Downey and myself immediately jumped up to take our guns; mine was the nearest, and I had just laid hold of it when I heard a roar, like thunder, and saw an immense tiger spring on the unfortunate Munro, who was sitting down. In a moment his head was in the beast's mouth, and he rushed into the jungle with him, with as much ease as I could lift a kitten, tearing through the thickest bushes and trees, everything yielding to his monstrous strength. The agonies of horror, regret, and, I must say fear (for there were other tigers, male and female) rushed on me at once. The only effort I could make was to fire at him, though the poor youth was still in his mouth. I relied partly on Providence, partly on my own aim, and fired a musket. I saw the tiger stagger and agitated, and cried out so immediately. Mr Downey then fired two shots and I one more. We retired from the jungle, and, a few minutes after, Mr Munro came up to us, all over blood, and fell. We took him on our backs to the boat, and got every medical assistance for him from the *Valentine* East India Main, which lay at anchor near the Island, but in vain. He lived twenty four hours in the extreme torture; his head and skull were torn and broke to pieces, and he was wounded by the claws all over the neck and shoulders; but it was better to take him away, though irrecoverable than leave him to be devoured limb by limb. We have just read the funeral service over the body, and committed it to the deep. He was an amiable and promising youth. I must observe, there was a large fire blazing close to us, composed of ten or a dozen whole trees; I made it myself, on purpose to keep the tigers off, as I had always heard it would. There were eight or ten of the natives about us; many shots had been fired at the

34

place, and much noise and laughing at the time; but this ferocious animal disregarded all. The human mind cannot form an idea of the scene; it turned my very soul within me. The beast was about four and a half feet high, and nine long. His head appeared as large as an ox's, his eyes darting fire, and his roar, when he first seized his prey, will never be out of my recollection. We had scarcely pushed our boats from the shore when the tigress made her appearance, raging mad almost, and remained on the sand as long as the distance would allow me to see her.

This scene of the humanly unthinkable, tiger and fire, may have partially inspired Blake. It did most certainly inspire Tipu Sultan. Sir Hector, the boy's father (and ancestor of Hector Hugh Munro, "Saki," whose stories are full of animals attacking people) was the archenemy of Tipu's father, Haidar Ali. At the news of the boy's death—which Tipu gleefully interpreted as a sign that his fellow tigers were joining the struggle against the British—he ordered the construction of a large mechanical toy, now in the Victoria and Albert Museum, to commemorate the event.

It is a lifesize wooden tiger crouched on a prone Englishman. They face each other; the man's left hand touches the tiger's face. They might be mistaken for lovers, but the tiger's teeth are sunk in the man's neck. ("Tipu Sultan," after all, means "Tiger Conqueror of Passion.") Wound up, the toy, simultaneously emits roars and hideous groans. Keats, in "The Cap and Bells," called it the "Man-Tiger-Organ."

Y.

After the fall of Seringpatam, tiger-killing became the standard measure in India of a Britisher's valor and innate superiority. And after the Empire forced peaceful co-existence onto the normally warring princely states, the maharajahs could only display their power and manhood in British terms. No visit to a palace by a distinguished foreigner was complete without a tiger hunt. That the guest would be neither endangered nor disappointed, the tigers were often drugged beforehand with opium-laced meat to ensure a safe and unerring shot.

George Yule of the Bengal Civil Service killed 400 then stopped counting. Colonel Rice killed 93 in four years. Montague Gerard killed 227. The Maharajah of Surguja killed 1,150. The Maharajah Scindia killed at least 700. The guests of the Maharajah Scindia killed at least 200. The Maharajah of Gauripiur killed 500 then stopped counting.

As early as 1827, one Capt. Mundy could write, with unintentional irony:

> Thus in the space of about two hours, and within sight of the camp, we found and slew three tigers, a piece of good fortune rarely to be met with in these modern times, when the spread of cultivation, and the zeal of the English sportsmen have almost exterminated the breed of these animals.

G.

The Bali tiger: *extinct since 1975.*
The Caspian tiger: 15–20 left, *extinction inevitable.*
The Java tiger: 6–10 left, *extinction inevitable.*
The Sumatra tiger: 700–800 left, *preservation possible.*
The Siberian tiger: 180–200 left, *extinction possible.*
The Chinese tiger: 50–80 left, *extinction probable.*
The Indo-Chinese tiger: 4500–5000 left, *declining rapidly.*
The Bengal tiger: 2500 left, *preservation possible.*
Estimated population of the Bengal tiger, *c.* 1900: 40,000.
Estimated world population of tigers, *c.* 1920: 100,000.

Cleansed, the tiger appears in Eliot's "Gerontion" as Christ.

E

Tigers eat men only when they are starving or are too old or sick to catch more elusive prey. In parts of India, it is believed that man-eating tigers are not tigers at all, but men who have transformed themselves into tigers to commit, for their purposes, masked acts of murder. These counterfeit tigers, the man-eaters, are recognizable to the villagers, as they would have been to Freud: they have no tails.

R.

Jorge Luis Borges, from his half-century of blindness, writes:

> In my childhood I ardently worshiped tigers . . . I used to linger endlessly before their cage at the zoo; I judged vast encyclopedias and books of natural history by the splendor of their tigers. (I still remember those illustrations: I who cannot quite recall the eyes or the smile of a woman.)

nominated by Sulfur

POLAND OF DEATH

by ALLEN GROSSMAN

From THE BRIGHT NAILS SCATTERED ON THE GROUND
(New Directions)

I

I hear my father underground scratching with a nail. And I say,
"Father, here is a word." He says, "It does not help. I am
Scratching my way with a nail ever since you dug me down
In the grave, and I have not yet come to Poland of death."
And I hear my mother saying, "Sing me something about the
Forest primeval." So I say, "Mother, here is a story."
And she says, "I have a pain in the blind eye, the left one
Which is dead."
          I hear my father scratching with a nail again,
And I offer him the words of a song, first one word and then
Another, and he refuses them. He says, "It is not a word," or
"It is just a word," or "It is not what you feel." "What
Do you feel?" Poland of death! Ever since I put my father
In the grave he has been scratching a way, and has not yet
Got under the sea, and mother has a pain in her blind eye.

So I tell her the story of a woman named Irene: How when she
Walked into a hayfield behind her house the animals shrieked.
How when she crossed over to the other side of the field
The clothes in the bluing froze, and all the yeast died
In the potato water. How when she reached the edge of the forest
Everything went up in flames in the farm she had left behind.
Then my father underground says, "Do not be bewildered by

38

The surfaces. In the depths, everything is law." And I say,
"My true love in the grave-deep forest nation is a forester."
And mother says, "This is the forest Primeval." Poland of death!

II

As not in life my father appeared to me
Naked in death and said, "This is my body."
So I undressed and faced him, and we were
Images of one another for he

Appeared to me at the same age I am.

Then he said, "Now I am in Death's country."
And I saw behind him in the dogmatic
Mirror of our death a forest of graves
In morning light. The smoky air was full
Of men and women sweeping the stone sills.
"Since you dug me down in America,"
He said, "I've been scratching a way with a nail,
And now I have come to Poland of Death."

And I saw the keepers of the graves moving
Among the shadows and the lights like lights.

Then he said to me—and not for the first time—
"Give me a word." And again, "Who are you?"
And then, after a long silence, "Write me
The Black Book of the world." And I replied,
"Louis, here is my body." And then one
Of us grew erect, and the cries began—
Like the weak voices of disembodied children
Driving crows from the cornfields.
                                        —He showed me
The severed head of a mother in her tears
Kissing and eating the severed head of a child;
And one familiar spirit like a snarled hank
Of somebody's black hair. And he showed also
A bloody angle of the wires where groans
Of men and women drowned the roar of motors

And mounted to a prophecy. Then he gave me
A sharp look and said, "Thank God, I have no children,"
And ran off with a cry down an alley of
That place like one who remembered suddenly
The day of his own death—

A short, pugnacious man, but honest and reliable.

Night fell and the mirror was empty for a while.
Then appeared, or half-appeared, Beatrice, my mother,
In the bed of her great age.
When she sleeps her human eye closes, and rests:
But her blind eye—the dead one—stares out
As if to say, "This is the forest primeval.
This is Death at last."

And I saw again the keepers of the graves
Moving among the shadows and the lights.

nominated by Michael Dennis Browne,
Edward Hirsch and Michael Ryan

OYSTER BAR
ON THE ROAD TO
MURURUA

by GEORGE STARBUCK

from PLOUGHSHARES

"But where will Marcos go?"

It's Bruce Lee, last of the Chieu Hois.
Taro reading: the Haoles are losing their pois.
The barfed-on offer their excusez-mois
Hey hey. Thanks for the memo. Un; deux; trois;

Banjoist kotoist jingoist Maoist Hoist,
the one-man all-girl hula group gets boistrouser and boistrouser half Piaf half ois-
eau-lyre half Rose La Rose half Blanche Dubois.

Not half bad for a honky-junkie-bourgeois
novelty act from Winnetka, Illinois.
Fabulous quick split. Great pair of borzois.
Woh woh the way she wears that car-wash chamois.

But clue me in. Envoi to end envois.

41

Is that you under that grass skirt, François?
I know it's one big commie-racist-judeois-
lamic plot out there but make me its connoisseur. Is it Christo back from dying the Simoïs

red? Does he giftwrap Diamond Head? Is it Lois
Lane to the rescue? Are these cold-stoned Iroquois
part of the schmeer? Am I getting the patois?
After we ticket Greenpeace do we hoist

anchor again for the dreaded Marco Is.?
Are we the head-on of the hoi pollois
while the great brains in basements hunch like Korchnois
or just a late-night case of the 2001s?

nominated by Michael Dennis Browne

BELA

by GERALD STERN

from AMERICAN POETRY REVIEW

This version of the starving artist
has him composing his last concerto
while dying of leukemia. Serge Koussevitsky
visits him in his hospital room
with flowers in his hand, the two of them
talk in tones of reverence, the last
long piece could be the best, the rain somewhere
makes daring noises, somewhere clouds are bursting.
I have the record in front of me. I drop
the needle again on the famous ending, five
long notes, then all is still, I have to imagine
two great seconds of silence and then applause
and shouting, he is in tears, Koussevitsky
leads him onto the stage. Or he is distant,
remembering the mountains, there is Boston
facing the wild Americans, he closes
his eyes so he can hear another note,
something from Turkey, or Romania, his mother
holding his left hand, straightening out the fingers,
he bows from the waist, he holds his right hand up.
I love the picture with Benny Goodman, Szigetti
is on the left, Goodman's cheeks are puffed
and his legs are crossed. Bartok is at the piano.
They are rehearsing Bartok's *Contrasts*. I lift
my own right hand, naturally I do that;
I listen to my blood, I touch my wrist.

If he could have only lived for three more years
he could have heard about our Mussolini
and seen the violent turn to the right and the end
of one America and the beginning of another.
That would have given him time enough to brood
on Hungary; that would have given him time
also to go among the Indians
and learn their music, and listen to their chants,
those tribes from Michigan and Minnesota,
just like the tribes of the Finns and the Urgo-Slavics,
moaning and shuffling in front of their wooden tents.
There is a note at the end of the second movement
I love to think about; it parodies
Shostakovitch; it is a kind of flutter
of the lips. And there is a note—I hear it—
of odd regret for a life not lived enough,
everyone knows that sound, for me it's remorse,
and there is a note of crazy satisfaction,
this I love, of the life he would not change
no matter what—no other animal
could have such pleasure. I think of this as I turn
the music off, and I think of his poor eyes
as they turned to ice—his son was in the room
and saw the change—I call it a change. Bartok
himself lectured his friends on death, it was
his woods and mountain lecture, fresh green shoots
pushing up through the old, the common home
that waits us all, the cycles, the laws of nature,
wonderfully European, all life and death
at war—peacefully—one thing replacing another,
although he grieved over cows and pitied dogs
and listened to pine cones as if they came from the sea
and fretted over the smallest of life. He died
September 28, 1945,
just a month after the war was over.
It took him sixty days to finish the piece
from the time he lay there talking to Koussevitsky
to the time he put a final dot on the paper,
a little pool of ink to mark the ending.
There are the five loud notes, I walk upstairs

to hear them, I put a silk shawl over my head
and rock on the wooden floor, the shawl is from France
and you can see between the threads; I feel
the darkness, I was born with a veil over
my eyes, it took me forty years to rub
the gum away, it was a blessing, I sit
for twenty minutes in silence, daylight is coming,
the moon is probably near, probably lifting
its satin nightgown, one hand over the knee
to hold the cloth up so the feet can walk
through the wet clouds; I love that bent-over motion,
that grace at the end of a long and furious night.
I go to sleep on the floor, there is a pillow
somewhere for my heavy head, my hand
is resting on the jacket, Maazel is leading
the Munich orchestra, a nurse is pulling
the sheet up, Bartok is dead, his wife is walking
past the sun room, her face is white, her mind
is on the apartment they lost, where she would put
the rugs, how she would carry in his breakfast,
where they would read, her mind is on Budapest,
she plays the piano for him, she is eighteen
and he is thirty-seven, he is gone
to break the news, she waits in agony,
she goes to the telephone; I turn to the window,
I stare at my palm, I draw a heart in the dust,
I put the arrow through it, I place the letters
one inside the other. I sleep, I sleep.

nominated by Linda Bierds and James Baker Hall

ON THE MEANING OF LIFE

fiction by IRINA RATUSHINSKAIA

from A TALE OF THREE HEADS (Hermitage Press)

ONCE UPON a time there lived a vegetarian boa constrictor. He never ever ate meat. Not out of moral conviction and for no particular reason, he simply didn't. It just wouldn't have seemed right. Instead, he ate only cucumbers and bananas; they were easier to swallow. Besides, the material things in life generally didn't interest the boa constrictor. For, his all-consuming passion (and you can imagine what it's like when passion consumes a boa constrictor!) was rabbit-watching.

Now just hold on a minute before you start snickering! He was a vegetarian. And he just watched. He watched them platonically. You perhaps, might find it difficult to comprehend, but think about it for a minute: a little white ball of fur just sitting there wiggling his nose and twitching his ears. . . . What a little cutie-pie!

You're doing it again. But when you were three years old and your over-emotional aunt would take you in her arms and say "I'm going to gobble you up," you never suspected her of doing anything of the sort, right? You were able to tell the difference, right?

Well, and so the boa constrictor loved and suffered a great deal. But he suffered mostly because he saw rabbits extremely rarely, only about twice a year! And, really, where can you find a rabbit these days? Some idiot told the boa constrictor he ought to slither down to the market early in the morning, where, true, he did find a rabbit, but you can imagine what shape it was in: splayed out on a dirty counter in front of a grubby peasant woman, five rubles a kilo—and subject to all sorts of abuse—for what! I won't even describe how the boa constrictor felt. Any sensitive person would understand.

From that time on the boa constrictor generally preferred not to go out in public. But rabbits appeared on television only rarely, and when they did, it just wasn't the same. So, strange as it may seem, the fact is that on Friday, March 18, the boa constrictor suddenly turned up in the crowd at the circus, and that evening changed the course of his life.

I'll spare you a description of the first half of the show—the usual stuff—but the second! The second half, for that matter, started out banally enough. A typical magician in a typical rustling black cape. With a magic wand, of course, and wearing a top hat. But then he took off the top hat, stuck his pale hand inside, and pulled it out. A little white ball of fur! With little paws and beady little eyes, and, most important of all, cute little ears! Sitting on a wooden stool and nibbling a carrot! That evening the boa constrictor's heart so overflowed that he noticed nothing else. He was happy, he loved everyone; he still loved everyone even on the way to the coatroom (you of all people would know it's practically impossible to love a coatroom crowd!). Far from getting annoyed, he was radiant and meek, and somehow he could only pity those around him. Poor, poor people! Here they are pushing and shoving and getting angry, but where will they be fifty years from now?

At home that night the boa constrictor didn't sleep a wink. The next morning he rushed off without drinking his coffee to buy a top hat, stopping only once on the way to say a kind word to an early morning yardkeeper hosing down the rosy street. By seven o'clock he was already in front of the store. Yes, you're absolutely right: the stores don't open until ten! Of course, in a rational state of mind it's not so difficult to figure that out, to wake up at the usual time, brush your teeth, eat breakfast, look yourself over in the mirror on the way out, and later, towards ten, take off from work. Of course! Who's arguing?

But the boa constrictor pined and ached in front of the store a full three hours while, you can be sure, no exceptions were made for him, and not only was he not admitted a second early, but the doors opened a full three and a half minutes late. Naturally, there were no top hats. The boa constrictor was only wasting his breath when he offered to take any size, just so long as it was satin and black; without even turning to face him, that blonde bitch of a salesgirl just rattled off her usual "we never carry them . . ., we never carry them. . . ." Need I mention that the boa constrictor left the other stores empty-handed as well, even after offering to pay extra and to purchase items he didn't need.

With heavy heart he returned home and coiled up in a corner. That day he ate no cucumbers and no bananas. Not the next day either. He ate nothing at all, while his still unfinished cup of coffee stood untouched on the kitchen table. At long last his friends started to worry, made the rounds, pulled a few strings, and after considerable finagling and by juggling a long series of outstanding favors, they came up with a black satin top hat. I don't know where they got it, perhaps from a theatrical costume dealer or a museum. But it was the real thing. With a white lining. And the elated boa constrictor, without even saying thank you, rushed towards his dream of dreams, then froze in quiet expectation. But no wiggling ears, absolutely nothing, appeared over the rim. The top hat was empty, cold, and formal, as it should be.

The boa constrictor, contrary to expectations, did not lose heart, and his friends' worst fears were hardly justified. Rather, he grew calm in spirit, more focused, and at least superficially returned to his former way of life. For he knew that great passion could alter the course of fate.

For hours on end he would stare at the top hat, aware that he still didn't know the Right Look, yet never for an instant doubting that one marvelous day he would find it. And, of course, that day came and marvelous it was.

Wiggling and white, out of the top hat it hopped (all four paws right onto the tablecloth!), looked the boa constrictor straight in the eye, then, in a moment of self-oblivion, edged towards him! Suddenly something snapped. The rabbit hopped uncertainly around the boa constrictor—something, obviously, just wasn't right—while the boa constrictor, noticing nothing, gazed lovingly, tenderly at the rabbit, at his ears and his cotton tail. Do you know that a rabbit foot brings good luck?

The rabbit grew more and more perplexed, though nothing was really happening, and finally, in a trance, with no idea what he was doing, he went outside and headed down the street. Something troubled him, some vague debt or calling, and for the rest of his life the rabbit would wander restlessly, wracking his little brain for answers, never knowing where or how to apply his energies. He craved a cause, cognizance that life on this earth is not in vain, but by evening, when a sense of moribundity and alarm began to set in, everything around him seemed so banal and petty, and the feeling that no one needed him, that nothing lay ahead for him, that his soul was completely empty, reduced him to anything but rabbit tears. At moments he glimpsed another world, a world distant and radiant, where there were no doubts and where everything flourished and overflowed with meaning. But where was the way there?

All the while every evening the boa constrictor, joyous and calm, continued to gaze at the top hat, and every evening a rabbit would crawl out, hop around, and, finally, leave in a daze. Somewhere, probably, those rabbits would run into each other, heave a common sigh, talk about one and the same thing, and clasp their weak little paws.

Translated by Diane Nemec Ignashev
nominated by Heritage Press

JACK OF DIAMONDS

fiction by ELIZABETH SPENCER

from THE KENYON REVIEW

ONE APRIL AFTERNOON, Central Park, right across the street, turned green all at once. It was a green toned with gold and seemed less a color of leaves than a stained cloud settled down to stay. Rosalind brought her bird book out on the terrace and turned her face up to seek out something besides pigeons. She arched, to hang her long hair backwards over the terrace railing, soaking in sunlight while the starlings whirled by.

The phone rang, and she went inside.

"I just knew you'd be there, Rosie," her father said. "What a gorgeous day. Going to get hotter. You know what I'm thinking about? Lake George."

"Let's go right now," Rosalind said.

The cottage was at Bolton Landing. Its balconies were built out over the water. You walked down steps and right off into the lake, or into the boat. In a lofty beamed living room, shadows of water played against the walls and ceiling. There was fine lake air, and chill pure evenings. . . .

The intercom sounded. "Gristede's, Daddy. They're buzzing."

Was it being in the theater that made her father, whenever another call came, exert himself to get more into the first? "Let's think about getting up there, Rosie. Summer's too short as it is. You ask Eva when she comes in. Warm her up to it. We'll make our pitch this evening. She's never even seen it . . . can you beat that?"

"I'm not sure she'll even like it," Rosalind said.

"Won't like it? It's hardly camping out. Of course, she'll love it. Get it going, Rosie baby. I'm aiming for home by seven."

50

The grocer's son who brought the order up wore jeans just like Rosalind's. "It's getting hot," he remarked. "It's about melted my ass off."

"Let's see if you brought everything." She had tried to give up presiding over the food after her father remarried, but when her stepmother turned out not to care much about what happened in the kitchen, she had cautiously gone back to seeing about things.

"If I forgot, I'll get it. But if you think of something—"

"I know, I'll come myself. You think you got news?"

They were old friends. They sassed each other. His name was Luis—Puerto Rican.

It was after the door to the service entrance closed with its hollow echo, and was bolted, and the service elevator had risen, opened, and closed on Luis, that Rosalind felt the changed quality in things, a new direction, like the tilt of an airliner's wing. She went to the terrace, and found the park's greenness surer of itself than ever. She picked up her book and went inside. A boy at school, seeing her draw birds, had given it to her. She stored it with her special treasures.

Closing the drawer, she jerked her head straight, encountering her own wide blue gaze in her bedroom mirror. From the entrance hall, a door was closing. She gathered up a pack of cards spread out for solitaire and slid them into a gilded box. She whacked at her long brown hair with a brush; then she went out. It was Eva.

Rosalind Jennings's stepmother had short, raven black glossy hair, a full red mouth, jetty brows and lashes. Shortsighted, she handled the problem in the most open way, by wearing great round glasses trimmed in tortoise shell. All through the winter—a winter Rosalind would always remember as The Stepmother: Year I—Eva had gone around the apartment in gold wedge-heeled slippers, pink slacks, and a black chiffon blouse. Noiseless on the wall-to-wall carpets, the slippers slapped faintly against stockings or flesh when she walked—spaced, intimate ticks of sound. "Let's face it, Rosie," her father said, when Eva went off to the kitchen for a fresh drink as he tossed in his blackjack hand. "She's a sexy dame."

Sexy or not, she was kind to Rosalind. "I wouldn't have married anybody you didn't like," her father told her. "That child's got *the* most heavenly eyes," she'd overheard Eva say.

Arriving now, having triple-locked the apartment door, Eva set the inevitable Saks parcels down on the foyer table, and dumped her jersey jacket off her arm onto the chair with a gasp of relief. "It's turned so hot!" Rosalind followed her to the kitchen where she poured orange juice and soda over ice. Her nails were firm, hard, perfectly painted. They resembled, to Rosalind, ten small creatures who had ranked themselves on this stage of fingertips. Often they ticked off a pile of poker chips from top to bottom, red and white, as Eva pondered. "Stay . . ." or "Call . . ." or "I'm out . . ." then, "Oh, damn, you, Nat . . . that's twice in a row."

"I've just been talking on the phone to Daddy," Rosalind said. "I've got to warn you. He's thinking of the cottage."

"Up there in Vermont?"

"It's in New York, on Lake George. Mother got it from her folks. You know, they lived in Albany. The thing is, Daddy's always loved it. He's hoping you will too, I think."

Eva finished her orange juice. Turning to rinse the glass in the sink, she wafted out perfume and perspiration. "It's a little far for a summer place. . . . But if it's what you and Nat like, why then—" She affectionately pushed a dark strand of Rosalind's hair back behind her ear. Her fingers were chilly from the glass. "I'm yours to command." Her smile, intimate and confident, seemed to repeat its red picture on every kitchen object.

Daughter and stepmother had got a lot chummier in the six months since her father had married. At first, Rosalind was always wondering what they thought of her. For here was a new "they," like a whole new being. She had heard, for instance, right after the return from the Nassau honeymoon:

Eva: "I want to be sure and leave her room just the way it is."

Nat: "I think that's right. Change is up to her."

But Rosalind could not stop her angry thought: *You'd just better try touching my room!* Her mother had always chosen the decor, always the rose motif, roses in the wallpaper and deeper rose valances and matching draperies. This was a romantic theme with her parents, accounting for her name. Her father would warble "Sweet Rosie O'Grady," while downing his whiskey. He would waltz his little girl around the room. She'd learned to dance before she could walk, she thought.

"Daddy sets the music together with what's happening on the stage. He gets the dancers and actors to carry out the music. That's different from composing or writing lyrics." So Rosalind would explain to new friends at school, every year. Now she'd go off to some other school next fall, still ready with her lifelong lines. "You must have heard of some of his shows. Remember So-and-So, and then there was. . . ." Watching their impressionable faces form their cries. "We've got the records of that!" "Was your mother an actress?" "My stepmother used to be an actress—nobody you'd know about. My mother died. She wasn't ever in the theater. She studied art history at Vassar." Yes, and married the assistant manager of his family firm: Jennings's Finest Woolen Imports; he did not do well. Back to his first love, theater. From college on they thought they'd never get him out of it, and they were right. Some purchase he had chosen in West Germany turned out to be polyester, sixty percent. "I had a will to fail," Nat Jennings would shrug, when he thought about it. "If your heart's not in something, you can't succeed," was her mother's reasoning, clinging to her own sort of knowing which had to do with the things you picked, felt about, what went where. Now here was another woman with other thoughts about the same thing. She'd better not touch my room, thought Rosalind, or I'll . . . what? Trip her in the hallway, hide her glasses, throw the keys out the window?

"What are you giggling at, Rosie?"

Well might they ask, just back from Nassau at a time of falling leaves. "I'm wondering what to do with this leg of lamb. It's too long and skinny."

"Broil it like a great big chop." Still honeymooning, they'd be holding hands, she bet, on the living room sofa.

"Just you leave my room alone," she sang out to this new Them. "Or I won't cook for you!"

"Atta girl, Rosie!"

Now, six months later in the balmy early evening with windows wide open, they were saying it again. Daddy had come in, hardly even an hour later than he said, and there was the big conversation, starting with cocktails, lasting through dinner, all about Lake George and how to get there, where to start, but all totally impossible until day after tomorrow at the soonest.

"One of the few unpolluted lakes left!" Daddy enthused to Eva. It was true. If you dropped anything from the boat into the water, your mother would call from the balcony, "It's right down there, darling," and you'd see it as plainly as if it lay in sunlight at your feet and you could reach down for it instead of diving. The caretaker they'd had for years, Mr. Thibodeau, reported to them from time to time. Everything was all right, said Mr. Thibodeau. He had about fifteen houses on his list, for watching over, especially during the long winters. He was good. They'd left the cottage empty for two summers, and it was still all right. She remembered the last time they were there, June three years back. She and Daddy were staying while Mother drove back to New York, planning to see Aunt Mildred from Denver before she put out for the West again. "What a nuisance she can't come here!" Mother had said. "It's going to be sticky as anything in town, and when I think of that thruway!"

"Say you've got food poisoning," said Daddy. "Make something up."

"But Nat! Can't you understand? I really *do* want to see Mildred!" It was Mother's little cry that still sounded in Rosalind's head. "Whatever you do, please don't go to the apartment," Daddy said. He hadn't washed dishes for a week; he'd be ashamed for an in-law to have an even lower opinion of him, though he thought it wasn't possible. "It's a long drive," her mother pondered. "Take the Taconic, it's cooler." "Should I spend one night or two?"

Her mother was killed on the Taconic Parkway the next day by a man coming out of a crossover. There must have been a moment of terrible disbelief when she saw that he was actually going to cross in front of her. Wasn't he looking, didn't he see? They would never know. He died in the ambulance. She was killed at once.

Rosalind and her father, before they left, had packed up all her mother's clothing and personal things, but that was all they'd had the heart for. The rest they walked off and left, just so. "Next summer," they had said, as the weeks wore on and still they'd made no move. The next summer came, and still they did not stir. One day they said, "Next summer." Mr. Thibodeau said not to worry, everything was fine. So the Navaho rugs were safe and all the pottery, the copper and brass, the racked pewter. The books would all be lined in place on the shelves, the music in the Victorian music rack just as it had been left, Schumann's "Carnaval" (she could see it still) on top. And if everything was really fine, the canoe would be dry, though dusty and full of spiderwebs, suspended out in the boat house, and the roof must be holding firm and dry, as Mr. Thibodeau would have reported any leak immediately. All that had happened, he said, was that the steps into the water had to have new uprights, the bottom two replaced, and that the eaves on the northeast corner had broken from a falling limb and been repaired.

Mention of the fallen limb recalled the storms. Rosalind remembered them blamming away while she and her mother huddled back of the stairway, feeling aimed at by the thunderbolts; or if Daddy was there, they'd sing by candlelight while he played the piano. He dared the thunder by imitating it in the lower base. . . .

"Atta girl, Rosie."

She had just said she wasn't afraid to go up there alone tomorrow, take the bus or train, and consult with Mr. Thibodeau. The Thibodeaus had long ago taken a fancy to Rosalind; a French Canadian, Mrs. Thibodeau had taught her some French songs, and fed her on tourtière and beans.

"That would be wonderful," said Eva.

"I just can't let her do it," Nat said.

"I can stay at Howard Johnson's. After all, I'm seventeen."

While she begged, her father looked at her steadily from the end of the table, finishing coffee. "I'll telephone the Thibodeaus," he finally said. "One thing you aren't to do is stay in the house alone. Howard Johnson's is okay. We'll get you a room there." Then, because he knew what the house had meant and wanted to let her know it, he took her shoulder (Eva not being present) and squeezed it, his eyes looking deep into hers, and Irish tears rising moistly. "Life goes on, Rosie," he whispered. "It has to."

She remembered all that, riding the bus. But it was for some unspoken reason that he had wanted her to go. And she knew that it was right for her to do it, not only to see about things. It was an important journey. For both of them? Yes, for them both.

Mr. Thibodeau himself met her bus, driving up to Lake George Village.

"Not many people yet," he said. "We had a good many on the weekend, out to enjoy the sun. Starting a baseball team up here. The piers took a beating back in the winter. Not enough ice and too much wind. How's your daddy?"

"He's fine. He wants to come back here now."

"You like your new mother? Shouldn't ask. Just curious."

"She's nice," said Rosalind.

"Hard to be a match for the first one."

Rosalind did not answer. She had a quietly aware way of closing her mouth when she did not care to reply.

"Pretty?" pursued Mr. Thibodeau. Not only the caretaker, Mr. Thibodeau was also a neighbor. He lived between the property and the road. You had to be nice to the Thibodeaus; so much depended on them.

"Yes, she's awfully pretty. She was an actress. She had just a little part in the cast of the show he worked with last year."

"That's how they met, was it?"

To Rosalind, it seemed that Eva had just showed up one evening in her father's conversation at dinner. "There's somebody I want you to meet, Rosie. She's—well, she's a she. I've seen her once or twice. I think you'll like her. But if you don't, we'll scratch her, Rosie. That's a promise."

"Here's a list, Mr. Thibodeau," she said. "All the things Daddy wants done are on it. Telephone, plumbing, electricity . . . maybe Mrs. Thibodeau can come in and clean. I've got to check the linens for mildew. Then go through the canned stuff and make a grocery list."

"We got a new supermarket since you stopped coming, know that?"

"I bet."

"We'll go tomorrow. I'll take you."

The wood-lined road had been broken into over and over on the lake side, the other side, too, by new motels. Signs about pools, TV, vacancy, came rudely up and at them, until, swinging left, they entered woods again and drew near the cutoff to the narrow winding drive among the pines. "Thibodeau" the mail box read in strong, irregular letters, and by its side a piece of weathered plywood nailed to the fence post said "Jennings," painted freshly over the ghost of old lettering beneath.

She bounced along with Mr. Thibodeau, who, his black hair grayed over, still had his same beaked nose, which in her mind gave him his Frenchness and his foreignness. Branches slapped the car windows. The tires squished through ruts felted with fallout from the woods. They reached the final bend. "Stop," said Rosalind, for something white had passed beneath the wheels which gave out a sound like dry bones breaking. She jumped out. It was only birch branches, half rotted. "I'll go on alone." She ran ahead of his station wagon, over pine needles and through the fallen leaves of two autumns, which slowed her motion until she felt the way she did in dreams.

The cottage was made of natural wood, no shiny lacquer covering it; boughs around it, pine and oak, pressed down like protective arms. The reach of the walls was laced over with undergrowth, so that the house at first glance looked small as a hut, not much wider than the door. Running there, Rosalind tried the knob with the confidence of a child running to her mother, only to find it locked, naturally; then with a child's abandon, she flung out her arms against the paneling, hearing her heart thump on the wood until Mr. Thibodeau gently detached her little by little as though she had got stuck there.

"Now there . . . there now . . . just let me get hold of this key." He had a huge wire ring for his keys, labels attached to each. His clientele. "Des clients, vous en avez beaucoup," Rosalind had once said to him as she was starting French in school. But Mr. Thibodeau was unregretfully far from his Quebec origins. His family had come there from northern Vermont to get a milder climate. Lake George was a sun trap, a village sliding off the Adirondacks toward the lake, facing a day-long southeast exposure.

The key ground in the lock. Mr. Thibodeau kicked the base of the door, and the hinges whined. He let her enter alone, going tactfully back to his station wagon for nothing at all. He gave her time to wander before he followed her.

She would have had to come someday, Rosalind thought, one foot following the other, moving forward: the someday was this one. It wasn't as if anything had actually "happened" there. The door frame which opened from the entrance hall into the living room did not face the front door but was about ten feet from it to the left. Thus the full scope of the high shadowy room, which was the real heart of the cottage, opened all at once to the person entering. Suddenly, there was an interior world. The broad windows opposite, peaked in an irregular triangle at the top, like something in a modernistic church, opened onto the lake, and from the water a rippling light, muted by shade, played constantly on the high-beamed ceiling. Two large handwoven Indian rugs covered the central area of floor; on a table before the windows, a huge pot of brown and beige pottery was displayed, filled with money plant which had grown dusty and ragged. There were

57

coarse-fibered curtains in off-white monk's cloth, now dragging askew, chair coverings in heavy fabric, orange and white cushions, and the piano, probably so out of tune now with the damp it would never sound right, which sat closed and silent in the corner. An open stairway more like a ladder than a stair, rose to the upper floor balcony, with bedrooms in the wing. "We're going to fall and break our silly necks someday," she could hear her mother saying. "It is pretty, though." The Indian weaving of the hawk at sunrise, all black and red, hung on the far left wall.

She thought of her mother, a small quick woman with bronze close-curling hair cut short, eager to have what she thought of as "just the right thing," wandering distant markets, seeking out things for the cottage. It seemed to Rosalind that when she opened the door past the stairwell into the bedroom which her parents had used, that surely she would find that choosing, active ghost in motion over a chest or moving a curtain at the window, and that surely, ascending the dangerous stair to look into the two bedrooms above, she would hear the quick voice say, "Oh, it's you, Rosalind, now you just tell me. . . ." But everything was silent.

Rosalind came downstairs. She returned to the front door and saw that Mr. Thibodeau had driven away. Had he said something about going back for something? She closed the door quietly, reentered the big natural room and let the things there speak.

For it was all self-contained, knowing and infinitely quiet. The lake gave its perpetual lapping sound, like nibbling fish in shallow water, now and then splashing up, as though a big one had flourished. Lap, lap against the wooden piles which supported the balcony. Lap against the steps, with a swishing motion on the lowest one, a passing-over instead of an against sound. The first steps were replaced, new, the color fresh blonde instead of worn brown. The room heard the lapping, the occasional splash, the swish of water.

Rosalind herself was being got through to by something even less predictable than water. What she heard was memory: voices quarreling. From three years ago they woke to life. A slant of light—that had brought them back. Just at this time of day, she had been coming in from swimming. The voices had climbed the large clear windows, clawing for exit, finding none, had fled like people getting out of a burning theater, through the door to the far right that opened out on the balcony. She had been coming up the steps from the water, when the voices stampeded over her, frightening, intense, racing outward from the panic within. "You know you do and you know you will . . . there's no use to lie, I've been through all that. Helpless is all I can feel, all I can be. That's the awful part . . . !" "I didn't drive all this way just to get back into that. Go on, get away to New York with dear Aunt Mildred. Who's to know, for that matter, if it's Mildred at all?" "You hide your life like a card in the deck and then have the nerve—! Oh, you're a great magician, aren't you?" "Hush, she's out there . . . hush, now . . . you must realize. . . ." "I do nothing but realize. . . ." "Hush . . . just . . . no. . . ." And their known selves returned to them as she came in, dripping, pretending nothing had happened, gradually believing her own pretense.

The way she'd learned to do, all the other times. Sitting forgotten, for the moment, in an armchair too big back in New York, listening while her heart hurt until her mother said, "Darling, go to your room, I'll be there in a minute." Even on vacation, it was sometimes the same thing. And Mother coming in later, as she half-slept, half-waited, to hold her hand and say, "Just forget it now, tomorrow it won't seem real. We all love each other. Tomorrow you won't even remember." Kissed and tucked in, she trusted. It didn't happen all the time. And the tomorrows were clear and bright. The only trouble was, this time there hadn't been any tomorrow, only the tomorrow of her mother's driving away. Could anybody who sounded like that, saying those things, have a wreck the very next morning and those things have nothing to do with it?

Maybe I got the times mixed up.

("She had a little part in the cast of the show he did last year. . . ." "So that's how they met, was it?") ("Your mother got the vapors sometimes. The theater scared her." She'd heard her father say that.)

I dreamed it all, she thought, and couldn't be sure this wasn't true, though wondered if she could dream so vividly that she could see the exact print of her wet foot just through the doorway there, beside it the drying splash from the water's runnel down her leg. But it could have been another day.

Why not just ask Daddy?

At the arrival of this simple solution, she let out a long sigh, flung her hands back of her head and stretched out on the beautiful rug which her mother had placed there. Her eyes dimmed; she felt the lashes flutter downward. . . .

A footstep and a voice awakened her from how short a sleep she did not know. Rolling over and sitting up, she saw a strange woman—short, heavyset, with faded skin, gray hair chopped off around her face, plain run-down shoes. She was wearing slacks. Then she smiled and things about her changed.

"You don't remember me, do you? I'm Marie Thibodeau. I remember you and your mom and your dad. That was all bad. *Gros dommage*. But you're back now. You'll have a good time again, eh? We thought maybe you didn't have nothing you could eat yet. You come back with me. I going make you some nice lunch. My husband said to come find you."

She rose slowly, walked through shadows toward the woman, who still had something of the quality of an apparition. Did she think that because of her mother, others must have died too? She followed. The lunch was the same as years before: the meat pie, the beans, the catsup and relish and the white bread taken sliced from its paper. And the talk, too, was nearly the same: kind things said before, repeated now: chewed, swallowed.

"You don't remember me, but I remember you. You're *the* Nat Jenning's daughter, used to come here with your folks." This was what the boy said, in Howard Johnson's.

"We're the tennis ones . . . Dunbar," said the girl, who was his sister, not his date; for saying "tennis" had made Rosalind remember the big house their family owned—"the villa," her father called it—important grounds around it, and a long frontage on the lake. She remembered them as strutting around, smaller then, holding rackets which looked too large for their bodies. They had been allowed on the court only at certain hours, along with their friends, but even then they had wished to be observed. Now here they were before her, grown up and into denim, like anybody else. Paul and Elaine. They had showed up at the entrance to the motel restaurant, tan and healthy. Paul had acquired a big smile; Elaine a breathless hesitating voice, the kind Daddy didn't like, it was so intended to tease.

"Let's all find a booth together," Paul Dunbar said.

Rosalind said, "I spent half the afternoon with the telephone man, the other half at the grocery. Getting the cottage opened."

"You can come up to our house after we eat. Not much open here yet. We're on spring holidays."

"They extended it. Outbreak of measles."

"She made that up," said the Dunbar boy who was speaking straight and honestly to Rosalind. "We told them we had got sick and would be back next week."

"It's because we are so in-tell-i-gent. . . . Making our grades is not a problem," Elaine said in her trick voice.

"We've got the whole house to ourselves. Our folks won't be coming till June. Hey, why don't you move down with us?"

"I can't," said Rosalind. "Daddy's coming up tomorrow. And my stepmother. He got married again."

"Your parents split?"

"No . . . I mean, not how you think. My mother was killed three years ago, driving to New York. She had a wreck."

"Jesus, what a break. I'm sorry, Rosalind."

"You heard about it, Paul. We both did."

"It's still a tough break."

"Mr. Thibodeau's been helping me. Mrs. Thibodeau's cleaning up. They're coming tomorrow." If this day is ever over.

She went with them after dinner. . . .

The Dunbar house could be seen from the road, a large two-story brick house on the lake, with white wood trim. There were two one-story wings, like smaller copies of the central house, their entrances opening at either side, the right one on a flagstone walk, winding through a sloping lawn, the left on a porte cochère, where the Dunbars parked. Within, the large rooms were shuttered, the furniture dust covered. The three of them went to the glassed-in room on the opposite wing and put some records on. They danced on the tiled floor among the white wicker furniture.

Had they heard a knocking, or hadn't they? A strange boy was standing in the doorway, materialized. Elaine had cried, "Oh, goodness, Fenwick, you scared me!" She moved back from Paul's controlling rhythm. They were all facing the stranger. He was heavier than Paul; he was tall and grown to the measure of his big hands and feet. He looked serious and easily detachable from the surroundings; it wasn't possible to guess by looking at him where he lived or what he was doing there.

"Fenwick . . ." Paul was saying to him. What sort of name was that? He strode over to the largest chaise longue, and fitted himself into it. Paul introduced Rosalind to Fenwick.

"I have a mile-long problem to solve before Thursday," Fenwick said. "I'm getting cross-eyed. You got a beer?"

"Fenwick is a math-uh-mat-i-cul gene-iyus," Elaine told Rosalind. The record finished and she switched off the machine.

"Fenwick wishes he was," said Fenwick.

It seemed that they were all at some school together, called Wakeley, over in Vermont. They knew people to talk about together. "I've been up about umpteen hours," Rosalind said. "I came all the way from New York this morning."

"Just let me finish this beer, and I'll take you home," said Fenwick.

"It's just Howard Johnson's," she said.

"There are those that call it home," said Fenwick, downing beer.

They walked together to the highway where Fenwick had left his little old rickety car. The trees were bursting from the bud, you could practically smell them grow, but the branches were still dark, and cold looking and wet, because it had rained while they were inside. The damp road seamed beneath the tires. There were not many people around. She hugged herself into her raincoat.

"The minute I saw you I remembered you," Fenwick said. "I just felt like we were friends. You used to go to that little park with all the other kids. Your daddy would put you on the seesaw. He pushed it up and down for you. But I don't guess you'd remember me."

"I guess I ought to," Rosalind said. "Maybe you grew a lot."

"You can sure say that. They thought I wasn't going to stop." The sign ahead said Howard Johnson's. "I'd do my problem better if we had some coffee."

"Tomorrow maybe," she said. "I'm dead tired." But what she thought was, He likes me.

At the desk she found three messages, all from Daddy and Eva. "Call when you come in. . . ." "Call as soon as you can. . . ." "Call even if late. . . ." She called.

"So it'll be late tomorrow, maybe around dinner. What happened was—" He went on and on. With Nat Jennings, you got used to postponements, so her mother always said. "How's it going, Rosie? I've thought about you every minute."

"Everything's ready for you, or it will be when you come."

"Don't cook up a special dinner. We might be late. It's a long road."

In a dream her mother was walking with her. They were in the library at Lake George. In the past her mother had often gone there to check out books. She was waiting for a certain book she wanted, but it hadn't come back yet. "But you did promise me last week," she was saying to somebody at the desk; then she was walking up the street with Rosalind, and Rosalind saw the book in her shopping bag. "You got it after all," she said to her mother. "I just found it lying there on the walk," her mother said, then Rosalind remembered how she had leaned down to pick up something. "That's nice," said Rosalind, satisfied that things could happen this way. "I think it's nice, too," said her mother, and they went along together.

By noon the next day her work was done, but she felt bad because she had found something—a scarf in one of the dresser drawers. It was a sumptuous French satin scarf in a jagged play of colors, mainly red, a shade her mother with her coppery hair had never worn. It smelled of Eva's perfume. So they had been up here before, she thought, but why—this far from New York? And why not say so? Helpless was what her mother said she felt. Can I, thought Rosalind, ask Daddy about this, too?

In the afternoon she drove up into the Adirondacks with Elaine and Paul Dunbar. They took back roads, a minor highway that crossed from the lakeshore road to the thruway; another beyond that threaded along the bulging sides of the mountains. They passed one lake after another: some small and limpid, others half-choked with water lilies and thickly shaded where frogs by the hundreds were chorusing, invisible among the fresh lime green; and some larger still, marked with stumps of trees mysteriously broken off. From one of these, strange bird calls sounded. Then the road ran upward. Paul pulled up under some tall pines and stopped.

"We're going to climb," he announced.

It suited Rosalind because Elaine had just asked her to tell her "all about the theater, every single thing you know." She wouldn't have to do that, at least. Free of the car, they stood still in deserted air. There was no feel of houses near. The brother and sister started along a path they apparently knew. It led higher, winding through trees, with occasional glimpses of a rotting lake below, and promise of some triumphant view above. Rosalind followed next to Paul, with Elaine trailing behind. Under a big oak they stopped to rest.

Through the leaves a small view opened up; there was a little valley below with a stream running through it. The three of them sat hugging their knees and talking, once their breath came back. "Very big deal," Paul was saying. "Five people sent home, weeping parents outside offices, and everybody tiptoeing past. About what? The whole school smokes pot, everybody knows it. Half the profs were on it. Remember old Borden?"

Elaine's high-pitched laugh. "He said, 'Just going for a joint,' when he pushed into the john one day. Talking back over his shoulder."

"What really rocked the boat was when everybody started cheating. Plain and fancy."

"What made them start?" Rosalind asked. Pot was passed around at her school, too, in the upper eighties, but you could get into trouble about it.

"You know Miss Hollander was heard to say out loud one day, 'The dean's a shit.' "

"That's the source of the whole fucking mess," said Paul. "The stoopid dean's a shit."

"Is he a fag?" asked Rosalind, not too sure of language like this.

"Not even that," said Paul, and picked up a rock to throw. He put down his hand to Rosalind. "Come on, we got a little further to climb."

The path snaked sharply upward. She followed his long legs and brown loafers, one with the stitching breaking at the top, and stopping for breath, she looked back and discovered they were alone. "Where's Elaine?"

"She's lazy." He stopped high above to wait for her. She looked up to him and saw him turn to face her, jeans tight over her narrow thighs and flat waist. He put a large hand down to pull her up, and grinned as she came unexpectedly too fast; being thin and light, she sailed up so close they bumped together. His face skin was glossy with sweat. "Just a little farther," he encouraged her. His front teeth were not quite even. Light exploded from the tips of his ears. Grappling at roots, avoiding sheer surfaces of rock, gaining footholds on patches of earth, they burst finally out on a ledge of rough but fairly flat stone, chiseled away as though in a quarry, overlooking a dizzying sweep of New York countryside. "Oh," Rosalind caught her breath. "How gorgeous! We live high up with a terrace over Central Park," she confided excitedly. "But that's nothing like this!"

Paul put his arm around her. "Don't get too close. You know some people just love heights. They love 'em to death. Just show them one and off they go."

"Not me."

"Come here." He led her a little to the side, placing her—"Not there, here"—at a spot where two carved lines crossed, as though Indians had marked it for something. Then, his arm close round her, he pressed his mouth down on hers. Her long brown hair fell backward over his shoulder. If she struggled, she might pull them both over the edge. "Don't." She broke her mouth away. His free hand was kneading her.

"Why? Why not?" The words burrowed into her ear like objects.

"I hadn't thought of you ... not for myself."

"Think of me now. Let's just stay here a minute."

But she slipped away and went sliding back down. Arriving in the level space with a torn jacket and a skinned elbow, she found Elaine lying back against a rock, apparently sleeping. A camera with a telescope lens was resting on the canvas shoulder bag she had carried up the hill.

Elaine sat up, opening her eyes. Rosalind stopped, and Paul's heavy stride, overtaking, halted close behind her. She did not want to look at him, and was rubbing at the blood speckled out on her scratched arm where she'd fallen against a limb.

"Paul thinks he's ir-ree-sisty-bul," Elaine said. "Now we know it isn't so."

Looking up, Rosalind could see the lofty ledge where she and Paul had been. Elaine picked up the camera, detached the lens, and fitted both into the canvas bag. "Once I took a whole home movie. That was the time he was screwing the waitress from the pizza place."

"Oh, sure, get funny," said Paul. He had turned an angry red.

In the car, Elaine leaned back to speak to Rosalind. "We're known to be a little bit crazy. Don't you worry, Ros-ul-lind."

Paul said nothing. He drove hunched forward over the wheel.

"Last summer was strictly crazy, start to finish," said Elaine. "Wasn't that true, Paul?"

"It was pretty crazy," said Paul. "Rosalind would have loved it," he added. He was getting mad with her now, she thought.

She asked to hop out at the road to the cottage, instead of going to the motel. She said she wanted to see Mr. Thibodeau.

"Sorry you didn't like the view," said Paul from the wheel. He was laughing now; his mood had changed.

Once they'd vanished, she walked down the main road to the Fenwick mailbox.

From the moment she left the road behind she had to climb again, not as strenuously as up to the mountain ledge, but a slow winding climb up an ill-tended road. The house that finally broke into view after a sharp turn was bare of paint and run-down. There was a junk car in the wide yard, the parts just about picked off it, one side sitting on planks, and a litter of household odds and ends nearby. A front porch, sagging, was covered with a tangle of what looked to be hunting and camping things. From behind, a dog barked, a warning sound to let her know who was in charge. There was mud in the path to the door.

Through the window of a tacked-on wing to the right, there was Fenwick, sure enough, at a table with peeling paint, in a plain kitchen chair, bending over a large notebook. Textbooks and graph papers were scattered around him. She rapped on the pane and summoned his attention, as though from another planet. He came to the door.

"Oh, it's you, Rose."

"Rosalind."

"I'm working on my problem." He came out and joined her. Maybe he was a genius, Rosalind thought, to have a fellowship to that school, making better grades than the Dunbars.

"I've been out with Paul and Elaine."

"Don't tell me Paul took you up to that lookout."

She nodded. They sat down on a bench that seemed about to fall in.

"Dunbar's got a collection of pictures—girls he's got to go up there. It's just a dumb gimmick."

"He thinks it's funny," she said, and added, "I left."

"Good. They're on probation, you know. All that about school's being suspended's not true. I'm out for another reason, studying for honors. But—"

A window ran up. A woman's voice came around the side of the house. "Henry, I told you—"

"But I need a break, Mother," he said, without turning his head.

"Is your name Henry?" Rosalind asked.

"So they tell me. Come on, I'll take you back where you're staying."

"I just wanted to see where you lived." He didn't answer. Probably it wasn't the right thing. He walked her down the hill, talking all the way, and put her into his old Volkswagen.

"The Dunbars stick too close together. You'd think they weren't kin. They're like a couple dating. They make up these jokes on people. I was there the other night to help them through some math they failed. But it didn't turn out that way. Know why? They've got no mind for work. They think something will happen, so they won't have to." He hesitated, silent, as the little car swung in and out of the wooded curves. "I think they make love," he said, very low. It was a kind of gossip. "There's talk at school. Now don't go and tell about it."

"You're warning me," she said.

"That's it. There's people living back in the woods, no different from them. Mr. Thibodeau and Papa—they hunt bear together, way off from here, high up. Last winter I went, too, and there was a blizzard. We shot a bear but it looked too deep a snow to get the carcass out, but we did. We stayed with these folks, brother and sister. Some odd little kids running around.

"If they get thrown out of Wakeley, they can go somewhere else. Their folks have a lot of money. So no problem."

"But I guess anywhere you have to study," said Rosalind.

He had brought her to the motel, and now they got out and walked to a plot where shrubs were budding on the slant of hill above the road. Fenwick had speculative eyes that kept to themselves, and a frown from worry or too many figures, just a small thread between his light eyebrows.

"When I finish my problem, any minute now, I'll go back to school."

"My mother died three years ago, in June," said Rosalind. "She was killed in a wreck."

"I knew that. It's too bad, Rosalind. I'm sorry."

"Did you know her?" Rosalind experienced an eagerness, expectation, as if she doubted her mother's ever having been known.

"I used to see her with you," said Fenwick. "So I guess I'd know her if I saw her." His hand had appeared on her shoulder. She was at about the right height for that.

"Nobody will ever see her again," she said. He pulled her closer.

"If I come back in the summer, I'd like to see you, Rosalind."

"Me too," she said.

"I've got some stuff you can read." He was squinting. The sun had come through some pale clouds.

"Things you wrote?" She wondered at him.

"I do a lot of things. I'll have the car." He glanced toward it doubtfully. "It's not much of a car, though."

"It's a fine car," she said, so he could walk off to it, feeling all right, and wave to her.

Rosalind was surprised and obscurely hurt by the message she received at the motel: namely, that her father and stepmother had already arrived and had called by for her. She had some money left over from what her father had given her, and not wanting to call, she took a taxi down to the cottage.

Her hurt sprang from thwarted plans. She had meant to prepare for them, greet them, have dinner half done, develop a festive air. Now they would be greeting her.

In the taxi past Mr. Thibodeau's house, she saw a strange car coming toward them which made them draw far to one side, sink treacherously among loose fallen leaves. A Chevrolet sedan went past; the man within, a stranger, was well dressed and wore a hat. He looked up to nod at the driver and glance keenly within at his passenger.

"Who was that?" Rosalind asked.

"Griffin, I think his name is," the driver said. "Real estate," he added.

There had been a card stuck in the door when she had come, Rosalind recalled, and a printed message: "Thinking of selling . . .? Griffin's the Guy."

Then she was alighting, crying, "Daddy! Eva! It's me!" And they were running out, crying, "There she is! You got the call?" Daddy was tossing her, forgetting she'd grown; he almost banged her head

68

against a beam. "You nearly knocked my three brains out," she laughed. "It's beautiful!" Eva cried, about the cottage. She spread her arms wide as wings and swirled across the rugs in a solo dance. "It's simply charming!"

Daddy opened the piano with a flourish. He began thumping the old keys, some of which had gone dead from the damp. But "Sweet Rosie O'Grady" was unmistakably coming out. They were hugging and making drinks and going out to look at the boat, kneeling down to test the still stone-chill water.

"What good taste your mother had!" Eva told her, smiling. "The apartment . . . now this!" She was kind.

In the late afternoon Rosalind and her father lowered and launched the canoe and, finding that it floated without a leak and sat well in the water, they decided to test it. Daddy had changed his gray slacks and blazer for gabardine trousers and a leather jacket. He wore a denim shirt. Daddy glistened with life, and what he wore was more important than what other people wore. He thought of clothes, evidently, but he never, that she could remember, discussed them. They simply appeared on him, like various furs or fleece that he could shed suddenly and grow just as suddenly new. Above button-down collars or open-throated knit pullovers or turtlenecks or black bow ties, his face, with its slightly ruddy look, even in winter, its cleft chin and radiating crinkles, was like a law of attraction, drawing whatever interested, whatever lived. In worry or grief, he hid it, that face. Then the clothes no longer mattered. Rosalind had sometimes found him in a room alone near a window, still, his face bent down behind one shoulder covered with some old faded shirt, only the top of his head showing and that revealed as startlingly gray, the hair growing thin. But when the face came up, it would seem to resume its livingness as naturally as breath, his hair being the same as ever, barely sprinkled with gray. It was the face for her, his gift.

"Did you see the real estate man?" Rosalind asked, over her shoulder, paddling with an out-of-practice wobble.

"Griffin? Oh yes, he was here. Right on the job, those guys."

They paddled along a stone's throw from the shore. To their right the lake stretched out wide and sunlit. One or two distant fishing boats dawdled near a small island. The lake, a creamy blue, flashed now and again in air that was still sharp.

"Daddy, did you know Eva a long time?"

There was a silence from behind her. "Not too long." Then he said what he'd said before. "She was a member of the cast. Rosie, we shouldn't have let you go off by yourself. I realized that this morning. I woke up early thinking it, and jumped straight out of bed. By six I'd packed. Who've you been seeing?"

"I ran into the Dunbars, Paul and Elaine, down in the big white house, you know. They're here from school. I have to run from Mrs. Thibodeau. She wants to catch and feed me. And then there's Fenwick."

"Some old guy up the hill who sells junk . . . is that the one?"

"No, his son. He's a mathematical genius, Daddy."

"Beware of mathematical geniuses," her father said, "especially if their fathers sell junk."

"You always told me that," said Rosalind. "I just forgot."

When they came in they were laughing. She and Eva cooked the meal. Daddy played old records, forgoing gin rummy for once. That was the first day.

"Wait! Look now! Look!"

It was Eva speaking while Daddy blindfolded Rosalind. They had built a fire. Somebody had found in a shop uptown the sort of stuff you threw on it to make it sparkle. The room on a gloomy afternoon, though shut up tight against a heavy drizzle, was full of warmth and light. Elaine and Paul Dunbar were there, sitting on the couch. Fenwick was there, choosing to crouch down on a hassock in the corner like an Indian, no matter how many times he was offered a chair. He had been followed in by one of the Fenwick dogs, a huge German shepherd with a bushy, perfectly curling tail lined with white, which he waved at times from side to side like a plume, and when seated furled about his paws. He smelled like a wet dog owned by a junk dealer.

At the shout of "Look now!" Daddy whipped off the blindfold. The cake had been lighted—eighteen candles—a shining delight. They had cheated a little to have a party for Rosalind; her birthday wasn't till the next week. But the idea was fun. Eva had thought of it because she had found a box full of party things in the unused bedroom: tinsel, sparklers, masks, and a crepe paper tablecloth with napkins. She had poured rum into some cherry Koolaid and floated orange slices across the top. She wore a printed off-the-shoulder blouse with a denim skirt and espadrilles. Her big glasses glanced back fire and candlelight. The young people watched her lighting candles for the table with a long, fancy match held in brightly tipped fingers. Daddy took the blue bandana blindfold and wound it pirate-fashion around his forehead. He had contrived an eye patch for one eye. "Back in the fifties these things were a status symbol," he said, "but I forget what status they symbolized."

"Two-car garage but no Cadillac," Paul said.

Daddy winked at Elaine. "My daughter's friends get prettier every day."

"So does your daughter," Paul said.

Eva passed them paper plates of birthday cake.

"*She's* getting to the dangerous age, not me. Hell, I was there all the time."

Everyone laughed but Fenwick. He fed small bites of cake to the dog and large ones to himself, while Rosalind refilled his glass.

The friends had brought her presents. A teddy bear dressed in blue jeans from Elaine. A gift shop canoe in birchbark from Paul. The figure of an old man carved in wood from Fenwick. His father had done it, he said. Rosalind held it up. She set it down. He watched her. He was redeeming his father, whom nobody thought much of. "It's grand," she said, "I love it." Fenwick sat with his hand buried in the dog's thick ruff. His nails, cleaned up for coming there, would get grimy in the dog's coat.

Rosalind's father so far had ignored Fenwick. He was sitting on a stool near Elaine and Paul, talking about theater on campuses, how most campus musicals went dead on Broadway, the rare one might survive, but usually—Eva approached the dog, who growled at her. "He won't bite," said Fenwick.

"Is a mathematician liable to know whether or not a dog will bite?" Eva asked.

"Why not?" asked Fenwick.

"You've got quite a reputation to live up to," Eva pursued. She was kneeling near him, close enough to touch, holding her gaze, like her voice, very steady. "I hear you called a genius more often than not."

"You can have a genius rating in something without setting the world on fire," said Fenwick. "A lot of people who've got them are just walking around doing dumb things, the same as anybody."

"I'll have to think that over," Eva said.

There came a heavy pounding at the door, and before anybody could go to it, a man with a grizzled beard, weathered skin, battered clothes and a rambling walk, entered the room. He looked all around until he found Fenwick. "There you are," he said.

Rosalind's father had risen. Nobody said anything. "I'm Nat Jennings." Daddy put out his hand. "This is my wife. What can we do for you?"

"It's my boy," said Fenwick's father, shaking hands. "His mother was looking for him, something she's wanting him for. I thought if he wasn't doing nothing . . ."

"Have a drink," said Nat.

"Just pour it straight out of the bottle," said Fenwick's father, who had taken the measure of the punch.

Fenwick got up. "That's OK, Mr. Jennings. I'll just go on with Papa."

The dog had moved to acknowledge Mr. Fenwick, who had downed his drink already. Now the boy came to them both, the dog being no longer his. He turned to the rest of the room, which seemed suddenly to be of a different race. "We'll go," he said. He turned again at the living room entrance. "Thanks."

Rosalind ran after them. She stood in the front door, hidden by the wall of the entrance from those in the room, and leaned out into the rain. "Oh Mr. Fenwick, I love the carving you did!"

He glanced back. "Off on a bear hunt, deep in the snow. Had to do something."

"Goodbye, Fenwick. Thanks for coming!"

He stopped to answer, but said nothing. For a moment his look was like a voice, crying out to her from across something. For the first time in her life, Rosalind felt the force that pulls stronger than any other. Just to go with him, to be, even invisibly, near. Then the three of them—tall boy, man and dog, stairstepped together—were walking away on the rainy path.

When she went inside, she heard Paul Dunbar recalling how Nat Jennings used to organize a fishing derby back in one of the little lakes each summer. He would get the lake stocked, and everybody turned out with casting rods and poles to fish it out.

(Rosalind remembered: she had ridden on his shoulder everywhere, till suddenly, one summer, she had got too big for that, and once it had rained.) "And then there were those funny races down in the park—you folks put them on. One year I won a prize!" (Oh, that too, she remembered, her mother running with two giant orange bows like chrysanthemums, held in either hand, orange streamers flying, her coppery hair in the sun.) "You ought to get all that started again."

"It sounds grand, but I guess you'd better learn how yourselves," Eva was saying. "We'll probably not be up here at all."

"Not be here!" Rosalind's cry as she returned from the door was like an alarm. "Not be here!" A silence was suddenly on them.

Her father glanced up, but straightened out smoothly. "Of course, we'll be here. We'll all have to work on it together."

It had started raining harder. Paul and Elaine, though implored to stay, left soon.

When the rain chilled the air, Eva had got out a fringed Spanish shawl, embroidered in bright flowers on a metallic gold background. Her glasses above this, plus one of the silly hats she'd found, made her seem a many-tiered fantasy of a woman, concocted by Picasso, or made to be carried through the streets for some Latin holiday parade.

Light of movement, wearing a knit tie, cuff links on his striped shirt ("In your honor," he said to Rosalind), impeccable blue blazer above gray slacks, Nat Jennings played the country gentleman with pleasure to himself and everyone. His pretty daughter at her birthday party was his delight. This was what his every move had been saying. And now she had gone to her room. He was knocking on its door. "Rosie?"

"I'm drunk," said Rosalind.

He laughed. "We're going to talk at dinner, Rosie. When you sober up, come down. Did you enjoy your birthday party, Baby?"

"Sure I did."

"I like your friends."

"Thank you."

"Too bad about Fenwick's father. That boy deserves better."

"I guess so."

She was holding an envelope Paul had slipped into her hand when he left. It had a photo and its negative enclosed, the one on the high point, the two of them kissing. The note said, "We're leaving tomorrow, sorry if I acted stupid. When we come back, maybe we can try some real ones. Paul."

There won't be any coming back for me, she lay dazed, thinking, but this was your place, Mother. Mother, what do I do now?

He was waiting for her at the bottom of the stairs and treating her with delightful solemnity, as though she was the visiting daughter of an old friend. He showed her to her place and held the chair for her. Eva, now changed into slacks, a silk shirt, and nubby sweater, came in with a steaming casserole. The candles were lighted again.

"I'm not a grand cook, as Rose knows," she smiled. "But you couldn't be allowed, on your birthday . . ."

"She's read a hole in the best cookbook," said Daddy.

"I'm sure it's great," Rosalind said in a little voice, and felt tension pass from one of them to the other.

"I'm in love with Fenwick," Eva announced, and dished out coq au vin.

"Won't get you anywhere," Daddy said. "I see the whole thing: he's gone on Rosie, but she's playing it cool."

"They're all going back tomorrow," Rosalind said. "Elaine and Paul were just on suspension, and Fenwick's finished his problem."

They were silent, passing dishes. Daddy and Eva exchanged glances.

"Rosie," said Daddy, filling everyone's wine glass, "we've been saving our good news till after your party. Now we want you to know. You remember the little off-Broadway musical I worked with last fall? Well, Hollywood is picking it up at quite a hefty sum. It's been in negotiation for two months. Now, all's clear, and they're wanting to hire me along with the purchase. Best break I ever had."

"I'm so happy I could walk on air," said Eva.

"Are we going to *move* there?" Rosalind felt numb.

"Of course not, Baby. There'll be trips, some periods out there, nothing permanent."

Before Rosalind suddenly, as she glanced from one of them to the other, they grew glossy in an extra charge of flesh and beauty. A log even broke in the fireplace, and a flame reached to some of the sparkler powder which was unignited, so that it flared up as though to hail them. They grew great as faces on a drive-in movie screen, seen floating up out of nowhere along a highway; they might mount skyward any minute and turn to constellations. He had wanted something big to happen, she knew, for a long time. "They never give me any credit," was a phrase she knew by heart. Staying her own human size, Rosalind knew that all they were saying was probably true. They had shoved her birthday up by a week to tidy her away, but they didn't look at it that way, she had to guess.

"Let's drink a toast to Daddy!" she cried, and drained her wine glass.

"Rosalind!" her father scolded happily. "What does anyone do with an alcoholic child?"

"Straight to AA," Eva filled in, "the minute we return."

"Maybe there's a branch in Lake George," Daddy worried.

"I'll cause spectacles at the Plaza," Rosalind giggled through the dizziness of wine. "I'll dance on the bar and jump in the fountain. You'll be so famous it'll make the *Daily News*."

"I've even got some dessert," said Eva, who, now the news was out, had the air of someone who intends to wait on people as seldom as possible. The cottage looked plainer and humbler all the time. How could they stand it for a single other night? Rosalind wondered. They would probably just explode out of there by some chemical process of rejection, which not even Fenwick could explain.

"If things work out," Daddy was saying, "we may get to make Palm Beach winters yet. No use to plan ahead."

"Would you like that?" Rosalind asked Eva, as if she didn't know.

"Why, I just tag along with the family," Eva said. "Your rules are mine."

That night Rosalind slipped out of her upstairs room. In order to avoid the Thibodeaus, whose house had eyes and ears, she skirted through the woods and ran into part of the lake, which appeared unexpectedly before her, like a person. She bogged in spongy loam and slipped on mossy rocks, and shivered, drenched to the knees, in the chill night shade of early foliage. At last she came out of shadow onto a road, but not before some large shape, high up, had startled her, blundering among the branches. A car went past and in the glancing headlights she saw the mailbox and its lettering and turned to climb the steep road up to the Fenwicks. What did she expect to happen there? Just who did she expect to find? Fenwick himself, of course, but in what way? To lead her out of here, take her somewhere, take her off forever? Say she could stay on with him, and they'd get the cottage someday and share it forever? That would be her dream, even if Fenwick's daddy camped on them and smelled the place up with whiskey.

She climbed with a sense of the enveloping stillness of the woods, the breath of the lake, the distant appeal of the mountains. The road made its final turn to the right, just before the yard. But at that point she was surprised to hear, as if growing out of the wood itself, murmurous voices, not one or two, but apparently by the dozen, and the sound of a throbbing guitar string, interposing from one pause to the next. She inched a little closer and stopped in the last of the black shade. A fire was burning in a wire grating near the steps. Tatters of flame leaped up, making the shadows blacker. High overhead, the moon shone. Fenwick, too, was entitled to a last night at home, having finished some work nobody else could have understood. He would return that summer. He was sitting on the edge of the porch, near a post. Some others were on the steps, or on chairs outside or even on the ground.

They were humming some tune she didn't know and she heard a voice rise, Mrs. Thibodeau's, beyond a doubt! "Now I never said I knew that from a firsthand look, but I'd have to suppose as much." Then Mr. Thibodeau was joining in: "Seen her myself . . . more than a time or two." The Thibodeaus were everywhere, with opinions to express, but about what and who? All went foundering in an indistinct mumble of phrases until a laugh rose and then another stroke across the strings asked them to sing together, a song she'd never heard. "Now that's enough," a woman's voice said, "I ain't pitching no more tunes." "I've sung all night, many's the time." "Just you and your jug."

From near the steps a shape rose suddenly; it was one of the dogs, barking on the instant of rising—there had been a shift of wind. He trotted toward her. She stood still. Now the snuffling muzzle ranged over her. The great tail moved its slow white fan. It was the one she knew. She patted the intelligent head. Someone whistled. It was Fenwick, who, she could see, had risen from his seat.

Something fell past him, out of the thick-bunched human shapes on the porch. It had been pushed or shoved and was yelling, a child. "Stealing cake again," some voice said, and the body hit the ground with a thump. The mother in the chair, not so much as turning, said, "Going to break ever' bone in her one o' these days." "Serve her right," came from the background—Mr. Fenwick. It was young Fenwick himself who finally went down to pick her up (by the back of her shirt, like a puppy), Mrs. Thibodeau who came to dust her off. The yelling stopped. "Hush now," said Mrs. Thibodeau. Rosalind turned and went away.

"Who's there?" Fenwick was calling toward the road. "Nobody," a man's voice, older, said. "Wants his girl friend," said the father. "Go and git her, fella."

The mountain went on talking. Words faded to murmurs, losing outline; as she stumbled down turns of road, they lost even echoes. She was alone where she had not meant to be, but for all that, strangely detached, elated.

Back on the paved road, she padded along in sneakers. Moonlight lay bright in patterns through the trees. Finally the Dunbar house rose up, moonlight brightening one white portico, while the other stood almost eclipsed in darkness. In a lighted interior, through a downstairs window, she could see them, one standing, the other looking up, graceful hands making gestures, mouths moving—together and alone. Great white moths circling one another, planning, loving maybe. She thought they were like the photographs they took. The negative is me, she thought.

Far up the road, so far it tired her almost as much to think of it as to walk it, the old resort hotel looked out on Lake George with hundreds of empty windows, eyes with vision gone, the porticos reaching wide their outspread arms. Water lapped with none to hear. "No Trespassing," said the sign, and other signs said "For Sale," like children calling to one another.

Rosalind looked up. Between her and the road, across the lawn, a brown bear was just standing up. He was turning his head this way and that. The head was small, wedge-shaped. The bear's pelt moved when he did, like grass in a breeze. Pointing her way, the head stopped still. She felt the gaze thrill through her with long foreverness, then drop away. On all fours, he looked small, and moved toward the lake with feet shuffling close together, rather like a rolling ball, loose and tumbling toward the water. The moon sent a shimmering, golden path across the lake. She was just remembering that her mother, up here alone with her, claimed to have seen a bear late at night, looking through the window. Daddy didn't doubt she'd dreamed it. He didn't think they came so close. Rosalind knew herself as twice seen and twice known now, by dog and bear. She walked the road home.

Voices sounding in her head, Rosalind twisted and turned that night, sleepless. She got up once and taking the red scarf she had found from the drawer, she put it down on the living room table near the large vase of money plant. Then she went back up and slept, what night was left for it.

Daddy came in for Eva's coffee and then they both appeared, he freshly shaved and she perfect in her smooth makeup, a smartly striped cassock flowing to her ankles. Rosalind had crept down in wrinkled pajamas, her bare feet warping back from the chill floor. "Today's for leaving," her father said. When Rosalind dropped her gaze, he observed her. They were standing in the kitchen before the stove. They were alone. He was neat, fit, in slacks, a beige shirt checked in brown and blue, and a foulard—affected for anyone but him. His amber eyes fixed on her blue ones, offered pools of sincerity for her to plunge into.

"What's this?" Eva asked. She came in with the scarf.
"I found it," said Rosalind. "Isn't it yours?"
Eva looked over her head at Nat. "It must have been your mother's."
"No," said Rosalind. "It wasn't."

After breakfast, by common consent, Rosalind and her father rose from the table and went down to the boat. Together they paddled out to the island. They had done this often in the past. The island was inviting, slanted like a turtle's back, rich with clumps of birch and bushes, trimmed with gray rock. Out there today, their words came out suddenly, like thoughts being printed on the air.
"We aren't coming back," said Rosalind. "This is all."
"I saw you come in last night."
A bird flew up out of the trees.
"Did you tell Eva?"
"She was asleep. Why?"
"She'll think I just sneaked off to see Fenwick. But I didn't. I went off myself . . . by myself."

He played with rocks, seated, forearms resting on his knees, looking at the lake. "I won't tell."

"I wanted to find Mother."

"Did you?"

"In a way . . . I know she's here, all around here. Don't you?"

"I think she might be most everywhere."

Maybe what he was saying was something about himself. The ground was being shifted; they were debating without saying so, and he was changing things around without saying so.

"I let you come up here alone," he went on, "because I thought you needed it—your time alone. Maybe I was wrong."

"If you'd just say you see it too."

"See what?"

"What I was saying. That she's here. No other places. Here."

The way he didn't answer her was so much a silence she could hear the leaves stir. "You didn't love her." The words fell from her, by themselves, you'd have to think, because she hadn't willed them to. They came out because they were there.

"Fool! Of course, I did!"

Long after, she realized he had shouted, screamed, almost. She didn't know it at the moment because her eyes had blurred with what she'd accused him of, and her hearing too had gone with her sight. She was barely clinging to the world.

When her vision cleared, she looked for him and saw that he was lying down on gray rock with his eyes closed, facing upward, exactly as though exhausted from a task. Like the reverse picture on a face card, he looked to be duplicating an opposite image of his straight-up self; only the marked cleft in his chin was more visible at that angle, and she recalled her mother holding up a card when they were playing double solitaire once while waiting for him for dinner: "Looks like Daddy . . ." "Let me see . . . sure does . . ." She had seen the florid printed face often enough, the smile affable, the chin cleft. "Jack of Diamonds," her mother said. For hadn't the two of them also seen the father's face turn fixed and mysterious as the painted image, unchanging from whatever it had changed to? The same twice over: she hadn't thought that till now. He reached up and took her hand. The gesture seemed to say they had blundered into the fire once, but maybe never again.

The scent of pine, the essence of oak scent, too, came warm to her senses, assertive as animals. She rubbed with her free hand at the small debris that hugged the rock. In former times she had peeled away hunks of moss for bringing back. The rock was old enough to be dead, but in school they said that rocks lived.

"You're going to sell it, aren't you? The cottage, I mean."

"I have to. I need the money."

"I thought you were getting money, lots."

"I'm getting some. But not enough."

So he had laid an ace out before her. There was nothing to say. The returned silence, known to trees, rocks and water, went agelessly on.

Nat Jennings sat up lightly, in one motion. "What mysteries attend my Rosalind, wandering through her forest of Arden?"

"I was chased by a bear," said Rosalind, attempting to joke with him, but remembering she had almost cried just now, she blew her nose on a torn Kleenex.

"Sleeping in his bed, were you? Serves you right."

He scratched his back where something bit. "I damned near fell asleep." He got to his feet. "It's time." It's what he'd said when they left that other time, three years ago. He put out his hand.

Pulling her up, he slipped on a mossy patch of rock and nearly fell. But dancing was in his bones; if he hadn't been good at it, they would have fallen. As it was they teetered, clung and held upright.

Rosalind and her father got into the boat and paddled toward the cottage, keeping perfect time. Eva, not visible, was busy inside. They found her in the living room.

She had the red scarf wound about her head gypsy-fashion. Above her large glasses, it looked comical, but right; sexy and friendly, the way she was always being. She had cleared up everything from breakfast and was packing.

"You two looked like a picture coming in. I should have had a camera."

"Oh, we're a photogenic pair," Nat said.

"Were you ever tempted to study theater?" Eva asked her.

"I was, but—Not now. Oh, no, not now!" She stood apart, single, separate, ready to leave.

Startled by her tone, Nat Jennings turned. "I think it was her mother," he quickly said. "She didn't like the idea."

nominated by Mary Hood and
Robert Phillips

AGAINST *JOIE DE VIVRE*

by PHILLIP LOPATE

from PLOUGHSHARES

Over the years I have developed a distaste for the spectacle of *joie de vivre*, the knack of knowing how to live. Not that I disapprove of all hearty enjoyment of life. A flushed sense of happiness can overtake a person anywhere, and one is no more to blame for it than the Asiatic flu or a sudden benevolent change in the weather (which is often joy's immediate cause). No, what rankles me is the stylization of this private condition into a bullying social ritual.

The French, who have elevated the picnic to their highest civilized rite, are probably most responsible for promoting this smugly upbeat, flaunting style. It took the French genius for formalizing the informal to bring sticky sacramental sanctity to the baguette, wine and cheese. A pure image of sleeveless *joie de vivre* Sundays can also be found in Renoir's paintings. Weekend satyrs dance and wink; leisure takes on a bohemian stripe. A decent writer, Henry Miller, caught the French malady and ran back to tell us of *pissoirs* in the Paris streets (why this should have impressed him so, I've never figured out).

But if you want a double dose of *joie de vivre*, you need to consult a later, hence more stylized version of the French myth of pagan happiness: those *Family of Man* photographs of endlessly kissing lovers, snapped by Doisneau and Boubat, not to mention Cartier-Bresson's icon of the proud tyke carrying bottles of wine. If Cartier-Bresson and his disciples are excellent photographers for all that, it is in spite of their rubbing our noses in a tediously programmatic "affirmation of life."

Though it is traditionally the province of the French, the whole Mediterranean is a hotbed of professional *joie de vivrism,* which they have gotten down to a routine like a crack *son et lumière* display. The Italians export *dolce far niente* as aggressively as tomato paste. For the Greeks, a Zorba dance to life has supplanted classical antiquities as their main touristic lure. Hard to imagine anything as stomach-turning as being forced to participate in such an oppressively robust, folknik effusion. Fortunately, the country has its share of thin, nervous, bitter types, but Greeks do exist who would clutch you to their joyfully stout bellies and crush you there. The *joie de vivrist* is an incorrigible missionary, who presumes that everyone wants to express pro-life feelings in the same stereotyped manner.

A warning: since I myself have a large store of nervous discontent (some would say hostility) I am apt to be harsh in my secret judgments of others, seeing them as defective because they are not enough like me. From moment to moment, the person I am with often seems too shrill, too bland, too something-or-other to allow my own expansiveness to swing into stage center. "Feeling no need to drink, you will promptly despise a drunkard" (Kenneth Burke). So it goes with me—which is why I am not a literary critic. I have no faith that my discriminations in taste are anything but the picky awareness of what will keep me stimulated, based on the peculiar family and class circumstances which formed me. But the knowledge that my discriminations are skewed and not always universally desirable doesn't stop me in the least from making them, just as one never gives up a negative first impression, no matter how many times it is contradicted. A believer in astrology (to cite another false system), having guessed that someone is a Saggitarius, and then told he is a Scorpio, says "Scorpio—yes, of course!" without missing a beat, or relinquishing confidence in his ability to tell people's signs, or in his idea that the person is somehow secretly Saggitarian.

1. The Houseboat

I remember the exact year when my dislike for *joie de vivre* began to crystallize. It was 1969. We had gone to visit an old Greek painter on his houseboat in Sausalito. Old Vartas's vitality was legendary and it was considered a spiritual honor to meet him, like getting an audience with the Pope. Each Sunday he had a sort of open house, or open boat.

My "sponsor," Frank, had been many times to the houseboat, furnishing Vartas with record albums, since the old painter had a passion for San Francisco rock bands. Frank told me that Vartas had been a pal of Henry Miller's, and I, being a writer of Russian descent, would love him. I failed to grasp the syllogism, but, putting aside my instinct to dislike anybody I have been assured I will adore, I prepared myself to give the man a chance.

Greeting us on the gang plank was an old man with thick, lush white hair and snowy eyebrows, his face reddened from the sun. As he took us into the houseboat cabin he told me proudly that he was seventy-seven years old, and gestured toward the paintings that were spaced a few feet apart, leaning on the floor against the wall. They were celebrations of the blue Aegean, boats moored in ports, whitewashed houses on a hill, painted in primary colors and decorated with collaged materials: mirrors, burlap, life-saver candies. These sunny little canvases with their talented innocence, third-generation spirit of Montmartre, bore testimony to a love of life so unbending as to leave an impression of rigid narrowmindedness as extreme as any Savonarola. Their rejection of sorrow was total. They were the sort of festive paintings that sell at high-rent Madison Avenue galleries specializing in European schlock.

Then I became aware of three young, beautiful women, bare-shouldered, wearing white *dhotis*, each with long blond hair falling onto a skyblue halter—unmistakably suggesting the Three Graces. They lived with him on the houseboat, I was told, giving no one knew what compensation for their lodgings. Perhaps their only payment was to feed his vanity in front of outsiders. The Greek painter smiled with the air of an old fox around the trio. For their part, they obligingly contributed their praises of Vartas's youthful zip, which of course was taken by some guests as double-entendre for undiminished sexual prowess. The Three Graces also gathered the food-offerings of the visitors to make a mid-day meal.

Then the boat, equipped with a sail, was launched to sea. I must admit it gave me a spoilsport's pleasure when the winds turned becalmed. We could not move. Aboard were several members of the Bay Area's French colony, who dangled their feet over the sides, passed around bunches of grapes and sang what I imagined were Gallic camping songs. The French know boredom, so they would understand how to behave in such a situation. It has been my observation that many Frenchmen and women stationed in America have the attitude of taking it easy, slumming at a health resort, and nowhere more so than in California. The émigré crew included a securities analyst, an academic sociologist, a museum administrator and his wife, a modiste: on Vartas's boat they all got drunk and carried on like redskins, noble savages off Tahiti.

Joie de vivre requires a *soupçon* of the primitive. But since the illusion of the primitive soon palls and has nowhere to go, it becomes necessary to make new initiates. A good part of the day, in fact, was taken up with regulars interpreting to firsttimers like myself certain mores pertaining to the houseboat, as well as offering tidbits about Vartas's Rabelaisian views of life. Here everyone was encouraged to do what he willed. (How much could you do on a becalmed boat surrounded by strangers?) No one had much solid information about their host's past, which only increased the privileged status of those who knew at least one fact. Useless to ask the object of this venerating speculation, since Vartas said next to nothing (adding to his impressiveness) when he was around, and disappeared below for long stretches of time.

In the evening, after a communal dinner, the new Grateful Dead record Frank had brought was put on the phonograph, and Vartas danced, first by himself, then with all three Graces, bending his arms in broad, hooking sweeps. He stomped his foot and looked around scampishly at the guests for appreciation, not unlike a monkey-grinder and his monkey. Imagine, if you will, a being whose generous bestowal of self-satisfaction invites and is willing to receive nothing but flattery in return, a person who has managed to make others buy his somewhat senile projection of indestructibility as a Hymn to Life. In no sense could he be called a charlatan; he delivered what he promised, an incarnation of *joie de vivre*, and if it was shallow, it was also effective, managing even to attract an enviable "harem" (which was what really burned me).

A few years passed.

Some Dutch TV crew, ever on the lookout for exotic bits of Americana that would make good short subjects, planned to do a documentary about Vartas as a sort of paean to eternal youth. I later learned from Frank that Vartas died before the shooting could be completed. A pity, in a way. The home movie I've run off in my head of the old man is getting a little tattered, the colors splotchy, and the scenario goes nowhere, lacks point. All I have for sure is the title: The Man Who Gave *Joie De Vivre* A Bad Name.

"Ah, what a twinkle in the eye the old man has! He'll outlive us all." So we speak of old people who bore us, when we wish to honor them. We often see projected onto old people this worship of the life-force. It is not the fault of the old if they then turn around and try to exploit our misguided amazement at their longevity as though it were a personal tour de force. The elderly, when they are honest with themselves, realize they have done nothing particularly to be proud of in lasting to a ripe old age, and then carrying themselves through a thousand more days. Yet you still hear an old woman or man telling a bus driver with a chuckle, "Would you believe that I am eighty-four years old!" As though they should be patted on the back for still knowing how to talk, or as though they had pulled a practical joke on the other riders by staying so spry and mobile. Such insecure, wheedling behavior always embarrassed me. I will look away rather than meet the speaker's eyes and be forced to lie with a smile, "Yes, you are remarkable," which seems condescending on my part and humiliating to us both.

Like children forced to play the cute part adults expect of them, some old people must get confused trying to adapt to a social role of indeterminate standards, which is why they seem to whine: "I'm doing all right, aren't I—for my age?" It is interesting that society's two most powerless groups, children and the elderly, have both been made into sentimental symbols. In the child's little hungry hands grasping for life, joined to the old person's frail slipping fingers hanging onto it, you have one of the commonest advertising metaphors for intense appreciation. It is enough to show a young child sleeping in his or her grandparent's lap to procure *joie de vivre* overload.

2. The Dinner Party

I am invited periodically to dinner parties and brunches—and I go, because I like to be with people and oblige them, even if I secretly cannot share their optimism about these events. I go, not believing that I will have fun, but with the intent of observing people who think *a dinner party* a good time. I eat their fancy food, drink the wine, make my share of entertaining conversation, and often leave having had a pleasant evening. Which does not prevent me from anticipating the next invitation with the same bleak lack of hope. To put it in a nutshell, I am an ingrate.

Although I have traveled a long way from my proletarian origins and, like a perfect little bourgeois, talk, dress, act and spend money, I hold onto my poor-boy's outrage at the "decadence" (meaning, dull entertainment style) of the middle and upper-middle classes; or, like a model Soviet moviegoer watching scenes of pre-revolutionary capitalists gorging caviar, I am appalled, but I dig in with the rest.

Perhaps my uneasiness with dinner parties comes from the simple fact that not a single dinner party was given by my solitudinous parents the whole time I was growing up, and I had to wait until my late twenties before learning the ritual. A spy in the enemy camp, I have made myself a patient observer of strange customs. For the benefit of other late-starting social climbers, this is what I have observed:

As everyone should know, the ritual of the dinner party begins away from the table. Usually in the living room, hors d'oeuvres and walnuts are set out, to start the digestive juices flowing. Here introductions between strangers are also made. Most dinner parties contain at least a few guests who have been unknown to each other before that evening, but whom the host and/or hostess envision would enjoy meeting. These novel pairings and their interactions add spice to the *post-mortem:* who got along with whom? The lack of prior acquaintanceship also ensures that the guests will have to rely on and go through the only people known to everyone, the host and hostess, whose absorption of this help-lessly dependent attention is one of the main reasons for throwing dinner parties.

Although an after-work "leisure activity," the dinner party is in fact a celebration of professional identity. Each of the guests has been pre-selected as in a floral bouquet; and in certain developed forms of this ritual there is usually a cunning mix of professions. Yet the point is finally not so much diversity as commonality: what remarkably shared attitudes and interests these people from differ-ent vocations demonstrate by conversing intelligently, or at least glibly, on the topics that arise. Naturally, a person cannot discourse too technically about one's line of work, so he or she picks precisely those themes that invite overlap. The psychiatrist laments the new breed of ego-less, narcissistic patient who keeps turning up in his office—a beach bum who lacks the work ethic; the college professor bemoans the shoddy intellectual backgrounds and self-centered ignorance of his students; and the bookseller parodies the customer who pronounced "Sophocles" to rhyme with "bifocles". The dinner party is thus an exercise in locating ignorance—elsewhere. Whoever is present is *ipso facto* part of that beleaguered remnant of civilized folk fast disappearing from Earth.

Or think of a dinner party as a club of revolutionaries, a technocratic elite whose social interactions that night are a dry run for some future takeover of the State. These are the future cabinet members (now only a shadow-cabinet, alas) meeting to practice for the first time. How well they get on! "The time will soon be ripe, my friends. . . ." If this is too fanciful for you, then compare the dinner party to a utopian community, a Brook Farm supper club, where only the best and most useful community-members are chosen to participate. The smugness begins as soon as one enters the door, since one is already part of the chosen few. And from then on, every mechanical step in dinner-party process is designed to augment the atmosphere of group *amour-propre*. This is not to say that there won't be one or two people in an absolute torment of exclusion, too shy to speak up, or else suspecting that when they do, their contributions fail to carry the same weight as the others'. The group's all-purpose drone of self-contentment ignores these drowning people—cruelly inattentive in one sense, but benign in another: it invites them to join the shared ethos of success any time they are ready.

The group is asked to repair to the table. Once again they find themselves marvelling at a shared perception of life. How delicious the fish soup! How cute the stuffed tomatoes! What did you use for this green sauce? Now comes much talk of ingredients, and credit is given where credit is due. It is Jacques who made the salad. It was Mamie who brought the homemade bread. Everyone pleads with the hostess to sit down, not to work so hard—an empty formula whose hypocrisy bothers no one. Who else is going to put the butter dish on the table? For a moment all become quiet, except for the sounds of eating. This corresponds to the part in a church service which calls for silent prayer.

I am saved from such culinary paganism by the fact that food is largely an indifferent matter to me. I rarely think much about what I am putting in my mouth. Though my savage, illiterate palate has inevitably been educated to some degree by the many meals I have shared with people who care enormously about such things, I resist going any further. I am superstitious that the day I send back a dish at a restaurant, or make a complicated journey to somewhere just for a meal, that day I will have sacrificed my freedom and traded in my soul for a lesser god.

I don't expect the reader to agree with me. That's not the point. Unlike the behavior called for at a dinner party, I am not obliged sitting at my typewriter to help procure consensus every moment. So I am at liberty to declare, to the friend who once told me that dinner parties were one of the only opportunities for intelligently convivial conversation to take place in this cold, fragmented city, that she is crazy. The conversation at dinner parties is of a mind-numbing calibre. No discussion of any clarifying rigor—be it political, spiritual, artistic or financial—can take place in a context where fervent conviction of any kind is frowned upon, and the desire to follow through a sequence of ideas must give way every time to the impressionistic, breezy flitting from topic to topic. Talk must be bubbly but not penetrating. Illumination would only slow the flow. Some hit-and-run remark may accidentally jog an idea loose, but in such cases it is better to scribble a few words down on the napkin for later, than attempt to "think" at a dinner party.

What do people talk about at such gatherings? The latest movies, the priciness of things, word-processors, restaurants, muggings and burglaries, private versus public schools, the fool in the White House (there have been so many fools in a row that this subject is getting tired), the undeserved reputations of certain better-known professionals in one's field, the fashions in investments, the investments in fashion. What is traded at the dinner-party table is, of course, class information. You will learn whether you are in the avant-garde or rear guard of your social class, or, preferably, right in step.

As for Serious Subjects, dinner-party guests have the latest *New Yorker* in-depth piece to bring up. People who ordinarily would not spare a moment worrying about the treatment of schizophrenics in mental hospitals, the fate of Great Britain in the Common Market, or the disposal of nuclear wastes, suddenly find their consciences orchestrated in unison about these problems, thanks to their favorite periodical—though a month later they have forgotten all about it and are onto something new.

The dinner party is a suburban form of entertainment. Its spread in our big cities represents an insidious Fifth Column suburbanization of the metropolis. In the suburbs it becomes necessary to be able to discourse knowledgeably about the heart of the city, but from the viewpoint of a day-shopper. Dinner-party chatter is the communicative equivalent of roaming around shopping malls.

Much thought has gone into the ideal size for a dinner party—usually with the hostess arriving at the figure eight. Six would give each personality too much weight; ten would lead to splintering side-discussions; eight is the largest number still able to force everyone into the same compulsively congenial conversation. My own strength as a conversationalist comes out less in groups of eight than one-to-one, which may explain my resistance to dinner parties. At the table, unfortunately, any engrossing *tête-á-tête* is frowned upon as anti-social. I often find myself in the frustrating situation of being drawn to several engaging people, in among the bores, and wishing I could have a private conversation with each, without being able to do more than signal across the table a wry recognition of that fact. "Some other time, perhaps," we seem to be saying with our eyes, all evening long.

Later, however—to give the devil his due—when guests and hosts retire from the table back to the living room, the strict demands of group participation may be relaxed, and individuals allowed to pair off in some form of conversational intimacy. But one must be ever on the lookout for the group's need to swoop everybody together again for one last demonstration of collective fealty.

The first to leave breaks the communal spell. There is a sudden rush to the coat closet, the bathroom, the bedroom, as others, under the protection of the first defector's original sin, quit the Party apologetically. The utopian dream has collapsed: left behind are a few loyalists and insomniacs, swillers of a last cognac. "Don't leave yet," begs the host, knowing what a sense of letdown, pain and self-recrimination awaits. Dirty dishes are, if anything, a comfort: the faucet's warm gush serves to stave off the moment of anesthetized stock-taking—Was that really necessary?—in the sobering silence which follows a dinner party.

3. *Joie's Doppelgänger*

I have no desire to rail against the Me Generation. We all know that the current epicurean style of the Good Life, from light foods to Nike running shoes, is a result of market research techniques developed to sell "spot" markets, and, as such, a natural outgrowth of consumer capitalism. I may not like it but I can't pretend that my objections are the result of a high-minded Laschian political analysis. Moreover, my own record of activism is not so noticeably impressive that I can lecture the Sunday brunchers to roll up their sleeves and start fighting social injustices instead of indulging themselves.

No, if I try to understand the reasons for my antihedonistic biases, they come from somewhere other than idealism. It's odd, because there seems to be a contradiction between this curmudgeonly feeling inside me and my periodically strong appetite for life. I am reminded of my hero, William Hazlitt, with his sarcastic grumpy disposition on the one hand, and his capacity for "gusto" (his word, not Schlitz's) on the other. With Hazlitt, one senses a fanatically tenacious defense of his individuality and independence against some unnamed bully stalking him. He had trained himself to be a connoisseur of vitality, and got irritated when life was not filled to the brim. I am far less irritable—before others; I will laugh if there is the merest *anything* to laugh at. But it is a tense, pouncing pleasure, not one which will allow me to sink into undifferentiated relaxation. The prospect of a long day at the beach makes me panic. There is no harder work I can think of than taking myself off to somewhere pleasant, where I am forced to stay for hours and "have fun." Taking it easy, watching my personality's borders loosen and dissolve, arouses an unpleasantly floating giddiness. I don't even like water-beds. Fear of Freud's "oceanic feeling," I suppose. . . . I distrust anything which will make me pause long enough to be put in touch with my helplessness.

The other repugnance I experience around *joie-de-vivrism* is that I associate its rituals with depression. All these people sitting around a pool, drinking margaritas, they're not really happy, they're depressed. Perhaps I am generalizing too much from my own despair in such situations. Drunk, sunbaked, stretched out in a beach-chair, I am unable to ward off the sensation of being utterly alone, unconnected, cut off from the others.

An article on the Science Page of the *Times* about depression (they seem to run one every few months) described the illness as a pattern of "learned helplessness." Dr. Martin Seligman of the University of Pennsylvania described his series of experiments: "At first mild electrical shocks were given to dogs, from which they were unable to escape. In a second set of experiments, dogs were given shocks from which they could escape—but they didn't try. They just lay there, passively accepting the pain. It seemed that the animals' inability to control their experiences had brought them to a state resembling clinical depression in humans."

Keep busy, I always say. At all costs avoid the trough of passivity, which leads to the Slough of Despond. Someone—a girlfriend, who else?—once accused me of being intolerant of the depressed way of looking at the world, which had its own intelligence and moral integrity, both obviously unavailable to me. It's true. I don't like the smell of depression (it has a smell, a very distinct one, something fetid like morning odors), and I stay away from depressed characters whenever possible. Except when they happen to be my closest friends or family members. It goes without saying that I am also, for all my squeamishness, attracted to depressed people, since they seem to know something I don't. I wouldn't rule out the possibility that the brown-gray logic of depression *is* the truth. In another experiment (also reported on the Science Page), pitting "optimists" against clinically diagnosed "depressives" on their self-perceived abilities to effect outcomes according to their wills, researchers tentatively concluded that depressed people may have a more realistic, clear-sighted view of the world.

Nevertheless, what I don't like about depressives sometimes is their chummy I-told-you-so smugness, like Woody Allen fans who treat an hedonia as a vanguard position.

And for all that, depressives make the most rabid converts to *joie de vivre*. The reason is, *joie de vivre* and depression are not opposites but relatives of the same family, practically twins. When I see *joie de vivre* rituals, I always notice, like a TV ghost, depression right alongside it. I knew a man, dominated by a powerful father, who thought he had come out of a long depression occasioned, in his mind, by his divorce. Whenever I met him he would say that his life was getting better and better. Now he could run long distances, he was putting healthy food in his system, he was more physically fit at forty than he had been at twenty-five, and now he had dates, he was going out with three different women, he had a good therapist, he was looking forward to renting a bungalow in better woods than the previous summer. . . . I don't know whether it was his tone of voice when he said this, his sagging shoulders, or what, but I always had an urge to burst into tears. If only he had admitted he was miserable I could have consoled him outright instead of being embarrassed to notice the deep hurt in him, like a swallowed razor cutting him from inside. And his pain still stunk up the room like in the old days, that sour cabbage smell was in his running suit, yet he wouldn't let on, he thought the smell was gone. The therapist had told him to forgive himself, and he had gone ahead and done it, the poor shlemiehl. But tell me: why would anyone need such a stylized, disciplined regimen of enjoyment if he were not depressed?

4. In the Here-And-Now

The argument of both the hedonist and the guru is that if we were but to open ourselves to the richness of the moment, to concentrate on the feast before us, we would be filled with bliss. I have lived in the present from time to time, and I can tell you that it is much over-rated. Occasionally, as a holiday from stroking one's memories or brooding about future worries, I grant you, it can be a nice change of pace. But to "be here now" hour after hour would never work. I don't even approve of stories written in the present tense. As for poets who never use a past participle, they deserve the eternity they are striving for.

Besides, the present has a way of intruding whether you like it or not; why should I go out of my way to meet it? Let it splash on me from time to time, like a car going through a puddle, and I, on the sidewalk of my solitude, will salute it grimly like any other modern inconvenience.

If I attend a concert, obviously not to listen to the music but to find a brief breathing-space in which to meditate on the past and future, I realize that there may be moments when the music invades my ears and I am forced to pay attention to it, note after note. I believe I take such intrusions gracefully. The present is not always an unwelcome guest, so long as it doesn't stay too long and cut into our time for remembering.

Even for survival, it's not necessary to focus one's full attention on the present. The instincts of a pedestrian crossing the street in a reverie will usually suffice. Alertness is alright as long as it is not treated as a promissory note on happiness. Anyone who recommends attention to the moment as a prescription for grateful wonder is only telling half the truth. To be happy one must pay attention, but to be unhappy one must also have paid attention.

Attention, at best, is a form of prayer. Conversely, as Simone Weil said, prayer is a way of focusing attention. All religions recognize this when they ask their worshipers to repeat the name of their God, a devotional practice which draws the practitioner into a trancelike awareness of the present, and the objects around oneself. With a part of the soul one praises God, and with the other part one expresses a hunger, a dissatisfaction, a desire for more spiritual contact. Praise must never stray too far from longing, that longing which takes us implicitly beyond the present.

I was about to say that the very act of attention implies longing, but this is not necessarily true. Attention is not always infused with desire; it can settle on us most placidly once desire has been momentarily satisfied, like after the sex act. There are also periods following over-work, when the exhausted slave-body is freed and the eyes dilate to register with awe the lights of the city; one is too tired to desire anything else.

Such moments are rare. They form the basis for a poetic appreciation of the beauty of the world. However, there seems no reliable way to invoke or prolong them. The rest of the time, when we are not being edgy or impatient, we are often simply *disappointed,* which amounts to a confession that the present is not good enough. People often try to hide their disappointment—just as Berryman's mother told him not to let people see that he was bored, because it suggested that he had no "inner resources." But there is something to be said for disappointment.

This least respected form of suffering, downgraded to a kind of petulance, at least accurately measures the distance between hope and reality. And it has its own peculiar satisfactions: Why else do we return years later to places where we had been happy, if not to savor the bittersweet pleasure of disappointment?

Moreover, it is the other side of a strong, predictive feeling for beauty or appropriate civility or decency: Only those with a sense of order and harmony can be disappointed.

We are told that to be disappointed is immature, in that it presupposes having unrealistic expectations, whereas the wise man meets each moment head-on without preconceptions, with freshness and detachment, grateful for anything it offers. However, this pernicious teaching ignores everything we know of the world. If we continue to expect what turns out to be not forthcoming, it is not because we are unworldly in our expectations, but because our very worldliness has taught us to demand of an unjust world that it behave a little more fairly. The least we can do, for instance, is to register the expectation that people in a stronger position be kind and not cruel to those in a weaker, knowing all the while that we will probably be disappointed.

The truth is, most wisdom is embittering. The task of the wise person cannot be to pretend with false naiveté that every moment is new and unprecedented, but to bear the burden of bitterness which experience forces on us with as much uncomplaining dignity as strength will allow. Beyond that, all we can ask of ourselves is that bitterness not cancel out our capacity still to be surprised.

5. Making Love

If it is true that I have the tendency to withhold sympathy from those pleasures or experiences which fall outside my capabilities, the opposite is also true: I admire immoderately those things I cannot do. I've always gone out with women who swam better than I did. It's as if I were asking them to teach me how to make love. Though I know how to make love (more or less), I have never fully shaken that adolescent boy's insecurity that there was more to it than I could ever imagine, and that I needed a full-time instructress. For my first sexual experiences, in fact, I chose older women. Later, when I slept with women my own age and younger, I still tended to take the stylistic lead from them, adapting myself to each one's rhythm and ardor, not only because I wanted to be "responsive," but because I secretly thought that women—any woman—understood love-making in a way that I did not. In bed I came to them as a student; and I have made them pay later, in other ways, for letting them see me thus. Sex has always been so impromptu, so out of my control, so different each time, that even when I became the confident bull in bed I was dismayed by this surprising sudden power, itself a form of powerlessness because so unpredictable.

Something Michel Leiris wrote in his book, *Manhood*, has always stuck with me: "It has been some time, in any case, since I have ceased to consider the sexual act as a simple matter, but rather as a relatively exceptional act, necessitating certain inner accommodations that are either particularly tragic or particularly exalted, but very different, in either case, from what I regard as my usual disposition."

The transformation from a preoccupied urban intellectual to a sexual animal involves, at times, an almost superhuman strain. To find in one's bed a living, undulating woman of God knows what capacities and secret desires, may seem too high, too formal, too ridiculous or blissful an occasion—not to mention the shock to an undernourished heart like mine of an injection of undiluted affection, if the woman proves loving as well.

Most often, I simply do what the flood allows me to, improvising here or there like a man tying a white flag to a raft that is being swiftly swept along, a plea for love or forgiveness. But as for artistry, control, enslavement through my penis, that's someone else. Which is not to say that there weren't women who were perfectly happy with me as a lover. In those cases, there was some love between us outside of bed: the intimacy was much more intense because we had something big to say to each other before we ever took off our clothes, but which could now be said only with our bodies.

With other women, whom I cared less about, I was sometimes a dud. I am not one of those men who can force himself to make love passionately or athletically when his affections are not engaged. From the perplexity of wide variations in my experiences I have been able to tell myself that I am neither a good nor a bad lover, but one who responds differently according to the emotions present. A banal conclusion; maybe a true one.

It does not do away, however, with some need to have my remaining insecurities about sexual ability laid to rest. I begin to suspect that all my fancy distrust of hedonism comes down to a fear of being judged in this one category: Do I make love well? Every brie and wine picnic, every tanned body relaxing on the beach, every celebration of *joie de vivre* carries a sly wink of some missed sexual enlightenment which may be too threatening to me. I am like the prudish old maid who blushes behind her packages when she sees sexy young people kissing.

When I was twenty I married. My wife was the second woman I had ever slept with. Our marriage was the recognition that we suited one another remarkably well as company—could walk and talk and share insights all day, work side by side like Chinese peasants, read silently together like graduate students, tease each other like brother and sister, and when at night we found our bodies tired, pull the covers over ourselves and become lovers. She was two years older than I, but I was good at faking maturity; and I found her so companionable and trustworthy and able to take care of me that I could not let such a gold mine go by.

Our love-life was mild and regular. There was a sweetness to sex, as befitted domesticity. Out of the surplus energy of late afternoons I would find myself coming up behind her sometimes as she worked in the kitchen, taking her away from her involvements, leading her by the hand into the bedroom. I would unbutton her blouse. I would stroke her breasts, and she would get a look in her eyes of quiet intermittent hunger, like a German shepherd being petted; she would seem to listen far off; absent-mindedly day-dreaming, she would return my petting, stroke my arm with distracted patience like a mother who has something on the stove, trying to calm her weeping child. I would listen too to guess what she might be hearing, bird calls or steam heat. The enlargement of her nipples under my fingers fascinated me. Goose bumps either rose on her skin where I touched or didn't, I noted with scientific interest, a moment before getting carried away by my own eagerness. Then we were undressing, she was doing something in the bathroom, and I was waiting on the bed, with all the consciousness of a sunmote. I was large and ready. The proud husband, waiting to receive my treasure. . . .

I remember our favorite position was she on top, I on the bottom, upthrusting and receiving. Distraction, absentminded-ness, return, calm exploration marked our sensual life. To be forgetful seemed the highest grace. We often achieved perfection.

Then I became haunted with images of seductive, heartless cunts. It was the era of the miniskirt, girl-women, Rudi Gernreich bikinis and Tiger Morse underwear, see-through blouses, flashes of flesh which invited the hand to go creeping under and into costumes. I wanted my wife to be more glamorous. We would go shopping for dresses together, and she would complain that her legs were wrong for these new fashions. Or she would come home proudly with a bargain pink and blue felt minidress, bought for three dollars at a discount store, which my aching heart would tell me missed the point completely.

She too became dissatisfied with the absence of furtive excitement in our marriage. She wanted to seduce me, like a stranger on a plane. But I was too easy, so we ended up seducing others. Then we turned back to each other and with one last desperate attempt, before the marriage fell to pieces, sought in the other a plasticity of sensual forms, like the statuary in an Indian temple. In our lovemaking I tried to believe that the body of one woman was the body of all women, and all I achieved was a groping to distance lovingly familiar forms into those of anonymous erotic succubi. The height of this insanity, I remember, was one evening in the park when I pounded my wife's lips with kisses in an effort to provoke something between us like "hot passion." My eyes closed, I practiced a repertoire of French tongue-kisses on her. I shall never forget her frightened silent appeal that I stop, because I had turned into someone she no longer recognized.

But we were young. And so, dependent on each other, like orphans. By the time I left, at twenty-five, I knew I had been a fool, and had ruined everything, but I had to continue being a fool because it had been my odd misfortune to have stumbled onto kindness and tranquility too quickly.

I moved to California in search of an earthly sexual paradise, and that year I tried hardest to make my peace with *joie de vivre*. I was sick but didn't know it—a diseased animal, Nietzsche would say. I hung around Berkeley's campus, stared up at the Campanile tower, I sat on the grass watching coeds younger than I, and, pretending that I was still going to university (no deeper sense of being a fraud obtainable), I tried to grasp the rhythms of carefree youth; I blended in at rallies, I stood at the fringes of be-ins, watching new rituals of communal love, someone being passed through the air hand to hand. But I never "trusted the group" enough to let myself be the guinea pig; or if I did, it was only with the proud stubborn conviction that nothing could change me— though I also wanted to change. Swearing I would never learn transcendence, I hitchhiked and climbed mountains. I went to wine-tasting festivals, and also accepted the wine jug from hippie gypsies in a circle around a beach campfire, without first wiping off the lip. I registered for a Free School course in human sexual response, just to get laid; and when that worked, I was shocked, and took up with someone else. There were many women in those years who got naked with me. I wish I could remember their names. I smoked grass with them, and as a sign of faith I took psychedelic drugs, and we made love in bushes and beachhouses, as though hacking through jungles with machetes to stay in touch with our ecstatic genitals while our minds soared off into natural marvels. Such experiences taught me, I will admit, how much romantic feeling can transform the body whose nerve-tendrils are receptive to it. Technicolor fantasies of one girlfriend as a señorita with flowers in her impossibly wavy hair would suddenly pitch and roll beneath me, and the bliss of touching her naked suntanned breast and the damp black pubic hairs was too unthinkably perfect to elicit anything but abject gratitude. At such moments I have held the world in my hands and *known* it. I was coming home to the body of Woman, those globes and grasses which had launched me. In the childish fantasy accompanying one sexual climax, under LSD, I was hitting a home run, and the Stars and Stripes flying in the background of my mind's eye as I "slid into home" acclaimed the patriotic rightness of my semenal release. For once I had no guilt about how or when I ejaculated.

If afterwards, when we came down, there was often a sour air of disenchantment and mutual prostitution, that does not take away from the legacy, the rapture of those moments. If I no longer use drugs—in fact, have become anti-drug—I think I still owe them something for showing me how to recognize the all-embracing reflex. At first I needed drugs to teach me about the stupendous-ness of sex. Later, without them, there would be situations—after a lovely talk or coming home from a party in a taxi—when I would be overcome by amorous tropism towards the woman with me. The appetite for flesh which comes over me at such moments, and the pleasure there is in finally satisfying it, seems so just that I always think I have stumbled into a state of blessed grace. That it can never last, that it is a trick of the mind and the blood, are rumors I push out of sight.

To know rapture is to have one's whole life poisoned. If you will forgive a ridiculous analogy, a tincture of rapture is like a red bandana in the laundry that runs and turns all the white wash pink. We should just as soon stay away from any future ecstatic experiences which spoil everyday living by comparison. Not that I have any intention of stopping. Still, if I will have nothing to do with religious mysticism, it is probably because I sense a susceptibility in that direction. Poetry is also dangerous. All quickening awakenings to Being extract a price later.

Are there people who live under such spells all the time? Was this the secret of the idiotic smile on the half-moon face of the painter Vartas? The lovers of life, the robust Cellinis, the Casanovas? Is there a technique to hedonism that will allow the term of rapture to be indefinitely extended? I don't believe it. The hedonist's despair is still that he is forced to make do with the present. Who knows about the success rate of religious mystics? In any case, I could not bring myself to state that what I am waiting for is God. Such a statement would sound too grandiose and presumptuous, and make too great a rupture in my customary thinking. But I can identify with the pre- if not the post-stage of what Simone Weil describes:

"The soul knows for certain only that it is hungry. The important thing is that it announces its hunger by crying. A child does not stop crying if we suggest to it that perhaps there is no bread. It goes on crying just the same. The danger is not lest the soul should doubt whether there is any bread, but lest, by a lie, it should persuade itself that it is not hungry."

So much for *joie de vivre*. It's too compensatory. I don't really know what I'm waiting for. I know only that until I have gained what I want from this life, my expressions of gratitude and joy will be restricted to variations of a hunter's alertness. I give thanks to a nip in the air that clarifies the scent. But I think it hypocritical to pretend satisfaction while I am still hungry.

*nominated by Kenneth Gangemi
and Ellen Wilbur*

SHRUBS BURNED AWAY

by DONALD HALL

from KENYON REVIEW

> What then are the situations, from the representation of which, though
> accurate, no poetical enjoyment can be derived? They are those in which the
> suffering finds no vent in action; in which a continuous state of mental distress
> is prolonged, unrelieved by incident, hope or resistance; in which there is
> everything to be endured, nothing to be done.
>
> MATTHEW ARNOLD

> Mi-t'o Temple after thirty li. A most desolate spot . . . For fear of them hiding
> tigers, all trees and shrubs have been burnt.
>
> HSU HSIA-K'O

Once a little boy and his sister—my mother lay
on top of the quilt, narrow and tense, whispering—
found boards piled up, deep in the woods, and nails,
and built a house for themselves, and nobody knew
that they built their house each day in the woods . . .
I listened and fell asleep, like a baby full of milk,
and carried their house into sleep where I built it
board by board all night, each night
from the beginning; from the pile of boards I built it,
painted it, put doorknobs on it . . .

As I sit by myself, middle-aged in my yellow chair,
staring at the vacant book of the ceiling, starting
the night's bottle, aureoled with cigarette smoke
in the unstoried room, I daydream to build
the house of dying: The old man alone in the farmhouse
makes coffee, whittles, walks, and cuts an onion
to eat between slices of bread. But the white loaf

on the kitchen table comes undone:—milk leaks
from its side; flour and yeast draw apart;
sugar and water puddle the table's top.

Bullied, found wanting, my father drove home
from his job at the lumberyard weeping,
and shook his fist over my cradle—He'll do
what he wants to do!—and kept to it twenty
years later, still home from work weeping, hopeless
in outrage, smoking Chesterfields, unable to sleep
for coughing. Forty years of waking to shallow light;
forty years of the day's aging; today
I observe for the first time the white hair
that grows from the wrist's knuckle.

I lay in the dark hearing trees scrape
like Hauptmann's ladder on the gray clapboard.
Downstairs the radio diminished, Bing Crosby,
and I heard voices like logs burning, flames
rising and falling, one high and steady, one
urgent and quick. If I cried, if I called . . . I called
softly, sore in the wrapped dark, but there was nothing,
I was nothing, the light's line at the closed door faint.
I called again; I heard her steps:—
light swept in like a broom from the opening door

and my head lay warm on her shoulder, and her breath
sang in my ear—A Long Long Trail A-winding,
Backward Turn Backward O Time in Your Flight . . .
In the next room a drawer banged shut. When my father
lay dying at fifty-one, he could not deliver
the graduation speech at Putnam Avenue School
near the house he was born in. Taking my father's
place, my head shook like a plucked wire.
I told the fourteen-year-olds:
Never do anything except what you want to do.

"I could not keep from staring out the window.
Teachers told my mother that I was an intelligent girl,
if I would only apply myself. But I continued

to gaze at hills pushing upward, or to draw with my crayons.
In the third grade Mr. Bristol came on Wednesdays;
he said I was the best young artist in the township.
At home when my mother made Parkerhouse Rolls
she let me mold scraps of dough on the oilcloth
of the kitchen table, and I shaped my first soft
rising edible sculptures.

"The year after my father burned in the wrecked car,
my mother came home early from the job she hated
teaching bookkeeping at the secretarial college.
Sometimes she wept because she had flunked someone
she caught cheating. Each day I comforted her;
I was fifteen years old. I cooked supper for her—
hamburgers and hot dogs, baked beans, corn niblets.
Once I took a recipe from Confidential Chat,
using asparagus soup, Ritz crackers, and water chestnuts.
She said I would make some man happy.

"That was the year I stopped drawing. Sometimes at night
when she fell asleep I would look at my old portfolio
and cry, and pick up a pencil, and set it down.
Every night before supper we played Chinese checkers
and I beat her; she trembled lifting the marbles, only forty
years old. She came home exhausted not wanting to play.
After a while we played no more checkers,
and she collapsed early with her Agatha Christie
in the blue leather lounger, with the vodka that ruptured
her liver through her abdomen ten years later."

Closing my eyes I collect the others.
One is an actor, homosexual, in a rent-controlled apartment
near Sullivan Square; he waits for the telephone:—
two weeks in General Hospital as a kindly
thoracic surgeon. In Woodbridge outside New Haven
another lives—ironic, uxorious, the five children
grown and gone; he waters his lawn with irony; he works
forty hours of irony a week and lives to retire.
Another died dropping from the parking structure in April,
climbing the parapet drunk with purpose.

"When I was twelve I spent the summer on the farm,
painting watercolors all morning, all afternoon hoeing
the garden with my grandmother who told stories.
We fed the hens; we gathered eggs. Once we discovered
four hen-husks drained dry by a weasel.
That summer I painted One Hundred Views
of house, hill, and covered bridge. When my grandmother
woke me at six o'clock with black coffee,
the day lay before me like a green alley over the grass
of a meadow I invented by setting my foot to it.

"When my mother came home from drying-out hospital,
still convulsive, she took pills and talked without stopping.
She told me about her first breakdown
when she was nine years old. She had a nightmare
over and over again: Bearded men who looked like the tramps
who asked for bread and butter at the porch door,
or the gypsies who camped in their wagons every summer,
made a circle around her, and the circle grew smaller
as the bearded men shuffled close. Every night
she woke up screaming, unable to stop. She knew:

"They wanted to cut her up for a patchwork quilt. Her mother
and father set a small cot beside their bed, and when she woke
screaming they comforted her. The circle of men
came closer; even when she was awake in her mother's arms,
the circle tightened; she heard her grandfather
tell somebody on the porch, 'We're going to lose
our little girl.' When she stopped crying her mother
pumped a cup of water. She remembered once
her mother brought water in an unwashed coffee cup
and there was sugar stuck in the bottom of the cup."

The Bee Gee, huge engine and tiny stub wings,
snapped around pylons in the Nationals; each year
they clipped more wing off. "On the Fourth of July,
I turned nine years old. I was playing in the woods
with Bingo and Harold Johnson; Bingo had a crush on me.
We were chasing each other and ran into a clearing
and found Bingo and Harold's father and my mother

drunk, rolling in the grass with their clothes off."
Douglas Corrigan took off from Long Island, flight plan
filed for California, plane heavy with gasoline,

and flew to Ireland—Wrong-Way Corrigan:
A mistake, he claimed; no sense of direction . . .
"Later we returned to the house with the grown-ups
and my father threw his Old Fashioned in my mother's face.
When I tried to run outside my uncle caught me
and set me on his lap; I kept on watching in my blue
shirt over my lace birthday blouse." For three years
David Palmer worked weekends in his garage to build
an airplane using the motors from six lawnmowers.
The CAB refused a license; a strut washed up on Catalina.

"My father ran from the house with a glass in his hand.
When he backed out of the driveway,
he knocked the mailbox over. My mother got my uncle
to chase him along dirt roads at midnight,
very fast;—I sat in the back seat, frightened.
He lost us but we knew where he was going." Wiley Post
and Will Rogers flew from the Walaka Lagoon; Inuits
found their bodies. In the Pacific, Navy patrol planes
searched for Amelia Earhart while her Lockheed sank
through fathoms with its cargo of helmeted corpses.

The old man walks on blacktop, farm to post office,
beside a ditch gray with late August grass. He is
a boy carrying a scythe over blacktop to join
his grandfather on the mowing machine in the hayfield
where he will trim around rocks. He tilts his blade
toward German prisoners sleeping by day in ditches
who escaped last week from the Canadian prison-camp.
When he returns an old man to the farmhouse
by the strong cowbarn, past Aunt Bertha's cottage,
blonde prisoners drink schnapps in the livingroom.

I told my wife: Consider me a wind
that lifts square houses up and spins them
into each other; or as a flood loosening houses

from their cellarholes; or as a fire that burns white
wooden houses down. I was content in the dark
living room, fixed in the chair with whiskey.
I claimed that the wind was out of control
while I looked through a window where the June tree
blew in the streetlight at two o'clock; leaves broke
from their stems, and the trunk did not split open.

I declared that everywhere at two in the morning
men drank in yellow chairs
while wives lay awake on beds upstairs, necks rigid.
Last night at the reception I glimpsed the made-up faces
of women I knew elsewhere—pale, shaking,
passionate, weeping. We understood together:
The world is a bed. In discontented peace,
in boredom and tolerance, only adultery proves
devotion by risk; only the pulse of betrayal
makes blood pelt in the chest as if with joy.

At the exact millisecond when two cells fused
and multiplied, I started this house. Through years
of milk and potty I constructed foundations. In Miss Ford's
classroom I built it; in vacant lots hopeless at football,
by Blake's Pond hunting for frogs and turtles,
under the leaf's breath, in rotted leaves I built it;
in months at the worktable assembling model airplanes,
at the blackboard doing sums, in blue summer
painting watercolors at my grandmother's I built this house.
I build it now, staring at the wrist-knuckle.

Who is it that sets these words on blue-lined pads?
It is the old man in the room of bumpy wallpaper.
It is the girl who sits on her drunken mother's lap
or carries her grandmother's eggs. It is the boy who reads
The Complete Tales of Edgar Allan Poe. It is
the middle-aged man motionless in a yellow chair,
unable to read, daydreaming the house of dying:—
We take comfort in building this house which does not exist,
because it does not exist, while we stare at the wrist's
hair, drinking Scotch in a yellow chair.

There was the dream of the party: a French farce,
frolic behind curtains, exits and entrances—
like a child fooling parents. I departed
alone on a bus that bumped down the white staircase
of the mansion over the bodies of three women
who stood complacent and pretty in the bus's way,
their faces familiar as photographs. When I looked
back from the bus's rear window at their bodies,
they waved to me although they were dead:—
They forgave me because no one was driving the bus.

My daughter curled in my lap, wailing and red,
eight years old. My thirteen-year-old son's long legs
writhed from a chair as tears fell on his spectacles.
Their father was leaving them . . . I
was leaving them. Their muscles contracted
knees to chin, as I watched from my distance,
and their limbs twitched and jerked in the velvet room.
My daughter wanted to see the place I had rented
to move to. She whirled among cheap furniture,
over bare linoleum, saying, "Cozy, *cozy* . . ."

It rains on Sunset Boulevard. I walk with the collar
of my jacket turned up. Topless go-go dancers twist
at the back of a bar, while men on the wet sidewalk
peer into the doorway at the young women's bodies,
their smooth skin intolerably altered by ointments
and by revolving orange and purple lights.
Lights bruise their thighs:—for three thousand years
these lights and ointments . . . I discarded
the comforts I contrived for myself; or I exchanged them
for a rain of small faces on the abandoned street.

I am a dog among dogs, and I whine
about waking to the six o'clock sun of summer
or brag about Sinbad's adventures, for which I left
houses excessive with shrubbery, carpets, and mirrors.
Justifying myself I claim: from the breathless blue
of my father's face I chose
the incendiary flower, yellow fire and therefore

106

rain on the Boulevard. Now in the gray continuous
morning, water drips from the cindery house that wanted
to bloom in the night. I stay up all night

at the Hollywood-La Brea Motel looking at television,
black-and-white war movies, Marines at Iwo,
sailors and blondes, B-24s; I do not understand
what happens. I listen to shills in blazers
with sixpenny London accents pitch acrylic while I drink
Scotch from the bottle. Studying a bikini'd
photograph on a matchbox, I dial BONNIE FASHION
MODEL AVAILABLE at four in the morning
from my vinyl room, and the answering service tells me
that Bonnie is out to lunch . . .

"I wait for the plane inside a blockhouse
at the airport's edge; then the cement walls vibrate
as if an earthquake shook them. I understand at once:
The plane from Ireland has crushed trying to land.
Immediately I watch a conveyor belt
remove bodies covered with brown army blankets
from the broken snake of the fuselage. One of the dead
sits up abruptly, points a finger at me,
and stares accusingly. It is an old man with an erection;
then I notice that all of the dead are men."

Another self sits all day in a watchpocket
of cigarette smoke, staring at the wrist-knuckle,
in repetitious vacancy examining the ceiling, its cracks
and yellowed paint, unprinted emptiness rolling
as continuous as the ocean, no ship or landfall anywhere,
no bird or airplane. I climb from the yellow chair
to the bare bedroom and lie on my back smoking
and staring . . . until ice in a glass, golden whiskey,
euphoria, falling down, and sleep with two yellowjacketed
Nembutols pave the undreaming gilt road to nothing.

Therefore I envy the old man hedging and ditching
three hundred years ago in Devon. I envy the hedge
and the ditch. When my father came home

from the lumberyard, head shaking, fingers
yellow with Chesterfields, I begged him to play catch
with me. He smacked the pocket
of a catcher's mitt: "Put her there!"—and I threw
a fastball ten feet over his head. As he trotted
after the ball I waited, ashamed of being
wild: enraged, apologetic, unforgiving.

Now I prepare to walk the dirt road by the pond.
I prepare to enter the sand. I endure
the present of Laurel Canyon among the middle-aged
rich who eat shrimp curled on ice, who wear tartan
jackets and earrings coded to shoes. They do not notice
when I go back down to the cellar under the kitchen
where a mirror hangs in the gloom. I make out
a white beard and glasses that reflect nothing:
But when I touch my chin my face is smooth.
I rejoin the party; I smile; I am careful drinking . . .

Nothing remains except a doll strangled on fence wire.
Night after night I sleep on pills
and wake exhausted. Rage scrapes its iron across my chest.
I cannot enter the farmhouse in the hills, or find the road
vanished under burdock. I burn another house
and self-pity exhausts me. I pour the first tumbler
over ice cubes that dull the taste. Roots of my hair
go numb. Numbness spreads downward
over the forehead's wrinkles past bloody eyes
to stomach, to wrist's white hair, to dead penis.

The world is a bed, I announce; my love agrees.
A hundred or a thousand times our eyes encounter;
each time the clothes slough off, anatomies
of slippery flesh connect again
on the world's bed, and the crescent of nerves
describes itself again in the wretched
generality of bliss. If we are each the same
on the world's bed, if we are each manikins of the other,
then the multitude is one and one is the multitude;
many and one we perform procedures of comfort.

I am very happy. I dance supine on my bed laughing
until four in the morning when the bottle is empty
and the liquor store closed on Hollywood and La Brea.
I must not drive the car for cigarettes;—
therefore I lurch a mile to the All-Nite Laundro-Mart
and falter back coughing. In the morning I lie
waking dozing twisted in the damp clothes
of lethargy, loathing, and the desire to die.
My father's head shakes like a plucked wire.
Never do anything except what you want to do.

"I am sad in the convenient white kitchen, dreaming
that I weep as I start making dinner.
The children themselves weep, bringing their sentences
on small folded squares of blue paper.
They will take pills to die without disturbance.
I help them count the pills out, and arrange
pillows for their comfort as they become sleepy.
While I slice onions and peppers on the breadboard,
someone whose identity hovers just out of sight, the way
a beekeeper's mask darkens a face,

"walks up the busy street and enters the kitchen
to instruct me in butchering the children.
The visitor picks up the long rag doll and with scissors
carefully cuts the doll's limbs at the joints,
teaching me expertly, with anatomical explanations
and a scientific vocabulary, while cutting and preparing
the model, then places the doll's parts
on a high shelf, arranged with the gaps of dismemberment
visible, so that I may consult it while cutting,
as I must do, as it seems that I want to do."

nominated by Laura Jensen

THAT THEY WERE AT THE BEACH —AEOLOTROPIC SERIES

by LESLIE SCALAPINO

from AMERICAN POETRY REVIEW

Playing ball—so it's like paradise, not because it's in the past, we're on a field; we are creamed by the girls who get together on the other team. They're nubile, but in age they're thirteen or so—so they're strong.

(No one knows each other, aligning according to race as it happens, the color of the girls, and our being creamed in the foreground—as part of it's being that—the net is behind us).

———————

A microcosm, but it's of girls—who were far down on the field, in another situation of playing ball—so it was an instance of the main world though they're nubile but are in age thirteen or so.

My being creamed in the foreground—so it's outside of that—by a girl who runs into me, I returned to the gym.

———————

It's in the past—yet is repressed in terms of the situation itself, poor people who're working, the division is by color. We're not allowed to leave the airport on arriving—others not permitted to stop over—we're immature in age, so it's inverted.

(Therefore receded—we get on the bus going to the city and look around, seeing people dressed shabbily).

A man—I was immature in age—was a stowaway so not having been active, taken from the ship we're on in a row boat.

'A sailor had fallen out of the row boat then, was embarrassed. So it's like paradise—the embarrassment, therefore it's depressed—seen by his waving at us as the other sailors are coming to him).

The class period ending—it's evanescence not because it's in the past, they'd stamped their feet while seated since the teacher hadn't been able to discipline them. She's old—the red hair coloring had been mocked—they're inactive.

(So it's evanescent because they're inactive. Though I am as well. She'd asked me to pull on her hair to indicate it was her real hair, which I do—them being unaware of this—as the class is disbanding, composed of girls and boys).

It is also an instance in the past, so it's depressed—yet the people on the bus aren't nubile, rather are mature.

We're girls—have to urinate which is unrelated to immaturity—refusing to do so in front of others; we require the bus to leave us. Therefore there aren't other people, we urinate, and then look around.

(So it's inactive—is depressed).

Tall, though they are nubile—playing leap frog is out of place; we're required to do so. It's contemporary in time so it's not depressed—I was immature, thirteen in age or so; responding to the other girls kicking as they jumped over some of us.

(So it's not depressed—but not as being active. I'm creamed, until the crowd of girls is pulled off by an instructor who's in the gym).

Attending a funeral—it's contemporary in time, not being in itself depressed; taking a ridiculous aspect—birds that sing loudly in the

111

chapel where the funeral service is being held. The birds are mechanical—so it's being creamed.

(Like in the earlier episode of playing ball. Our being creamed in the foreground of the field by the other girls).

A microcosm, but it's of sailors—though I'm given attention standing in pictures with one or two of the men. They've come into a port at one time—I'm immature in age—it doesn't occur for that reason but is inverted, the sailors flirted with girls.

(Which is contemporary in time therefore. And being mechanical since I'm interested in the sailors, then merely interest).

A boy was actually at the funeral—so it's inverted—was later playing ball, really occurring.

(Inverted also because of being at the funeral, mechanical birds part of it; so it isn't creamed in the future—not because of that).

The boy who was actually at the funeral—corresponds to work as a chimney sweep which I had for a short time—is inverted.

(I didn't take the job seriously since it was in the past—I was supposed to do it awhile, was contemporary. So it's related to the boy; I got sick from the soot—so my leaving after working only two days stemmed from that).

Someone else driving—the funeral having taken place—is getting speeding tickets, with us in the car—we're older than he

So we don't say anything because we're older. Not about the police stopping him, the drive is several hundred miles at night—which is like him later going below the border

●

Him not being sentient

A man whoring—it's from the standpoint of a girl, is a situation of trying to finance going below the border to whore and staying down there as long as he can before having to return to get some job.

(It's a microcosm, is also inverted—not retroactive).

We're thirteen in age or so—they're nubile—so I wouldn't say that ever in describing myself

We're bicycling as are they. Other girls who come on us from a side road. There are fields around, they race us—almost sarcastic seen while bicycling (so it's retroactive; isn't just in relation to their being nubile—contemporary in time)

—so it's mechanical birds though it's in the past

Not really being ill, but thinking he is, (it's also the mechanical birds), the man's deeply embarrassed—he's not old—at it turning out to be viewed this way after having others take him to hospitals.

(So it's the mechanical birds because he isn't old. Nor is there a funeral—but not related to one he's taken from a swimming pool, goes in an ambulance).

Not really being ill—corresponds to the man who mugged me, not the one I mistook for him—it's depressed.

The real thief running away from the telephone booth is in my side vision, I don't realize it while blaming a boy standing in front of me. They're boys really—so it's inverted—though the one who'd stayed behind for a minute while I cursed him flirted with me.

A man mugging me—therefore inverted, not just in relation to maturity—seeing I'm frightened is almost considerate by not hitting me when I struggle with him, though finally giving him the purse.

The naiveté—on my part—he's depressed

He's depressed—by mugging me—corresponds to my having a job

Having an employer, I'd make jokes seen by him to be inappropriate, had offended him—I make jokes because it's in the past (is therefore sentient—I'm fairly immature in age and my offending him is unintentional).

Winos were lying on the sidewalk, it's a warehouse district; I happen to be wearing a silk blouse, so it's jealousy, not that they're jealous of me necessarily.

They're not receded, and are inert—as it happens are bums—so it's being creamed; because it's contemporary in time—jealousy because of that.

The bums happen to be lying in the street, it really occurs that I wear a silk blouse.

So it's mechanical—because of the winos being there—not from the blouse which I'd happened to wear though going into the warehouse district.

Stevedores—I'm immature in age—who are now made to live away from their families to work, the division is by color; they're allowed to form unions but not act—so it's evanescent.

(Because it's inactive—not just in the situation itself. Or in their later not coming to the docks—so they were striking, regardless of them being fired which occurs then).

The man having been in government—it's evanescent because it's inactive, our being immature in age—he's assassinated at an airport where we happen to come in that morning. We get on a bus which goes to the ocean—it's also beefcake but not because of the man already having died, is mature.

(We haven't seen him—as with the sailors it's contemporary in time).

A microcosm, but it's of sailors—so it's in the foreground, is beefcake—is in the past

(Therefore is contemporary in time while being seen then—so beefcake is in the past—similar to the situation of the other girls also refusing as I had to walk out onto the field, my then being immediately required to—not just in relation to them cooperating then).

It's the mechanical birds because of my having gone out on the field then—is the men

So it's sexual coming—anyone—but corresponds to the floating world, seeing men on the street

---

not in relation to there being too many of them standing around on a job

●

It's hot weather—so it's recent—corresponds to them

(though the floating world was in the past). To others as well—is in the setting of me being on a boardwalk seeing crowds of people walking or rollerskating. Some happening to be immature in age—it's not retroactive

●

Being in the past—is jealousy on my part—in general

Not in relation to the people I happened to see who were immature in age—on the boardwalk—necessarily

●

Their not being sentient

The reserves—they weren't using the police, so it's inverted—were wearing battle-gear, it's beautiful weather—they were old—is crowded

not occurring now—and their being frightened of the crowd, so it's inverted because of that—I'm there but jealousy on my part, in general—stemming from that

_____

I'm not retroactive—corresponds to making jokes because it's in the past

(Not retroactive because of the beautiful weather. And taking the car to be repaired; the mechanic coming out to test drive, its tires have gone flat in the short time I was in the shop. The man and I get out of the car, laugh, I walk somewhere else to have its tires filled, drive away. Buying a dip stick then, I'd done what was necessary to it myself apparently).

_____

Beginning to honk, because a man in a car behind me looked as if he were going to take my parking place, it's near shops, is crowded—I honked before seeing that he's old. And it appearing he hadn't wanted the parking place.

(His being old not mattering because it's crowded—which is transparent, regardless of there being the one parking place—so it isn't sentient)

_____

The background had been in the selling of the car—almost giving it away

though it's not that, but seeing it again sitting by the highway—I'm weeping because of something, am driving back from the city—so it's transparent, crowded but my being miserable; which had occurred anyway. The man who'd bought the car cheating me though saying it was worthless—it is—having occurred earlier

_____

Corresponding to having a job—and going below the border

On the vacation—I'm fired after I returned though the employer had consented to the vacation—we get to a small town in the desert. There are mines. It's at night. We've driven very fast. A crowd of men are in the store buying liquor who are poor—so it's evanescent (it's evanescent though we're buying liquor as well)

Someone else, who's middle aged—so it's not the man with the boy, getting gasoline

—being miserable, had put his head on the steering wheel, corresponds to there being the one parking place, though he's not going then. So isn't in that one. And weeping unrestrainedly because of his life—isn't necessarily related to his age

---

Other people not being retroactive—because of the beautiful weather—so it's recent

people said to be working for subsistence complimented for being willing to—in a naive way by the plant owner—is then inactive

•

The construction workers whistling or catcalling at women who go by the construction site, at each woman going by—they're not sentient

(We're not—either are they)

It's hot weather—so it's reversed, is contemporary as with the sailors

(beefcake is in the foreground)

---

is naive—corresponds to the floating world

---

isn't knowledgeable of myself therefore—is the boys—who happen to be standing on a street corner, they're unemployed though it's Sunday anyway. It's necessary that they not have jobs. We're downtown driving—so there's no one else there

(is not sentient—but which is the mechanical birds, because of the weather)

---

so it would be transparent in the past, crowded but my being miserable

—as it happens—and have it not occur now

●

Their not being sentient

Seeing a crowd of people—we'd gone to a gallery as it happened— so they're not at their jobs

---

that they were at the beach—aren't retroactive

The floating world was courtesans though

It was in a man's divorce, (he's the father of a man who'd earlier gone below the border)—and him just taking off to the south one day to be near the border for good, not wanting his job anyway— not clarifying

(it's therefore sentient—isn't for him)

isn't for me

taking a cab, the driver seems frightened, seen by him not speaking to me—stemming from his job—unfamiliar because of the streets

---

A crazy, recognized by people around because he is always on the street—staying outside is it being crowded, though the man isn't old.

I'm going by when fraternity boys are shouting at him, making fun—didn't realize he could've shouted first, occurring to me when I saw him shouting by himself one time

Alcohol not enabling someone to be in paradise, being what he was saying

therefore inverted. A man getting out of a car, another transient coming by who begins to shout for some reason, addressed the man by the car (though it's not necessarily to him)—who also shouted, but not making fun of him

---

It having to be some time ago—was related to the bus driver, we're in school. The driver is surly, in general—turning a corner driving he hits a girl because she's not out of the way, thinking she should run

he hasn't drunk anything—so it isn't dislike

●

and isn't dislike for him—so afterwards we'd always make the sound in the bus of it hitting her at that corner

---

which is their wanting to take the money I might have on me

two muggers—though they were not together—who both followed me for a time aware of each other and that I see them. I was walking quickly with my suitcase which would mean to them that I'd just arrived in the city, it's crowded with passers-by (so not enabling someone to be in paradise—is regardless of the money I might have on me).

A transient—so it's not necessary to be it—the other men in the restaurant throw him out

because he's noisy, being drunk—but having no arms so removing him is inverted, another transient comes in who has arms, is also drunk—and therefore thrown out as well (that man had reentered carrying a cat before being thrown out again).

The floating world was courtesans though

●

A girl at the time—the insects which is inverted, in a situation in

119

which she's on the deck of a boat on the Nile, there was a swarm of locusts, coming on her suddenly—she's a friend

really the friend of a relative

●

It'd have to be some time ago—I got cake on me, handed to me by my mother, we're in a taxi. Men in another car—beside me, I'm somewhat immature in age—whistled and called to me customary stemming from seeing me eating the cake

(so I'm embarrassed)

Climbing a mountain—it's Fuji—there are marines having to climb it for exercise; easily able to get far ahead of us, which we don't realize, we're girls, they wait when we have to rest—

it isn't creamed for us—though dissolution not occurring. And not occurring in the situation with the marines.

---

it's regardless—I was immature in age, so that is mechanical

Holding one end of a jump rope, the other end is tied to a tree—a boy who was a bully riding his bicycle is going to ride across the jump rope; I pull the rope slightly as it's lying on the sidewalk before he gets to it so he sees that and knows I can do it—so it isn't mechanical in that sense

---

is so our being fairly immature in age, we're students—the man who's discovered in the crowd—he's there to observe it, is in the F.B.I., had been in it in my childhood living nearby since he was a neighbor

Though the people in the crowd don't call to him saying they know who he is because of that—but it's mechanical because of that

---

it being reversed

●

It's obvious—occurring recently

The checkers falling behind—after chasing a man out shouting that he has stolen, he ran far away from the supermarket—a woman I know rode after him on a bicycle (for the reason given by the checkers)

●

I went on up the street, seeing a transient who had his things with him sitting near-by—there are men pouring cement in a site, he's watching them—so isn't sentient

because of occurring recently

---

stemming from that—

I take her to the hospital—meaning the landlady who's in her nineties—to visit a tenant who's fallen down having been drunk

We walk a block, the street flooding since it's raining. It isn't creamed—in the sense of her age

as it is being caught in the rain with bags of groceries—no one's around

It's pouring, I'm on the street corner unable to carry them further—it's funny because I should have known better. But though taxis are never in the neighborhood, one goes by and I go home in it

---

So it's the bicyclist, cursing—which occurs when I almost hit a bicyclist, he says so following my car for a block afterwards—

So I'm sentient—he is not

I'm in a packed courtroom, a crowd is outside; the man sitting there—having been informed on as communist in a ridiculous situation—the other members of the cell had been F.B.I. So there not having been understanding on his part, he was embarrassed—in expression—

Therefore dissolution not occurring—my being fairly immature in age. Not creamed for me afterwards.

I'd gotten into the hearing—of the man—because of the crowd's pushing and the police admitting me into the courtroom

though my friends had been left outside, were more aware than I—so it's the landlady because of them being amidst the crowd

---

as it is working for a lawyer only slightly older than I, I'm fairly immature in age—I offend him unintentionally by making a joke when he says he'd like to get into working for trusts

It's dumb work, temporary for me—so that is the landlady

---

it's temporary work—he's the lawyer who's slightly older than I, I was fairly immature in age

He doesn't speak to me for a week once, we're in the car mostly—because I'd made jokes; I hadn't meant to offend him—so it's the landlady in that sense

●

which is like selling my car—having an ad

I have the feeling I wouldn't have luck without the car, though it won't run—but nevertheless sell it to a man who puts the money on the grass. I'd bent down to get it giving him the chance to grab me—picking me up in his arms isn't the reason he buys the car—it's to repair it

---

Seeing my old car parked on the street—I'm driving by and had

already been unhappy—regardless of the feeling that I wouldn't have luck without the car, so that is then the landlady

●

The lawyer and I, he's only slightly older than I—working have to have dinners; though I've unintentionally offended him—

which is the landlady for that reason. We're in expensive restaurants, he and I fairly immature in age

---

my being fairly immature in age—we dock, there are lines of stevedores, men coming onto the ship—we can't get off in that port, it's the port's authority, because a few people on the ship had become sick

but the stevedores can

—making jokes

was making fun of the lawyer, our both being fairly immature in age—though I didn't realize it

●

We're—the lawyer and I—in the car, I had made the jokes before this, he's gotten beer

but we hadn't opened it yet; he backed into a tree, driving away from the grocery

●

The thought that there is no riot—isn't going to be any

is connected to the stevedores

There is no riot—associated with the stevedores—the man to whom I sold my car, he'd taken me for a drive in the hills deciding on it, had driven it recklessly

he's trying to frighten me so I'll give him the car—which I do, though I realize it

---

nominated by American Poetry Review

THE BIRTHING

fiction by PATRICIA HENLEY

from FRIDAY NIGHT AT SILVER STAR (Graywolf Press)

ONE SHOT and the killing was over, quickly as trimming a thumbnail. Morgan walked away from the alfalfa field toward the dead goat. It was early evening and the sun had long ago loosened its hold on the canyon.

Angel came running from behind the house. She wore a loose white shirt and was barefooted and soil crept up her ankles like socks. Her braids flew behind her.

"Why the hell did you *do* that?" she said.

Morgan stood near the dead gray nanny goat and with one hand he absently thinned green apples from the dwarf tree. He held the .22 in the other hand, the barrel at an angle to the ground.

"Told her I would if she didn't keep her penned," he said. "Here. You take this back to the house." He handed her the rifle and lifted the goat in his arms and began walking toward the county road, toward the goat woman herself who had heard the shot and was waiting in the middle of the gravel road, but near her house, a quarter mile farther toward the lake. Morgan could see her waiting, arms akimbo, in a long skirt and a big picture hat. The pine woods behind her were blackening and the goat was still warm in his arms.

IT WAS their custom to hold meetings to resolve disputes among their kind. The authorities had never been called in. At the meeting Morgan showed no remorse. He had changed his shirt, wet his head under the garden hose, and slicked back his wavy blond hair. He sat nudging loose tobacco into the careful crease of a

124

rolling paper, his feet propped on an applewood stool next to the cold woodstove.

Angel stood up first thing and defended him. "Morgan was forced to do this. He didn't want to do it." She sat down then on the sagging sofa and pulled the nearest young child into her lap, murmuring to his neck and smoothing his forehead.

The schoolhouse was lit by kerosene lamps with soot-black globes and the light was a little skittish, like a feline creature among them.

Georgia, the goatherd, sat in an overstuffed chair surrounded by her four children. She tapped her boots on the linoleum floor and, head bent, stared at Morgan through slitted eyes. Theirs was a longstanding feud. When the little one named Banjo whimpered, she put him to the breast to quiet him.

After Angel spoke no one said anything for a long time. A coyote howled from the rimrock and two dogs wrangled on the schoolhouse porch, their growls low and menacing. At last a tall woman in an old band uniform jacket stood and spoke. "We've got to think about what we're trying to do. We can't be shooting one another's animals." Her hands were grimy with garden soil and she ran them through her frizzy red hair. "What do we believe in?" she said.

Everyone started talking at once and no one was accorded attention. Morgan said nothing and Angel didn't look at him. She didn't like to think the father of her unborn child would kill a neighbor's goat just for eating apples.

"Hold it. JUST HOLD IT, PEOPLE," Sam hollered, his arms high, gesturing for their attention. The jabbering subsided, like air seeping out of a balloon.

Sam was respected, a leader, a hard worker, a strong wiry man people rarely challenged.

"I can't sit here all night listening to this," he said. "I've got chores. I'll wager most of you do, too." He wiped his face with a blue bandana. There were murmurs of assent.

"Okay," Sam said. "I'm going to ask Morgan to relinquish his .22 for three months. All we can do is let him know we disapprove." No one disputed him.

"What about the goats?" Morgan asked.

"And we will put pressure on Georgia to pen up the goats. I will help you build a pen," Sam said directly to the goatherd before she could say one word in defense of animals running free. She slumped in her chair, defeated. The lines were deep around her mouth and eyes.

"Meeting adjourned," Sam said. The people filed out of the schoolhouse, resuming conversations and laughing, drifting home in the cool night, quick to forget the conflict. Angel and Morgan were last. They stood on the porch and looked at the stars while the others dispersed. The cloying smell of the lilac bush was thick in the night air.

"Want to feel the baby moving, Morgan?" Angel said. She reached for his calloused hand.

"Sure, Sugar," Morgan answered, dutifully placing his hand on her abdomen. He kept it there until the baby kicked. Then he hugged her with the baby like a bundling board between them.

"Are you scared about the baby?" Morgan said.

"Scared?" Angel loved for Morgan to ask her how she was feeling. He didn't ask her often since they had quit courting and settled down to have a baby. She was nineteen. He was twenty-four. They had met a year ago at a healing gathering in British Columbia, linking hands in a circle of two hundred people dancing and not letting go.

"I mean scared of the delivery," he said.

"No," Angel said. "So many ladies have done it before me. It must be almost foolproof."

"Let's go home," Morgan said, and he took her hand to guide her in the shadows to the red house beside the rushing creek.

THE HOLY FOLKS came the first of July when the sun was relentless and the people sometimes gathered in the afternoon to soak in the deepest part of the creek, watching the water striders skim across the water and the nightshade curling around the cottonwood roots. They drove into the canyon in a rattletrap Ford stationwagon, circa 1956, blue and white beneath Arizona and California dust, and overloaded. The tailpipe scraped the first real bump the car came to off the blacktop and the tailpipe was lost, so that the holy folks made quite an entrance, a noisy entrance disturbing the quiet rising of the heat waves.

Morgan watched from the grove of aspens shielding the creek pool. They stopped by the mailbox and all three piled out of the car, two women and one man, dressed in graying, once-white clothing. Morgan stepped from the shade and waved them in his direction.

The three strangers walked abreast down the lane, kicking up small dust clouds. They stepped into the shade where they had seen Morgan. Morgan, Angel, and Sam soaked in the creek.

"Come on in here," Morgan said. He was sitting on a submerged log, thigh deep in the cool water, the lingering branches of a willow trailing around him. Angel's freckled breasts bobbed in the water like some lush riparian fruit.

The three strangers sat down beside the creek, but didn't get in. The women pulled their skirts above their knees and hung their legs over the bank so that their feet splashed in the water. The man sat a little away from them and took off his raggedy straw hat and fanned himself. He was young, younger than the women, perhaps Morgan's age, and slender and white-skinned, as if he ate too many vegetables and not enough meat. His shirt was open to the waist and a brass fish hung on a thin chain around his neck. His chest was hairless and white as wax. The faces of the women were lined and creased. Morgan reckoned they were in their thirties, though one seemed older than the other. They looked alike, slightly plump, with the same dull black hair in braids. There were rings of dirt around their necks and wrists, as though they hadn't been able to bathe in a long time.

"My name's Adam and this here is my family, these women," he said, and he gestured with an open palm toward the women, who lowered their eyes in a modest way. "Greta and Gail." He had a slur of an accent.

"Where'd you come from?" Morgan said. He was curious, but not wary. They were used to strangers passing through.

"We been on the road awhile. Started in east Texas. Tennessee before that," Adam said. "We're lookin' for a place to settle down a bit."

Morgan and Sam exchanged glances and Sam shrugged and nodded his head. The milk cow mooed long and loud close to the barbed wire fence on the other side of the creek.

"We got a spot not far over there—across the road—where we allow folks to camp for a few days," Morgan offered. "It's right by the creek and off in the woods you can have a little privacy."

"We'd appreciate it," Adam said.

"I'll take you over there if you like," Sam said.

"That's mighty friendly of you," the older woman said, her voice thick and sweet.

THE HOLY FOLKS set up a tipi before dark, a bright canvas structure like a temple in the juniper woods. That night they had a campfire and the people heard the rhythm of a tambourine and singing, a strange high wail and syllabic chanting in a language they could not decipher.

Angel went to visit them the next morning and took a pint of pickles as a gift. When she came home, Morgan was watering the rhubarb, wearing only cut-offs and sandals.

"How was it?" he said.

"How was what?" Angel said.

"The visitors," Morgan answered. He held his thumb over the end of the hose so the water sprayed and made a fine prism.

"They're okay. They deliver babies, Morgan." She knelt beside the first row of onions and pulled some pigweed.

"Deliver babies?"

"One of 'em's a midwife," Angel said.

"Do they all sleep together?" Morgan said.

"How should I know? They call one another 'brother' and 'sister'."

Morgan absorbed this information in silence.

"Morgan," Angel said, still squatting, "we're going to need a midwife soon."

"Maybe they came here for that reason," Morgan said.

Angel stood up satisfied and went into the house. "Maybe so," she said.

That night Angel baked a rhubarb-strawberry pie and presented it to Morgan. He insisted they whip the last bit of cream. The sun gave way to evening and they ate supper on the narrow deck of the red house. The cool air soothed them. Morgan talked enthusiastically about planting more fruit trees and maybe raising turkeys next year. Angel liked it when he talked about the future.

Nighthawks swooped and rose like rags on the grassy slope before the alfalfa field began. From away high on the canyon wall they heard the coyote cries of children at play. Angel felt the baby flutter inside her. An owl sang from the shadows and Angel held her breath and listened for the holy folks. They were so far away, a

128

quarter mile at least, and she couldn't tell if she heard them or just imagined she heard them.

Morgan went into the house and returned with a sweater for each of them. "Here," he said, "it's chilly already."

Angel just draped the sweater around her shoulders.

"He's a man of the Lord, Morgan," she said.

"Who?"

"Adam. You know," Angel said.

"Oh yeah?"

"He talks about the Lord's will and the Lord's love all the time."

"Talk's cheap, Angel," Morgan said.

Angel seethed inside. "You don't believe in anything, Morgan Riley."

Morgan didn't respond and after a minute Angel went into the house. Morgan followed her and in the loft under the blanket he said, "I do believe in you and me and our land, Angel." He put his arms around her and cradled her head in his hand.

THE HOLY FOLKS stayed into August and became almost a part of the community. Greta and Gail offered to help with the barn repairs. They didn't seek out a winter dwelling, so no one figured they would stay past the first frost, if that long.

One rare rainy day Angel went to make the final arrangements to have Greta, the older of Adam's women, deliver her baby. Her time was near and she needed assurance. She found the holy people inside the tipi with a small fire crackling in the center fire ring. The younger woman, the quiet one, was working yarn around two sticks, weaving a rainbow god's eye. Greta stirred a blackened pot near the edge of the fire while Adam sat, back straight, legs crossed, with fingertips resting on his knees.

"May I come in?" Angel said.

"Come in before you soak to death," Greta said.

Angel settled beside Adam on a rag rug. He placed his white hand on her belly. "You'll be delivering soon," he said. His touch was warm through her thin shirt and Angel was uncomfortable with the touch. He was the only man besides Morgan to touch her like that.

"Yes," Angel said, and he took his hand away. "I need someone to help me."

"I'll help you. I already told you that," Greta said. She had a cocoon-like voice, enveloping Angel, making her feel safe. She was motherly, with soft large breasts free under her dress and a body that looked as though she had given birth herself.

"Morgan says to find out what you want for helping me."

"Not a thing. Just a healthy baby."

"Well, we'll give you something," Angel said.

"Whatever," Greta said, and she began to hum some Bible song, as if to end the discussion.

On the way home Angel looked in the give-away box in the schoolhouse and found a pink dress. She took it home and bleached it in a bucket for three days. Scrubbed and pressed, it was near white with just a wash of color left in the seams like the petals of a rose down close to the stem. She bathed and plaited her hair and wore the dress to the tipi one evening. The holy folks welcomed her as one of their own and together they shared tea and made their plaintive music long into the night. Near ten o'clock, as the moon was setting, they were joined by Georgia, the goatherd. It seemed it was her habit to join them, and Angel felt a tug of loyalty to Morgan, as though she should leave the gathering when Georgia arrived, but she could not bring herself to leave. She felt ecstatic whirling in her cotton dress as the fire danced on her bare legs.

When she went home in the dark, she felt her way along the lane with her bare feet and knew the pleasure of her familiarity with each rock and ridge. The baby was kicking up a storm and Angel suddenly realized Morgan might be lying awake in the loft waiting for her.

She closed the screen door, cushioning its slam with her hand. She pulled the white dress over her head and laid it on the sofa before she climbed the loft ladder to the bed. It was black in the loft, but she knew the way by heart and lifted the blanket on her side and crept under. Morgan rolled over and nested against her back and said, "Let's get to sleep. We got plenty work to do tomorrow, Angel."

Another evening when Angel returned from the tipi she found Morgan under the truck in the day's last light.

"What are you doing under there, Morgan?" she asked. Her voice sounded dreamy, even to herself. She just stood beside the left front wheel, since squatting and rising had become strenuous.

Morgan stuck his head out from under the truck. "Fixin' the

brakes, 'case we have to take you to town," he said. His hands and bearded face were streaked with grease.

"Sure is a nice night tonight," Angel said. She sighed and looked toward the creek, keeping her hands folded on her belly. "I saw the heron that lives back there."

Morgan disappeared under the truck again. Angel heard the gravelly sound of him scooting in the dirt on his back. The sky and the horizon seemed to meld in a blue wash and she thought she saw the silhouette of a deer in the alfalfa field.

"Adam plays a silver flute, Morgan," she said.

"Is that right," Morgan said. His voice was faint, disinterested.

"He says he can heal the sky after rain with his flute."

"You got a package today, Angel," Morgan said. "From your mother."

Angel's eyes opened wide. "Where is it?"

"In the house by the radio. Sam brought it from town."

Angel walked to the house and Morgan worked on the brakes until dark.

IT WAS the end of August and the grass was brown as palominos. The people were beginning to journey into the fir woods to gather firewood. Each day Angel and the other women laid out sliced apricots and peaches and pears to dry in the sun. Against the coming barrenness they stored great glass jars full to the brim with the leathery fruit. Batches of wine were begun in clay crocks and the smell attracted insects to the sweet rot. Tomatoes were bending their mother stems and even melons ripened despite the short growing season. There was a sense of accomplishment among the people. They had worked the land and the land had yielded a good harvest. Weather had been with them.

Angel's water broke at high noon while she gathered small green eggs from her chickens. The wetness spilled down her left leg and she remembered wetting her pants as a child and feeling ashamed.

"Morgan. Morgan," she shouted from the fenced-in chicken yard. Morgan looked up from the black plastic pipe emerging from the showering tank he was repairing. The hens chattered around Angel and she waved like someone arriving home.

"My water broke," she said. Then she shooed the chickens and slipped through the gate and locked it.

131

Morgan met her on the path and put one arm around her shoulders.

"I feel a tightening down there," she said. She held one hand on the underside of her belly.

"Does it hurt?" Morgan said, squinting in the sun.

"No, it doesn't hurt," she said. "I'll take the eggs to the house. You go tell Greta."

"You want me to go to the house with you first?"

"No, I'm okay," Angel said. She lifted the egg basket and then said, "Morgan, I want to have it here. No hospital."

"We will, Angel," Morgan said and he walked down the path toward the country road. He didn't look back. His worn workshirt was the same color as the bachelor buttons bordering the path.

Angel carefully placed the eggs in a cardboard carton and set them in the cooler in the shade of the back porch. The creek curved behind the house, silver from the sun, gurgling incessantly in a comforting way. Rude Steller jays hawked at Angel and she knew a small sadness, an awareness that she would never be the same again, that time was passing, that something irrevocable was about to occur. She went in the house ravenously hungry and ate two banana muffins with butter. Then she sat rocking and rocking next to an open window with the pocket watch on the cedar chest beside her.

"I'm coming, Angel," Greta said, as she slammed the screen door.

"No hurry," Angel said.

Greta unloaded a woven shopping bag on the kitchen counter, then turned to Angel with her hands on her hips. She wore a pale shirtwaist that nearly trailed the floor. Her hair was braided and pinned like a helmet against her head. She was sunburned, the skin at her neck fleshy and wrinkled.

"Are you timing the contractions?" she asked.

"Uh-huh," Angel said. "They're not real regular yet."

"Well, keep timing. They'll most likely get regular as they get closer."

"Where's Morgan?" Angel said. She glanced out the open window.

"Checking something on the truck," Greta said. "Where are the sterile linens?"

"Up there," Angel said, and she nodded toward the high shelf of the pantry, above the canned peaches and cherries and pickles.

Greta reached high and brought down the brown grocery bag which Angel had stapled shut and baked in a slow oven. It contained two white sheets and several towels.

"What about the floss and scissors?" Greta asked.

"Right here on the cedar chest," Angel answered. "We got plenty of time." She smiled at Greta in a shy way, then lowered her eyes and folded and unfolded the hem of her smock. It barely reached her knees and she wore nothing underneath.

"Did you buy the shepherd's purse?" Greta said.

"Yes. It's in the little brown crock."

"I'll make a tea of it just in case we need it. Won't hurt to let it boil and boil. You'll need a strong brew if there's much bleeding." And Greta set to work building a fire in the cookstove.

The two rooms were joined by a step up and a double open doorway and Angel could see Greta as she bustled around the kitchen, crumpling newspaper for firestarter, poking around for kindling. It felt good to have someone there to build a fire, make tea, and keep her company. Angel gathered a bundle of yellow yarn from the floor and began crocheting, the shiny silver hook slipping in and out of the yarn like a cat. She was making a bootie the length of a matchstick.

After a while Morgan came in with an armload of split wood. He stacked the wood, then came and stood between the kitchen and the main room. Angel stopped rocking.

"How are you?" he said. He seemed far away.

"Okay. Twenty minutes apart," she said. "Maybe it's a false alarm."

"Do you think so?"

"No, not really, Morgan. This is it."

"Do you need me yet? I thought since Greta was here I could finish fixing the shower and maybe do some other chores."

"I guess I don't need you yet."

"Okay. Just holler, Greta, if she gets close," Morgan said, and he was gone, out the front door into the sun's glare. Angel watched him until he walked out of sight past the garden's tall corn stalks.

"He'll be back," Greta said from the kitchen. "You got a ways to go yet."

"I know," Angel said, and she commenced rocking again and was comforted by the rocker's squeak.

Greta made a cool hibiscus tea with raw honey and the two women sat suspended in the afternoon, in the shade of the main room, gossiping and sharing a secret now and then, a shard of the past. It might have been any lazy afternoon, two women drinking tea and talking, but for the pocket watch ticking away Angel's innocence. The contractions grew closer and more intense so that when one came Angel's speech was slow and distant and she would still be telling her story but it was as if another person spoke and she, Angel, had gone way inside, concentrating on the force certain as moontide, the force that would wash the child into the world.

When evening came and the nighthawks began their ritual swing across the yard, Angel had reached a plateau and her contractions grew no closer.

"I should fix Morgan's supper," she said.

"Don't you worry 'bout his supper," Greta said. "He'll eat somewhere, no doubt. Or I'll fix him something when he comes home."

"Where is he, I wonder?" Angel said.

"I'm home," Morgan shouted, a grin on his face. "Thought I'd never get through at Sam's. They fed me, then I felt obliged to help with the milking."

Angel met him at the door and hugged him hard.

"I'm glad you're here," she said. In the back of her throat her voice flinched in fear.

"I figured Greta would call if you needed me," he said.

"I would have," Greta said. She dealt herself a hand of solitaire on the kitchen table.

"Why, you haven't even made the bed yet," Morgan said. He had built a plywood platform for a single mattress because he didn't want her climbing the loft ladder.

"We don't do that until it's real close," Angel said. "To keep the sheets sterile." She held his large, stained hand as though it were an anchor in rough sea. The light around them dimmed and Angel danced into her next contraction.

Greta silently picked up the watch and noted the time.

"Does it hurt?" Morgan said.

"Yes. Yes, it hurts," Angel said. "But maybe that means it'll be over soon."

"Let me clean up a bit, Sugar. Then I'll sit with you," he said, and he untangled her hands from his arm.

Morgan went into the kitchen and Angel lit a lamp beside the single bed. She sat on the bed for a moment, but then moved to the rocker. She liked to think of rocking the baby to sleep in her arms. And she would sing.

Greta finished her cards and sat shuffling the deck.

"How long could this go on?" Angel asked.

"First babies generally take their time," Greta said. "We might as well settle in for the night."

The night was a long one. At first Morgan and Angel and Greta tried to play hearts, but Angel could not concentrate and Morgan's presence disturbed the intimacy the two women had earlier established, so the talk was dull and desultory. Morgan grew restless and often went to the porch to watch the stars in the sky. Angel sweated and her hair grew tangled and she was alternately subdued and fretful. Once when Morgan was outside fetching kindling—they had let the fire die out—he heard a sharp cry and he ran to the door, but only looked in and saw Angel was still in the rocker and the bed still unmade, so he returned to his task.

In the dark hour before dawn, Greta made the bed with the sterile sheets and Angel, spent and trying to breathe in the proper way, but often crying out, went into the bed and bathed herself with wheat germ oil to lessen the chance of tearing. Her contractions were two minutes apart. They waited and her screams reverberated around the small house, shaking the salvaged barnboard walls and Morgan's heart.

Roosters fiddled at the skywash and Venus pinned the pink shell above the canyon. It was a cool morning, portending autumn. Morgan had dozed fitfully, unable to stay awake during the last hour. Angel longed for sleep and release from the pain. And still the baby would not be born. Greta had held her hand all night and once said, "You've got the hands of a child." The words stuck in Angel's mind.

When the morning grew light enough to see, Greta stirred from Angel's side and blew out the lamp.

"Greta," Morgan said, "don't you think she needs a doctor?"

"Not yet," Greta answered. "It's just hard work, Morgan."

Angel looked as though she had worked hard, her eyes puffy, her face pale. She lay on the bed with her legs bent and apart, the sheet covering her like a tent. The tent was open at her feet and Greta reached under now and then and measured her dilation.

"Four fingers," Greta announced. "Morgan, she needs you now. You stay by her. I must go out for a moment." And she left the house in a hurry, her skirts switching.

"Morgan, it hurts so bad. I can't believe how much it hurts," Angel said. She spoke quickly, desperately.

Morgan took her hand but didn't answer. When her body clenched, she clenched his hand, but it was limp and his eyes avoided hers.

"I want Greta," Angel said.

"She'll be back."

"Morgan." She screamed his name. "Mor-GAN!" and her body tensed, her back and legs arching in the pain and she could not believe it hurt the way it did. She wished to die.

When Greta returned, she had Adam with her. He walked in as though he belonged there and he was fresh and clean in white pants and a white shirt. He was like a vision to Angel. He went to her side.

"You're having a hard time, Angel?"

"Yes, God, yes, it's awful," Angel said, and she cried.

"When did this labor begin?" Adam asked.

"Yesterday noon," Morgan said.

"We've got to help her have this baby. She's wearing herself down," Adam said.

"Listen, Adam, I want to take her to the hospital," Morgan said. His hands shook like aspen leaves.

"No. NO," Angel screamed.

"We can do it here," Adam said.

Then Morgan saw the other man's eyes lock with Angel's and his heart spoiled within, ripe with bitterness.

"Adam, I'm afraid," Angel said. She groped for his hand.

"There's nothing to be afraid of," Adam said. "Be strong."

"I said I'm taking her to town," Morgan blurted. He spread his feet in a defensive stance.

"She needs a coach, someone to help her through. It won't take long," Adam said. "I can do it."

Morgan felt as though he were invisible.

"Yes. Yes," Angel said, breathless and panting and up on her elbows. "Adam, stay with me."

Then she cried in longing, a cry so raw with want and need that Morgan turned away.

"Son-of-a-bitch," he whispered, beating his fist into his palm.

His face was flushed and contorted in anger. He slammed the door and rode the morning like a man in a foreign country, a man with no home, working to obliterate the sound of Angel screaming.

And even as she held the waxy child, so new, with sky and clouds in each pale eye, Angel could hear the dull thud of Morgan splitting sugar pine as he had split her.

nominated by Andre Dubus and
Joyce Carol Oates

MR. GOLDBAUM

fiction by GORDON LISH

from RARITAN: A QUARTERLY REVIEW

Picture Florida.

Picture Miami Beach, Florida.

Picture a shitty little apartment in a big crappy building where my mother, who is a person who is old, is going to have to go ahead and start getting used to not being in the company of her husband anymore, not to mention not anymore being in that of anybody else who is her own flesh and blood the instant I and my sister can devise good enough alibis to hurry up and get the fuck out of here and go fly back up to the lives that we have been prosecuting up in New York, this of course being before we were obliged to drop everything and get down here yesterday in time to ride along with the old woman in the limo which had been set up for her to take her to my dad's funeral.

It took her.

It took us and her.

Meaning me and my sister with her.

Then it took us right back here to where we have been sitting ever since we came back to sit ourselves down and wait for neighbors to come call—I am checking my watch—about nine billion minutes ago.

Picture nine minutes in this room.

Or just smell it, smell the room.

Picture the smell of where they lived when it was both of them that lived, and then go ahead and picture her smelling to see if she can still smell him in it anymore.

I am going to give you the picture of how they walked—always together, never one without the other, her always the one in front, him always shuffling along behind her with his hands up on her shoulders, him always with his hands reaching out to my mother like that, with his hands up on her shoulders like that, her looking like she was walking him the way you would look if you were walking an imbecile, as if there was something wrong with the man, wrong with the way the man was—but there was nothing wrong with the way my father was—he just liked to walk like that when he went walking with my mother and he never went walking without my mother.

I mean, that's what they did, that's how they did it when I saw them—that's what I saw when I saw my parents get old and when I came down to Florida and had to see my old parents walk.

Try picturing more minutes.

I think I must have told you that we made it on time.

Only it wasn't anything like what I had been picturing when I sat myself down on the airplane and started keeping myself busy picturing the kind of funeral I was going to be seeing when I went to the funeral my father was going to have.

Picture this.
It was just a rabbi that they went ahead and hired.

To my mind, he was too young-looking and too good-looking. I kept thinking he probably had me beat in both departments. I kept thinking how much he was getting paid for this and would it come to more or would it come to less than my ticket down and ticket back.

I felt bigger than I had ever felt.

I didn't know where the ashes were. I didn't know how the burning was done. There were some things which I knew I did not know.

But I know that I still felt bigger than I had ever felt.

139

As for him, he took a position on one side of the room, he stood himself up on one side of the room, and me and my sister and my mother, we all went over to where we could tell we were supposed to go over on the other side of the room, some of the time sitting and some of the time standing, but I cannot tell you how it was that we ever knew which one to do.

I heard: "Father of life, father of death."
I heard the rabbi say: "Father of life, father of death."

I heard the guy who was driving the limo say, "Get your mother's feet."

Picture us back in the limo again. Picture us stopping off at a delicatessen. Picture me and my mother sitting and waiting while my sister gets out and goes in to make sure they are going to send over exactly what we ordered.

Maybe it would help you to picture things if I told you that what my mother has on her head is a wig of plastic hair that fits down over almost all of her ears.
It smells in here.
I can smell the smell of them in here.
And of every single one of the sandwiches that just came over from the delicatessen.

Now picture it like this—the stuff came hours ago and so far that is all that has. I mean, the question is this—where are all the neighbors which this death was ordered for?

I just suddenly realized that you might be interested in finding out what we finally decided on.
The answer is four corned beef on rye, four turkey on rye, three Jarlsberg and lettuce on whole wheat, and two low-salt tuna salad on bagel.
Now double it—because we're figuring strictly half-sandwiches.

Here is some more local color.
The quiz programs are going off and the soap operas are coming

140

on and my sister just got up and went to go lie down on my mother's bed and I can tell you that I would go and do the same thing if I was absolutely positive that it wouldn't be against my religion to do it—because who knows what it could be against for you to go lie on your father's bed—it could be some kind of a curse on you that for the rest of your life it would keep coming after you, until, ha ha, just like him, you're dead.

My mother says to me, "So tell me, sonny, you think we got reason to be nervous about the coffee?"

My mother says to me, "So what do you think, sonny, you think I should go make some more extra coffee?"

My mother says to me, "I want you to be honest with me, sweetheart, you think we are taking too big a chance the coffee might not be more than plenty?"

My mother says to me, "So what is your opinion, darling, is it your opinion that we could probably get away with it if I don't put on another pot?"

Nobody could have pictured that.

Or have listened to no one calling and imploring us to hold everything, keep the coffee hot, they're right this minute racing up elevators and down stairways and along corridors and will be any second knocking at the door because there is a new widow in the building and an old man just plotzed.

You know what?
I don't think that you are going to have to picture anything.

Except for maybe Mr. Goldbaum.

Here is Mr. Goldbaum.
Mr. Goldbaum is the man who sticks his head in at the door which we left open for the company which was on the way over.
Here is Mr. Goldbaum talking.
"You got an assortment or is it all fish?"

141

That was Mr. Goldbaum.

My mother says, "That was Mr. Goldbaum."

My mother says, "The Mr. Goldbaum from the building."

Now you can picture a whole different thing, a whole different place.

This time it's the Sunday afterwards.

So picture this time this—my sister and me the Sunday afterwards. Picture the two different cars we rented to get out from the city to Long Island to the cemetery. Picture the cars parked on different sides of the administration building which we are supposed to meet at to meet up with the rabbi who has been hired to say a service over the box which I am carrying of ashes.

Picture someone carrying ashes.

Not because I am the son but because the box is made out of something too heavy.

Here's a picture you've had practice with.
Me and my sister waiting.
Picture my sister and me standing around where the offices are of the people who run the cemetery, which is a cemetery way out on Long Island in February.

I just suddenly had another thought which I just realized. What if your father was the kind of father who was dying and he called you to him and you were his son and he said for you to lie down on the bed with him so that he could hold you and you could hold him and you could both be like that hugging each other to say goodbye before you had to actually go leave each other and you did it, you did it, you got down on the bed with your father and you got up close to your father and you got your arms around your father and your father was hugging you and you were hugging your father and there was one of you who could not stop it, who could not help it, but who just got a hard-on?
Or both did?

Picture that.

Not that I or my father ever hugged like that.

Here comes the next rabbi.

This rabbi is not such a young-looking rabbi, not such a good-looking rabbi, is a rabbi who just looks like a rabbi who is cold from just coming in from outside with the weather.

The rabbi says to my sister, "You are the daughter of the departed?"

The rabbi says to me, "You are the son of the departed?"

The rabbi says to the box, "Those are the mortal remains of the individual who is the deceased party?"

Maybe I should get you to picture the cemetery.

Because it's the one where we all of us are getting buried in—wherever we die, even if in Florida.

I mean, our plot's here.

My family's is.

The rabbi says to us, "As we make our way to the gravesite, I trust that you will want to offer me a word or two about your father so that I might incorporate whatever ideas and thoughts you have into the service your mother called up and ordered?"

Okay, picture him and me and my sister all going back outside in February and I am the only one who cannot get his gloves back on because of the box, because of the canister—because of the motherfucking urn—which is too heavy for me to handle without me holding onto it every single instant with both of my hands.

The hole.

The hole I am going to have to help you with.

The hole they dug up for us is not what I would ever be able to picture in my mind if somebody came up to me and said to me for me to do my best to picture the hole they make for a grave.

I mean, the hole was more like the hole which you would dig for somebody if the job they had for you to do was to cover up a big covered dish.

Like for a casserole.

And that's not the half of it.

Because what makes it the half of it is the two cinder blocks which I see are already down in it when I go to put the urn down in the hole.

And as for the other half?
That's the two workmen who come over from somewhere I wasn't ready for anybody to come from and who put down two more cinder blocks on top of what I just put in the hole.

You know what I mean when I say cinder blocks?
I mean those blocks of gray cement or of gray concrete that they call cinder blocks.

Four of those.
Whereas I had always thought that what they did was fill things back in with what they took out.
Unless they took cinder blocks out.

You can go ahead and relax now.
It is not necessary for you to lend yourself to any further effort to create particularities that I myself was not competent to render.
Except it would be a tremendous help for me if you would do your best to listen for the different sets of bumps the different sets of tires make when we all three of us pass over the little speed bump that makes sure cars go slow before coming into and going out of the cemetery.
Three cars, six sets of tires—that's six bumps, I count six bumps and a total of twenty-six half-sandwiches—six sounds of hard cold rubber in February.

Or hear this—the rabbi's hands as he rubs the wheel to warm the wheel where he has come to have the habit of keeping his grip in place when he puts his hands on the wheel to steer.
But who hears him think this?
"Jesus shit."

144

That's it. I'm finished. Except to inform you of the fact that I got back to the city not via the Queens Midtown Tunnel but via the Queensboro Bridge (since with the bridge you beat the toll), that and the fact that I went right ahead and sat myself down and started trying to picture some of the things which I just asked you to picture for me, that and the fact that I had to fill in for myself where the holes were sometimes too big for anybody to get a good enough picture of them, the point being to get something written, get anything written, and then get paid for it, this to cover the cost of Delta down and Delta back, Avis at their Sunday rate, plus extra for liability and collision.

One last thing—which is that no one told me.

So that I just took it for granted that where it was supposed to go was down in between them.

nominated by Amy Hempel

SOME SNAPSHOTS FROM THE SOVIET UNION

by WILLIAM H. GASS

from THE KENYON REVIEW

THE DISMAL DANES had lost our bags . . . cartons of books . . . gifts to our hosts. A darling blond "girl scout" in an SAS coat had assured us we might leave any unessential burdens at the airport while we rested overnight in our Copenhagen hotel. "It will be sent on," she said. "Why carry it back and forth to your rooms?" Because it will be lost, I did not answer. So we entrusted a dozen boxes of books to some airport storeroom. Muriel Murphy and William Gaddis threw in a couple of suitcases they would therefore not see for a while. British Air had already delayed Harrison Salisbury's London luggage, so he missed the opportunity to have it mislaid in Stockholm. Since our unnecessaries were a constant visual comfort, even when not in use, neither my wife Mary nor I would let go of a single handle. The books, however, were only books, and would not mind the cold of collective storage. Let them seek the safety of the Swedes. The consequence of this fallacious reasoning was that many of us arrived in Moscow without either literature or fashion. When he learned of his luck, Gaddis looked at the heaven he did not believe was there. It was a gesture which would be called for often.

Meanwhile, Gaddis and Gass had their picture taken at the airport giggling under a sign that said: "Spies."

Upon landing in Moscow we pushed our way past the intense young men who scrutinized our passports. They were not to be hurried, nor did the hollered greetings which our hosts passed through the gate more readily swing them wide. Allen Ginsberg's face was many times reread and his picture compared. But compared to what? Was his examiner acquainted with the rabbinical look? In the room beyond, there was literally a throng. They really do wear those fur coats and hats, I thought. It multiplies any group by two. My official gave me a nasty, noncommittal glance and slid my passport back. Shortly Yevtushenko was embracing Allen, I was being introduced to my translator (each of whom, not to further weaken our feeble Western grip on things, had been given names like Svetlana and Misha and Nellie); someone was asking someone else whether they had been in the Soviet Union before; still another voice was saying, "I have read your Mr. JR, Mister Gaddis," while tracers were being fired back over an entire snow-covered country.

Apparently the Russians could not believe the Danes had bungled things. It was equally impossible that the Swedes . . . Therefore our bags had arrived and had only to be reunited with their owners. So they counted and recounted everything. Carts were loaded up, unloaded down, and then heaped high again. We went one by one into a little office to point at silhouettes of luggage like charts of ships or enemy aircraft. We were asked to describe our effects. Frequently, words failed. We greeted our hosts several more times as if we had just descended from the plane. I was learning what it meant "to mill around." Have you been to the Soviet Union before? Only on overflights, I answered, drawing a thin straight line across my interrogator's face. A message had been received from Stockholm, I was told, which said my books were safe and would be sent on, just as the untrustworthily trim young troop leader had alleged. Why mine? Chance never favored me with so much as a sly wink. Nor would I willingly get in the ring with adversity. Yet Norman Cousins (who specialized in such struggles, and smiled with such insistent serenity at Difficulty it dropped its D to acknowledge possibilities it had but a moment before forebade) would never see his gifts again. Fate, of course, is perverse, for mine were paltry old paperbacks of prose—storage and stack worn—about whose actual whereabouts I was finally indifferent; whereas Allen's, for instance, were his *Collected Poems*, thick as a brick, dolled up in fresh jackets and still smelling of ink.

Mary took my picture standing beside a fire extinguisher case

147

whose design she admired. The fire extinguisher in the case was called Gloria. To me, the case looked more like one made to show what was customarily in such cases rather than one which actually contained the objects there so educationally displayed. That is, it looked as if it were meant to be looked at, not used. We did not dispute this until later. Indeed, it did not look that way to me, either, until later. Thought, at that time, was the furthest thing from my mind. What mattered at the moment was the Russianness of the walls, the clock, the baggage carts, the signs, the recognizable but indecipherable speech, the case, the carts—even when they weren't particularly anything but Tech. They were in Russia and we were in Russia, too, and that was simply unbelievable; it was simply amazing; it was. . . . We had not come to see the Soviet Union. We had not come to see communism in inaction. We had not come to be critical or picky. We had come to the Russia of our dreams, with their sound tracks of romantic, sometimes barbarous music; to the Russia of subtle intrigue, of grandeur, of cruelty, of astonishment, apathy, and loss; to the Russia, in short, of our reading, a Russia which the regime had perhaps reduced to ash, but which was still aflame in the memories we had of *Anna Karenina* or *The Brothers Karamazov*, those novels Henry James called "loose and baggy monsters"; or perhaps it was the quiet tales of Chekhov or Turgenev we remembered; in any case, it was that Russia we were bound by literary love and loyalty to come to, and not to the Soviet Union, even though our more recent reading might have been in *The First Circle* or *The Yawning Heights*.

Nor was it possible for either Mary or me to set aside our memories of a comparable trip we had taken to the People's Republic of China the previous year. None of the ordinary objects in the baggage room of the Beijing Airport was particularly Chinese, nor was the long inexplicable wait for our luggage anything but international, yet we were waiting *in* China, and the smiling faces beyond the distant barriers *were* Chinese—that was the miracle.

Meanwhile, above us all, floated the furry hats of Harrison Salisbury and Arthur Miller. Clearly, they had been to Russia before, and would not be asked if or whether. Jerome Lawrence was wearing a spiffy red vest, and Gaddis went about in a camel hair coat no writer should have been able to afford. Yevtushenko looked unsovietly slim in a topcoat and red scarf, with his familiar flat cloth cap on his head—one of a kind my father wore to drive his '32 Dodge.

I halt a moment to mention that these are not merely fashion notes, because the overcoat in a Russian winter becomes what is most familiar about a person, and I can now no more disengage my memories of Adele Auchincloss's bulky blue quilted coat, or her light blue knitted tam, from her indoor self than I would ask her to take them off in the wind of Red Square. Allen Ginsberg wore a hooded white jacket—when he wasn't on the phone—that might have been surplus from the Finnish War. Norvel Young's coat was of an almost priestly black—very impressive against a bank of snow—and Mary's long red scarf often served the same function for us as a tour guide's little plastic flag. I wore a nondescript gray Burberry, which dated from before the Conquest, and went about bareheaded, as Inge Morath often did, her cameras slung like bandoliers about her, since, of course, we camera carriers had more fortitude and gumption than the others. Anyway, Inge was all intelligence, energy, and resource, and I fell in love with her at once.

By now, each of us had gone twice to the tyanetbl. In Mary's uneasily tilted photo of the fire-fighting equipment, I am wearing rumpledumples and holding a few cellophaned stems of flower. They, the case, and the contents of the case, all glint.

I consider scratching the final sentence of the previous paragraph in order, like Shakespeare, to conclude my scene with a couplet, but the strap of my camera case is cutting uncomfortably into my neck, and in the picture I have passed beyond such refinements into a sullen stomachache.

The ideal fire hydrant, I would argue back home at our dinner table, shifting the example slightly like a golf ball from a bad lie, should epiphanize the fire hydrant, so that one glance would be enough to stabilize within the soul the essence of the object. The ordinary fire hydrant would be helpless before such a task. Open its valve and only water, not realization, would pour out; whereas the ideal fire hydrant would not properly be subject to touch, let alone the rape of the wrench or the disgusting disgorge of the hose. Our scruffy American hotel hoses, looking like the badly coiled guts of an elephant, cried out to be fooled with, unrolled, poked into smoke. The glinty equipment in the airport case, so anally in place, said, "mustn't touch," especially Gloria. Before she became

149

an architect, Mary regarded my Platonism with amused tolerance, as you might someone who persisted in ordering crême caramel in a White Castle. Now her work went on in a crowd of worldly requirements, elbow to elbow with expediency, efficiency, economy, and other riffraff. Anyway, it was for this aspect of the word, "before," that the phrase, "once upon a time," was invented.

Muriel Murphy was met at the airport by a young friend who was in Moscow to help set up Ted Turner's TV Olympics. She had been waiting a spell—not unusual—and now, as she waited while we waited, she told us how she and another American woman had gone to an "animal fair" in Moscow where all sorts of creatures, both common and strange, could be sold or bought; there her friend had purchased a kitten to keep her company. Out of care for the cold, she had carried the kitten to the car beneath her coat, but once inside the car the cat had suddenly slipped down a sleeve and disappeared into the terra incognita behind the glove compartment and the dash. Indeed, it so successfully vanished into the front and center of things that, although the Volkswagen's engine was in the rear, they nevertheless hesitated to put the car in gear for fear of clipping off pieces of its precious felinity. They had to take the dash apart, fishing in among the wires for a responsive nip or scratch or hoping for a traceable meow. Finally, after much dismantlement, the kitten was recaptured and recontained in her friend's fur.

Cat stories, like cats, wonderfully pass the time.

So once more into the tyanetbl, dear friends.

The Russians give it up. We carry away whatever we've got hold of to the bus. Dusk follows close upon the dawn this time of year, and darkness is beginning to float up from the snow like shadows cast upon the sky. We won't see much of Moscow until morning.

II

Not even then. Our arrival is to be prolonged. We are driven to Moscow's domestic airport past miles of Hong Kong high rises, or Cairo, or Beijing, or Titograd high rises, past Anywhere City, past seemingly endless piles of flats, by clumps of towers made of frozen gray gruel, ugly without interest, ugly without relief, unindividuatedly ugly (floor upon floor like the syllables of my adverb), creating without further assistance a meanspirited and tightfisted squalor, with not a single touch of Sicilian carelessness or the Mediterranean's gift for contamination, but past organized and sternly disposed and brutal New Towns such as those of postwar England and Germany, where mass destruction by building not by bombing has occurred, with results uglier even than the Pruit-Igoes we blew up in Saint Louis, along with their systems of central humidity. In Cairo, it is dust; in Beijing, it is coal smoke; whereas, in Moscow, a cold wind runs between their stilty feet. Only bureaucrats could have built these: these temples to expediency, efficiency, and economy. I hope it is where they have to live. The badly mixed and poorly poured concrete will soon shale, and the pebbly surface that is then exposed will grime so effectively no soot will reach the street, and every wall will seem covered with gloomy Belgradean stucco, as though each building along the avenues was a drawn shade. The Chinese architect we spoke to in Shanghai explained patiently: the people have to have a place to live. Indeed—I did not say—a place. One might have been on Bochum's dour university campus, in Leeds, or caught in Chicago Circle in an eddy of people, trash, and weeds, a hardness underfoot like the hardness of life, as if we needed reminding.

There was ice on the airfield in Vilnius, so we began our day by waiting. I walked about outside. Across the street was a barracks-like assemblage of buildings. There were large notice boards with the photographs of exemplary people stuck upon them—some sort, I supposed, of reward. I risked taking shots of innocuous objects: an Aeroflot plane put out to memorial pasture; then a fence, grill, and gate, grouped together like three mourners at a grave; one which failed to capture the way the gray tarmac ran off into the gray sky; and a metallic outdoor urn for cigarette ashes which came out, when developed, with an uneasy tilt to it. Could we get nothing level in this country? Flakes of snow would materialize, then melt in the milk, and the wind, too, would nip at you suddenly. Was it absolutely necessary to walk about without a hat? So I—we—read our guidebooks once again. Perhaps a visit to the tyanetbl? We purchased small sandwiches from large grim women who gave them up reluctantly. At any moment, we were told. Soon. Shortly. No thanks, I don't chew gum. Or suck savers. And what do you teach at the University? Have you been to the States, then? Ah, that often?

The airport was apparently divided into an area for all-points

Russian, another for all-points Republican, because one end of the long set of adjoining buildings was active and crowded—there you might see heads in kerchiefs or many members of the military—while our end was almost empty except for ourselves: no business for the Baltic, little for the Ukraine. We caucused in the tiny snack bar, where the sandwiches were relinquished, to consider a telegram to be composed, signed, and sent to the Summit, supporting Peace and the noble efforts of Our Leaders. I have little patience with such presumptions. And I sincerely wished, for our noble leaders, only severe cases of William Tell's revenge. I took another walk "around the block." We met again, later, to let our hosts know whether we were interested in visiting Leningrad, for we now learned we were scheduled for Minsk, and unless we changed our tickets and lengthened our stay, Leningrad was out of the question. This was dismaying news. Seeing Leningrad was, for most of us, the main aim of our journey. Yet what aim, when the entire target was about to be removed? Mr. Sagatelyan appeared to be in charge. He was a journalist (an expert in foreign relations, his fact sheet said), but looked as pink and polished as a banker, with a genial, chubby, trustworthy face and a puddle of baldness like a tonsure. Almost any minute now, he said; it won't be long. In Vilnius, as the day wore on, the ice wore out. From the kiss of the sky, I opined. No luck. I offered to compose an obscene limerick in support of the Summit. My offer was silently declined even though I promised to employ the phrase, "star whores." Our translators were a young lot; I felt they might have smiled, even though the Americans were serious about patting Our Leaders' Behinds; but our translators had been sent on to Vilnius ahead of us to smooth our way and ice the field. Have a piece of candy. Smoke? There were Professors from Moscow University and other institutions in our company. They, too, had never been to Vilnius, where the airfield was now only damp and mildly skiddy. Could we manage the extra days, we asked ourselves and one another. Why had the Soviets waited until now to extend our stay, we grumped. Except for Allen Ginsberg, who was eager to go to Minsk, and whose free time was evidently greater than ours (he had been angling for an extension of his visit from the moment he got off our Stockholm plane), we all leaned to Leningrad. But members of the Minsk Writers' Union were waiting with set alarms and other preparations. Most of us decided it would be foolish to fly so far, lose our luggage, wait so patiently, attend to the titular and ceremonial talk we would have to listen to during the next few days, and not see Leningrad—the Venice of the frozen north, the hallowed hermitage of the Impressionists.

Four pink-cheeked young women waiting in the snow held out red carnations to us when we eventually deplaned in Vilnius. They were in costumes of violet and lilac, beaded and beribboned, with violet vests over their embroidered white blouses, in pleated skirts of the same material and colors as their vests, and wearing bellhop hats from whose rear a lively clutch of ribbons dangled like—of course—a pony's tail. I was not used to this. When I arrived anywhere by plane, I usually received the handshake of a graduate student who would try to take my briefcase away from me and then forget where he had parked the car.

Norman Cousins was surrounded by the press. Harrison Salisbury was surrounded by the press. Microphones and cameras beseeched us for a word, a smile. An edible ear of pink spun sugar passed so near it might have felt my breath. My sigh was as long as the ribbons. Arthur Miller was surrounded by the press. Bill Gaddis was surrounded by his camel hair coat. At last we really had arrived.

III

During the three weeks I was in the Soviet Union three different Americans told me the following joke, although they each altered details in order to individualize it. In the unlikely event a Russian had related it, I doubt he would have taken the trouble. According to the common kernel of the story, a Russian is showing an American visitor the Moscow Metro, of which the city is quite justifiably proud. "Look at the spacious main corridors," he says, "experience the swiftness of the escalators, note the many differences in decoration when you change stations, the art glass inserts in the columns, the mosaics in the small domes which vary and enliven the concourse ceilings, the cleanliness of every floor and stairway, the quality of workmanship and materials, the statues of Lenin and other notables which enrich the way—for nothing is too fine for the workers." "Everything you have mentioned is indeed excellent," the American says, after inspecting his surroundings and being duly impressed, "but we've been standing here for twenty minutes and there's been no train." "So—well—," the Russian replies heatedly, "and what about your extermination of the Red Indians?"

The joke (which can refer as easily to blacks, migrant workers, or massacres in Vietnam) slanders the subway, for during rush hour trains arrive and depart as frequently as three a minute. By comparison, descending into the New York subway is like being swallowed by a worm. There, art glass would last less than half an hour by a fast watch. And most Russians would take that fact to be a significant sign of the superiority of their culture. Nor do I think they are entirely wrong. Nevertheless, the story, which is not all that funny in itself, is such an appropriate one I soon understood why I heard it so often, and it sums up the exchanges which took place between Soviet and American writers in Vilnius about as accurately as any brief resume could.

Led by Norman Cousins, these meetings have been going on since 1976, so some of the participants—like Nikolai Federenko, the Secretary of the Writers' Union who led the Soviet delegation, Harrison Salisbury, who worked for many years as a journalist in the Soviet Union, David Kugultinov, a poet from Kalmykia, and the playwright Jerome Lawrence, as well as Norvel Young, the emeritus chancellor of Pepperdine University which hosted the Russian group last year and was one of the United States organizers of this one—were veterans of these peculiar ceremonial tournaments. Others of us, at least William Gaddis, Louis Auchincloss, Charles Fuller, Sylvie Drake, and myself, were neophytes and amateurs, while Arthur Miller and Allen Ginsberg, as I think of them, were old hands at everything.

The decision (whoever made it) to hold the seventh meeting between the writers of the two nations in Vilnius was somewhat a surprise, for Lithuania is not a place citizens of other Republics in the Soviet Union can visit very readily, and quite a few members of the Soviet delegation (those who flew from Moscow with us, for example) were as much tourists in the territory as we were. The Lithuanian language is very ancient. Its alphabet is like ours, its roots resemble Sanskrit, and the people who speak it are passionately alive to their tongue and proud of their rich graphic and musical heritage. The various Republics of the Soviet Union are by no means moving in accord with some preestablished harmony, and the Baltic States, I was told, were among the most edgy. They have had a strongly anti-Soviet, even pro-German, history. Walking about, I felt I received more than just a whiff of Austria.

Vilnius, furthermore, had been the center of one of the culturally richer Jewish communities in Europe. The former ghetto is now no more than a wide place in the street, with perhaps a few blocks of old houses being restored as shops, museums, and tourist offices. Memories are not so easily repainted. The Catholic Church is still strong, although most places of worship inside the Soviet Union have been turned to secular uses (wedding halls, mostly, but in at least one case, an Atheist Museum), and the training of priests has been carefully curtailed. Many of the houses near our hotel were still privately owned, and everything one experienced reinforced the feeling that here were a people fiercely determined to retain their individuality, their language, their culture. It was clear from the outset, and not merely from the costumed airport greeting, that the Lithuanians intended to be warmly generous hosts, and they certainly succeeded, although not a few of us felt after a while as stuffed with good things as a Christmas goose.

Our late arrival wiped out most of the activities scheduled for the first day (8.13 Meeting of the guests. 9.30 Breakfast. 13.30 Dinner. 14.30 Departure from Hotel Draugysté. 15.00 Opening ceremony at the Art Workers' Palace). Alas, we were nevertheless in time to attend a speech by the newly elected chairman for the region which took place at the Presidium of the Lithuanian SSR Supreme Soviet. I was informed that this was his inaugural address to the officials of the Party, so if we were included, as I correctly guessed, he could bore two birds with one drone. The talk consisted mainly of the recital of those strange facts called "figures," or in baseball lingo, "stats." The State's stats, I understood, were good, and getting better. I would learn that such recitations were a Soviet habit, as we would be told later how many pupils were studying English, how many cows were eating grass, how many tractors were encouraging the earth, how many clouds had a silver lining, how many villages had been demolished by the Nazis, how many watts of power poured out of this or that Electrograd on an average day, how many books there were in libraries, or, indeed, how many American books were in print in Lithuania alone [Th. Dreiser (20 books; 917 thousand copies), E.

Hemingway (16; 428), J. London (14; 206,6), Mark Twain (13; 281,5). It was said that children especially doted on W. Disney (9; 730) and J. F. Cooper (10; 285)].

It was a very ceremonial occasion, but not too ceremonial for Fanta, bottles of which sat like tall toy soldiers in groups containing mineral waters at appropriately handy intervals along the table—a little orange to wet a drying ear, I supposed, as the speechmaking went on like a chinook. Vodka is no longer served at State functions, so that the circumstances of civility, one realizes, are reduced. But what a reduction. Arabs, Egyptians, Eastern Europeans, American children, Mormons, even Chinese, drink pop with lunch. For a snob, a nose of the nubby sort I have is an embarrassment, and I should have liked to borrow Louis Auchincloss's perfectly proportioned beak in order to look down its fine aristocratic length upon the Finns' crudely colored fizz. The ban was to be bemoaned, too, because vodka, in its original Russian version, is delicious, and should neither be drunk ice cold nor socked back—the advice of barbarians. Sipped from numerous small bottles, it is, I found, quite moderate in its effects. Furthermore, it made us friendly. How can one feel at one's ease standing in the middle of a ballroom with a paper cup of Pepsi in one hand and a jellied cracker in the other? Vodka is not made from potatoes, as is alleged, but has been distilled from centuries of old toasts. It is thus the perfect vehicle for such salutes, taking the place of sincerity with a success no one wants to query. Try "I raise a glass of goop to all our healths." And what to do about despair, mankind's most epidemic epidemic? No. The new arrangements distinctly would not do. However, private bottles would appear at banquets from time to time, ministering to our needs like teams of Red Cross. And the wiser of us laid away a few fifths within the bits of baggage that hadn't been stolen by the Swedes.

In the morning, in the minutes between breakfast and meeting, Mary and I escaped routine to walk up the road which passed in front of the hotel. Immediately our spirits lightened. We were, at last, in Lithuania, not in a bus or building which happened to be sitting in Lithuania. It was a neighborhood of modest frame houses surrounded by small yards. In that sense the sight was familiar. But most windows had shutters, the outside stairs were covered, and the roofs were of corrugated metal. The pitch was steep. There was a lot of fretwork. And most of the houses were painted green from the same can. It had been, we surmised, a harsh green once, but age had powdered and faded the paint until now it resembled verdigris—whole buildings seemed built of bronze. It was a green so beautiful it tinted the breath it took away. I boldly stepped into a back yard to take a picture of a pump. A horn hooted a few blocks back. It was the bus.

Our conference began propitiously, everybody said, since it coincided with the Summit, although the mound we made was more like a hummock. Our visit to the Union of Soviet Socialist Republics also concluded on a symbolic note, because, as the last remnants of the United States party left Moscow for the West, we witnessed Yelena Bonner, released at last (although on a tether), having her baggage checked through customs and thoroughly but politely searched. My photograph of the event, blurry in the bad light, made every movement appear frantic, when, in fact, it was patient waiting which was everybody's ardent occupation. Omens are, like horoscopes, only trivially amusing, and they lent no real weight to our endeavors; however, Norman Cousins reminded us that these meetings of American and Soviet writers constituted the only cultural exchange presently taking place between our two countries.

The subject of the conference was "The Writer and Preservation of Universal Human Values," a subject vague enough as to seem no subject at all, but as noble sounding as a Wagnerian trumpet. To the Soviets it mostly meant: "How can the writers of the two countries promote the cause of peace?" whereas, to the Americans, who tended to take the shared problem of peace for granted, it meant: "How can we further the cause of freedom for all people, especially writers?" In an impressive palace where Napoleon had overnighted his horse, if not himself, we gathered around a long U-shaped assemblage of tables, trying to alternate nationalities the way, at home, we often feel obliged to separate husbands and wives. Norman Cousins and Secretary Federenko sat at the head (or, as I prefer to think, the bottom of the U), while at the open end a young woman was stationed, like a ball girl at a tennis match, to move microphones rapidly around. Translators crouched in windowed hutches at the edge of the room where rows of chairs along the wall were also arranged and silently occupied by Lithuanian authors of all kinds except youthful or female—there to audit. Nikolai Federenko, in the chair, emphasized the fact that the

Soviet writers, although some had official station, were in every case speaking for themselves, and all of them did, indeed, use their own voices. It was suggested that we begin by talking about our own work, moving clockwise around the table, a procedure designed, I thought, to produce a maximum of flatulent vanity and eat up our hours without seriously touching on the topic (for two days we went from tick to tock in this fashion). I later learned that Norman Cousins had suggested this strategy some years before in order to encourage the Soviets to depart from the set speeches they were customarily delivering, and that, at first, it had seemed to work. Now, however, they had mastered the format and were comfortable with it. I was familiar with their tactics. At the Serbian Writers' Conference in Belgrade which I had attended only a month earlier, two Russian poets had arrived, dutifully denounced Star Wars, and retired to their rooms to stay drunk for the week, as the Yugoslavs maliciously reported. Mostly I remembered how stony-faced they were, as if they had fallen from a church.

Anyway, the arrangement was one in which even Oscar Wilde would have been boring, and we did not, on the whole, disappoint one another. Although each Soviet writer spoke in favor of peace as if no one else had, or was likely to, the Americans did try, quite delicately I thought, to poke small holes in the vacuity.

Harrison Salisbury began, for instance, by mentioning that he had grown up in the region of the United States where many Jews from Lithuania and Byelorussia had fled to avoid persecution, and he went on to discuss his new book on the Chinese Communists' Long March, comparing one of its aims (to celebrate human struggle and heroism) with his history of the siege of Leningrad, *The 900 Days*. Our hosts were perhaps no more pleased to remember the plight of the Jews than they were to hear about the courage of the Chinese, or to be reminded of the history of their own epic battle through a book banned by them now since 1969 because, while it spoke well of the people, did not sufficiently flatter Stalin and the Party.

Between us, almost every point but ecology and peace was a sore one. Louis Auchincloss's brief but elegant description of the problematic center of his new novel involved the critical distinction between legal rights and moral obligations, a distinction which the Soviet spokesmen would consistently refuse to recognize. How was it possible, his novel wonders, for reasonably responsible and decent people to have supported and prosecuted our war in Vietnam? Was a negative Puritanism still alive in this age of unbelief? Had we lost our faith in virtue and salvation, but none of our grim certainties about sin and damnation? My own wonderment was what the Communist authors made of these observations, for didn't a similar situation exist in both of our countries, where the realization of our national aspirations, by now, was surely despaired of, although their failure was still feared? Weren't continued discipline and obedience the last reflexive spasms of such great dreams as both of us had dreamed? In every Utopia, as it turns out, nightmare is the very stuff of real life.

The Soviets had had their innings, too, of course, but had mostly been content, it seemed to me, to pop up. They were not about to start something. However, there were moments when they showed the edge of the reactionary knife they would later unsheath. Eduardas Meželaitis, for instance, a Lithuanian poet with a philosophical bent, argued that today poetry was too preoccupied with itself. Poetry needs to be more concerned with man and less with cosmetics. It would benefit both if poetry sided with man and came to man's defense. Decoded, he was saying that poetry ought to pay less attention to form in order to promote Marxist humanism. It was clear that "man" was Eduardas Meželaitis's favorite word. His best known poem is entitled *Man*, and he received the Lenin Prize for it. One stanza (as translated by Tom Botting and quoted in *Baltic Literature* by Aleksis Rubulis) goes like this:

So I stand—
Majestic, wise and steadfast,
Broad of shoulder and potent.
The bright sun I've encompassed, so great is my stature.
I project on our planet
The smiles of sunlight
Both eastwards and westwards,
To north and to south.
So I stand—
For I am Man,
A Communist.

Due to obligations which would take him away from the table, Chinghiz Aitmatov, a Kirghizian writer many of the Americans knew about and admired, asked to speak out of turn, as Agathon had in Plato's *Symposium* when Aristophanes was overcome by hiccups. Since many of his own stories are based on popular tales and legends, I imagine no one was surprised when he praised Latin American literature for showing how local myths and folklore could be raised to the level of international consciousness. Such a consciousness can be realized only in society, and individualism cannot contribute to this process. Moreover, he said (expressing a concern which his compatriots seemed to share), each of our works must contain an antidote for the plague of consumerism which is everywhere threatening to destroy the spiritual quality of life. Since "individualism" is always regarded by the Soviets as essentially selfish, disruptive, and antisocial, there was no surprise in these remarks either.

William Gaddis spoke warmly of his personal indebtedness to nineteenth-century Russian literature. This honestly positive note was struck several times, especially by Sylvie Drake and Jerry Lawrence, and might have been ground enough to build on, but if we read each others' worlds so differently, how differently do we read each others' works? The Russians not only revere Walt Whitman, but Jack London as well. The cult we have made of Chekhov has bewildered more than one Russian critic. Perhaps Theodore Dreiser's illiteracies are smoothed out in translation so that all you read about are social problems and the ruination of the worker. Perhaps all of Dostoyevski's infelicities similarly disappear to leave only rant and melodrama. What is romantic to us, may be realism to the Russians. These confusions are not confined to our two countries. We need only recall Poe's fad in France, or that of Erskine Caldwell. As for myself, I am quite weary of the worldwide interest in Mark Twain. When Gaddis expressed his enthusiasm for Gogol, did our hosts believe he was doing so simply because Gogol said some unpleasant things about the Russian soul?

And how would one go about explaining that it was difficult to celebrate the great Russian novelists in our country just now, not because of some widespread prejudice against communism, but because such praise was often offered for reactionary literary reasons?

Gaddis tactfully suggested that since bureaucratic corruption can go anywhere and arrive with its luggage in any era, he and the earlier Russian writers had the same target, and that he was attempting to save his version of an acceptable country as they were endeavoring to redeem theirs. Mr. Gaddis's good news was that there was much more stupidity than malice in the world, but the bad news was that stupidity was such a hard habit to break.

Allen Ginsberg began his remarks by reading a moving poem by one of the Vilnius group of Yiddish poets whose voices were largely stilled when the ghetto there was destroyed. (I discovered later that this particular poet had fortunately escaped to Israel.) He went on to outline the aims of the Beat poets with whom he has been so closely associated, but in such a way there could be no doubt of the immediate relevance of his remarks. What is the difference between public pronouncement and private speech, he asked, and if private speech is eloquent and public speech is constricted, what is the remedy? It isn't necessary to be right all the time—infallibility is a tyrant's tune—what is necessary is that we be open and frank and honest with one another. Candor, gentleness, and vulnerability can lead to an unprejudiced use of the intelligence. It was in the service of these ideas (the conviction that private life was more interesting than public life, for instance) that he wrote *Howl* and *Kaddish*, subjective and personal poems which later became objective for others. Public talk tends to be shaped for the ear of its listeners, and cut to make the speaker's figure fashionable. In this way, it becomes false talk and failed communication. Homosexuality was sometimes on his mind, and so he unashamedly spoke of it. The shame would have been not to. But it was generally of ideals associated most closely with Whitman—those of frankness, liberality, and freedom for all people, not simply people who were gay, that he supported.

What the Soviets said tended to be translated for us in unqualified phrases, shattered pieces of telegraphese, especially when speakers spoke rapidly, and I suppose our statements received the same treatment; thus it was either out of willfulness or because the translation was faulty that the "other side," as they had increasingly become, decided that Allen Ginsberg had claimed the individual was more important than society. This interpretation was embraced with such satisfied self-righteousness that I was provoked to reply that the individual was certainly more important than *this* society. My childish blurt was tactfully not translated, if it was heard, and I repeat it here only to report my state of mind, which was one of increasing irritation. David Kugultinov, a poet from

Kalmykia, with a Rabelaisian presence, roundly averred (as we would have said in an earlier, more accurate, age) that he loved women, women only, and that in the republic which he represented there was not a single homosexual to be found. I think he felt congratulations were in order, yet I could not be certain whether he was mainly being smug or jocular.

In a country and in a time of year when the only things black were the silhouettes of coats and hats against the snow, Charles Fuller walked through the streets of the Soviet Union in a perhaps sacred but uncomfortable circle of stares, and I think he may have longed for a little of that despised invisibility associated with Ralph Ellison whom he began his brief presentation by quoting. All People ought to have the right to define themselves in their culture and in their nation. From the beginning he hoped his own playwriting would help put an end to the denigration of blacks in American literature. During the sixties, anger and resentment became confrontational, and the work of that period tended to produce new stereotypes, presenting blacks as violent, reactionary people unable to reason or pursue anything abstract or intellectual. Now he believed that black writing could best help the people it most immediately represented by no longer insisting so fanatically on speaking only for them, but instead by moving confidently into the mainstream of American society and its literature. Blacks don't have to stay inside the confines of a color. They can speak—as well as anyone—for anybody.

If the Soviet authors still held to their views of a few years ago (and who knew what they really thought?), then Charles Fuller's standpoint (as strong, accurate, and enlightened as I felt it was) would be another sad example of what they call "abstract humanism." For them, it designates work which avoids a particular Soviet reality in favor of less committed generalizations. Man, in Eduardas Meželaitis's poem, is, after all, a Communist.

If Ambassador Federenko, a title he retained from the days of his appointment as Ambassador to Japan, was the first apparatchik on my bird list, Mikhail Sagatelyan, the journalist who had flown to Vilnius with us, was surely the second "chicken of the apparatus," as I rendered the Russian. If, in sour defense of my sanity, I thought of Ambassador Federenko as a rather uncomically menacing W. C. Fields, I called Mikhail Sagatelyan "moonface" in my mind, not simply because his face was quite round, but because you never knew what phase he might be in. He was often full—beaming and benevolent—at other times harvest red, or largely dark. As he spoke, really warming to his topic, his voice taking courage from its own rising tone, and as I sorted out his sentences into some point of view, I realized that here was someone who was really speaking at least part of his mind, and that mind was distressingly familiar: "moonface" was a member of the Moral Majority.

When Clark Gable uttered his "I don't give a damn" in *Gone with the Wind*, Mr. Sagatelyan said, there was an outcry from concerned citizens in the United States. But what has happened since? Nothing but sex and violence of the most depraved kind everywhere. All the barriers are down. American literature has lost its power of influence; it has lost its moral grandeur. And like a source of infection, this libertinage has been spreading rapidly all over the world.

During the days that followed, in those hollow hours of waiting in lobbies or on buses, I asked myself exactly where my differences with Mr. Sagatelyan lay, since I believe I could have offered reasons for my distaste of America's popular culture which he would have found agreeable. Religion is not the only opiate of the masses, and in the United States popcult is as political as the Party. Like the Party, it treats the people to a parade of false gods, not all of them embalmed like Lenin or merely of the living dead like Elvis Presley; like the Party, it encourages, through sports, the illusions of strength, skill, and success; like the Party, it fosters a false tranquillity, and avoids the truly disagreeable; like the Party, every immediate value is expedient and may change on the morrow; like the Party, for those who are willing to purr, it puts down saucers of sweetened feeling you have to go to your knees to lap up. Unlike the Party, it achieves its aims by appearing to be freely chosen—merely offering itself like a whore in a doorway; unlike the Party, it has no single line, but, aside from the general promotion of consumerism, is content to distract what is left of the mind; unlike the Party, it can be opposed without grievous punishments, attacked and avoided.

What Mr. Sagatelyan was unwilling to say straight out was how ready he was to sacrifice his own freedom of expression in order to prevent others from having theirs. The freedoms of others are no doubt disagreeable things; they do such damnably stupid things

163

with them (hell *is* other people, as Sartre's play says), but they must be suffered, if one is to continue, justly, to enjoy one's own.

What Mr. Sagatelyan was unwilling to admit is that kitsch is kitsch whatever camp it comes from. As Stanislaw Baranczak wrote in the November 26, 1984, issue of the *New Republic*: " . . . certain TV commercials (those of the 'no-more-ring-around-the-collar' or 'you'll-never-go-back-to-thick' variety), while basically unknown as a genre in the Communist bloc, have too much in common with the general mindlessness and bad taste of what is a surrogate for mass culture there."

I think it is fair to say that Americans characteristically come to such conferences prepared to be critical of their own country. It is, of course, a tradition with us, a part of our way of being, and never implies an absence of loyalty or commitment, but we customarily receive for our flagellations a few more licks from the other guys. From them, however, no similar self-criticism is ever forthcoming. By the time our visit was over, many of us were quite fed up with the absolute absence of other people's problems.

Allen Ginsberg, who tried to distinguish between kinds of pornography, and point out the criminal sources of some of the worst of it, was immediately chastised by Ambassador Federenko, in a tone suitable for addressing small boys, as a "well-known sidetracker." We were being led away from the purely literary subject of our meeting. This moment was for me, as they say of games, a turning point in our discussions, for the real and profound differences between us were emerging in ways it would prove increasingly difficult to cover over or patch up, although efforts to restore amity were certainly made.

What the Soviets looked upon as "purely literary," we were inclined to regard as "purely political." Certainly, the avowed subject of our conference was entirely political in intent. If their sidetracks were our mainlines, our mainlines were their stone walls, as the Soviet response to Arthur Miller's painfully pertinent remarks made plain. What Miller said, in sum, was: we have writers who write pornography (an activity which we deplore), and you have writers you have put in prison (an activity you refuse to acknowledge).

The United States, he said, had been spared the hierarchies and subordinations of feudalism. It is a country where everybody, in principle, has a chance to make money, not just a few, though it may turn out that only a few succeed. Pornography, in his view, was the exploitation of sex for commercial purposes, and it was something of which he disapproved, but censorship was not a satisfactory solution. At this point he brought up the allegations by Pen International concerning writers punished and jailed in the Soviet Union for their work.

You have said America was saved from feudalism, Chairman Federenko responded. What about the slave trade?

The bulk of the body of American law was and is antifeudalistic, Arthur Miller replied.

What about the American Indians?

Chairman Federenko acknowledged that the issue of punished writers had also been raised at a recent writers' conference in Budapest, but no one there could name anything these so-called writers had written. They had read nothing by them. They could not even pronounce the names of these people they passed off as writers. These names were wholly unknown to literature, and they had left no mark on the literary scene. Some people violate laws in the United States. We (the Soviets) don't give these people the status of writers and then accuse you of lying about them. We should put in a good word for our fellow writers, but this is not a literary topic. This is outside any literary area.

How unamusing the subway joke seemed now in front of its actual rival. We all knew, of course, that to be recognized as a writer in the Soviet Union you had to be a member of the Writers' Union. These imprisoned people were not members of the Writers' Union, hence not writers. Nor could you continue to publish unless you were a member of the Writers' Union, so it became difficult to make any mark on anything but the wall of your cell. The matter seemed to them to be entirely internal, and we were merely meddling. They did not recognize, let alone honor, the distinction between legal and moral obligations which Louis Auchincloss had introduced earlier. Furthermore, both sides knew who some of these unknown writers were, and some of the Americans, at least, had read them. One writer, also a physicist, is a woman, Irina Ratushinskaya, who, on March 5, 1983, was sentenced to seven years' hard labor, to be followed by five years of internal exile, for writing and circulating poems with the purpose, the court said, "of subverting or weakening the Soviet regime." The fall, 1985, issue of *Formations* magazine contains two of her poems (adapted by Frances Padorr Brent and translated by Carol Avins). One is dated December 1983, and is about the snow which whitely covers the tracks of our lives. But we must, she says, continue to go on, even if we go on only "like an epilogue."

> But leaving the stamp
> of stubborn footprints
> to rise on frozen steps—
> just to the executioner's block.
> But the severe cold
> of a clean shirt
> falls like comfort
> on weak shoulders.

To compare these lines with those I quoted earlier is unfair, yet unavoidable. We have to ask ourselves who the true poet is, and how the true poet fares. And we must learn how to pronounce her name: Irina Ratushinskaya.

One of the barriers to American and Soviet friendship, Arthur Miller said, is our belief that it is possible to be arrested in the Soviet Union for writing, speaking, and protesting. This is not merely an American perception. Why not repair this problem which is like an unhealed wound?

But listen to your friends, the Soviet writers, Chairman Federenko said. This Pen list is not a clean source. Of the people in question, one is a chemist, another is a physicist. It is not for literary reasons they are in jail. It is often for drugs, or for subversion.

Allen Ginsberg said he knew of many similar cases in the United States, where protesters, unpopular agitators, interesting writers who spoke of little-known social injustices, were hassled or arrested on drug accusations. He hoped that the Soviet Union was not imitating the West in arresting people on drug pretexts.

It was then agreed to suspend public discussion of this issue, but to continue it in private if we desired.

IV

Away from the table and its perilous U-turn, we were in nearly another world. When our hosts invited us to a Lithuanian play which was presently being performed at the Young People's Theater in Vilnius, I must confess, although I realized the obligation to attend, the words, "Young People's Theater," and "Lithuanian play," disheartened me. We were told that what we were to see was an epic adaptation of Chinghiz Aitmatov's novel, *The Day That Lasted One Hundred Years*, and the word "epic" disheartened me still further. It was an interesting title, but one which lent itself rather easily to a bad review. However, Mary and I have a rule which we have carried over from our WASP upbringing: try everything. Or else. Would you like to go to the ballet? yes; the circus? yes; the museum? sure; a play? absolutely; a concert? you bet. So, disheartened though we were, we went. The theater was crowded and expectant. Aitmatov would be in the audience. He had seen this dramatization of his novel in Moscow, but not in Vilnius, and not by this company—a company whose character was beginning to be transmitted to us almost by osmosis. At the meetings, Aitmatov, who is a large, large-headed, man, had mostly practiced looking glum. He looked glum now. If he is glum, why should I be happy, I thought. I don't remember seeing other members of the Soviet delegation, although our translators and some journalists were there. We had a row of seats to ourselves as befitted foreign dignitaries or folks with a disease. I rather enjoy being treated like a VIP, although I can never believe I am one. The play would be translated through earphones for us into Russian and English. Fortunately, this was not a theater of speech. A pinched, remote voice uttered inarticulate sounds, and the earpieces were uncomfortable. I took them off. Would people think I had simply tuned out and gone for a snooze? Probably.

The play begins. We are far away, at a whistle stop; it might have been somewhere in our West. It is no doubt Kirghizia. There is a track running across the rear of the stage, a man with a lamp. There have been trains. The man with the lamp walks heavily about. His footfalls echo. The echoes are elements. A cough. Intrusive. Also an element. Light fall. An action. The train, when it passes this place, will shake things up. The shaking is a situation. The development is slow, deliberate, ritualized. Drama is being kicked into another dimension. Quite a few of my colleagues felt the first act dragged, but I was mesmerized almost immediately. I was ashamed of myself at the same time. Where was my critical distance, my objectivity? However, this was theater the way I believed writing ought to be written. It was baroque Beckett.

Props, in this play, did not live up to their name. Instead, they became the play itself. The setting was precisely not that: a place the action went in and out of, like patients at a doctor's office. It was more like a nest a bird might build, and part of being a bird. The qualities of any performance of this kind are hard to pin down, difficult to characterize. The actors did not act. They moved past realism into mime. They would turn somersaults or shinny up a pole. So there was something of the acrobat here, of the circus as well. Still, if I say that the actors did wondrous things with a rope and a rug which they made believe was a camel more successfully than the animal or the cigarette ever could, what would it mean? One might as well stand in front of a painting and scream.

During intermission, and afterward, we repaired to a small room where there was coffee and cake and eventually members of the cast to be devoured too; then an intense young man with a satanic hairline, dressed as if entirely in black leather though he was not, appeared with an entourage, and this young man, I was told, was the director. With his arms folded protectively across his chest (a black sweater, not leather, I believe), he seemed exceedingly ill at ease. The smile he smiled he smiled in passing, as if it were not his but unpleasantly encountered like a hair in one's food. I asked one of the translators to point to his name on the program. Her finger went, unfortunately, in quite a wrong direction, even to the wrong page, for she did not know Lithuanian either, and it was the Lithuanian version I held out to her.

Cingizas AITMATOVAS

ILGA KAIP ŠIMTMEČIAI DIENA

2-ju daliu spektaklis
Inscenizacijos autorius—G. KANOVIČIUS
Režisierius—LTSR valstybines premijes laureatas
Eimuntas NEKROŠIUS
Scenografas—Adomas JACOVSKIS
Kompozitorius—Faustas LATENAS

Had I read it carefully, and with some confidence in myself, I should have figured the matter out: *realization*—Eimuntas Nekrošius. Furthermore, Nekrošius felt like the right name for this play. And a laureate. But what did "režisierius" really mean? Anyway, I got it wrong in my piece on the conference for the *New York Times*.

In the second act a man is sewn into an animal skin which is then shrunk. Its grip on his head makes an idiot of the man before it kills him. The scene is played by a man confined in a wicker basket, as if inside his own skeleton. Both the torture and its consequences are thus suggested, acted, mimed, symbolized, danced. Even uttered. And the effect is dazzling. In the grip of custom, in the hands of repeated tyranny, the playwright seems to say, time is shrunk in the same way as the body, and we begin to grasp the meaning of Aitmatov's title. So compressed, a period of a hundred years takes place in the space of a single day, at the same time preserving the classical Unities. Generations of tyrants with their tortures all wear Joe Stalin's coat.

The cast met Arthur Miller, Charles Fuller, and Jerome Lawrence, each of whom praised the play, particularly its second half. I think Arthur told them he thought the opening was a trifle slow. It may have been then that they hatched their little plot.

V

The final hours of the conference were occupied by long statements from our chairs-in-chief. The translation we were given of Nikolai Federenko's almost endless concluding oration didn't make much sense. He was clearly still troubled by allegations of various kinds that had been made at other conferences—in Budapest, in Sofia. He seemed upset to me. His hands trembled. Maybe they always did and I hadn't noticed. He appeared to skip a few pages of his prepared text. Like any disciplined doctrinaire's, his talk was so larded with authoritative quotes they became the meat. It was not merely the Fundamentalist preacher's technique, it was fully medieval. He called the roll of American writers. Norman Mailer, William Styron, and Joseph Heller were invoked. The past decade, he said, showed some significant sliding away from the proper ideals of the writer. A lot of Western literature has been invaded by violence, sex, and apocalyptic thought, and everywhere there is a conflict between the literature of despair and that of hope. E. L. Doctorow was quoted. Romain Rolland. Numerous OK Russians. Henri Barbusse. I waited for a statement from John Gardner, but for some reason it was not forthcoming.

I was not in the mood to look upon the Secretary, our Chairman, the Ambassador, as a good guy. I began to feel he was eating up our time deliberately, covering our differences with coded platitudes.

It is the sacred duty of the writer to warn people against moral corruption, the Secretary was saying. Sure, I thought, I am ready to do just that, if you will shut up and allow me the opportunity, and I knew that William Gaddis, at the end of the table, was chewing his nose in a state of transcendental disgust; but we were to be effectively silenced by the long winds.

So each of the regular participants, both American and Soviet, would have come to Vilnius to speak for ten minutes about the most harmless things.

The Secretary finished finally. Then the Ukrainian poet, Ivan Drach, as if he were feeding a fish to a seal, asked the Chairman why he hadn't spoken of himself as others had, and urged him, unnecessarily, to do so.

He did so.

A representative of the Lithuanian writers, the group who had sat silently along the wall for three days, was invited to speak. This seemed reasonable and courteous, but this gentleman not only seized his opportunity, he slew it, and carried its corpse around the room. The tactics of the Soviets were proving to be quite successful.

The final moments of the conference were chaotic. The press was suddenly allowed in a half hour before it had been ruled they would be. At precisely that moment, whether by accident or design I don't know, the Americans raised the problem of the imprisoned writers once more. The Soviets reacted very strongly to what they believed (not without reason) was a breach of promise. Nor did they want this discussion to go on in front of the press, even if the press could not report it. Chairman Federenko said that of course we could continue our talks beyond their scheduled time, but our Lithuanian hosts had prepared an entertainment for us, and there were many costumed young people waiting outside. He said again that he resented the way the Americans were attempting to meddle in the internal affairs of the Soviets. Norman Cousins replied that writers all over the world had a common bond, and that if something like jailing writers were to happen in the United States, he felt that we would welcome the Soviet writers' comradely concern.

I was struck then, and I am struck again now, by the differences between this conference and the ones I attended in China and Yugoslavia in recent years, as well as the meeting between Chinese

170

and American writers which was held in Malibu this May (1986). In Belgrade, the Yugoslavs made a brave and vigorous appeal for an end to all censorship, and I had spoken there about the kinds of censorship we had to endure in the United States—market pressures and neglect, mostly. Exchanges were lively and relatively free. At our first meetings with the Chinese in Beijing, there had been some ceremonial stiffness, to be sure, but the general warmth was evident; there was a real willingness to exchange ideas on both sides, and the Chinese spoke quite openly (and I thought with great and genuine understanding, even forgiveness) of the experiences they had undergone in prison or in exile during the Cultural Revolution. The American delegation was not so naive as to suppose that the People's Republic had become a capitalist country (nor did any of us wish this catastrophe to overtake them), but one would have had to be stonier than their ancient statues not to have sensed the enthusiasm and excitement of the people. The Chinese writers who came to Malibu in May, as we returned their hospitality, were, on the whole, younger than those whom we had met in Beijing—full of wit, curiosity, and energy—in every way the opposite of the frozen figures who had sat (as we had sat frozen too) around the U-2 table (as I was calling it) to pass platters of platitudes from place to place—platters we inspected with that dim regard and tepid interest one has for picnic food on plastic plates.

It was agreed to conclude and listen to the entertainment. Chairman Federenko closed the conference, then, by saying that the Soviets would be ready to continue such conversations in the future, provided further meetings met the highest needs of the nation and of peace. These struck me as two rather large provisos.

In a moment there was folk dancing and folk singing and folk: young ladies and gentlemen whirled us around and issued other orders to our bodies. The grand room finally contained the artificial gaiety that suited it, and my ire ebbed as I practiced obedience and tried to keep up.

VI

There was to be a reception for us in the evening, but the Young People's Theater had requested our presence for another performance. We regretted our previous commitment, but there it was: to

171

be is to be received. They suggested we come only for the first act. We could then return to the reception in good time. This, in effect, put Fat in Skinny's coat, but our natural interest, and our desire to do the right thing—to please all parties—prevailed, while our official hosts were reluctant though agreeable. So a number of us bused off to see the first act of a play called *Pirosmani* . . . *Pirosmani* . . ., also directed by E. Nekrošius, and performed by his company. Its action concerned the last day in the life of Pirosmani, a fabulous folk painter from Georgia (who, like Ambrose Bierce, did not die so much as disappear). The day was therefore an invention, and consisted of a set of short monologues encircled and crisscrossed by gestural mimes, actions, and acrobatics, whose every movement was slowed and intensely considered; and by tableaux and icons, pictographs which were so visually immediate, original, and emotionally charged they came alive, enlarging the list of actors, in order, literally, to become the play. It was as if a style of painting had been performed, and it was a remarkable achievement. When the promised cultural exchange between our two countries begins, I should be ready to give up several suburbs of Saint Louis for another Glimpse of the art of Eimuntas Nekrošius and his gifted troupe.

The curtain did not come down. If last night's play was called an epic, what was this? The company continued the first act into the second so smoothly that for a time I did not realize what was happening. The invitational phrase, "after the first act," was to mean, "after the play." The cast was determined that we should see *Pirosmani* . . . *Pirosmani* . . . not just *Pirosmani* . . . and so we did; we drank it in; we ate it up; and all of us were lavish in our praise. I wonder what the Lithuanian audience thought when the first act ran past its stop. I also wonder whether this remarkable ensemble will remain in Lithuania, unseen even by the rest of the Soviet Union. Were they punished or applauded for their ruse, because it certainly set back the reception a bit, and miffed the bosses. I was triply pleased: by the play, by the resolution of the players, by the miff of our masters. It is moments such as these that warrant a million meetings.

Mary and I went to the reception tired but in good spirits, and teased the Russians by telling them how good the Lithuanians were, and how sly. A captive audience is not the best kind, one remarked. It is if it has Arthur Miller in it, I said with a mean grin.

VII

Muriel and Bill were without clothes. Still. The rest of us suggested suitable substitutes: bearskins, vodka, virtue. In Saint Louis I had packed some shirts directly from the laundry, and now I offered a blue one to Gaddis, whose gratitude was tempered by the fact that, though I am certainly thicker through the torso than he, the shirt fit him like a corset. It turned out that it was not my shirt but someone else's—a callow youth's perhaps—which I had received by mistake. Now fate had put it upon an unfortunate writer's back in Vilnius, Lithuania. When I went to the laundry to wonder where *my* blue shirt had got to, the fussy ladies who worked there wanted to know where *their* blue shirt was, inasmuch as its owner desperately desired knowledge of its location. I was able to tell them that their shirt had gone to Paris and was not likely to return. The existence of *my* blue shirt was denied.

We had been seeing the sights of Vilnius—museums, churches, lovely old streets, painted shutters, pigeons, vines, memorials, squares—when one of our translators announced that we were going to visit a school. Arthur Miller said he'd seen children before, and had been to school once himself. The school was expecting him, he was told. It won't hurt you, Mr. Miller. Mr. Miller wasn't sure of that. Already clouds were beginning to occlude the mind. The best propaganda was the people in the streets, but propagandists never understand that.

More kids in costume. I hoped I'd not have to dance. Lots of beautiful, shy, beaming, curious faces. We straggled from room to room: here is history, see the map of America; here is music; here is math. We went into each class, looked at the walls, smiled at the children, asked inane questions, got detailed answers, peeked at our watches, hung back. Mr. Miller especially hung back. Inga and Adele were, as usual, all energy and interest. They were the two I always tried to emulate, looking where they looked, moving as they moved, but this time I was not up to it (a condition about which Allen has written some good poems). Now we were in the English classroom. There was Jack London. There was a map of the United States. There was Mark Twain. Mark Twain has a lot to answer for. The students were curious, shy, beautiful, beamish, and in the seventh grade. I wish my girls were going to a school like this, I thought. The propaganda was working. Upon the teacher's desk was an anthology of American poetry. Allen Ginsberg naturally wanted to know: was he in it? and began to leaf through. Yes. There he was. And he stood behind the teacher's desk and suddenly began to recite in a voice that reached booming by the third line.

> Bare skin is my wrinkled sack
> When hot Apollo humps my back . . .

Allen's delivery will not faze these children, for the Russians read with loud emotion and much gestural activity. They have to hold huge halls of people spellbound the way Allen used to manage crowds. The children watch with wide eyes and try to follow. The poem is about a derelict who lives under a bridge.

> I sup my soup from old tin cans
> And take my sweets from little hands . . .

Allen huffs the lines out and the teacher turns a little toward the wall, small fist held against her cheek. The theme of the poem is beginning to sink in like water through sand.

> Who'll come lie down in the dark with me

Allen concludes,

> Belly to belly and knee to knee
> Who'll look into my hooded eye
> Who'll lie down under my darkened thigh?

Then we flow from the room as though a cork's been popped, and Arthur Miller has a grin on his face that goes clear around his head like a scarf. Well done, I don't say. Allen would provide us with other glorious moments.

VIII

We board the bus for the collective farm. I have the same aversion for collective farms as Arthur Miller has for schoolhouses,

174

although I have never seen a collective farm. The Soviets must still be living in the thirities, we think. They are still in the persuasion business. Police cars form up ahead and behind us. They don't want us to come to harm, we say. In Malibu we couldn't get a bus to come for the group when they were supposed to. Here— presto!—an entourage. Presto! a collective farm. We stop at a place called Panèvežys and pull up in front of what is probably the city hall, although it looks like a school. Yes. Girls in the costumes of the country, with tambourines and ribbons flying. They dance on the front walk and the steps of the building. Just the place. We stand on the steps and watch them whirl, smiles on our faces to welcome our welcome. At the moment it is not snowing, but the sky is gray as gruel. Our leader, Norvel Young (for Norman wisely saves himself from these occasions), receives a large brown ceremonial loaf of bread. Still on the steps, on the steps still, we are given pieces of bread and sticks of hard salty cheese— both delicious. I chew cheese and vainly focus my camera—wholly in no hurry—I hope I'll not have to dance.

A long room with long windows along one side, in the center long tables dotted with bowls of fruit, and candies and small gifts at innumerable places. The local apples are excellent. Unlike some of the popular varieties in America, they taste as if they had actually come from trees. The manager of the farm, I take it, or the mayor of the town (I am never clear about these things), addresses us. It is a Soviet habit. Taken to see something, you are bused to a building, ceremoniously escorted inside, and then lectured. What you witness you witness through bus or school windows. But I realize now that I am not here to observe a collective farm, but to hear about one. The Soviets would make fine baseball fans; they have the requisite passion for statistics. Some of us think of questions to ask. Louis always has something civil to say. It comes of being civil. I am not civil. I am silent. Gaddis is silent as well. I feel we live on the same wavelength like clothes on a stretch of wash. I am waiting for the sun to come out. My film is in color and too slow for winter. I am wondering why the Soviets still want to persuade us of their success, show things off in this fashion. Are they that insecure? Would insecurity account for the defensiveness of their writers, their arrogance? Yet the Americans were arrogant and touchy too. Did I want to screw those bulbs into the same sockets? Inge, who has a camera for every occasion, is a vegetarian and is constantly pelted with fruit. She relishes her apple. Why

175

not, she has a film speed for every winter light, for every mist, and early nightfall. The sun dies like a spring fly. Inge relishes her second apple. No. Numbers are not for me. I have lost count. The mayor / manager makes another point. Everyone feels quite benevolent, but the forms our feelings are required to fill falsify them, force them into lies. The mayor / manager makes another point. All rise.

Another factor contributes to the general uneasiness of our hosts. The Soviet side of them wishes to say, see: Communism Works. We have improved the lot of the Lithuanians. Prior to our coming, their condition was X, now it is X plus Y. The Lithuanians, on the other hand (and sometimes the hands are the same), want to remind us that they exist; that they are a people with their own history, their own language, their own culture.

While in Vilnius, we were all repeatedly photographed, repeatedly interviewed. But one question (I remember now) was put to me twice. Did I think of the Soviet Union as a Western or an Asian country? Surrounded by the streets and people of Vilnius, I had thoughtlessly replied: European, of course. The second time, more alert, I had answered with my own question: European civilization goes precisely as far as the Greeks got. Here, how far did the Greeks get?

At the farm we see a bunch of bison but not one cow. There are plowed fields on either side of the road. Wow. What modernization! Soon we encounter some brightly colored storage silos. I want them. I must have them. They are magnificent. And shortly out of sight. Near the silos is an airstrip on which an old Dakota sits parked. An old Dakota? Might we look at that? Around the edge of a small lake a number of small houses are arranged. We shall descend from the bus to inspect the interior of one of them. All the furniture is new and neat and nailed in place. The latest in oilcloth, plastic, formica, other resins. No more lived in than a coffin. Of course, after the hordes have gone, a newspaper may be flung on the floor, a bit of cup spilled into a saucer, a new rug replaced by a worn one, and then the humans may cautiously return to their former haunt. Sniffing for Air Wick. There are fascinating outbuildings, tools hanging on exterior walls, barrels and basins. We are to visit another school, but now I am determined to take a few pictures, and I want those basins, that pitchfork, here and there a rusty unknown. So I set off down the road with my camera, walking into a back yard to look at a lean-to. There is activity on the highway behind me. The police cars are in motion, and at first I think they are simply repositioning themselves for our return. They are parked in driveways, one ahead of me, one behind me. I try to concentrate on my pictures. The light is lousy. But I have to explain the placement of the police cars to myself, nevertheless, which is annoying: the road is now open for the bus, and the police cars will simply fall in, fore and aft, as it passes. Unbeknownst to me, unbeknownst to my shutter, my film has grown so brittle in this cold, some click ago it snapped, and I am aiming myself at nothing: black on black. As I move down the road, though, the police cars move too, parking themselves a house ahead, a house behind. What to do about that? Nothing. I walk on. We repeat the figures of our dance. I am, of course, happy, intent, oblivious to their behavior, grossly innocent. Except that I am acutely self-conscious, and exaggerate every movement so I feel in slow motion. The bus bleats, calling me home. I dawdle back, free to the last. How am I free? I stop to pet a dog.

IX

We board the bus for a journey to Kaunas. There is more snow on this road, and our escort is aggressive. Apparently we have a tight timetable today, because soon we are astraddle the centerline, blue police lights whirling, shoving the cars and trucks going our way to one side, tossing oncoming traffic onto berms and snowy shoulders, zipping through intersections, losing no time. As the Americans become aware of what is happening, they grow exuberant, even gay. It is hard to look elsewhere than at the broad swath of our blade. It's wheeee-city. Only the President might get away with this in America, one of us observes. We multiply inanities. It's the parting of the Red Sea, I'm afraid I say. Will there be anyone foolish enough not to give way? But it's like playing chicken with a wolf. Jerry Lawrence sways back and forth in the center of the bus, trying to take a picture of our hoggishness. Jerry must be as trusting as he is kind, for he will throw open his shutter for any object and expect an image to materialize. What speck of light would want to disappoint him?

Our arrogant charge down the highway is an appalling display of privilege, and we love it. We revel in our power, in a VIPness we

177

would otherwise never possess or dare, in this fashion, to express, but which we can now show without shame, because none of it's our doing, none of it's our blame. Such roadway overlordship is as rare in the United States as reason is in the Senate. After all, how do the so-called lower classes in our country realize the democracy of the motorcar if not by climbing onto their slutcycles, into their vandalvans, into their pimpmobiles, and painting rubber on the road.

We pass a beautiful pale blue church—pale blue with paler trim—and I regret, aloud, that we cannot stop, at least to go— click! if not to go—look! We are on timetable, I am told, but perhaps when we return along the same road it can be arranged. And when we return, it is arranged. The bus stops and some of us descend into the dusk. Our morning mist, it seems, will stay the night. Gaddis will have a cigarette. Behind us the police have halted traffic in both directions. I fail to feel like Caesar. We dutifully put our cameras to our eyes, make click, and, embarrassed, hurry back to our howdah. Adele and I had cried out "oh!" simultaneously, thinking blue an odd color for a church. At that time neither of us had seen the Cathedral of the Resurrection at Smolny Institute. Deep blue and white. Like a plate.

Looking at the slide, I see two structures. The one in front looks like a steeple tower that's been taken from its perch and set upon the ground. This tower is connected by a narrow wooden passage to the main building, which is squarish, and surmounted by a small classical rotunda and an onion-shaped dome. So, like the horseman, it seems to be offering its head to the highway. But I shall always remember this church because, just to take its picture, we caused a small pause in the proceedings of the world.

This day, we are to learn, is to be devoted to the memory of Boche brutality. There would be a number of such days. Like our visits to the school or to the collective farm, there was a propaganda point to be made. The point was: you Americans do not know how we suffered. And everywhere we went we certainly encountered scars of the war: memories of the war, memorials to the war, museums for the war, acts said to have been required by the war, beliefs said to have been grounded in the experiences of the war, dates measured from the war, fears, hopes, energies as well, pride, hate, resentment—feelings carried over from that terrible time, now refocused, reformulated, refelt.

I think Americans suffer one special advantage when they travel abroad in representational groups like this: they are taken for dummies. Oh boy, were we taken for dummies. We had things explained like Helsinki is in Finland. Like Leningrad used to be called Petrograd, and before that Saint Petersburg. Like the Hitler-Stalin Pact bought time. As if we hadn't read at least Harrison Salisbury's books. As if he weren't a member of the delegation. But what would they know of the contents of these volumes, since Harrison's books are banned in the Soviet Union? So we knew a few things we weren't supposed to know: of the unsavory history of Lithuanian loyalties, for example. Our hosts certainly thought we could be led to overlook one massacre by pushing our noses into another. Anyway, we knew how they had suffered—at least, somewhat. What we did not know was how they still felt about that suffering. It remains a patriotic necessity with them to feel angry, outraged, heroic, and unappreciated.

Although the Great Patriotic War was the worst of times, it was (unlike Stalin's Purge of the Party) the best of times as well, because the people heroically threw back the enemy and defeated the Fascists. During the Purges the bureaucracy fed upon itself, not simply chewing its own nose for spite, but gnawing at genitals and fingers, playing both Prometheus and vulture, so that today's torturer would be tomorrow's victim. During the Great Patriotic War, however, success followed sacrifice, and the Party demonstrated its strength and utility to the rest of the world.

Perhaps because I am a dummy, what sank in finally—listening to the way our guides spoke, observing the way museum plaques and pamphlets were worded, after reading written testimonies, histories, interpretations—was the fact that, for members of the Party, it was always the Party that won, lost, or suffered; it was the Party that was let down or upheld. Occasionally there would be references to the sacrifices of the people, but that was the wording of Party propaganda. Even Eugenia Ginzburg, in *Journey into the Whirlwind,* writes about how, during the Purges, she came to feel that Stalin had betrayed the Party. Never a word about the Nation.

In the United States such a division of loyalties would be called treason. Party is what, precisely, we expect people of principle to be above. And as Harrison has shown, the Party did not write that many glorious pages during the Great Patriotic War. I began to wonder whether, in the Soviet Union, there are not some who are loyal Russians—or loyal Latvians, Ukrainians, or Lithuanians—and others who are loyal to the Party, but few who are loyal to the Union. Whether these thoughts have any merit, clearly the propagandists had missed their target once again.

During one of the many interviews I had in Vilnius (the press certainly "covered" us, though with what I'm not sure), a reporter for Moscow Radio asked me what recent Russian writers I had read. After a moment, with a wry smile which I hoped was disarming, I replied that I had read writers like Sakharov, Solzhenitsyn, Aksyonov, Ginzburg, Mandelstam, and Zinoviev. The reporter, in a tone of voice and with a facial expression blanker than the sky, corrected my pronunciation of Zinoviev. She went on to the next question: what did I hope the conference would accomplish? My answer was an optimistic *cliché garni*. It is no wonder, of course, that the Soviets feel "misrepresented." And it is not surprising that they try to correct these "misrepresentations." For our part, we did not want to be "dummies," and to be "taken in." As Clive James wrote in his volume of essays and reviews, *From the Land of Shadows* (a book William Gaddis put in my hands after our return to the States):

> To speak only of the arts, and of the arts to speak only of literature, it can be taken for granted that any writer over the last fifty years who has not been persecuted by the State is simply not worth reading. Learning to read Russian brings rich benefits, but the prospective student should be warned that he will not be able to retain any comfortable illusions he might have about this century being as fruitful as the last. It is like walking out of a garden into a desert. The catastrophe was already in the making before Stalin came to power. Those gullible Western authors who go on junkets to Moscow and Leningrad at the invitation of the Soviet Writers' Union, and who come home to declare themselves impressed with how *many* poets are published in *Literaturnaya Gazeta* and how *many* copies of his new book a Soviet poet is accustomed to see printed, are kept safe by the language barrier, as well as by their natural obtuseness, from realising that the Writers' Union is an organisation

which exists in order to seek out talent and make certain
that it is expunged.

(London: Picador, 1983, p. 260)

On our way we passed the new city of light, Electrènai, where
there were clusters of new flats and many wires and what I took to
be distant cooling towers. But behind all these modern buildings
and the image of efficiency and serious work they presented, I saw,
to my immense surprise, the structurally harmonious figure of a
great Ferris Wheel.

X

We came to the concentration camp (the Ninth Fort of Kaunas)
through a heavy mist. Nearby these forbidding doors and bars and
murder chambers is an interesting memorial museum in modern
style, but just up a gently sloping walk, with a vast unmarked
meadow behind it where a mass grave is located, is a huge
outcropping of manmade rock from whose jagged facets human
fists and faces burst. This stone comes from the ground as if
screamed, as if every edge were a knife's held against the throat of
the sky, and our day's dark air lay like a curtain behind the slate
gray irruption, perfectly setting it off, completing the mood of the
moment, closing it for all time in the grip of death.

The novel that ran after Party truth may have exhausted itself,
but we had seen an actor like Vladas Bagdonas (who played
Pirosmani), a director like Nekrošius, and now a sculptor like A.
Ambraziunas (who executed the design for this Memorial to the
Victims of Fascism), creating works as original, powerful, and
genuine as any. Completed in 1985, it is composed of three broadly
striated stone expulsions which also manage to resemble tilted
trunks, and which together form massive triangles through which a
distant tree or two can be seen when the fog lifts. These are the
anonymous headstones of hundreds, fossilized heaps of human
feeling, the harsh embodiment of every anguished outcry, and I
was reminded of the dark cone of agony that, in Picasso's paintings
sometimes, issues from the mouth of the picador's gored horse.

Another magnificent memorial, at Khatyn, near Minsk, is as
dispersed over as vast a distance as the one at Kaunas is com-

pressed. At Kaunas, space is held in a single meadow like liquid in a bowl, while its balancing solidity is massed and grouped in the steel armature and board-formed concrete of the tomb's three intrusive stones. Even a sweeping glance can capture one of its dramatic ensembles. The Khatyn monument commemorates, most immediately, the destruction by fire of a Byelorussian village of 149 inhabitants, most of whom were killed when the barn into which they had been herded was burned. That building is represented by a similarly shaped block of polished but broken stone that stands where the barn once stood. The architects, Yu. M. Gradov, V. P. Zankovich, and L. M. Levin (who deservedly received the Lenin Prize for this moving work in 1970), laid out their memorial the way the village was laid out, so that what was formerly the main street is now marked by a footpath of broad concrete slabs designed to lead the visitor past the visible foundations of twenty-six symbolically demolished houses, their gates standing forever ajar, and where, from within, a tormented ash gray chimney rises, not to a cross, of course, but to a bell, as though a final note of hearth smoke had been caught there during the firing of the house. These bells ring irregularly with the others so that they sound—now here, now there—throughout the great clearing, and you are never out of the touch of their tolling, as you are never out of sight of the stele they ring from.

At the entrance to this cemetery town (which has since given its name to all the others that were similarly destroyed, so they are called "khatyns") is a large statue of a man, bones melted by pain and tears, holding like a wet towel the lifeless body of a child draped over his outstretched arms. The sculptor, S. I. Selikhanov, has created an appropriate and powerful greeting; however, the figure is composed and sited in such a way that the silhouette is equally arresting from every side, and seems like a black gash against the sky, a shadow that has stood up from the snow. The people who lived here were burned alive on March 22, 1943. Two hundred and nine towns and nine thousand two hundred additional villages were destroyed. Rows of symbolic graves mark these communities, each small square filled with earth taken out of the ground where the dead town stood, and brought here, when the memorial was dedicated, by survivors from each place. Such as there were.

A deeply notched wall holds reminiscences of nearby crematoria, concentration, detention, and other camps, and it leads us alongside a square containing three birches and an eternal flame: the three-quarters of the people who were spared, and the one quarter who were slain. Finally we reach a fence constructed of the names of the few who were buried under gunned-down bodies, and thus overlooked, or who were given the *coup de grâce* through their caps, and left for dead, or who fell through the wall of a burning building, rolling clothing over in the dirt until its flames were out, or those who, wounded, reached underbrush or other hiding anyway, and who probably believe (against the Party's propaganda and every other reason) they see God's hand in their rescue, and only Hitler's in their ruin.

This knowledge—of how one hog throws its wash upon another—terminally depresses me.

The Soviets have made a movie of this dreadful "incident" called *Come and See,* an invitation which I hope many Americans will accept when it is finally shown in the United States. One might wish to quarrel with the way some bits of it have been bitten, but on the whole it is a beautiful and dismaying film. We were shown it in Minsk, along with the War Museum there. These two additional events nearly completed our education concerning the Great Patriotic War. We would warm our hands at still another eternal flame in Leningrad. Millions dead there too—though from other causes.

At Khatyn, as between lovers, no touch was too trivial to be undirected. Our guide was dressed entirely in mourning: black leather boots, long black coat, shiny black fur stole, black fur hat and black suede gloves, black shoulder bag. I didn't hear much of what she said, for I had already learned the two things to avoid in the Soviet Union: tour guides and roosters of the apparatus. It is the habit of the former to lecture you on everything from Marxist-Leninism to the decline of churchgoing, and to do so in a strident, no-nonsense, nonstop voice that brooks no interruption, while you peer helplessly out the halted bus at the sight you would like to see if the overly energetic lady would ever pause and the bus door poooosh itself open. What a welcome sound—that poooosh.

Prior research had apprised us of the fact that Khatyn, the village the Nazis burned, and Katyn, the site of the alleged massacre of thousands of Polish officers by the Soviets, bear remarkably similar names, so that the sound of the first—Khatyn—

might successfully blot out the sound of the second—Katyn. It may be that the noble rhetorical statement this promenade through murder makes has its subtler, less noble sotto voce side.

So we bade adieux to the grim delights of death. Moscow would be next. More and more, too, our days would be occupied by the obvious, pleasant as that was: Red Square, the Kremlin, the Metro, the Metro joke, a hotel in a style called Stalinist Gothic, unarriving elevators.

XI

I did not regard it as ominous when Gass and Gaddis had difficulty getting served in the Moscow Writers' Union. The plate of kasha we finally got was good even if that was all we got. Gaddis and Gass let their tongues hang out, but the wine and beer went to those tables uncontaminated by Americans. I did not take it amiss, although the Soviet Union is the sort of country that makes you wonder about such things. Gaddis was freshly appareled, too, his baggage having finally come some days before. Lunch was simply like the baggage—an accident of Fate.

Norman Cousins had returned to the United States, and Harrison Salisbury had flown, I think, to Italy, so that there were perhaps seven of us in the group when we arrived for our appointment at the Translation Center. We were blandly informed, while our coats were being hustled out of reach, that all the people we had hurried to meet were unavoidably "in conference." Not to worry, Mr. Bland said, he would talk to us for a bit, and he, and a young man I identified as a graduate student, took us into a small room for a chat. "We've been naughty," Louis whispered, "and we're being punished." The conversation limped along familiar lines. Look at all the writers we Soviets have translated, not only classics like Whitman, Masters, Frost, Sandburg, Hill (who?), MacLeish, and so on, but many of your contemporary poets as well, for instance, Ferlinghetti, eh? Creeley, eh? Snyder, um, and you, too, Mr. Ginsberg, whereas . . . "Dissidents," I said. "We do well by dissidents. . . . whereas what have you . . . ?" "Two or three poems in an anthology don't count," Allen said, flourishing the offending volume. I wondered whether it was the same one he had read from. "I have been a famous poet for thirty years, and you haven't done a single book." Allen brought the book down with a bang. "Fuck you guys! I'm sick of having this shit laid on us! Fuck you!" Allen's outburst was abrupt and unexpected, but these common words expressed, I think, some common feelings. Mr. Bland was more than equal to the occasion. "We'll just treat this as another one of your theatricals, Allen," he said blandly, and we all tiptoed on to the end of our appointment time.

Quite circumstantially, the service at the Writers' Union immediately improved.

XII

We are going to go to Leningrad by evening train, but before that Thanksgiving must befall us, as it befalls Americans everywhere. Christmas we share with others. Thanksgiving we have to ourselves. At an elegant dinner at the American Ambassador's residence in Moscow, I find myself at a table with a correspondent for the *Washington Post*. Clearly, he is unaware of the writers' meeting in Vilnius. In the United States we keep literary matters in proper perspective—namely, distant and dim. As we talk, he grows increasingly more alert, and he begins to pump us a bit. Ah, I thought, we are being taken for dummies again, this time by one of our own countrymen. My hunch was that the reports of our meeting by both sides would be as if written by Mr. Bland, and so, when I was pumped, I leaked. The correspondent made a few phone calls between bites of turkey and pumpkin. And the report in the *Post* was acceptably sour. Dinner was not only tasty, it was fun. I decided I liked leaking.

XIII

The Red Arrow Express. What romantic words! It is midnight in Moscow when we board the train. It will be eight o'clock in the morning when we arrive in Leningrad. Our compartment is clean and comfortable. Nightcaps are numerous. It is snowing as we slide out of the station, and the train begins to move past platforms covered by snow and lit by flakes of falling light. During the Great Patriotic War, this train was nearly the last link between a beleaguered Moscow and a besieged Leningrad. Its wheels and engines were heroic. Heavily hatted figures move in and out of sight in the snow. The world we observe through the windows is the Russia of legend and fable, silent and dark. The woods arrive, now and then a farmhouse light shines all alone like a star. The world and the word, for a while, are one. We have dreamed the land we ride through. This little bratty boy from Warren, Ohio, is actually riding on the Red Arrow. It is not possible. And in the morning a warm woman will bring us glasses of hot tea, and we will watch our arrival in Leningrad with the same disbelief as our departure from the capital. If we have dreamed the land we ride through, what better way to pass it than in sleep?

Moscow was not nearly as dull and gloomy as people had told me it would be. When Russians rehab, they restore everything but the Czar, and the redone Arbat District is especially handsome, with Tuscan earth tones everywhere, as well as some beautiful blues, the color now of Pushkin's house—far too fancy a place for a poet. Now the bright yellow and orange walls of the Bulvar tint the snow according to the rules for coloring shadows laid down by Claude Monet. While the group warms itself in one of the shops, in a courtyard off the avenue, I photograph a very cold Russian cat and a few barrels covered with snow and a faded door or two. A burly gentleman suddenly appears who wants to know . . . something. Just spying, I did not cheerfully say while in graceful retreat. In the States, where I usually photograph, the very walls are awash with suspicion and every window is wary. I have been chased by heads which have appeared from behind drapes, and threatened by landlords and warned away by guards and thoroughly intimidated by a circle of sullen faces.

All out again into the sunburned snow. The camera has a glorious release; it shutters me not to shop. If I am told one more time how frozen my feet must be because I have no boots, or how frozen my fingers must be because you can't photograph through gloves, or how frozen my ears must be because I have no hat, it will turn out to be true. We walk farther down this street cut from a Christmas card, my eyes turning cartwheels, Soviet citizens resolutely paying no mind to the tourists. Our tireless translators, before we leave for the States, will take Mary and me to see some of the great modernist masterpieces in Moscow. An apartment block by Corbusier and a workers' club by Mel'nikov were impressive even in the always failing light and bitter unilluminating wind.

But Leningrad . . . ah, exclamation point. My eyes were caught in the Neva ice, and would not be free till spring. That's the pinnacle of the Peter and Paul Fortress! And that's the Admiralty's needlelike spire! I tried to imagine old emaciated women dragging corpses on sleds through these immediate streets, but the images in the eye were too real; it was inconceivable that so beautiful a city should have been thus brutalized—to become a city of death. How many of the world's great cities have been built on reclaimed land, on swamps? Would that woman never stop talking and let us out to circle ourselves around the Alexander Column?

XIV

The Hermitage. Of course. Miles of masterpieces. We agree to dissolve the group into a dew and disappear in all directions including evaporation. Our interests are too diverse. And this way, guidedom will have no dominion. We only have a few hours, so Mary and I decide to concentrate upon the buildings themselves, rather than upon their contents. Nevertheless the magic of the Hermitage is such that it tends to turn the world into a work of art. One side of it faces the Neva, another the Palace Square with its huge Alexander Column and the great arch of the General Staff Building across the way. As I pointed my camera out the windows, often heavily frosted and reflecting the chandeliers within like a burst of fireworks in the sky without, I realized that, thus framed, these landscapes and buildings and beautifully pruned winter trees were even more impressive; for now, somehow, they were no longer simply real, but were raised the way the camera elevates its images to the status of the fly in amber, to the status of standstill; since nothing in the cold glass seemed to move, but to be eternal the way the inner courtyards of the Hermitage appeared to be etched on the pane like an engraver's plate, twigs and limbs and walks done in fine dark lines, their benches draped with snow as though the Czar had ordered them covered while the court was away on vacation; the Palace Square was filled with an emptiness which the Square itself had chosen, and was not simply bare because of the time of day, the wind, the rhythm of arrival of the buses; and down the melting streets the tracks of the traffic showed as if everything were on a slow exposure; for on film the suggestion is that any movement it might contain has at last arrived at its moment of fulfillment, has come to this stillness like a train to its destination, so it may halt now, now that relevant lines, and relevant masses and hues and postures, and each active sign of the scene, are in an exalted position: the position of perfect repose and integration.

Quite the opposite attitude and effect was the one possessed and sought by our hosts when they led our bemused group to the location of Raskolnikov's room in a Leningrad apartment building. There was almost no light left, and the wind had grown, like the one in *Hamlet*, into a nipping and an eager air. We pulled up in front of a bleak building on an empty street. Not here. Around the corner. Perhaps. Now I was ready to have some bossy babe open her mouth like a book and print her breath upon my ear (that would be sexy), while I rested in the warmth of the bus and counted the number of dark doorways indenting the dark street. But we were to be counting footsteps soon—not doorways. "Misha, nip round the corner like the wind and see what's there." Wrong block.

Earlier in the afternoon, we had visited Dostoyevski's apartment, had seen the room he'd died in. There Gaddis had added up his years and with a wan smile weakly thumped his smoker's chest. Memorabilia, unless they have an interest of their own, rarely move me; nevertheless there was something touching about the isolation of Dostoyevski's little cigarette box where it lay all alone at the middle of a small rug-covered table in a pool of reddish light; however, my sentimentalities had not overcome my sense of the ontologically ridiculous, so it was with the greatest reluctance I followed our leader into a gloomy cold courtyard, and watched him while he sniffed the corners looking for the correct stairs. Absurdity is not a feeling I survive well. It was as if my soul, in the sorry shape it was in, was being shamed into going skinny-dipping.

"His garret was under the roof of a high, five-storied house and was more like a cupboard than a room," Misha related, translating from the Russian for us and holding the book awkwardly toward the little light the sky still held. "Here we are," our leader (a Leningrad novelist and critic) said, passing through a door and turning up a stairs. Because of the triumph of the Workers' Revolution, the Soviet Union may no longer contain unsavory slums. If not, this was a savory one. We went up a flight. Had anyone, I asked, been hunting for the snark? A young woman passed us, warmly dressed. Was she in the novel too? Raskolnikov's landlady in her youth? Another landing. And another. The room at the top. The room without a view. I had slipped through the mirror as Alice had done, and I was not in a page of Russian fiction. Yet Alice could do what she did because she was fictional to begin with. That's the trouble with Russia, I decided, screwing on my flash attachment. After generations of Czarist-Leninist-Stalinist lies, they don't know the difference. I'd take a few compromising photos of these fictional forms. Each with a red nose. Only Muriel's beautiful slavic profile seemed appropriate, yet wholly out of place. There was the garret, by god, more like a cupboard than a room.

According to our leader, the flat of the money lender was precisely umpteen paces away. At first, when people had tried to find it, he explained, they had gone astray because Dostoyevski, trained as an engineer and architect, remember, had used an engineer's measure, and when the searchers' paces matched those he had presumably stepped off, it became possible to locate it precisely. "Ah . . . I see . . ." I said, in tones of incredulous Yankee wonder. We would follow in Raskolnikov's murderous footsteps. Don't drop the axe, you'll dull the blade, I didn't say, as we descended.

Out and down in the indented street toward another courtyard. "The staircase leading to the old woman's room was close by, just on the right of the gateway," Misha read. Already we were on the stairs. The stairs were quite deserted. All the doors were shut. We met no one. We lost Gaddis, who had more consideration for his lungs than I for my lunacy. "Let's go get her; let's clobber the old Jew," I said to Allen, who was into this, and ignored me.

"And here was the fourth story," as the book said, "here was the door, here was the flat opposite, the empty one." In front of the door at which the professor pointed, returning the situation to its symbol like a good samaritan a lost purse, sat a battered green slop bucket. So, finally . . . in all of wide Russia . . . this was my subject . . . here was my shot.

XV

Another romantic moment. The Auchinclosses and the Gasses are being driven in a black taxi out of Moscow into the country, actually all the way to Peredelkino, to see Yevgeny Yevtushenko, who has very kindly asked us to visit him at his dacha. Allen and

Misha are in another car. It is our last night, and we have been to a concert, so the hour is already a bit ungainly. It is snowing slightly, and our headlights bore a hole in the bleak and the blear a bit like an automobile in the movies; consequently the snow looks white only when it's being run over. Eventually we turn off the road onto a narrower one lined with fences and trees. We are following Allen's car which obviously does not know the way either. The snow is as deep as a dog's muzzle here, and we can see buildings beyond the road, short trees I believe bear snowballs in the summer, snowballs which fly straight and strike a shoulder softly. If you were a Russian writer, Adele tells Louis, you might have a dacha out here—think of it—near Pasternak's grave. We'd be in prison counting thaws like Irina Ratushinskaya, I answer for him.

Our drivers ask directions from a couple encountered on the road. They point behind us. We back over our tracks. The last will be first, I do not say. One reason I love Louis so is that he can smile at the unsaid and understand. Our back bumper, our trunk, arrives. Here is the house. A dog begins to run toward us, but Yevtushenko has him in hand. He and the dog greet us, not both by wagging, and we enter a cheerful, unpretentious country cottage. We meet a young woman too, discreet as a searchlight. The floors where our boots will puddle are of bare wood and linoleum. Coats cling to a coat rack like survivors of a sinking. In another room a long trestle table covered with communities of food awaits us. At the other end of the space are chairs and a sofa, a TV monitor as well, that looks longingly at its audience. The atmosphere would be completely and serenely rustic except that on one wall there is a huge horse's head by Pirosmani, on others drawings by Picasso and Matisse, signed like photos from the stars, and, all about, objects of honest interest—gifts galore. I try to be, as the kids used to say, swayve, but a good gawk is not beyond me.

Yevtushenko gestures us to the table where we shall sample his household's winter fare: hunks of pickled cabbage, salt-cured green apples and the season's last tomatoes, sausage, cheese in large salty chunks, coarse dark bread and a loaf of crusty white, some homemade wine from Georgia, and also from the same Republic a large jar of bootleg vodka, as soft and chewable as an earlobe. From my garden, he says proudly, as I swallow bites of green tomato, preserved by a process of which I was unaware, and so delicious the teeth dance.

Yevtushenko's thin, alert face is somewhat lined, but his eyes leap and his gestures are expansive. I am not unmindful of the fact that two of the world's most famous poets of that generation whose common spark last crossed the gap between our countries are in a conversation I can overhear; that this is the almost mythical Peredelkino; that we have come from Moscow in black taxis which might have been nicknamed "Red Arrows." Yevtushenko is wholly self-absorbed, but he has a self to be absorbed by. Mary is swallowing this scene which is, in its way, as full of remembrance as our mouths are: sentiments that time and tears have cured. Yevtushenko is speaking of his first wife, Bella Akhmadulina, who is now living in Georgia. Ah . . . but . . . is she still a poet? He claps both hands to the sides of his head. Allen . . . Allen . . . I've such family problems! Well you might, I think, with a wife and family living in Moscow and a lovely young woman out here living in. The poet plays a few stories for us it would be unwise to repeat, juicy as the apples. I love the sawing sound a bread knife makes as little bits of crust shower to the board. The cheese is dense and rich and green as the tomatoes. What is earth in a bourgeois mouth but more myth? The good old days march by like a parade. This is Mary's decade, her Topsy time, the Fifties which these poets are now renovating. Yevtushenko squeezes a feeling by hugging himself. The young woman, who speaks no English and must have been bored, has disappeared.

Would we like to see some uncut tapes from those days, videocassettes of old newsreels of poetry readings in Leningrad and Moscow, here and there over the whole country? The crowds, the enthusiasms, the ideas, the dreams, the song . . . Yevtushenko has the proper equipment, Japanese, he says with a grin, from New York. We slide down the room a little and soon the screen goes gray with youth. There is Bella. Quite beautiful, we agree. The camera pans over the crowd. Ah, how beautiful we were in those days. Quite, we agree. Now Yevtushenko is reading, his thin face unmarked, unwise. Look at those faces. He claps his hands to his head. Time makes him remorseful. Look at me. Ah. You don't understand what I'm saying? what I've said? What a moment! See those faces. Wonderful! Now it is Voznesensky's turn at the mike. And the camera runs up and down the audience like a hand on an arm. What would Henry James make of this, I wonder, or Edith Wharton?—the past preserved from the freeze of winter, the harshness of history, and served to our eyes now like the food on the table. I look at Louis who looks as steadfastly benign as the Pope. "Narcissus as Narcissus" is, if I remember right, the title of a poem by Paul Valéry. The room is filled with applause.

Would we like to see a few frames of Yevtushenko's movie—a new one—as recently made as a roll—based upon his autobiography—a film he will show in New York in February? No, I do not say. Nor, it is late, but thank you for a lovely repast. Yes, Mary says. Oh yes, she says, yes. All nod. Do Mandarins like me have no memories? I search my mind. The answer is: no—we do not. Is that because we have never been important? Very probably. Yevtushenko will show us two scenes: the first is of peasant people celebrating a wedding (the bridegroom is going off to war), and the second will be of his mother (played by the young woman whose acquaintance we have just made) dancing naked in the snow after a sauna—a moment in the movie he especially prizes.

The young star is recalled so that she may rewatch the scene, or watch us watch it, I suppose. And will we watch her watch us watch it? The two taxi drivers (members, I like to imagine, of some department of the Soviet alphabet) are asked to bring their mugs of tea from the kitchen to enjoy the movie too. They enter warily, stage right.

There are peasants in peasant dress to be sure, and local peasant people to wear them. This is Yevtushenko's ancestral village. Everything is authentic. He, himself, has a small part. The banquet tables undulate as if they were on a ship at sea, and the camera goes as quickly around a corner as a man can. There is the joy of anticipated union, the sadness of expected parting. Everything is authentic, though reenacted. But how about Yevtushenko's mother, now mother naked, and Yevtushenko, too, like a little jay, beclouded by the steam, and at eight or nine bemused by the sight of his mother running happily outside to sport in the snow, to roll over and over, tossing handfuls of snow into the snowy air, her body all white against the white, her dark pubic patch hopping about like a frantic black bird. Beautiful, Yevtushenko murmurs. Certainly authentic, I think. The room is filled with applause.

On the drive back I repeatedly wonder about two things. What makes my mistake—when I claim fact is fiction, and turn into low art the high view from a Hermitage window—any less hilarious or metaphysically absurd than the one the Russians commit when they clamber up flights of fictional stairs to look at a factual doorway, or, right before their eyes and mine, turn their films into seated people?

How do you deal with the knowledge that you've just gone to bed with the actress who's been playing your mother at your behest! then to show your mother's real invented nakedness to guests?

XVI

The events of the days immediately following our return from the Soviet Union (the initial refusal of Allen Ginsberg's request for a visa extension, then the approval of it, the galvanizing speech of Yevgeny Yevtushenko at the Soviets' own Writers' Conference, and the positive reception to his call for a lessening of censorship, the reported approval by Nikolai Federenko of its contents): these features form for our conference a happier face than it seemed to bear, and perhaps Secretary Federenko isn't one of the bad guys after all. Perhaps Yevtushenko was speaking his own mind, then perhaps he was merely turning with a new wind; perhaps these are signs of an increasing Soviet self-confidence and candor; perhaps the "liberals" are being flushed into the open for an easier shot. The Writers' Union did not deem it wise to send representatives to the Pen Conference held in New York in January. Was it just because some dissidents would be there? Or did they realize that their absence would encourage everyone to pick on the United States? In any case, one wishes that the curtain of concealment could be opened, and private speech could stroll calmly in public as though it were Sunday.

The room, I feel sure, would fill with applause.

But first we would have to believe we knew what was really going on.

nominated by The Kenyon Review

LE PETIT SALVIÉ

by C. K. WILLIAMS

from THE PARIS REVIEW

for Paul Zweig
1935–1984

1.

"The summer has gone by both quickly and slowly.
It's been a kind of eternity, each day spinning
out its endlessness, and yet with every look
back, less time is left . . ."

So quickly, and so slowly . . . In the tiny elevator of the flat you'd
    borrowed on the Rue de Pondicherry,
you suddenly put your head against my chest, I thought to show
    how tired you were, and lost consciousness,
sagging heavily against me, forehead oiled with sweat, eyes
    ghastly agape . . . so quickly, so slowly.
Quickly the ambulance arrives, mewling at the curb, the
    disinterested orderlies strap you to their stretcher.
Slowly at the clinic, waiting for the doctors, waiting for the
    ineffectual treatments to begin.
Slowly through that night, then quickly all the next day, your last
    day, though no one yet suspects it.
Quickly those remaining hours, quickly the inconsequential tasks
    and doings of any ordinary afternoon.

Quickly, slowly, those final silences and sittings I so regret now
not having taken all of with you.

2.

"I don't think we'll make the dance tonight," I mumble
mawkishly. "It's definitely worse," you whisper.
Ice-pack hugged to you, you're breathing fast; when you stop
answering questions, your eyes close.
You're there, and then you slip away into your meditations, the
way, it didn't matter where,
in an airport, a café, you could go away into yourself to work, and
so we're strangely comforted.
It was dusk, late, the softening, sweetening, lingering light of the
endless Paris evening.
Your room gave on a garden, a perfect breeze washed across your
bed, it wasn't hard to leave you,
we knew we'd see you again: we kissed you, Vikki kissed you,
"Goodbye, my friends," you said,
lifting your hand, smiling your old warming smile, then you went
into your solitude again.

3.

We didn't know how ill you were . . . we knew how ill but hid it
. . . we didn't know how ill you were . . .
Those first days when your fever rose . . . if we'd only made you go
into the hospital in Brive . . .
Perhaps you could have had another year . . . but the way you'd
let death touch your life so little—
the way you'd learned to hold your own mortality before you like
an unfamiliar, complex flower.
Your stoicism had become so much a part of your identity, your
virtue, the system of your self-regard.
If we'd insisted now, you might have given in to us, when we
didn't, weren't we cooperating
with what wasn't just your wish but your true passion never to be
dying, sooner dead than dying?

You did it, too: composed a way from life directly into death, the ignoble scribblings between elided.

4.

It must be some body-thing, some species-thing, the way it comes to take me from so far,

this grief that tears me so at moments when I least suspect it's there, wringing tears from me

I'm not prepared for, had no idea were even there in me, this most unmanly gush I almost welcome,

these cries so general yet with such power of their own I'm stunned to hear them come from me.

Walking through the street, I cry, talking later to a friend, I try not to but I cry again,

working at my desk I'm taken yet again, although, again, I don't want to be, not now, not again,

though that doesn't mean I'm ready yet to let you go . . . what it does mean I don't think I know,

nor why I'm so ill-prepared for this insistence, this diligence with which consciousness afflicts us.

5.

I imagine you rising to something like heaven: my friend who died last year is there to welcome you.

He would know the place by now, he would guide you past the ledges and the thorns and terror.

Like a child I am, thinking of you rising in the rosy clouds and being up there with him,

being with your guru Baba, too, the three of you, all strong men, all partly wild children,

wandering through my comforting child's heaven, doing what you're supposed to do up there forever.

I tell myself it's silly, all of this, absurd, what we sacrifice in attaining rational mind,

but there you are again, glowing, grinning down at me from somewhere in the heart of being,

ablaze with wonder and a child's relief that this after all is how astonishingly it finishes.

In my adult mind, I'm reeling, lost—I can't grasp anymore what I
  even think of death.
I don't know even what we hope for: ecstasy? bliss? or just release
  from being, not to suffer anymore.
At the grave, the boring rabbi said that you were going to eternal
  rest: rest? why rest?
Better say we'll be absorbed into the "Thou," better be consumed
  in light, in Pascal's "Fire!"
Or be taken to the Godhead, to be given meaning now, at last,
  the meaning we knew eluded us.
God, though, Godhead, Thou, even fire: all that is gone now,
  gone the dark night arguments,
gone the partial answers, the very formulations fail; I grapple for
  the questions as *they* fail.
Are we to be redeemed? When? How? After so much disbelief,
  will something be beyond us to receive us?

7.

Redemption is in life, "beyond" unnecessary: it is radically
  demeaning to any possible divinity
to demand that life be solved by yet another life: we're
  compressed into this single span of opportunity
for which our gratitude should categorically be presumed; this is
  what eternity for us consists of,
praise projected from the soul, as love first floods outward to the
  other then back into the self . . .
Yes, yes, I try to bring you to this, too; yes, what is over now is
  over, yes, we offer thanks,
for what you had, for what we all have: this portion of eternity is
  no different from eternity,
they both contract, expand, cast up illusion and delusion and all
  the comfort that we have is love,
praise, the grace not to ask for other than we have . . . yes and
  yes, but this without conviction, too.

8.

What if after, though, there is something else, will there be
  judgement, then, will it be retributive,

and if it is, if there is sin, will you have to suffer some hellish
    match with what your wrongs were?
So much good you did, your work, your many kindnesses, the
    befriendings and easy generosities.
What sort of evil do we dare imagine we'd have to take into those
    awful rectifications?
We hurt one another, all of us are helpless in that, with so much
    vulnerable and mortal to defend.
But that vulnerability, those defenses, our belittling jealousies,
    resentments, thrusts and spites
are the very image of our frailty: shouldn't our forgiveness for
    them and our absolution be assumed?
Why would our ultimate identities be burdened with absolutes,
    imperatives, lost discordant hymns?

9.

How ambiguous the triumphs of our time, the releasing of the
    intellect from myth and magic.
We've gained much, we think, from having torn away corrupted
    modes of aggrandizement and gigantism,
those infected and infecting errors that held sway over us and so
    bloated our complacencies
that we would willingly inflict even on our own flesh
    the crippling implications of our metaphysic.
How much we've had to pay, though, and how dearly
    had to suffer for our liberating dialectic.
The only field still left to us to situate our anguish and
    uncertainty is the single heart,
and how it swells, the heart, to bear the cries with which we used
    to fill the startled heavens.
Now we have the air, transparent, and the lucid psyche, and
    gazing inwards, always inwards, to the wound.

10.

The best evidence I have of you isn't my memory of you, or your
    work, although I treasure both,
and not my love for you which has too much of me in it as
    subject, but the love others bore you,

bear you, especially Vikki, who lived out those last hard years
   with you, the despairs and fears,
the ambivalences and withdrawals, until that final week of fever
   that soaked both your pillows.
Such a moving irony that your last days finally should have seared
   the doubt from both of you.
Sometimes it's hard to tell exactly whom I cry for—you, that last
   night as we left you there,
the way you touched her with such solicitude, or her, the
   desolation she keeps coming to:
*"I've been facing death, touched death, and now I have a ghost I
love and who loves me."*

11.

Genevieve, your precious Gen, doesn't quite know when to cry,
   or how much she's supposed to cry,
or how to understand those moments when it passes, when she's
   distracted into games and laughter
by the other kids or by the adults who themselves don't seem to
   grasp this terrible non-game.
At the cemetery, I'm asked to speak to her, to comfort her: never
   more impossible to move beyond cliché.
We both know we're helplessly embedded in ritual: you wanted
   her, I tell her, to be happy,
that's all, all her life, which she knows, of course, but nods to,
   as she also knows what I don't say,
the simplest self-revealing truths, your most awful fear, the brutal
   fact of your mortality:
how horribly it hurt to go from her, how rending not to
   be here as father and friend.

12.

Nothing better in the world than those days each year with you,
   your wife, my wife, the children,
at your old stone house in the Dordogne, looking over valleys one
   way, chestnut woods the other,
walks, long talks, visits to Lascaux and Les Eyzies,
   listening to each other read.

Our last night, though, I strolled into the moonless fields, it
 might have been a thousand centuries ago,
and something suddenly was with me: just beyond the boundaries
 of my senses presences were threatening,
something out of childhood, mine or man's; I felt my fear,
 familiar, unfamiliar, fierce,
might freeze me to the dark, but I looked back—I wasn't here
 alone, your house was there,
the zone of warmth it made was there, you yourself were there,
 circled in the waiting light.

13.

I seem to have to make you dead, dead again, to hold you in my
 mind so I can clearly have you,
because unless I do, you aren't dead, you're only living
 somewhere out of sight, I'll find you,
soon enough, no need to hurry, and my mind slips into this other
 tense, other grammar of condition,
in which you're welded to banalities of fact and time, the reality
 of what is done eluding me.
If you're accessible to me, how can you be dead? You are
 accessible to me, therefore . . . something else.
So what I end with is the death of death, but not as it would have
 been elaborated once,
in urgencies of indignation, resignation, faith: I have you neither
 here, nor there, but not not-anywhere:
the soul keeps saying that you might be here, or there—the
 incessant passions of the possible.

14.

Here's where we are: out behind the house in canvas chairs,
 you're reading new poems to me,
as you have so often, in your apartment, a park in
 Paris—anywhere: sidewalk, restaurant, museum.
You read musically, intensely, with flourishes, conviction: I might
 be the audience in a hall,
and you are unimaginably insecure, you so want me to admire
 every poem, every stanza, every line,

just as I want, need, you, too, to certify, approve, legitimize, and
all without reservation,
and which neither of us does, improving everything instead,
suggesting and correcting and revising,
as we knew, however difficult it was, we had to, in our barely
overcome but overcome competitiveness.
How I'll miss it, that so tellingly accurate envy sublimated into
warmth and brothership.

15.

Here's where we are: clearing clumps of shrub and homely brush
from the corner of your yard,
sawing down a storm-split plum tree, then hacking at the dozens
of malevolently armored maguey:
their roots are frail as flesh and cut as easily, but in the August
heat the work is draining.
Now you're resting; you're already weak although neither of us
will admit it to the other.
Two weeks later, you'll be dead, three weeks later, three months,
a year, I'll be doing this,
writing this, bound into this other labor that you loved so much
and that we also shared,
still share, somehow always will share now as we shared that
sunny late summer afternoon,
children's voices, light; you, pale, leaning on the wall, me tearing
at the vines and nettles.

16.

"A man's life cannot be silent; living is speaking, dying, too, is
speaking," so you wrote,
so we would believe, but still, how understand what the finished
life could have meant to say
about the dying and the death that never end, about potential
gone, inspiration unaccomplished,
love left to narrow in the fallacies of recall, eroding down to
partial gesture, partial act?
And we are lessened with it, amazed at how much our selfworth
and joy were bound into the other.

201

There are no consolations, no illuminations, nothing of that long
   awaited flowing toward transcendence.
There is, though, compensation, the simple certainty of having
   touched and having been touched.
The silence and the speaking come together, grief and gladness
   come together, the disparate fuse.

17.

Where are we now? Nowhere, anywhere, the two of us, the four
   of us, fifty of us at a *fête*.
Islands of relationships, friends and friends, the sweet, normal,
   stolid matrix of the merely human,
the circles of community that intersect within us, hold us, touch
   us always with their presence,
even as, today, mourning, grief, themselves becoming memory,
   there still is that within us which endures,
not in possession of the single soul in solitude, but in the
   covenants of affection we embody,
the way an empty house embodies elemental presences, and the
   way, attentive, we can sense them.
Breath held, heart held, body stilled, we attend, and they are
   there, covenant, elemental presence,
and the voice, in the lightest footfall, the eternal wind, leaf and
   earth, the constant voice.

18.

"The immortalities of the moment spin and expand; they seem to
   have no limits, yet time passes.
These last days here are bizarrely compressed, busy, and yet full
   of suppressed farewells . . ."
The hilly land you loved, lucerne and willow, the fields of
   butterfly and wasp and flower.
Farewell the crumbling house, barely held together by your
   ministrations, the shed, the pond.
Farewell your dumb French farmer's hat, your pads of yellow
   paper, your joyful, headlong scrawl.
The coolness of the woods, the swallow's swoop and whistle, the
   confident call of the owl at night.

202

Scents of dawn, the softening all night fire, char, ash, warm
   embers in the early morning chill.
The moment holds, you move across the path and go, the light
   lifts, breaks: goodbye, my friend, farewell.

nominated by The Paris Review
and James Baker Hall

THE PROMISE OF LIGHT

by RICHARD JACKSON

from THE GEORGIA REVIEW

In the background, steam rises from the snow patches,
and from the backs of horses nearly out of sight
yet making their way towards a hidden stream.
For a moment, the crowd that is gathered around the man
who drank himself to death does not know whether
to look at this and the other pictures he painted
at the end of this alley in perfect detail, or at the man.

I believe the artist painted his scenes from Gustav Mahler's
Pastoral, and it must be that by now the horses
would have found the stream, so much do they seem to trust
the artist's stroke which allows them all to turn
away, perhaps from shyness. Once, north of Atlanta,
I came upon two trailers in a wreck that had spilled
their horses, quiet and unnatural, on the wet pavement,

lit at intervals by the blue lights of the police cruisers.
No doubt these horses waiting to disappear into
the wall are those horses alive in a world we can't name,
and this man, who kept a photograph of a woman he never
knew, cut from a magazine, as his friends explain,
speaking his whole life to her, invented whatever
past, whatever future, he could trust to face the dark.

And surely he remembered, for the first time in years,
climbing the ladder down to the bottom of a pier—

the stars already fading—with a girl he hardly
knew, the wooden pilings coated with barnacles
and black seaweed, the tide low, the oil slicks
gathering on the harbor around driftwood, paper
cups, tin cans, dead fish—gathering towards

the darkness which was the other shore they swam for,
trusting luck, trusting the certainty of tides. He must
have remembered how long it takes to trust anything.
I remember reading how Mahler as a boy watched until dawn,
not believing in the burlap bags stuffed with the hair
of mice and human hair—charms his uncle hung
around the orchard because nuisance deer couldn't stand the
    smell.

Now, in silence, the crowd begins to break up. The artist
who had seemed only to be sitting asleep on a cinder
block he took from an empty lot next door is gone,
and I almost believe the fog on the walls might lift,
revealing the scene I read once where Mahler watched,
from a distance, a girl so awkwardly beautiful he couldn't
trust what he saw. The man with her lifted her blouse

and placed it across a branch, its arms spread
like antlers, or spread like the arms of another lover,
or her father, or even Mahler becoming too slowly the man
who would finally understand that whoever you love is
all of a sudden there, promising nothing but the next day,
the way fireflies would gather as they all began
to leave, promising nothing but their own brief light.

In those days, the imprints from tie beams in the shadow
of a railbed in Bohemia would be enough to take him anywhere.
Once, by tracks like those, I found and broke open a brown
    cocoon—
inside were hundreds of yellow spiders entangled in each
others' lives, the way our own lives and the lives
of so many we never knew, even this poor artist's,
become entangled by whatever stories we remember.

I remember the story of Gustav Mahler writing
his pastoral symphony in a world as silent as this wall,
instructing his wife to untie the bells from cows,
cut the rope to the village tower, teach singers
how to mime—and how she would try to silence the birds, keep
the horses from running—and how, later, he would lock himself
in a room waiting for his daughter to die, and how he would
    return

to the Danube to face his own lingering death. And I remember
Mike Connally, the sketch artist who played left field
with an old, stubby glove and whom we called "Sky" because of
    the long
fly balls he'd hit, and how he turned away, in the end, from
any sky to face the quiet of the Tennessee for three weeks before
they found him. I think he knew what the poet Delmore
    Schwartz meant
by the deafness of solitude, the world we are never able to hear—

Schwartz, who wrote on a restroom wall in Syracuse, New York,
"Give me $5 and the change and I'll go where the morning
and the evening can't hurt me," and who lay finally
for three days in a New York City morgue. We live
so seldom in the real world, he said, because we are
so often surprised by the deaths of friends, and cannot
understand, even from that, the meaning of our own deaths.

It may be that now I no longer wish to tell one event
from another, believing the stars which are moving away
yet reappear, like the stories of this artist, of Mahler, of Schwartz,
and of Mike Connally. On the far wall is a picture of wolves
who must have stalked a caribou to death for weeks,
trusting, even as the artist must have, in the terrible
meaning of that event, trusting, as we must, in the way

the mind and heart find each other out
despite our own fears, despite whatever details
we invent to divert ourselves, these stories or images
we make of the morning emerging from the fog where,

when we look carefully, one or the other of us is
also emerging, trusting whatever silence lingers,
knowing the world begins from where we are.

nominated by The Georgia Review, *Edward Hirsch,*
William Matthews, Sherod Santos, and David Wojahn

THE UNDERGROUND

by THOMAS McGRATH

from ANOTHER CHICAGO MAGAZINE

Cities arise . . .
Like bric-a-brac on mountains which have not yet been named.
Here, the Pioneers
Arrived, drugged and armed to the eyes, on high-flying
    bombers—
And most of them think they are still in the flat lands to the west.

Here, on the good days,
In those serious born-again apparently-sufficient imperialist
    climes—
Where all days are apparently good days the cities ornament
    them
Themselves:
Among the desolate monsters that sometimes appear after
    midnight
(Escaped from below) statues spring into being: presidents,
Generals at the center of circles and squares—stars where
    converging
Streets may be commanded by gunfire . . .
                     L'Etoile est plus belle, n'est ce pas?
Oui. Beautiful.
           Et le mittrailleuse de ma tante, aussi.
But my aunt's machine-gun does not command all vistas, for—
Meanwhile, below,
In stopes black as the bore of an outlaw Frontier Colt

(And among the mneumonic plagues of heuristic condemned numbers)
The miners are tearing gold out of the rocks
With their bare hands.

                   Down here all the machines have failed:
The machines with spark-plugs fired by patriotic clichés
And burning the blood of children in cylinders of law and homicide . . .

Aloft, from balconies spun from hallucinatory silk,
The ladies climb the vertiginous ladders of afternoon TV sex,
(Those same ladders which have only one end).
Their eyes, brilliant with boredom, gaze down the grand avenues
Toward Presidential palaces with their glowing facades of caviar.
The weather is petrified in its windless theater of ice,
And the seasons have been vanished and replaced by appropriate music.
Moon of hypocrites . . .
               light . . .
                      stiffened by black glass . . .
Tomorrow: high tea in the execution chamber.

Underground, the weather goes on in the dim streets:
Among marooned motorcycles dead of too much salvation.
(Mourned by the little cadenzas of torn-out tongues.)
Here are the immense catalogs of lost meat:
The broken wrists of black-gowned washerwomen
The blind tearing off the skin of their eyes to see
The starving child who has eaten his own arm to the elbow
The old who sit in the plaza with guitars full of plastic explosive
And unwanted sex—
                here the miners return from their last
Shot in the dark.
           Now the square is filled.
                  They await the *Indios* . . .

In the bat-freaking twilight, *crepuscule du soir*,
And down along the old soignée river, the rich
Salauds and assholes, on elite terraces, suffering, perhaps,
From imperfect coronary recall or attrition of the memory, see,

The necrotic marble of those clouds which are now being towed
Into the blood-warm skies of saltpetre and semen . . .

Yes, lovely twilight up there: the ladies, in electronic nightgowns,
Watch while a stone cutter, snatched by night from below,
Is chiselling in granite, over the graveyard entrance:
"NO IDEAS BUT IN THINGS."
                                        And right behind him, another,
(Free-lance) "AND NO THINGS WITHOUT SOME
GODDAMN KIND OF IDEA *ABOUT* THEM!"

                    Below in the underground square, the peasants,
Drawn by the silver bells of their tiny burros arrive
From the Capitalist & Cocaine dictatorships of imperialist
duchies,
Colonies of the dollar and longtime fiefdoms of the CIA.
Now, in the little fiesta of the damned, songs are exchanged,
And tentative sex, and stories are told and politics
Made clear.
                    The guns are given.
                                        The day of the Rising is set.

Meanwhile, above in the city,
The elite take to their arms the Commodity Fetish: in boudoirs
Where (the moonlight clotting among mythologies of power and
drugs)
The glaciers have set up their tents.

nominated by Reginald Gibbons and
Terrence Des Pres

AN EMBARRASSMENT
OF ORDINARY RICHES

fiction by MARTHA BERGLAND

from NEW ENGLAND REVIEW/BREAD LOAF QUARTERLY

W HEN YOU ARE AWAY, most of what happens to me happens in the supermarket. I like it. I wouldn't like it all the time, but sometimes I love to let myself go to seed, live unwashed, uncombed. I read in the sun on our unmade bed, eavesdrop, go to the Grand Union several times a day. And I eat too much— probably for want of talking and kissing on these long days in this apartment in this brand new suburb. The little tree trunks are still wrapped in tape and the scalp still shows through the grass. We are new here too, so I can't connect one name with one face in this town, except the names and faces of our neighbors—J. G. and C. E. Mazza, according to the mailbox. But when I hear them I never see them, and when I see them they never speak.

My days here when you are on the road selling are usually broken into two parts: (1) sinking, and then (2) hauling myself up out of my petty squalor. The first half of each day is disintegration, self-indulgence, slovenliness; the last half, furious reform, listmaking, housecleaning. In the mornings I go to the supermarket for white cake; in the afternoons, for vegetables. I try not to let myself go later than 3:00 or 4:00. If I disintegrate beyond late afternoon, the downward curving of the day and the weight of the falling light pull me down too far and I am in way over my head. So when the day begins to curl under, I have to act fast. I quickly wash and dress and clean up the place. I go to the supermarket, buy food for a healthful meal, cook the food carefully, set myself a place at the table, and try to eat slowly while I watch the news. Then I wash the dishes, make sure each room is in order, make a list for tomorrow, select some classic to read while I wait for you to call.

Occasionally I wake up organized, in a secular state of grace, but not usually. More often, there is something I go after in silence, indolence, eavesdropping, inaction. There is something I am waiting to hear or feel or come to. But I have never actually found out what it is. I lose my nerve (or maybe it's nerve I find) and I reform myself every day.

I woke up early this summer morning into the bird song and the chilly air with your pillow at my back instead of you. When you go away, this little domestic sea calms, and some other self of mine slowly floats to the surface. Instead of jumping out of bed at the first touch of light, I lie still, wait for more sun, conserve my warmth. I remember your warming me. I slow my breathing and sift carefully through each breath for smells of your hair, your mouth, your skin. I breathe in to see pictures of you—both all of you and parts of you. As the summer sun moves into our sparsely furnished bedroom, over the white walls, the bureau, the bed, a sweet breeze moves the Sears curtains. Oh love, where will we *be* next year? I *try* to remain calm and light on my feet. I do like traveling light. I calm down. In every city on earth there is a bedroom with a window facing east. I lie still and wait for the sun or the birds or the clock radio to wake the Mazzas.

Because I don't turn on the TV or stereo when you're gone, I hear all the sounds of the Mazzas living next door. When they make love or fight in their bedroom, I eat cake on our bed a yard or so away from them. When they are in their kitchen, I sit on our kitchen counter and listen. The female voice when they argue is low, sometimes inaudible, drones on and on; the male voice is more infrequent and louder and clearer: "I don't know what the fuck you're talking about," "I'm sick of hearing all this shit," and "What kind of a schmuck do you think I am?"—things on that order. Their arguments are dreary, but I love to hear them. Their walls are probably white as ours are. They fight in the same light we do. Their door slams have the same ring to them. In the lulls, she probably stands at the window and stares out at what I see: the parking lot and cars and vans; the little trees; the building just like this one facing us; and, at sunset, the great wide grey and salmon blazes in the sky—nutty to me above the mercury vapor lights' wan green glow, the false mansard roofs, and the electric-green subdivision grass.

This morning as I was waiting for them to wake up, I remembered last Wednesday when you were so frustrated and enraged at the committees and the shitheads who thwart your plans. When you came home, you could no longer hold back your invective and you paced and pointed from the time you walked in the door until supper. Even after supper when you sat down and let me rub your back and shoulders, your arms were still untamed. They jumped and tensed like horses under my palms. So when you finally went to sleep on the couch in my arms, my breathing, too, relaxed as I was released from your battering consciousness. As you slid jerkily into sleep, we began to trade places in the air of the room around us. I expanded up into the room as you receded into the sleeping body that I love so much. I was relieved, but I also missed you, as I miss you now. Waiting this morning for the Mazzas to come to, I was regretting my relief at that small loss of you to sleep.

Our neighbor, J. G. Mazza, is, as we have both remarked, an aristocratic-looking young man. He carries his head as though he alone feels with his face the currents of air we earthlings walk through. His straight and severe bearing, his large, light eyes, his high cheekbones and thin nose, his light hair all seemed to mark him as a WASP prince, but from listening I know he's Italian. We thought him a poet, a musician, a scholar, but, get this, he's an assistant manager in one of those stereo stores in the shopping mall. And I know that he's an angry man with a nasty temper. C. E. Mazza always looks to be in his tow when they walk to their Datsun in the parking lot. She looks like a lot of other women: medium-color hair, average weight for her average height, neither very pretty nor unattractive. Both Mazzas come from large families—his Italian, hers WASP—and neither one can stand the other's. She wanted to live near the family, but, since he's up-and-coming in the stereo-selling business, his career ladder brought them here. She's an unemployed high school music teacher. Her name is Cindy; his is Jerry.

When he goes to work at 9:00 after either hard words or politeness or horseplay or silence at breakfast, she goes back to bed and cries herself back to sleep, I think. I read magazines and novels in bed on the other side of the wall until she wakes up, washes and dresses, does the breakfast dishes. I think of her with fondness living her life parallel to mine—with almost the same views out the windows, in the same light at dusk, on the same carpet—though I am exasperated at her inability to make herself understood, at her ability to choose consistently the wrong metaphors and wrong tone of voice to make a point with him. She feels sorry for herself in this new place without her mother, her sisters, her career, her own money, without a house to take care of, and she doesn't like their friends here who are his friends. She talks out loud to herself. She asks herself questions: "What next? What am I going to do? Why does he have to be like that? What am I going to fix for supper?"

This morning before eight one of the teenagers who works here at Marshridge Acres began mowing the lawn right underneath our—and the Mazzas'—bedroom windows. I felt J. G. hit the floor, felt their window flung open, and probably all the other neighbors heard, too, J. G. above the sound of the mower call the boy down there a Goddamned little cocksucker who didn't even have the brains or the courtesy. . . . His voice—suddenly too loud—trailed off when the lawnmower turned without comment around the corner of the building. J. G. got back in bed.

After a few minutes of silence, I heard C. E. Mazza in a reasonable tone of voice request that he please not talk to the poor kid that way. J. G. then noted in a less reasonable tone that the kid was not a poor kid but a thoughtless putz and why couldn't he start his mowing someplace else. When C. E. observed that somebody would always have to get waked up first and why shouldn't it be them, J. G. requested that she please not use that fucking school teacher tone on *him*. Then there was some more about whether or not it was a fucking issue to be waked up 15 minutes ahead of time and whose fucking fault it was and whether or not they were getting fucked over by the management of this fucking place. After a while of this I heard C. E. get out of her side of the bed and I heard the bathroom door close. When she came out after a flush and a few minutes I could hear very distinctly a sentence which I think she rehearsed in the bathroom: "Jerry, I find your attitude toward the 'working man' very inconsistent." She should have stayed in the bathroom until she got that sentence in better shape.

"What the hell do you know about working man coming from

that big house full of WASP women with table manners? Don't talk to me about working man!"

Now they're slipping into their main argument, the one they've been perfecting for as long as I've been tuning in. And I could hear all the words.

"I wasn't trying to talk about anybody else; I was talking about you. I was making an observation about what I see as an inconsistency in *you*. Please, Jerry, listen to what I *said*." Her voice was wavering; her firm, reasonable tone giving way to something weaker, something guaranteed to lose her the bout. "Jerry," she went on, "I was just trying to . . ."

"I *know* what you were trying to do. I *know*. Don't you think I can tell by now what you are always trying to do to me?"

"I'm not trying to do anything to *you*. It's to us, I mean, *for* us. I'd do anything, say anything to keep us together."

"Really? Then why don't you spend less money on long distance phone calls to your mother to bitch about this place and on dishes to—as you say—make this place seem like a home. It *is* home because we live here and no amount of dishes is going to make it more so."

This caused C. E. to actually raise her voice: "I have *never*, I repeat, *never* bought one fucking dish we didn't need or one fucking dish that wasn't worth more than what I paid for it."

Now J. G. could be reasonable: "Don't you think this discussion of dishes is a bit off the subject? I believe you know what I was getting at."

Then C. E. called J. G. a son of a bitch and a few other things but I couldn't quite hear. Whatever it was made J. G. laugh—an infuriating laugh. Again it was quiet over there.

I think she was standing near the head of the bed, just on the other side of the wall, and I think he was lying on the bed staring at the ceiling. I ran into the kitchen to get a glass to put to the wall so I could hear better. When I came back, they were still in their same places. With the glass I could hear C. E. trying to calm down her breathing.

Then, in a different tone she was trying out, C. E. said, "I want this to work, honey, but I just *hate* it here. I gave up a lot for us."

That last was exactly the very worst thing she could have said. Out of all the possible combinations of words on this earth, she just picked the most inflammatory. J. G. was instantly on his feet. His tone was, as they say in the novels, menacing: "Don't start that fucking list again. Don't remind me again of what you came from down to this. If you know what's good for you, if you start that list one more time, if you begin to mention one item on that list, I will walk out that door and not come back. Do you hear me?"

Haven't they seen the movie? *Everybody* has seen this one at least ten times. This is the one about the pioneer couple in the Klondike or in the Oklahoma oil fields—one of those Godforsaken *raw* places. This is the one where there's money in it for them if they can just stick together. She had chosen to forsake all to support him in his cock-eyed scheme because she *believes* in him; she's left some big house with panelling in St. Louis or a position at a one-room schoolhouse in Ohio. It's all swell at first, but after a while, what with no trees and the dust and all, she gets bitchy and sad and homesick; she wants to bug out. But then the mine caves in and she almost loses him, or the gusher comes in and he is vindicated. So she comes to her senses and chooses all over again for love his choosing money for the both of them. It always works out OK.

Not much more got said. C. E. did not drop the other shoe. J. G. opened and closed the bureau drawers and C. E. cried on the bed. He got dressed and she just cried. Then the front door to the apartment opened and closed. J. G. had gone off to work with the last word but without any breakfast. C. E.'s crying stopped as soon as he was out the door.

But then the door opened again. J. G. came back in the bedroom and I could hear that he stood beside the bed. He had thought of something he wanted to say. C. E. was holding her breath. His voice was cold, cold. He said he changed his mind and that if anyone leaves it will be her since she is the one who hates it here. He pays the rent so if anyone walks out it will be her and she should, once and for all, make up her Goddamned mind. Then she suggested that he should go fuck himself and he left, slamming the door.

I was glad, as I thought of him driving to work, that he was going to a very safe occupation only three miles away. Because in the movies this is when the big accident happens to the man in the plot. But maybe this is the version where his fate arrives in the form of good luck; maybe this is J. G.'s lucky day and he will get promoted to manager in the Tampa, Florida store. In any case, C. E. and J. G. have finally completed a fight they've been working on for more than a year. Not too much mincing of words this time, and no premature apologies, though one could wish for a somewhat fuller expression of feelings and positions. J. G. and C. E. have for the first time pretty good ideas about where the other stands: she wants to leave but loves him and doesn't have the nerve; he can't stand the way she blames him and is not about to go anywhere on account of her. It isn't clear if he loves her or not.

As J. G. was driving to work to meet his fate, C. E. was sobbing on the bed. My ear was pressed to the glass against the wall.

"Oh Jerry, Jerry," she cried, "I love you, you bastard, you prick, you fuck." She cried and cried: "Scumbag. Cocksucker. Jerk. I love you, my Jerry, you shit."

C. E. sobbed on and on. My ear was getting numb. My legs were going to sleep from kneeling on the bed for so long. Finally she got up and blew her nose and went to the bathroom. Then I heard her go to the living room and I think she dialed the phone. This is where she lost me. I can't hear the living room very well. I bet she was calling her mother.

I wonder what you think of all this, of me eavesdropping on their most intimate moments. I venture a guess that you disapprove of my eavesdropping, see it as a feminine weakness. But as long as I know all this stuff, I might as well tell you. Right?

I left C. E. to talk to her mother. I tried to put J. G. and C. E. Mazza out of my mind. I knew that if I hung around here some of the substance of this fight would soak through my thin interest in mainly the form of it. I didn't want to hear apologies or packing or any more crying. When I caught myself beginning to list the fates that could keep you from coming back to me, I dressed fast, grabbed the car keys, and headed for the Grand Union.

I took the longer way, the back road, past the few farm houses, barns, and fields left in this fast-growing "bedroom" community.

I drove slowly with the windows down and the hot air off the asphalt blowing up through the sleeve of my tee shirt. The heat made me contemplative. I drove with one hand like a greaser, a day-dreamer, a teenager. There were plenty of teenagers out this summer morning. I didn't know they got up this early. They were driving or walking or riding bikes everywhere I looked. They're like me, I guess: no place in particular to go, but it's nice to get out of the house. (No, I am not complaining. I have everything I need, though, like most people, not what I've dreamed of. I'm a woman luckier than most. When you are here I have all the kissing and conversation and more that any girl could ask for. And when you're gone, I overhear plenty. What I have is an embarrassment of ordinary riches—you who love me and whom I love, a roof over my head, more than enough to eat, a car that gives me no trouble, a card at a good library, only a little housework to do, and good friends and a loving family—though they are far away.)

Teenaged girls—in twos and threes—walked on the shoulder in the shade of a long row of old maple trees (planted by some long-dead farmer who crosses nobody's mind when they cross his field). They stepped over the beer cans thrown out of cars last night by the boys their pants are hot for. They were heading for the shopping mall. This morning all these undersized females washed their hair and blew it dry. They dressed carefully in tube tops, fake gym shorts, high heels. They have clear skin, small hips, brown legs. They wear pink and blue like babies. Their little bottoms stick out of their tight shorts. They look like baby hookers.

I drove slowly past the teenaged virgins proceeding under the arch of the double line of maples, but even going this long way I still got to the Grand Union before they opened the doors and before I'd thought of a good reason to be there. There was a small clump of people waiting to be let into the Grand Union—serious shoppers with lists and with coupons to redeem, with places to go after this, with reasons and purposes up the ass. In a few minutes, though, the manager (his photo is above the Service Desk) opened the doors and we shoppers fanned out into the aisles, pushing carts with cold handles.

A lot more goes on in the supermarket than you might imagine, though what happens there is surely insignificant in the scheme of things, under the steel and salmon evening sky. I often overhear women speak in anger or in wonder to no one in particular: "So this is the way it's going to be" to the can of beans up nine cents from last week; "Those cocksuckers" the ladies say across the little babies sagging in the carts; "Heads will roll" murmurs a lady in a 200-dollar dress. And, amidst all this wonderful American illusion of choice and plenty, there is always the confusion of comparing apples and oranges, two-ply and one-ply, pitted and unpitted, boneless and boned. Under the Muzak and the green-white light we ladies try to imagine or organize or dream up or just want one more week with its meals. We choose over and over in the aisles—between our time and our money, or between our time and his money. Out of the chaos of plenty offered we try to select what could be significant, what could keep body and soul together and we choose whether to feed body or to feed soul. But the hardest choice of all is who do we feed and who do we choose for.

There in the supermarket, my love, couples and women and children and sometimes men trail like comets' tails the charged electric air of domestic situations, of wanting something they haven't got, of turning what they do have into enough. I am thankful that in all this confusion I don't have to compose my face in case I meet someone who knows me. Because anyone could read on my face that I am trying to read in the writing on the shelves if it is better to get a job or better to make straight the path through the shag, smooth the troubled brow, cook the good food. I try to read there if our strain is financial or neurotic or cultural or just plain cussedness. Should I look harder for work, even though I know we'll be here less than a year? Should I go back to school and become an unemployed something else? Should I introduce myself to my neighbors who do not introduce themselves to me? The practice of which virtues is appropriate in this place? And who should I do them on? My primary virtues are virtues of omission: I don't drink or take drugs; I don't make many long distance calls to my family or friends; I don't shop a lot or buy much or charge things or cost you very much money. I try to keep my bitter tongue in my mouth, though as soon as you come back—even though our voices are sweet when we speak long distance once a day—that mean tongue is the one I will use on you. My main virtues are practiced in bed. There among the cabbages, I wanted you back here, my love, so I could practice and practice on you.

Should I ask you what to do? Should you tell me?

I bought plain yogurt, an artichoke, scallions, Sara Lee pound cake, mushrooms, and the *Times*. As the checker picked up my artichoke she asked, "What do you do with one of them once it's on your plate?" So I told her how to take the leaves off and dip them in butter and how to draw the leaves between your teeth and how to take out the choke, and I told her how to eat the best parts, the hearts and the bottoms. "I guess I wouldn't have much use for one of them after all," she allowed.

I drove back here through the heat and put the groceries away. I closed up the windows and turned on the air conditioner to shut out any sounds of the Mazzas, to clear the air of the smells of the former tenant that this heat and humidity were drawing up out of the shag.

I decided to go for a walk. Though we have lived here for several months, I had only driven around the subdivision. I needed to make myself more at home, take a look around and see where it is really that we live.

Do you know that farmhouse right in the center of all these apartment buildings? I decided to walk over there. All of Marshridge Acres must have been at one time farmland, though not good farmland. Whoever owned that house must have owned this land.

I walked across grass and on asphalt. They made no provision here for people afoot, except around the pool and to and from the tennis courts. I breathed slow in the heat. The air conditioners made a terrific enclosing racket, drowning out nature and TVs and traffic.

When I got close to the farmhouse yard, I saw three workmen there clearing away debris—pieces of aluminum siding and pink bats of insulation, ladders, power tools—and putting all this stuff in a panel truck. The house had been re-sided. The old peeling clapboard had been replaced with wider, bright-white aluminum clapboard. I stood beside the fence to look for a minute when a workman came up to me and said, "She's home. Go in on the back porch and holler." I had intended to just walk around the perimeter of the yard, but I went right into the yard and onto the back porch.

A grandmotherly, cheerful old lady met me on the porch and wasn't at all surprised to see me. She was chewing something. "Come in, come in," she said, "come in, come in, come in." And she sort of shooed me through the kitchen, where I could smell something baking, into the dining room where she had evidently been eating her lunch. "Come in, come in, come in," a little too loud. The lady sat me down at her dining table. Then with one hand on my shoulder she poured me a glass of iced tea. I felt as if I had stepped through a looking glass.

In front of me, the dining table was cluttered with half-empty casserole dishes and with little dishes of leftovers. The nice lady set a clean plate in front of me, and, as she put on it a spoonful or two from each of those dishes, she told me what each of those leftovers was, who had made it, when they'd brought it over, and who all she'd given some to. She walked around the edge of the table dishing out for me, and reciting the history of lasagna, macaroni-and-cheese, applesauce, a green bean casserole, chicken-and-rice, pot roast, Swedish meatballs, and more—all cold. When my plate was full she sat down and picked up her fork, then put it down and looked at me: "Who are you anyway? From one of the insurance companies? One of the aluminum siding people?" Before I could say more than no, she started telling me about how they'd decided to sell the place and move south now that they could afford it since they'd sold all the rest of the farm to the developers. They'd decided—her and Jim—to fix it up and sell it. And Jim, being the shrewd businessman he was, called every one of the aluminum siding outfits in the Yellow Pages, *every one,* and had them come out and make him a written estimate. Even though most would have done business based on a word and a handshake, Jim was a smarter man than that. So he picked the lowest bid and she picked the color—white. And the one he picked was the fastest, too; they came out that same week. "But before they could get out here, Jim passed away. I woke up last Tuesday morning and he was dead. Went in his sleep. Simple as that."

She paused and I started to stand up. I said, "Oh no, I'm so sorry."

She said, "Sit down and eat your lunch." She took a few bites and I just sat there.

At the end of the dining room, centered between two long windows, was a big, white freezer which just then began to hum loudly. I noticed that the other end of the dining-room table was covered with newspapers and that the newspapers were covered with cooling cookies. They must have been what I'd smelled when I came in the door. I couldn't think of anything to say or a way to get out of there.

She said she'd given six dozen cookies to the aluminum men, as she called them. "It's my hobby—making cookies. Here, I'll show you."

She got up and opened the freezer and I could see that it was almost full of plastic containers with adhesive tape labels and she said the containers were all full of cookies. "What kind do you like? I got all kinds."

I said I didn't know.

She said, "Sure you do. Chocolate? Chocolate fudge? Chocolate chip? Peanut butter? Sugar? Sugar with walnuts? Oatmeal plain? Oatmeal with raisins? Macaroons?"

"Macaroons."

"Fine. I'll give you some. How many of you at your place?"

I told her one.

"One dozen then." She picked up her empty plate and carried it out to the kitchen, came back carrying a plastic bag from a shoe store and some more plastic containers. She began putting the fresh cookies into the plastic boxes and labelling them. "Taste one of these" or "Try this" she'd say now and then and I ate the still-warm cookies she handed me. Then she took out a box of frozen macaroons and counted out one dozen and put them in the shoe bag. The warm ones she put in the freezer. Finally she was finished and she handed me the bag: "These'll be thawed before you get home."

I started to cry.

"Now, honey, don't cry. You didn't even know Jim, did you? And besides he was an old man, it was his time, and he died a fairly rich man." She gave me a paper napkin off the sideboard to dry my eyes on and she stood beside me and patted me on the shoulder, though not with the same friendliness as before. She wanted this display over with.

"The kids down in Tucson wanted me to call off the aluminum people, but I said, 'No, Jim wanted this done and he signed on it.' I decided we'd just go ahead with it. So they came the day before yesterday, and, I think out of respect, they've finished up in close to no time at all. They're clearing up now. I've already given them their cookies and paid them in full now that the job's done. They got the full amount right away just like Jim would have done. He was a handsome man right up to his dying day. Come here, honey, I'll show you."

She took me by the elbow and led me into the living room where the shades were drawn. She sat me down on the sofa and sat down beside me. In front of us on a coffee table was a slide projector aimed at a white space over the fireplace where usually hung the

222

large picture of cows grazing in a meadow, now propped against a recliner. She turned on the projector and fiddled with it. I watched the white light above the mantel. When the colors finally came on and when she finally got them focussed, what I saw there was a picture of an old hawk-faced man lying dead in his casket. He had on rouge. He was holding a pearl rosary, surely for the first time. I was paralyzed.

She showed me a whole carousel of pictures taken of Jim's wake, his funeral, and the dinner after. There was slide after slide of Jim in his casket from different angles and the flowers and relatives and the limousines. There was one of her standing next to Jim in his casket: one of her hands rested lightly on the casket; the other held her black purse. She was smiling at the camera. There was one of the casket closed and the flowers piled around in front and in front of the flowers stood two scared little children, like Hansel and Gretel, holding hands. There was a picture of her dining room table laden with food no one had yet dipped into—some of the same casseroles I had just eaten a few bites of. She talked all the way through the slides, adding names and details to those weird friezes. I couldn't listen and I couldn't tear my eyes away, though I wanted to get up and run out of the house.

Finally she turned the projector off and opened the shades and then she looked hard at my face. "You have no cause to take it so hard, you know." This was a reprimand. "Death is just a part of life. Are you one of the aluminum people? From the bank? An insurance company?"

Again I said no, but I found myself saying that I had originally come here to see if she had a room to rent, but now that I saw it was out of the question . . .

"Out of the question? Who says? And who said I had a room to rent? Whatever made you think that in the first place? There's no sign out front and no advertisements anywhere and besides that it never occurred to me to *rent*, just to sell. But since you mention it, it might not be a bad idea, that is, until I do make up my mind who to sell to." She took me by the elbow again, "Come on, I'll show you what I've got and we can talk about it; you can choose."

First she showed me her (and Jim's) bedroom just off the living room, told me she didn't think she could rent me that one, even if it was the biggest one in the house and she could probably get the most for it. And anyway, she said I probably wouldn't want to sleep in a room where a man died last week as I looked pretty suggest-ible. She said it didn't bother her in the least because death was just the end of life, you know. I agreed that it was and said I would never even think of asking her to give up her own bedroom. There was a catch in my voice.

She grabbed my arm hard and shook it: "For heaven's sake! Jim was no prize. As a matter of fact, he was a perfect son of a bitch! I won't say I'm glad he's dead, but, frankly, I won't miss him, though he was a provider, I can say that for him. Why, when we moved here as newlyweds, we had nothing but his idea to have a dairy farm. Nothing. Now look at all this. I can go anywhere I want and get just about anything I could ever want. He was a provider. And a looker. Jim was a looker."

(My love, dead, this Jim looked like a wet hawk. Jim who? I didn't know their last name.)

I said, "What was his name, ma'am."

"Want," she said.

"What?"

"Want. Want. Jim Want. Want's our name."

"Oh."

"I know, it's odd. It used to be something else in some other country, but now it's Want. And has been for some time. W. A. N. T. Want." She was tired of having to explain her name. "What's yours?" she asked me.

"Mazza," I said. "Cynthia Elaine Mazza. M. A. Z. Z. A."

"What kind of name is that?"

"Shortened," I said. "It used to be something else too. In some other place."

Mrs. Want took me upstairs, by the arm, and showed me four bedrooms on the second floor and a funny little attic room on the third. The four bedrooms were crammed full of furniture and boxes of stuff, but the attic room, being too hard to get to, was almost empty. There was blue-flowered paper on the walls and moth-eaten white sheer curtains at the little window. I looked out and saw the aluminum men's van run over several of Mrs. Want's peony bushes, then lay some rubber across the parking lot. Mrs. Want was now telling me how she was going to clear out a lot of the junk downstairs, sell it (she offered to sell me a toaster oven, a mixmaster, a meat grinder), and rent out all these empty rooms for the time being. She was going to advertise, and repaper—if she absolutely had to—and get some other clean single ladies (besides me) in here. There were dollar signs in her eyes. She said, "Of course, when I do sell and move south, the deal's off." She named an outrageous sum for rent and I said I'd let her know.

She took me back downstairs and handed me the bag of macaroons and walked with me into the yard to admire her siding. "Never has to be painted," she said, "This is what they like, these young people. I don't blame them at all. Never have to paint. Never."

I started to leave.

"Where's your car?"

"I walked."

By then I was far enough so that she had to almost yell. "Walked?"

"Walked. Walked. Not far," and I pointed in the direction of Building 32.

I walked very fast away from the sound of her voice, toward our apartment, through the heat and the drowning sound of all the cooling systems. On the way, I threw the venal old grandmother's macaroons into a dumpster, and I thought about how to tell you about her so that we would both think this funny. I prayed to never be relieved to lose you, as Mrs. Want was to lose her Jim. I want no release, only grief.

When I got home to our air-conditioned apartment, I closed the curtains, took a bath, straightened each of the rooms, made the bed, made a list, got myself a peach, and got into bed. I turned on the TV to watch one of the soaps. Right away I went to sleep and, probably set off by the blue-flowered wallpaper in Mrs. Want's attic room, I had a very vivid dream of home.

I dreamed about Christmas when I was a girl in New Hampshire. I dreamed that I was lying in the little cherry bed that I slept in until I went away to college. I dreamed that I was breathing in the cold air of my unheated attic room, dreamed the moonlight shining through the frost on the window, and, outside, shining on the snow all around. I felt with my legs and my arms the cold cotton sheets, the heavy wool spread. I dreamed my parents and aunts and uncles and grandparents downstairs laughing. My sisters were in the next room breathing softly, and the mice—descendants of mice that haunted other generations of my family—were busy in the walls. We had lived on this farm in America for a long time, but

225

in this dream, around the house lay the hills of Bethlehem. Out in the moonlight beside their shadows, shepherds and sheep moved slowly across the snow toward a neighbor's yellow light.

When I woke up, it was very cold in our apartment. "Rockford Files" was on the TV. I had slept for hours.

I got up and turned off the TV and the air conditioner and opened the windows. The sun was setting. I stood shivering beside the living room window watching the orange glow in the west. As the sky darkened, I realized that part of the glow was close, not on the horizon, and was getting brighter. There was a fire and it was here in Marshridge Acres. One of the buildings in the complex was burning. I dressed quickly and grabbed a jacket.

In the hallway, I met the Mazzas—also dressed hurriedly for the fire, their faces flushed and excited. As we three—temporarily hooked together by disaster—made our way across lawns and parking lots, past the tennis courts and buildings just like ours, we kept expecting to see the building just beyond in flames. But the fire was not in one of the apartment buildings. Mrs. Want's house was on fire and was surrounded by fire trucks and hoses and men and equipment.

"Oh no," I found myself saying over and over. "Oh no oh no." I had never seen a house on fire. There were great roiling billows of dark smoke and violent orange tongues of flame from the upper windows and the roof. The noise was awful—the shouts of firemen and the sightseers, the pumps, the motors, water rushing, glass breaking, and, worst of all, the terrible roar that was fire consuming.

Mrs. Want's aluminum siding was holding up very well; it was turning her house into a furnace.

After a length of time that I cannot estimate, the flames died down. The streams of water were shut off, the hoses slackened, all pumps shut down. From the blackened shell columns of smoke or steam rose like beams of light into the still night above. Orange ·· · 1·· glowed and then went out like fireflies here and there on the blackened walls.

I overheard people now in the crowd talking about Mrs. Want and the recent death of Mr. Want. I saw the manager of Marshridge Acres rushing around acting like the host or the head mourner. No one seemed to know Mrs. Want and no one knew if she was in there or not. The firemen began to pack up their equipment. The ambulance left. The sightseers began to go home. In the morning when the ruins have cooled they will come back and sift through the ashes for Mrs. Want. She might be in there or she might not.

As I walked away, I saw ahead of me C. E. and J. G. Mazza walking slowly with their arms around each other. So they've seen the movie.

When I got back to the apartment the phone was ringing. It was you and all this is why I sounded funny and you see why I couldn't begin to go into it on the phone. I love your voice; it has the same textures as your skin. In it I hear the heft of your body.

I didn't sleep all night. I lay in our bed and waited for the sun to come up on another day you will come home. I stayed in bed and waited for the sun to replace my hard words with the lovely wordlessness of your long legs and back, your blue-eyed glance, your arms that are never still, your smile that teases. I teased myself with imagining what it would be like this time, how you would save my days, especially some very sweet hours.

Even though I know you become to me when you are away all my reasons and my refuge, I also know that your coming back and your going away are twin reliefs. I love my solitude but count the hours until you come home. I love you, not more, but better when you're away; my voice clears. Though I planned carefully what to feed you and what to wear, as I was lying there in the sun this morning, I could not keep away the sureness that when I hear your car in the parking lot, your step on the stair, your key in the lock, what will well up in me will be the same old voice and there I will be—the table set nice, all dressed up, and at my very worst.

When I got up and went to the window, I saw that the ground fog was rising in the low places and that the parking lot and the grass sparkled with silver. As I stood there, the street lights went out and the sun came up warm and ripe over this silent and motionless brand-new place.

Oh my love, my sweet difficult love, what resources, what muscles, what skills, what lobes, what ceremonies, what love play or foreplay, what work, what money—*what* can we use that we are not using to keep us together, to keep us—against such odds—loving and loving each other?

I know this: Under this morning sky which is beautiful and through this air which is thick, I see—and maybe it's a lack in my eyes, you tell me—only the buying and selling of barren land and striving, striving on tennis courts. I have tried in my small ceremonies to change what we have into enough, but I can't. You and I have set out across this weird suburban landscape without any supplies but money and love, air and light. I'm afraid and I want to go back.

nominated by New England Review/Bread Loaf Quarterly

THE GHOST OF SANDBURG'S PHIZZOG

fiction by NORBERT BLEI

from THE GHOST OF SANDBURG'S PHIZZOG (Ellis Press) and
STORYQUARTERLY

Now of course there are two Sandburgs . . .

—Borges

Sandburg rising, a prairie, a harvest of wheat to his hair, spewing out a dry weed stuck between his teeth . . . rubbing prairie rose from his eyes. Brushing both hands through his hair for that part, slightly to the right, combing each side down straight through his fingertips over the top of his ears.

Yawning, breaking, shoveling for his black shoes, his gray stockings. Baggy brown pants, wrap-around-twice worn leather belt, white shirt tucking-in back, sides, front. Galluses over the boney shoulders. Buttons. And a bow tie: blue.

Naw, I'll wear me a red bandanna today, gargling, sandpaper throat, bricklayer's hands . . . parting the clean curtains, checking his phizzog in the glass. That face he's got. Ah, the looking-glass man . . .

Time? The storyteller you can't shut up, he goes on.

Halsted Street, Harrison Street, Peoria Street . . . the traffic in his eyes. Broken faces, police whistles, iron fences, loving hunger, Grant on his bronze horse in Lincoln Park under snow, a man singing, streetcars, neighbors at work, washerwoman, fish crier, cripples, passers-by with silence written on mouths, killers, working girls, masses of asses in the fog.

We were the people, maybe.

Sandburg shaking it off . . . I wish to God I never knew you now.

Shaking off his phizzog, scattering myth in a puff of milkweed seed. Now cornhusker, haystack hair, cornflower eyes, golden squash skin, prairie wind stealing his songful breath.

I am, I am, I am . . . dust, laughter, stars, radishes, eggs, frost, crow, kiss, water, muskrat, nigger, pumpkin, river, railway, limestone, walnut, potato blossom, concertina, melon, eagle, loam, lover . . .

The ghost of Sandburg shoveling off to the streets, trailing a busted walnut guitar behind him. A bucket of mud, a pail of smoke, a pocket of Illinois prairie. No more.

I wish to God I never . . .

Stockyard slaughtered, hogbutcher heaven, skyscraper stillborn.

They tell me you are crooked, are wicked, are brutal . . . Yes, the people? The family of man? *Always the mob*.

Perish the people.

People putting handles on all the languages. Talk is cheap. Naming's become numbering. Hold. Still.

Shovel it all under, let me work.

I *was* the people, wasn't I? Chicago citizen, Illinois boy, Midwest meanderer.

Oh, I had a zoo inside me once . . .

There is a baboon in me . . .

I study the language of taverned souls, an intoxication still . . .

"The old lady left. I threw her out. Women go crazy in their change-of-life. She was drinking a bottle of VO a day. Tomorrow I go to traffic court. I left her the car, you see, and she's been gettin all these goddam traffic tickets. All parking tickets mostly. She didn't think I'd know. But I got a letter to appear in court the other day for all those goddam traffic tickets she's been gettin. Well, they're in for a big surprise if they think I'm goin to pay them. I'm just gonna tell them she left me, and she's got the car, and those tickets are all hers. What the hell can they do to me? If I get a nice judge, he'll understand. A good judge should understand about women. Hell, why should I have to pay for her mistakes?

"Three things happen to a woman when she goes through this. Either she hits the bottle for good, or she starts jazzin anything that moves, or she wises up. I know where she hangs out. Her

230

friends tell me what she's doin. I know what she's doin every night. Drinkin like a fish, jazzin like a mink. Not wisein up at all.

"I'm workin on a trap. I got this dolly all lined up. Just me and this babe somewhere, and then my wife all of a sudden comin in and catchin us.

"If that don't work, then I'll divorce her. That's all. That's all I can do."

Everybody loved Chick Lorimer . . . Nobody knows where she's gone . . .

Let us be honest about women . . . Ziegfeld girl, harlot, Mom, loving one easy, loving another hard . . . I loved only one . . . women of lights and nights and shadows, o beauty of no takers . . . old woman asleep in the hallway, woman with her head flung between her knees, gypsy gal, the mouths of women, river lady, girl with a rose in her hair, lady with a laugh . . . I know the birth of all your songs.

Mammy.

Sorrow shaken from white shoulders.

I wish to God, I wish to God, I wish to God . . .

There is an eagle in me . . .

The ghost of Sandburg sups. Nighthawk hopper. Shadow and light.

I have such a heart's hunger for you all . . .

"Yeah, but since I left Weight Watchers I'm on my own diet now, and I lost fifteen pounds all on my own. I eat everything. Almost everything. And I got a new pant suit, size eighteen, you should see me in it! I should wear it all the time. It's blue and it looks so nice on me. I'm happy in it. I could never wear anything like it before with my wide ass. Tonight I'm going dancing with my friend. He fixes watches. Yeah, so I gave him this watch to fix. I'm always breaking watches. You're supposed to shake them like this when they stop. When my husband was alive, he'd fix them like this, you know . . . bang the hell out of them on the table. And so I do the same thing. But my friend who fixes watches says you're not supposed to do that with watches. He taught me how to handle them. You're supposed to just shake them gently like this. But I can't. I still bang the hell out of them, and they still don't work. Naw, it's nothing serious. He's just a friend. He's a nice guy. We go to a lotta places together. We have a good time. No motels or nothing. We can go to my place for that if we want. Why spend money on a motel? How do you like this watch? It's hot. I spent five bucks on it. My watch-fixer thinks it's worth twenty-five bucks. He's different. I never went nowhere with my husband. He liked to just stay around the house. That was all right. And then he died. He was a policeman. We buried him in his uniform. It was real nice. He had his stamps and his coins . . . he had his own things to do. And when he was going to the hospital, the last thing he said was, 'Toodle loo.' He thought he was coming back, you know. And when they told me, I just screamed. That's all. But I kind of think he knew he was going, you know? The last few months he kept asking me about his policies. One of the kids wanted to cash in a policy for a car. And he kept asking me where that policy was for the kid. We don't have it, I told him. We have three twenty-year endowment policies, that's all. Three of them. And he was painting and fixing things around the house. He knew he was going to go. He made me an end table out of bricks. I always wanted an end table out of bricks and he never made me one. Make me an end table out of bricks, I'd tell him. I'm gonna make you an end table out of bricks now, he said, just before he went. And he did. It was so nice. I painted it white and decorated it with ivy and everything. It's funny how he was doing all these things like he wasn't gonna be around. My oldest kid is a mission-ary in Indochina. He was in Indochina all last year and this year he's coming home. Next year he's going back to Indochina. Last week me and my friend went to New Salem. I want to know all about Lincoln. Tomorrow me and my friend are going to the museum. I never knew so much was inside museums before. I want to find out about the laser beam. My kid knows all about it so I want to learn something about laser beams so I know what he's yaking about when I see him. Last year I went to the Planetarium around Christmas to see the star of the East. It's supposed to be in the same place it was when Christ was born. But I couldn't find it. Jesus, my car is really a wreck. Yesterday the muffler fell off, and the goddam thing was just hanging there. What am I gonna do? I yelled in the middle of the street. And then some kid on a bike came by and tied it up with his patrol belt. With his patrol belt! Jesus, I tell you I've been having more fun. I never went anywhere before, now I go everywhere. Tonight I'm going dancing. Do you know the new dances? There's nothing to them. You just keep moving. We never know when it'll be us, you know. We've all got to face the same battle. I like to move fast."

Neighborhood. Backyards, fences, gangways, alleys, street lamps, garbage cans, milk wagons, ice wagons, junk wagons . . . "Raaaaaggg-saaaaa-Lionnnnn," kick-the-can, cherry trees, robins, apple trees, sparrows, elms, Lombardy, catalpas with long thin black cigars for smoking, morning glories, gutters, wooden steps, front porches, back porches, Hide-and-Seek, "Here I come ready or not!" corner taverns, buckets of beer, pinochle, priest, parish, "Step on a crack and break your mother's back," woodsmoke, burning leaves, squirrel, robin, bluejay, screens, moths, crystal sets, radio, the polka hour, concertina, dumplings, sauerkraut, working-stiffs, homemade wine in the basement . . .

A light in the basement window . . . the ghost of old man Daruva turning the spigot on a fifty gallon barrel of homemade Yugoslav wine, filling a mason jar, slumping on a stool near the cement basin, feeling the presence of the past.

Daruva, slaughtering stockyard Slav, blood shoveler . . . the ghost of Sandburg sipping wine beside him, the work and the weary, taking up a song:

I dreamed I saw Joe Hill last night
Alive as you and me
"Why Joe, you're ten years dead," I said.
"I never died," says he.

Daruva squeezing the wine of the mason jar tight in both hands, steeped in blood . . . No vork, no money, vork, no money, is no good, nothing. Is same! Is always altogether same . . .

I knew that the WPA
Can't do a thing for me.

Daruva, a broken jar of wine at his feet, the stool upturned, dangling by a lampcord like a side of beef from the basement rafters.

"I never died," says he.

There is a fox in me . . .

I stand before the place that was once Minsky's burlesque.
I hang around a while, hankering for the drum roll and the baggy
    pants comic, the
screech of the curtain, the dancer with the moon in her hair.

AND NOW STRAIGHT FROM PARIS JUST BACK FROM A
  SWING
THROUGH SOUTH AMERICA HERE NOW LIVE ON
  STAGE
STORMY!

Oh, she was young, oh, she was blond, oh, she was beautiful,
  and oh, she could
dance a Lake Michigan moon out of the water and onto her hair.

Swaying in black velvet, she moved out of the river within me,
Oh, prairie night, oh, dark thunder, oh, shimmering woman, I
  am one of your boys.

For Stormy could bump and she could grind and she could
  bump
And she could grind, and she could promise you everything
Even up there in the last row of the highest balcony.

And she could bounce it to you and to you and to you
And you knew she could promise you everything and never
  deliver the goods.

Cause Stormy could bump and she could grind and she could
  put her hands
On her hips and guarantee all moveable parts cause Stormy
  vibrated the
Language of burlesque and had mastered the art of the bump
  and the grind
And the terrible taunting technique of the tease.

She bumped it to the boys in the first five rows,
She threw it to a mailman, ready to receive and deliver her
  message
In all kinds of weather.

Oh, she could bend and she could shake and she could throw her
  head
Right into your lap . . . She could dance until the Broadway
  Limited left

The next day, and she could bump all night moving freight
	through silent
Fields of tall corn, with only a whistle for song.

She could strip to the essentials, moving it barely at all,
Cause Stormy stripped clean was anti-climatic, cause Stormy all
	in
Her finery was burlesque bonafide . . .

. . . the boom-da-da-boomda-da-boom of the drums,
the drop of the gloves,
the swish of the hips,
the toss of the moonily hair,
the backside journey of a zipper,
the coyly turned head, and the wink,
the this-is-what-you've-been-waiting-for-boys,
as Stormy turns and bares to face all the world of Minsky's,
and the lights go out and the curtain and the curtain screeches
	shut,
and the music and the hand-clapping and the shouts,
and I tell you there was nothing in the world like this,
		but a wind died down.

The babbling tongues of the people, that was mine. I talked
turkey. I loved tongue . . . *I rise out of my depths with my*
language: gabby, plugged nickel, slam-bang, wigwag-ging, gazook,
babbler, pig-sticker, Dago, baboon, Hunky, riffraff, humdrum,
goofy, ooze, hugger-mugger, on the fritz, bunkshooter, Wop,
cockeyed, skiddoo, the little two-legged joker, lickety-split, pal,
ramshackle, ragtime jig, hoosegow, phooey, son-of-a-gun, coolie,
snootful, dopey, wrongheaded fool, gimme mazuma . . .
	You rise out of your depths with your language: persona, unreal,
I don't believe it, beautiful, fantastic, super, too much, cool, bad,
laid-back, doing, bottom line, viable, nuances, syndrome, uptight,
real person, doing your own thing, dynamite . . .
	Dynamite super farout laid-back me, doing poetry . . .
	Well, I'm doggone happy, a gabby mouth, my heart goes pit-a-
pat; I'm just a palooka, young feller, loony lingo, a broken face
gargoyle, a jabberer with a snootful of plain words, horsefeathers,

rubbernecks, no baloney . . . gimme Shee-caw-go, ragtag and
bobtail, the rabble, the peepul!
   Where to? What next? There are no handles upon a language.

Lines based on certain regrets that come with
rumination upon the painted faces of women on
North Clark Street, Chicago
   Women of the night, dark side, shadow light, back streets of the
black heart, painted women under the gas lamps luring the farm
boys . . . Businessmen, fathers, suburban church leaders, conven-
tioneers, policemen, firemen, Billy-Grahamed beings, small town
sheriffs, midnight poets all . . . all beating a path to Salvation, Your
name is Woman . . . They tell me you are wicked, and I can't
believe them . . .
   COMPLETELY NUDE . . . EXCITING YOUNG WOMEN . . .
   MANICURES . . . BODY PAINTING
"Hi," she says, leaning into the closed door.
Hello, I reply. I'm Carl Sandburg. You probably never heard of me
before.
"Nope."
I've had such a longin for a manicurin in this City of Big Shoulders.
"All right," she says without smiling. "I'll explain the rules."
Rules, Ma'am? I didn't come to play poker or write a sonnet.
"I undress completely, but there's no touching beneath the waist.
Remember that.
Did you come for a manicure or a body painting, did you say?"
Well, I came to finally realize a painted woman . . . but I do have
this bad case of writer's cramp, stiff joints . . .
"Okay. You've got fifteen minutes."
For what?
She smiles and proceeds to tell a poor poet what else a body can do
with itself, if a body cared to, while she disrobes, dismantles . . .
Did you ever hear of Minsky's?
She shakes her head, no.
I could maybe write a poem about you this way . . . luring the farm
boys, I think.
Cornstalk thin, dry, vulnerable, sad as a scarecrow.
Please, I can see all there is to see. Is this all a body's worth, fifteen
bucks? Don't you even dance?
"Just a look and a manicure, Buster."

Exciting young woman, these are sensitive fingers, careful now.

"Are you a doctor?"

No, a gabber, a babbler, a wordsmith.

"What's that?"

Someone who goes around and just keeps talking to himself, hoping others will hear how carefully he speaks to them.

"You're not law and order, are you?"

That's a fine question. I play tennis without a net, so it's been said.

"Do you want to paint me?" she asks, holding a palette of colors.

He dips his fingers in green paint and writes the word "prairie" just beneath her navel. He blows it dry, then touches his lips to it.

"Once I was painted with birds," she says. "Once with flowers. And there was a guy who came in here one time, a minister, who knelt before me, then painted the ten commandments on me from my neck to my knees."

There are some things even a poet can't imagine in his own city. Some things that make no sense at all and are best kept in the dark, in that zoo inside ourselves.

"Are you through, Buster? Cause your time is up.

God, what a phizzog you got."

There is a wolf in me . . .

Sandburg, beseiged by contemporary bullshitters, dressed in saffron robes, dressed in white, dressed in black, on all the contemporary Chicago corners . . . gimme mazuma or it's Hell's bell . . . Sandburg hightailing it for west Madison, pausing briefly beneath Claes Oldenberg's Batcolumn, smiling . . . *Here is a tall bold slugger* . . . then skedaddling for a mission on Madison, still searching for *the* word.

He takes a back seat. His phizzog lost in a sorrowful sea of faces, brother, can you spare a dime, waiting to be fed . . . but not just yet . . . first, the Word to fill the stomach, stem the hunger pains.

The Reverend Cracker appears singing, "Something Got a Hold of Me Last Night," urging every last man Jack to stand, I SAID STAND! while he and his cronies pray out loud. Cracker ascends a high platform studying every face, including Sandburg's phizzog.

"How many you men had the flu?" he hollers. "Some people tell me Heaven's like Chicago!" he taunts. "SOME PEOPLE TELL ME HEAVEN'S LIKE SKID ROW," he screams.

One crony plays a guitar, another a violin. One begins to sing,

"There's One Way, One Way to God," Cracker joining in. Sermon, song, sermon, song, sermon, song . . . the song of hungry stomachs.

Brother, I am fire . . . seethes Sandburg.

"Last Night I Dreamed an Angel Came," sings Cracker. A black man closes his eyes and sways gently with the song.

"Say 'Amen,' " says Cracker.

"Amen," say the men.

"THAT'S ALL YOU MEN ARE IS DIAMONDS IN THE ROUGH," screams Cracker. "THAT'S ALL. THAT'S ALL. AM I RIGHT, MEN? AM I RIGHT? HOW MANY YOU MEN THINK THE REVEREND CRACKER'S RIGHT? SEE? SEE? NOW ALL YOU MEN THERE SAY THE REVEREND CRACKER SPEAKS THE TRUTH, SAY IT! THERE . . . THERE . . . NOW ALL YOU MEN SAY, 'AMEN.' "

You come along squirting words at us, shaking your fist and calling us all damn fools so fierce the froth slobbers over your lips . . .

"HOW MANY YOU MEN THINK WE SHOULD THROW THAT MAN OUT? HOW MANY YOU MEN THINK HE SHOULD STAY BUT KEEP HIS MOUTH SHUT? . . . NOW ALL SAY, 'PRAISE BE THE LORD' . . . THAT'S RIGHT . . . THAT'S GOOD . . . YOU KNOW, THAT'S THE MOST SENSIBLE THING YOU SAID ALL DAY . . . There's NOBODY deserves to hear the truth TWICE if they heard it ONCE!"

I like to watch a good four-flusher work . . .

I will be the word of the people.
Mine will be the bleeding mouth
from which the gag is snatched.
I will say everything.

There is a fish in me . . .

Midnight. Sandburg at the bar in the Billy Goat Tavern, listening to a young newspaperman . . . "I was out of it. I found that if I could just make it to work in the morning and back home at night, that would be an accomplishment. Just to get there and to get back. The rest of the day was a haze. I could not function. And if a man cannot function, a man is totally lost.

"I was hallucinating. I was paranoid. There was no me, nothing whatsoever. I tried a psychologist. Ha, he was something. A few weeks after I began going to him, he shot his own wife.

"I know what the depths are, believe me. I know what hell is all about. I was so psychotic I could have killed a man. I'm sure of that. I wouldn't have done it. No, no, no . . . I wouldn't have killed a person. But I could have. And that's the frightening thing. I share every murderer's heart now. And that's the wonder, that we are brothers.

"I understand Hesse now, and all the business of being reborn. When you're down that far, something must happen. After my psychologist shot his wife I realized that no one, nobody was going to help me. If I was to survive, it would depend on me.

"So I began with just a few things, mundane tasks that I could accomplish. Like washing the windows, cutting the lawn. Little daily accomplishments. Gradually I built upon them. Physical things.

"Mind and body. That is really an important thing. I had let my body go to waste. I was fat, sloppy, ugly. So I began to work on this. Putting my body back in shape. That's why I took up diving. I discovered the significance of my body in the way my mind worked.

"I discovered all sorts of things about myself, about my life under water. Water is grace. Water is a way to live. It is such a fantastic world down there. I love to dive off the Keys in Florida. The clarity under water is so pure it is astounding. I can see for a half a mile or more.

"The fish swim right beside me. I've had a barracuda this long look right into my mask and turn, and swim right along with me. They are not startled. It is almost as if I am one of them. I love life under water."

And when has creative man not toiled deep in myth?
Sandburg sunrise . . . doffing his cap to the ghost of Daley in the

Civic Plaza . . . Sandburg bidding adieu, a Polaroid camera in hand, asking a city worker to take a shot of him under the Picasso.

Click . . . Sandburg's smiling phizzog . . . the black pools of Picasso's eyes shining down upon him . . . the dimple on Daley's double chin, winking.

Sandburg merging with morning down Dearborn, melting into mosaic Chagall, seesawing through Calder's red stabile, snapping photos of a free floating poem.

Sauntering Sandburg on LaSalle Street, tossing wooden nickels into the doorways of all the bank buildings . . . then rising to the heights of Sears Tower.

Sandburg quaffing a dark beer at Berghoff's . . .

Sandburg haunting Kroch's & Brentano's in search of himself . . .

Sandburg riding an Art Institute lion . . .

Sandburg sitting at a table, nodding off, reading himself in the Chicago Public Library:

Let me be monosyllabic today, O Lord . . .
    a crony of old men
    who wash sunlight in their fingers and
    enjoy slow-pacing clocks.

Sandburg on the bridge, Michigan and Wacker, perusing the Gothic heights of the *Chicago Tribune* building, laughing with his white teeth, turning to the *Chicago Sun-Times*, remembering the old *Daily News* . . . under the terrible burden of destiny laughing as a young man laughs . . . then boarding the Mercury Sightseeing Boat under the bridge for a last view from the lake, city of the floating shoulders, and a final winding farewell down the Chicago River, head singing so proud to be alive and coarse and strong and cunning . . . the ghost of Sandburg ascending on cat feet, river trailing from his shoulders in fog, nocturne in a deserted urban landscape, the Sandburg spectre floating Chagall blue rivernight; starnight, moonlight, merging all the waterways . . . Rock River, Fox River, Chicago River, Desplaines River, Kankakee River, Illinois River . . . downstate, O Sangamon, Kaskaskia, Little Wabash, Little Muddy . . . O home in Illinois.

I find myself in prairie . . . my peace, my past. I need prairie to pitch into, plant myself, dream myself corn, loam, wheat, grass, goldenrod, red rooster, yellow summer rain, oak, daisy, dark running water, farmer, flat land, horse, honey locust, purple thistle, crabapple, hollyhock, prairie rose, crow, meadow, dogwood, thrush, rock, violet, redbud, hawthorne, prairie woman, moss, barn, snow, owl, ice, seed, prairie man, blizzard, corncrib, wind, silo, chicken, dog, limestone, bushel basket, hazel nut, spade, goat, plow, Holstein cow, north star, bullfrog, graveyard, haystack, Abe Lincoln, prairie child . . .

The story lags.

The story has no connections.

The story is nothing but a lot of banjo plinka plinka plunks.

Time? The storyteller you can't shut up . . .

Son, you ain't seen nothin yet . . .

I lean into a prairie wind, plant an acorn, be an acorn, become an oak, spreading my arms into branches, holding hawk, owl, crow, cradling them gently, lifting them off, I am trees, I am woods, I am forests, wind dancer, twilight, horizon, first star, deepest night, harvest moon, daybreak, the rising sun . . .

Rooster crow, robin song, dog bark, the splash of a frog, the whir of a windmill, the neigh of a horse, the hum of an insect, the banging of a screen door, the smell of coffee perking . . .

I stretch and lie down in prairie grass, chuckle over my own phizzog in blue heaven looking glass, slip a long thin green weed between my teeth, play with it gently inside my mouth . . .

I extend my arms beside me beyond reach, working a pair of angel wings in earth as a child would do in snow, working my legs the same way . . . Kickapoo, I say, Chillicothe, papoose, caboose, hallelujah on top a dung pile, bypaths, gravestones, bandannas and a wagonload of radishes . . . plinka, planka, plunk, my guitar has strummed itself into bird . . .

Working myself on the earth, into earth, till the image is shrouded in prairie, the earth angel becomes shadow, becomes light while grasses rise all around once more—two prairie roses for what the eyes once saw, and wind tickling the longest thin straw held in a mouthful of roots, jabbering in me still.

nominated by Andre Dubus

AGAINST NATURE

by JOYCE CAROL OATES

from ANTAEUS

> We soon get through with Nature. She excites an expectation which she cannot satisfy.
>
> —Thoreau, Journal, 1854

> Sir, if a man has experienced the inexpressible, he is under no obligation to attempt to express it.
>
> —Samuel Johnson

The writer's resistance to Nature.

It has no sense of humor: in its beauty, as in its ugliness, or its neutrality, there is no laughter.

It lacks a moral purpose.

It lacks a satiric dimension, registers no irony.

Its pleasures lack resonance, being accidental; its horrors, even when premeditated, are equally perfunctory, "red in tooth and claw" et cetera.

It lacks a symbolic subtext—excepting that provided by man.

It has no (verbal) language.

It has no interest in ours.

It inspires a painfully limited set of responses in "nature-writers"—REVERENCE, AWE, PIETY, MYSTICAL ONENESS.

It eludes us even as it prepares to swallow us up, books and all.

* * *

I was lying on my back in the dirt-gravel of the towpath beside the Delaware-Raritan Canal, Titusville, New Jersey, staring up at the

242

sky and trying, with no success, to overcome a sudden attack of tachycardia that had come upon me out of nowhere—such attacks are always "out of nowhere," that's their charm—and all around me Nature thrummed with life, the air smelling of moisture and sunlight, the canal reflecting the sky, red-winged blackbirds testing their spring calls—the usual. I'd become the jar in Tennessee, a fictitious center, or parenthesis, aware beyond my erratic heartbeat of the numberless heartbeats of the earth, its pulsing pumping life, sheer life, incalculable. Struck down in the midst of motion—I'd been jogging a minute before—I was "out of time" like a fallen, stunned boxer, privileged (in an abstract manner of speaking) to be an involuntary witness to the random, wayward, nameless motion on all sides of me.

Paroxysmal tachycardia is rarely fatal, but if the heartbeat accelerates to 250–270 beats a minute you're in trouble. The average attack is about 100–150 beats and mine seemed so far to be about average; the trick now was to prevent it from getting worse. Brainy people try brainy strategies, such as thinking calming thoughts, pseudo-mystic thoughts, *If I die now it's a good death,* that sort of thing, *if I die this is a good place and a good time,* the idea is to deceive the frenzied heartbeat that, really, you don't care: you hadn't any other plans for the afternoon. The important thing with tachycardia is to prevent panic! you must prevent panic! otherwise you'll have to be taken by ambulance to the closest emergency room, which is not so very nice a way to spend the afternoon, really. So I contemplated the blue sky overhead. The earth beneath my head. Nature surrounding me on all sides, I couldn't quite see it but I could hear it, smell it, sense it—there is something *there,* no mistake about it. Completely oblivious to the predicament of the individual but that's only "natural" after all, one hardly expects otherwise.

When you discover yourself lying on the ground, limp and unresisting, head in the dirt, and helpless, the earth seems to shift forward as a presence; hard, emphatic, not mere surface but a genuine force—there is no other word for it but *presence.* To keep in motion is to keep in time and to be stopped, stilled, is to be abruptly out of time, in another time-dimension perhaps, an alien one, where human language has no resonance. Nothing to be said about it expresses it, nothing touches it, it's an absolute against which nothing human can be measured. . . . Moving through space and time by way of your own volition you inhabit an interior consciousness, a hallucinatory consciousness, it might be said, so long as breath, heartbeat, the body's autonomy hold; when motion is stopped you are jarred out of it. The interior is invaded by the exterior. The outside wants to come in, and only the self's fragile membrane prevents it.

The fly buzzing at Emily's death.

Still, the earth *is* your place. A tidy grave-site measured to your size. Or, from another angle of vision, one vast democratic grave.

Let's contemplate the sky. Forget the crazy hammering heartbeat, don't listen to it, don't start counting, remember that there is a clever way of breathing that conserves oxygen as if you're lying below the surface of a body of water breathing through a very thin straw but you *can* breathe through it if you're careful, if you don't panic, one breath and then another and then another, isn't that the story of all lives? careers? Just a matter of breathing. Of course it is. But contemplate the sky, it's there to be contemplated. A mild shock to see it so blank, blue, a thin airy ghostly blue, no clouds to disguise its emptiness. You are beginning to feel not only weightless but near-bodiless, lying on the earth like a scrap of paper about to be blown off. Two dimensions and you'd imagined you were three! And there's the sky rolling away forever, into infinity— if "infinity" can be "rolled into"—and the forlorn truth is, that's where you're going too. And the lovely blue isn't even blue, is it? isn't even there, is it? a mere optical illusion, isn't it? no matter what art has urged you to believe.

* * *

Early Nature memories. Which it's best not to suppress.

. . . Wading, as a small child, in Tonawanda Creek near our house, and afterward trying to tear off, in a frenzy of terror and revulsion, the sticky fat black bloodsuckers that had attached themselves to my feet, particularly between my toes.

. . . Coming upon a friend's dog in a drainage ditch, dead for several days, evidently the poor creature had been shot by a hunter and left to die, bleeding to death, and we're stupefied with grief and horror but can't resist sliding down to where he's lying on his belly, and we can't resist squatting over him, turning the body over . . .

. . . The raccoon, mad with rabies, frothing at the mouth and tearing at his own belly with his teeth, so that his intestines spilled out onto the ground . . . a sight I seem to remember though in fact I did not see. I've been told I did not see.

* * *

Consequently, my chronic uneasiness with Nature-mysticism; Nature-adoration; Nature-as-(moral)-instruction-for-mankind. My doubt that one can, with philosophical validity, address "Nature" as a single coherent noun, anything other than a Platonic, hence discredited, isness. My resistance to "Nature-writing" as a genre, except when it is brilliantly fictionalized in the service of a writer's individual vision—Thoreau's books and *Journal,* of course—but also, less known in this country, the miniaturist prose-poems of Colette *(Flowers and Fruit)* and Ponge *(Taking the Side of Things)*—in which case it becomes yet another, and ingenious, form of storytelling. The subject is *there* only by the grace of the author's language.

Nature has no instructions for mankind except that our poor beleaguered humanist-democratic way of life, our fantasies of the individual's high worth, our sense that the weak, no less than the strong, have a right to survive, are absurd.

In any case, where *is* Nature? one might (skeptically) inquire. Who has looked upon her/its face and survived?

* * *

But isn't this all exaggeration, in the spirit of rhetorical contentiousness? Surely Nature is, for you, as for most reasonably intelligent people, a "perennial" source of beauty, comfort, peace, escape from the delirium of civilized life; a respite from the ego's ever-frantic strategies of self-promotion, as a way of insuring (at least in fantasy) some small measure of immortality? Surely Nature, as it is understood in the usual slapdash way, as human, if not dilettante, *experience* (hiking in a national park, jogging on the beach at dawn, even tending, with the usual comical frustrations, a suburban garden), is wonderfully consoling; a place where, when you go there, it has to take you in?—a palimpsest of sorts you choose to read, layer by layer, always with care, always cautiously, in proportion to your psychological strength?

Nature: as in Thoreau's upbeat Transcendentalist mode ("The indescribable innocence and beneficence of Nature,—such health, such cheer, they afford forever! and such sympathy have they ever with our race, that all Nature would be affected . . . if any man should ever for a just cause grieve"), and not in Thoreau's grim mode ("Nature is hard to be overcome but she must be overcome").

Another way of saying, not *Nature-in-itself* but *Nature-as-experience*.

The former, Nature-in-itself, is, to allude slantwise to Melville, a blankness ten times blank; the latter is what we commonly, or perhaps always, mean when we speak of Nature as a noun, a single entity—something of *ours*. Most of the time it's just an activity, a sort of hobby, a weekend, a few days, perhaps a few hours, staring out of the window at the mind-dazzling autumn foliage of, say, Northern Michigan, being rendered speechless—temporarily—at the sight of Mt. Shasta, the Grand Canyon, Ansel Adams's West. Or Nature writ small, contained in the back yard. Nature filtered through our optical nerves, our "senses," our fiercely romantic expectations. Nature that pleases us because it mirrors our souls, or gives the comforting illusion of doing so. As in our first mother's awakening to the self's fatal beauty—

> I thither went
> With unexperienc't thought, and laid me down
> On the green bank, to look into the clear
> Smooth Lake, that to me seem'd another Sky.
> As I bent down to look, just opposite,
> A Shape within the watr'y gleam appear'd
> Bending to look on me, I started back,
> It started back, but pleas'd I soon return'd,
> Pleas'd it return'd as soon with answering looks
> Of sympathy and love; there I had fixt
> Mine eyes till now, and pin'd with vain desire.

—in these surpassingly beautiful lines from Book IV of Milton's *Paradise Lost*.

Nature as the self's (flattering) mirror, but not ever, no, never, Nature-in-itself.

* * *

Nature is mouths, or maybe a single mouth. Why glamorize it, romanticize it, well yes but we must, we're writers, poets, mystics

246

(of a sort) aren't we, precisely what else are we to do but glamorize and romanticize and generally exaggerate the significance of anything we focus the white heat of our "creativity" upon . . . ? And why not Nature, since it's there, common property, mute, can't talk back, allows us the possibility of transcending the human condition for a while, writing prettily of mountain ranges, white-tailed deer, the purple crocuses outside this very window, the thrumming dazzling "life-force" we imagine we all support. Why not.

Nature *is* more than a mouth—it's a dazzling variety of mouths. And it pleases the senses, in any case, as the physicists' chill universe of numbers certainly does not.

* * *

Oscar Wilde, on our subject: "Nature is no great mother who has borne us. She is our creation. It is in our brain that she quickens to life. Things are because we see them, and what we see, and how we see it, depends on the Arts that have influenced us. To look at a thing is very different from seeing a thing. . . . At present, people see fogs, not because there are fogs, but because poets and painters have taught them the mysterious loveliness of such effects. There may have been fogs for centuries in London. I dare say there were. But no one saw them. They did not exist until Art had invented them. . . . Yesterday evening Mrs. Arundel insisted on my going to the window and looking at the glorious sky, as she called it. And so I had to look at it. . . . And what was it? It was simply a very second-rate Turner, a Turner of a bad period, with all the painter's worst faults exaggerated and over-emphasized."

(If we were to put it to Oscar Wilde that he exaggerates, his reply might well be: "Exaggeration? I don't know the meaning of the word.")

* * *

Walden, that most artfully composed of prose fictions, concludes, in the rhapsodic chapter "Spring," with Henry David Thoreau's contemplation of death, decay, and regeneration as it is suggested to him, or to his protagonist, by the spectacle of vultures feeding off carrion. There is a dead horse close by his cabin and the stench of its decomposition, in certain winds, is daunting. Yet: ". . . the assurance it gave me of the strong appetite and inviolable health of

Nature was my compensation. I love to see that Nature is so rife with life that myriads can be afforded to be sacrificed and suffered to prey upon one another; that tender organizations can be so serenely squashed out of existence like pulp,—tadpoles which herons gobble up, and tortoises and toads run over in the road; and that sometimes it has rained flesh and blood! . . . The impression made on a wise man is that of universal innocence."

Come off it, Henry David. You've grieved these many years for your elder brother John, who died a ghastly death of lockjaw; you've never wholly recovered from the experience of watching him die. And you know, or must know, that you're fated too to die young of consumption. . . . But this doctrinaire Transcendentalist passage ends *Walden* on just the right note. It's as impersonal, as coolly detached, as the Oversoul itself: a "wise man" filters his emotions through his brain.

Or through his prose.

* * *

Nietzsche: "We all pretend to ourselves that we are more simple-minded than we are: that is how we get a rest from our fellow men."

* * *

> . Once out of nature I shall never take
> My bodily form from any natural thing,
> But such a form as Grecian goldsmiths make
> Of hammered gold and gold enamelling
> To keep a drowsy Emperor awake;
> Or set upon a golden bough to sing
> To lords and ladies of Byzantium
> Of what is past, or passing, or to come.

> —William Butler Yeats, "Sailing to Byzantium"

Yet even the golden bird is a "bodily form taken from (a) natural thing." No, it's impossible to escape!

* * *

The writer's resistance to Nature.

Wallace Stevens: "In the presence of extraordinary actuality, consciousness takes the place of imagination."

* * *

Once, years ago, in 1972 to be precise, when I seemed to have been another person, related to the person I am now as one is related, tangentially, sometimes embarrassingly, to cousins not seen for decades,—once, when we were living in London, and I was very sick, I had a mystical vision. That is, I "had" a "mystical vision"—the heart sinks: such pretension—or something resembling one. A fever-dream, let's call it. It impressed me enormously and impresses me still, though I've long since lost the capacity to see it with my mind's eye, or even, I suppose, to believe in it. There is a statute of limitations on "mystical visions" as on romantic love.

I was very sick, and I imagined my life as a thread, a thread of breath, or heartbeat, or pulse, or light, yes it was light, radiant light, I was burning with fever and I ascended to that plane of serenity that might be mistaken for (or *is*, in fact) Nirvana, where I had a waking dream of uncanny lucidity—

My body is a tall column of light and heat.

My body is not "I" but "it."

My body is not one but many.

My body, which "I" inhabit, is inhabited as well by other creatures, unknown to me, imperceptible—the smallest of them mere sparks of light.

My body, which I perceive as substance, is in fact an organization of infinitely complex, overlapping, imbricated structures, radiant light their manifestation, the "body" a tall column of light and blood-heat, a temporary agreement among atoms, like a high-rise building with numberless rooms, corridors, corners, elevator shafts, windows. . . . In this fantastical structure the "I" is deluded as to its sovereignty, let alone its autonomy in the (outside) world; the most astonishing secret is that the "I" doesn't exist!—but it behaves as if it does, as if it were one and not many.

In any case, without the "I" the tall column of light and heat would die, and the microscopic life-particles would die with it . . . will die with it. The "I," which doesn't exist, is everything.

But Dr. Johnson is right, the inexpressible need not be expressed. And what resistance, finally? There is none.

* * *

This morning, an invasion of tiny black ants. One by one they appear, out of nowhere—that's their charm too!—moving single file across the white Parsons table where I am sitting, trying without much success to write a poem. A poem of only three or four lines is what I want, something short, tight, mean, I want it to hurt like a white-hot wire up the nostrils, small and compact and turned in upon itself with the density of a hunk of rock from the planet Jupiter. . . .

But here come the black ants: harbingers, you might say, of spring. One by one by one they appear on the dazzling white table and one by one I kill them with a forefinger, my deft right forefinger, mashing each against the surface of the table and then dropping it into a wastebasket at my side. Idle labor, mesmerizing, effortless, and I'm curious as to how long I can do it, sit here in the brilliant March sunshine killing ants with my right forefinger, how long I, and the ants, can keep it up.

After a while I realize that I can do it a long time. And that I've written my poem.

nominated by Antaeus

Four from THE BAUDELAIRE SERIES

by MICHAEL PALMER

from ACTS

A man undergoes pain sitting at a piano
knowing thousands will die while he is playing

He has two thoughts about this
If he should stop they would be free of pain

If he could get the notes right he would be free of pain
In the second case the first thought would be erased

causing pain

It is this instance of playing

he would say to himself
my eyes have grown hollow like yours

my head is enlarged
though empty of thought

Such thoughts destroy music
and this at least is good

* * *

Words say, Misspell and misspell your name
Words say, Leave this life

From the singer streams of color
but from you

a room within a smaller room
habits of opposite and alcove

Eros seated on a skull as on a throne
Words say, Timaeus you are time

A page is edging along a string
Never sleep never dream in this place

And altered words say
O is the color of this name

full of broken tones
silences we mean to cross one day

* * *

Desire was a quotation from someone.

Someone says, This this. Someone says, Is.

The tribe confronts a landscape of ice.

He says, I will see you in the parallel life.

She says, A miser has died from the cold; he spoke all
his sentences and meant no harm.

My voice is clipped, yours a pattern of dots.

Three unmailed ones have preceded this, a kind of illness.

Now I give you these lines without any marks, not even
a breeze

dumb words mangled by use

like reciting a lesson or the Lord's Prayer.

How lovely the unspeakable must be. You have only to say
it and it tells a story.

A few dead and a few missing

and the tribe to show you its tongue. It has only one.

* * *

There is much that is precise
between us, in the space

between us, two of this
and three of that

(after Vallejo)

nominated by Paul Auster

THE ALIAS: A SURVEY

by ALBERT GOLDBARTH

from INDIANA REVIEW

You aren't you. You're sleeping. Now your bones are
marionette sticks in a dark heap, waiting morning.
We can't help but be to time this way as chameleons are
to color. In their world, degrees of the globe to the east,
the cells in the wild lime skin of one are dials tuning in
a tame rock-gray; another's a flower by now,
in a convocation of flowers wearing the deep carnelian robes
of authority and a golden anther crown. Nearby, a turtle
belly's a witch doctor's mask. A worm's the crest
of a tongue some fish lure other fish with. A john

could be a dog ("You're a dog," she says) at the feet
of a whore in dominatrix latex. "Lick my boots,"
she says, and "Wouldn't my little doggie like a pussy
to play with," and "Bark for it then." And then
he leaves—he's Boss at the office, Daddy at home, and
Honey Bear in bed that night for a reason that's none
of my snoopy poet's business or yours, though in that
dark, we all know, wives can lightly stroke their husbands' eyes
like field anthropologists who think they really understand
the whole of a culture behind its ceremonial masks. Who

knows? The gods have spoken through a court dwarf
tranced by candles, through a burly hulk out hauling
geese in from traps when he thinks he sees "a sign"

—and spoken alike. Through spots the size of indigo-purple
grapes, on a raw ram's liver. Through trees. Through
seizures. Through little idols sculpted from horn.
Through some of our skulls like an off-duty medic being
beeped to emergency business. The radar marker sweeps
around a weather-scope and it's only another oracle of the one
true universe showing us her folds. If a goose did

land in a baited field, frighten, and fly, the feather
left behind might enter the life of a tip kept ready
every day in a crystal well of ink—the former life of a tip
implanted in the quick amino acids of a living bird would be
its long-gone homeland. If an author lifts a quill to write
a credible novel of espionage, he'll use a nom de plume
—you have to be careful. One expatriate double agent
disguised as a birder paces the city park, and waits
for the operative only known as The Clown to bike up
whistling. Across the street from the park, the dominatrix

—her name is Lucy—is home at last, and brusquely pulls the
    curtains
closed to all of this. For a while she watches their green batiste
weave ripples from the sun. Then she goes to her father's
darkened room. She thinks she can actually smell the
cancer. The arm that's left is as spare as a sceptre; he
raises it, with a tired aplomb, admitting her. And then of
course the long routine of soiled pads and prescriptions. By
the time she's done, the living room curtains are gray. She
hates it. A late bird calls in the park, then stills. Her bourbon
lowers. She eases back to his room and sees

sleep make his face into someone she loves.

nominated by Linda Bierds

UNWRITTEN LAWS

by BILL TREMBLAY

from DUHAMEL: IDEAS OF ORDER IN LITTLE CANADA
(BOA Editions Ltd.)

You couldn't climb into Bernadino's garden and
just take vegetables. He'd throw a brick at you
with his Mighty Joe Young chest muscles from
hauling lead in a wheelbarrow between surprised-
looking ripped out fire hydrants in the Water
Supply Company's back lot and the white-hot
crucible, the plugs holding their twisted shapes
a minute before slipping like glacier walls into
a silver sea to be poured off again into molds.

When he came home after work to tend his tomatoes
neatly staked and tied with thin strips of white
cloth, he would know, or some enemy you didn't
know you had might tell on you because Jesus said,
"The least you do to mine you do to me," and it went
both ways. Then you'd get it. You had to mind
the priests. If you had diabetes so bad the Boston
doctors said having another baby would kill you,
you still had to because God wants new souls.
But if Jesus died to save us all, why didn't history
stop? The priests said that was a mystery.

You couldn't walk on the Fong's front lawn
because Sarge slept under the porch in criss-
crossed shadows. His slobbery lower jaw sputtered

as he snored off his last bucket of beer. If you
shook his ground, his K-9 training would wake him.
Everyone knew Sarge could bite through chains and
put gouges in your thigh that turned purple then
yellow. You couldn't even think of paying old lady
Guardino to poison his chow. He was a war hero.
He bit the butt of the Generalissimo. On Memorial
Days, Lyle Fong would leash him and march behind
Le Cercle Canadien Drum & Bugle Corps with a
doughboy helmet buckled to his head at a jaunty
angle with a cracked, dirt-brown leather chinstrap.

You couldn't play with yourself or you'd get like
Shakey Joe, spastic on the railroad tracks, and
what he did with his fly unbuttoned was awful red.

You couldn't swear within earshot of a dragonfly
or it would sew your lips up. That's why it's real
name was "flying needle." You had to mind the nuns
or they'd put you in the encyclopedia.

You couldn't go into the Central Avenue Spa.
Its show windows hadn't changed since the owners
went to New York City to celebrate Truman's miracle
come-from-behind victory over Dewey and saw stores
on 42nd Street with cheap telescopes lying tilted up
at fading stars warped on blue corrugated night sky—
its door the gateway to inside, whoosh of big electric
fan, a middle-aged man with a mustache waiting for
the counterman to stop serving two high school girls
cherry flips like he was asking them a big favor,
zipping panics at the window for cops who knew he'd
sell anything from behind the glass showcases with
their buck knives and Marine Band harmonicas.

A row of red plastic tuffets along the counter,
and beyond, two sets of booths where a rainbow mafia
jukebox gloomed the studs of leather jackets humped
over hamburgs from the grill black as a pagan altar,
floorboards showing through cratered tiles that

checkerboarded into darkness under the broken EXIT
sign and on out into God only knew what blind alley
where you would stagger some midnight because you
were only human in the hot beery stench of Dragon's,
lost, bricked in, melting, begging for another
chance, looking up at a narrow strip of stars in
the shape of a big capitol I.

nominated by Vern Rutsala

BEAUTIFUL

fiction by C. E. POVERMAN

from PLOUGHSHARES

LAST NIGHT Laura called and asked if I could stand in for her at Bloomingdale's. Lancôme was doing a promotion, and Laura was supposed to work at the cosmetics counter making up from three to eight.

I always do my own make-up, but one ad I did for BMW, they wanted a make-up artist. That's where I met Laura. The BMW shoot. Laura's a make-up artist.

In the BMW ad, I'm on a big black BMW, we're coming right into the camera, head on. I'm looking haughty and cool; there was an incredible response to that ad. Sales. Guys called BMW wanting to know who I was, where they could meet me. Men live in a dream world half the time: where they could meet me. . . .

After we shot the ad, I was knocked out. Everyone's always surprised, oh, you're exhausted, all they did was shot some pictures, but you're not just sitting there, you're projecting something. It takes pure energy. It's intangible, something you learn to do, to project energy, a look.

So I sat there glassy-eyed, and the photographer pulled out a mirror and we did some lines and then the guy who owns the BMW dealership pointed to the bike, yes? and we got on, why not? We're going along; over his shoulder I'm watching the speedometer, the tach, and this clock. The clock has a second hand that is still and jumps a couple of seconds and is still again. I was watching that. All of a sudden he laid it into a corner, I grabbed him hard around the waist, and he laughed and shouted back, "You're beautiful, but you're no different."

"What's your big problem?" I shouted. He just laughed. I couldn't wait to get away from him. Men have to make a run at you.

Anyway, Laura did my make-up for that BMW ad. Laura herself is nice, nothing much to look at, but she does understand make-up. She works for one of the theaters and a tv studio. I like her, but when she asked if I could stand in, I hesitated. It's only ten dollars an hour. And then, you never know what you're going to run into on something like that. I mean, it's probably women who are unhappy with themselves or have decided to change or maybe they just want a miracle. I figure whatever it is, I'm not going to be able to make them real happy. If their problems were fixable, would a few more cosmetics help?

But I sensed something in Laura's voice—an appeal. Maybe something between her and her old man. She told me about him. Sometimes he knocks her around. Long sleeves once on a hot day to cover the black and blue marks. I figured he gave her a black eye or something and that's why she couldn't go out. I heard it in her voice. Pain. The creep! She got married when she was nineteen and they've been married ten years and he's an up and comer in real estate and has her talked into one of these deals where he sees other women and tells her about it and she pretends she doesn't mind, very enlightened, right? though it's half killing her. I'd never put up with that crap. And any man hits me—and ever touches my face—I'll kill him. But Laura puts up with it. One time he asked her to leave town for a week so he could have some slut in and she did, she left, dumb! she pays half the rent on that place. When she called to say she was coming back, he asked her to stay away another two days. And when she finally let herself into the apartment, the bed was unmade, there were wineglasses and cigarette butts all over the night tables, the place still stank from the bitch's perfume.

I met the guy once, Laura's husband, and he is a little short nothing, a pure nothing. I wanted to smack him for what he was doing to Laura. I hate little men anyway. I can't look at a man who isn't at least taller than I am. At least. When I asked Laura why she put up with him, she just got this quiet faraway look in her eye, really sad, I felt so sorry for her, she seemed helpless, she must have a terrible self-image. So I figured Laura had a black eye and I said, okay, I'd do the Lancôme promotion.

So here I am at home, getting ready, doing my make-up. Sometimes when I'm in front of the mirror, I feel like I've been here forever, making up, but you can't be lazy. Every time you step out, you're advertising yourself, whether it's for a job, a go-see, whatever. Everything has to be right. Hair, make-up, stockings, every detail.

I stand naked in front of the mirror, curlers in my hair, and then I start. Lately, before I put my curlers in, I check my hair for gray or white hairs. That may sound odd, I'm only twenty-four, but my grandmother, my mother's mother, went gray early—in her twenties—and I look a bit like her. So I check for gray, first. I'm not sure what I'll do about it, but . . .

Then I put the curlers in, step back and look at myself. The goddamned pill puts the weight on me, my breasts and just above the curve of my hips, and the camera always adds another ten to fifteen pounds. Between the camera and the pill, I sometimes wonder if I stand a chance. I hate the pill, the diaphragm is a mess and a turn-off and you never really know, either. I don't trust it. I tried the i.u.d. for a while, but that gave me hellish cramps and an awful flow. And I don't think they're safe, i.u.d.s. I've heard horror stories of perforated uterus walls. And a friend of mine got pregnant with one of the damned things. The i.u.d. just disappeared in her. They couldn't find it. And she's pregnant. She decided to have the kid and when the kid is born, he has the i.u.d. in his hand.

So I'm on the pill. I hate the pill but the diaphragm . . .

One afternoon, Richie and I are suddenly in the mood and then, you know, I had to pull away and go get the thing and get it fixed up with the orthogoo and when I got back, I said, "Here, you put it in."

He was turned off, but tried to hide it. "What for?"

And I said, "To know me better, I want you to know everything about me."

He still looked uncomfortable. I said, "Don't you want to?"

He looked at the diaphragm and said, "Well, I'm not really sure how it fits, or what to feel for, or when it will be in place."

"That's okay, that's the point, for me to teach you about me." I put the diaphragm down and got a piece of paper and drew him a diagram of female anatomy, simple, really. The uterus, the cervix, the vagina, and I started explaining how the lip of the diaphragm hooked onto . . .

I glanced over. He was sitting there staring at the pad, looking a little squeamish and kind of puzzled.

"What's that look on your face?"

"What look?"

He stared at the diagram. I pointed. "What do you make of it?"

He took the pencil and in the middle of the uterus, he drew a question mark and smiled a little and said, "It looks like circles within circles."

"This is a joke to you, isn't it?"

"I just want you to leave me a little bit of mystery. You know, the Grand Inquisitor says, mystery, magic . . ."

"Don't give me that! I finished U.S.C., I know The Brothers K, too."

He's a big Princeton grad trying to turn all of his English lit into pop culture, he's trying to make it as a screenwriter, in the meantime he's doing PR for one of the studios. He did get something going last year, but it got put into turn-around after a few months. That's how we met. He was lining up some models for promotion work.

"A little mystery isn't so much to ask. . . ."

He stared at the sketch. I snatched it from him.

"Don't have your mystery on me. There's no goddamned mystery when I end up on a table with my legs spread and a vacuum sucking at my uterus."

I've never really seen anyone turn pale, though I've heard the expression, but he turned pale.

"Kim . . ."

"I'm the one, not you. Women are always being prodded, poked, having fingers stuck in us, whatever. You don't want to put the diaphragm in, but you don't mind sticking your cock into me, do you?" I grabbed the diaphragm. "Here, maybe you guys ought to have this thing stuck up your asses once in a while to know what it's like."

I got up and walked out leaving him with the diaphragm in his hand. I felt bad right away and went back and tried to kiss him and apologize, but he pushed me away. For a second I thought he was going to hit me—though he never has—and I said, "Don't hit my face, Richie!" He just looked at me with disgust, got dressed and walked out. We didn't talk to each other for a couple of days. I really don't know why I got so angry with him—and suddenly. Old patterns, I guess. Anyway, we got over it. And I don't use the diaphragm now. I'm not even sure I can blame him for not wanting to stick his hands into all that mess.

I'm still making up when Richie comes out of the bedroom. Except for my pantyhose, I'm naked.

"Got an ad, Sausage?"

Sausage. The squeezed way the pantyhose makes me look.

"Sausage, yourself. No, the Lancôme promotion. I told you last night. Don't you listen to me?"

"Right. Forgot."

"Do you think I'm getting fat?"

"No."

"Here?" I squeeze some around my hip.

"Nope."

"Five pounds."

"Nope, it's lady-like."

"Come here."

"I'm here."

"Closer. Stand next to me. Look at yourself in the mirror beside me. Aren't you a pretty man?"

He looks embarrassed. I look at him in the mirror with me. "See us. Look at you. You're pretty. Look, Richie."

"You look."

"I am looking. You look, too."

"If you want to look at me, why look in the mirror?" He tries to turn me toward him. "Why not look right at me? Here I am."

"It's different, that's all. Different perspectives. I've told you that before. Lenses, mirrors."

"But . . ."

"Oh, Richie, don't be a bore. Look at us. Together. I can't see us together without a mirror, that's all." I turn him back toward the mirror. But he doesn't look. I look. He can't. It embarrasses him for some reason. But I can look. I look at us. We are so different. They tell me I am beautiful, one of the prettiest women in L.A. They tell me I could make it in New York and maybe I'll go, I've been thinking about that. But beautiful or not, if I liked women, I wouldn't be the kind I'd go for. I'm just so pale. My skin is absolutely white and hardly ever tans. I have small precise features. Small features like mine are very photogenic. But I don't think I'd go for them. I look at Richie next to me. He's tall and slim and has incredibly soft skin, almost like a girl's. It's not fair for a man to have such soft skin. His skin is softer than mine, almost hairless, and a beautiful fawn color. He has long dark lashes and large eyes, also dark and soft, like a pretty colt or deer, and his face is full of colors, highlights, blushes, light and shadow. If Richie were a girl, he'd be the kind I'd like.

"Richie, you are pretty. Are you going to the studio?"

"In a while. They said I could work at home this morning, but to be there for a meeting at three. I'll be working late tonight. . . ." He trails off, points to the molding. "Pawprints."

Richie didn't care about the molding until he repainted the bungalow.

"I didn't do that."

"I sure don't use blue eyeshadow."

"Well, don't complain, you like the finished product."

"If you spent as much time reading as you did making up, you'd be . . ."

"I'd be some gimpy librarian."

He shrugs, turns, "I've got to change." He heads into the bedroom.

He kids me about make-up. He's got a little streak of the old Puritan ethic about cosmetics, but it kind of fascinates him, and a lot of times I'll look back in the mirror and catch him looking up from the paper and just staring at me. He'll smile shyly. I've tried to show him what I'm doing, each step, how it works, but he can't really let himself get into it. But once, when he got stoned, I told him I was going to make him up; he was just listening to the Moody Blues and hardly paying any attention, so I sat down and started, he didn't resist, he had a big faraway smile and was mumbling stony shit about the moon and stars, he is so sweet when he's stoned, and I just started putting the make-up on him, not really sure what I was looking for or where I wanted to go with it, but just putting on some basic contouring and seeing where it would lead, letting it take me where it would, and all of a sudden I knew just what I wanted, light, shadow, contouring, I saw this incredibly beautiful woman in him, I didn't want to scare him or threaten him, men are in a dream world half the time, anyway, so I started talking about a philosophy teacher I'd had and this thing he'd said

264

about looking for yourself in the other sex and Richie was nodding and then I said, and looking for the other sex in yourself, I kind of reworded it a little, and Richie said, "Did you sleep with him?"

I think I would have been furious if I hadn't been stoned, but Richie and I can talk to each other stoned, we get more accepting, and so I laughed and said, "No, no, I didn't sleep with him. . . ."

"Because," he said with that smile, "it would be alright, I'm just curious."

Not that I hadn't thought of it, sleeping with the philosophy teacher, he was very good-looking and had a real passion for philosophy—he made it seem like real life—but no, I decided to drop it and just kissed Richie and kept putting the blue eye shadow on him and he kept listening to the Moody Blues and when it was done, I stood back, I was really stunned, he was enormously beautiful, but still himself, completely a man, he played lacrosse at Princeton and has quarter-moon scars on one knee, inside and out, where he had cartilage removed, completely a man, but enormously beautiful, maybe he was the woman I would be with his fawn skin and beautiful large eyes, and I kissed him really gently and said, "God, you're beautiful, look at yourself," and he smiled from faraway; he was off into those Moody Blues and said, "I don't want to see," and I touched him a little gently to stir him and remind him he was a man and then brought over a mirror and put my arm around him and held up the mirror and said, "Look," and he looked a really long time with a trace of that faraway stoned smile and said, "Who is it, Kim?"

And I said, "It's you, and it's absolutely alright, it's you."

And he kept looking in the mirror, the Moody Blues turned up, saying, "Who is it, Kim?"

And I kept saying, "It's you, do you *see?*"

And he said, "Yes, I see, but *who* is it?"

And I said, "Never mind. Whoever. Don't ask those boring intellectual questions. That stuff's all a defense, anyway. It doesn't matter who it is. Don't worry. Whoever it is, it's beautiful."

I'm thinking about that as I'm finishing my eyes. When I look up, I see him standing behind me staring into the palette. "It's a regular rainbow in there." He's dressed and ready to go. "Here. Mind if I put this cigarette out. It's all ash. You always do this."

I shrug. "Put it out. Richie," I turn. "I don't want to scare these women. I mean, look too good."

He shrugs. "Then you've got a problem. Tell you what, I'll go with you and when they start to look a little scared, I'll tell them you snore and drool on the pillow and leave pawprints on the molding, that should help them. Okay? I've gotta go."

"Kiss me. Here." I point to my cheek. He kisses me. "I'll see you tonight."

"Yeah."

"Watch out for all those beautiful women, Richie. Women dig men like you. I shouldn't tell you that."

Then I kiss him, smear my mouth, and wipe his mouth with a tissue. He goes out and I'm alone. Suddenly, I look at myself in the mirror and I feel exhausted, absolutely exhausted, like something heavy is weighing down on me and I can hardly move, can hardly even breathe. I go in and lie down on the bed. I look over at the Chinese fern on the night table. Needs water. At the clock. I'm going to have to get moving, I'm already running a little late, but I don't know if I can move. If only it would let me go a little. One afternoon, I put on some make-up, highlight, foundation. . . . The mirror seemed so bright, I looked at my face, no eyeshadow, no mouth, just a smooth, even flesh tone, I looked at the colors, it just felt like too much, and I went in and washed my face. Richie acts like it's all me, a big joke, but it's not me, or just me, something in his vanity, he's got to share some of the responsibility. I lie here exhausted another few minutes and then I get up, water the fern, and start taking the curlers out of my hair.

By the time I get to the cosmetics counter there are already a couple of women waiting and I don't really have much time to think about it, I just set up—Mrs. Adams, the woman in charge, helps me. I take one of the women, who isn't too bad, sit her on a stool, give her a smile, ask her about herself, try to get her used to the idea that I—a stranger—am going to be touching her in a few moments. She's kind of average-looking, a few basic cosmetics might help her some, maybe they'll help her feel a little better about herself, more confident. I start making her up, explaining what I'm doing, asking her who she is, why she came today. She doesn't say much. Some women stop to watch, talk nervously, laugh, move on. When I finish, the woman looks at herself, shrugs, and starts to leave. Mrs. Adams calls her back and gives her a loaf of French bread and a blue canvas bag which says, LANCÔME, PARIS. They're part of the promotion.

The woman takes her blue bag and bread, and she disappears. I start on the next woman, then the next, and after a while I glance up and realize I've been working a couple of hours. The next woman is tense, but I get her to relax. Her face is actually starting to glow, she's talking about her job and her kids when she notices a group of women standing back and watching, studying her and making comments. She tenses up, says, stop, I say, never mind them, relax, you look fine, but I can't get her to relax and so I help her wipe the make-up off, she gathers her things and just about runs out of there. I kind of know how she felt, but you've got to be able to ignore stuff like that.

I take a break, drink some coffee, head for the ladies' room to straighten up. It's about five-thirty and I'm starting to feel hungry. I look at myself in the mirror. Whoever invented the fluorescent light didn't have skin in mind. What's wrong with some of these women anyway? They're so closed off to style, fashion. So afraid to try; is it immoral to be pretty, to try to make yourself beautiful? Is jewelry immoral? They act like it's the Russian Revolution or something. I've been half-expecting some of these dummies from the women's movement to come galloping up and issue a proclamation, let's scrub our faces with Ivory soap and wear blue jeans and feel self-righteous forever. I'm as independent—more!—than a lot of those whiners, and what a bunch of dogs. It's fashion, play. You accentuate what's good, what's strong—if you have a good feature, you display it. I read in the paper the other day how a woman met Cary Grant and said, "But you don't look like Cary Grant." And he smiled and said, "My dear, no one does." Cary Grant's not even his real name. Archibald Leach is Cary Grant, and Cary Grant knows that no one looks like Cary Grant. Not even Cary Grant.

When I get back to the counter, there's a black girl waiting, about sixteen, and I sit her down, she looks up at me, drops her eyes, we talk for a minute, and I start. She's real cute, has nice features, but I can tell she doesn't think she can be pretty, not really pretty, because she's black, so I start telling her what I'm doing and how nice it is to have such pretty skin, it allows her to use bright colors, wonderful colors, oranges, reds, lavender hues. I tell her she's really pretty, and she says, do you think so, do you really think so? and I know what she's really saying, she's surprised, I don't think anyone had ever told her she was pretty or could be; I tell her so, I hold up the mirror and say, you're beautiful, you're a real knockout, now remember what I told you about using bronze powder to set the whole thing, you're a real knockout, dynamite, and I am not lying. She leaves smiling.

The women keep coming, they're so vulnerable, they just come in and give themselves to me, they're asking for help, and it makes me care, feel responsible for them. I'm really hungry by now and my feet are tired, I've been standing up all this time, but someone brings me some coffee and I keep on working.

I'm just about ready to call it a night—I light a cigarette, take a sip of coffee, cold now. When I look up, I notice a girl standing off to one side. I look over at her, but she's kind of half-turned away and doesn't seem interested. I start cleaning up. When I glance over again, she's a little closer, but she still doesn't approach, and finally I ask, "Did you have an appointment?" She looks at me apologetically and nods, yes. I half-feel like telling her that I'm finished, my feet are killing me, it's not exactly a secret that high heels were not made for standing, not five hours, but I look at her, there's something sad about her, sad and timid and apologetic; it's in her posture, her eyes, her clothes, which do nothing to help, and so I say, "Well, come on," and pat the stool.

She says, "That's okay, if you're finished . . ."

I feel both sympathetic and annoyed, I almost feel like saying, look, do you or don't you want to do this?

But she comes over uncertainly and says, "It's just that you seem tired. . . ."

I hesitate and say, "It's not supposed to show, but I am. Sit down, anyway." I take her purse and set it behind the counter, "It'll be safe there." I smile at her. "Come on, sit down."

She sits and we try to make small talk while I look her over. She has large gray-green eyes—beautiful—long dark lashes, a nice nose, high, pronounced cheekbones, okay hair, a little on the mousy side, but that could be fixed, a pretty full mouth. She is almost beautiful, but there is something off, besides the fact that she is doing absolutely nothing to show off her beautiful eyes, show those cheekbones, the mouth. In another moment, I see it, of course, her chin, she has a receded chin, and so this beautiful face is not beautiful, but almost beautiful and gives the appearance and feeling of weakness. She looks at me hopefully, and I say, "What's your name?"

"Maureen."

When I tell her mine, she seems grateful. Just for that. I decide the best thing would be to build her confidence a little and so I tell her she has beautiful eyes, lovely cheekbones. She looks at me doubtfully, and I can see she's timid and so I ask her about herself and she starts talking while I apply highlight. The first time I touch her—just her cheek—she jumps, looks embarrassed. "I'm sorry."

"It's okay. I'm just going to rub this on, start beneath the eyes—it's highlight—then I'll put on this foundation. Okay?"

"Please go ahead. I'm sorry."

I ask her what she does and start putting the highlight on—it's really whiteface, pure and beautiful, and sometimes I think it would be nice to go around in just whiteface, so cool and calm, I'm thinking about what I'm going to do with her chin, she settles down, I go along, I'm listening to her, there's a sadness in her voice, an *if* to everything she says, I finish with the highlight and start the foundation, then the contour, explaining to her what I'm doing and how it works, she tells me she finished college a few years ago and was unsure of what to do next, so after working as a barmaid, working in a boutique, then as a landscape gardener, and a housepainter, she still didn't know what she wanted, so she began as a legal secretary, which is what she's doing now . . . just coming from there as a matter of fact.

I'm working on her eyes.

. . . but which is still not what she wants to do—legal secretary. She thinks she'd like to go back to school.

I nod. "Don't move. I don't want to poke you in the eye."

She stares straight ahead, but keeps talking. Her voice is a little stronger now, but there's that *if*. She loves her boyfriend, but she's not sure he's right or loves her right. She hesitates. She doesn't even know what she means by that, *right*. She'd like to change herself or make a change in her life, but somehow . . . she says she can remember a time when she used to be confident, really confident, sure of herself, but something happened, she's not sure what, or when it happened, or if anything at all even really happened, and now she's not sure. . . .

She hesitates. "Do you think men like make-up?"

"Mine acts like he doesn't. He jokes. Maybe it gets him a little nervous, but I think it turns him on. The playfulness, the invention . . ."

She nods uncertainly. "I've never done anything like what you're doing. Some eyeliner and lipstick, but nothing like this. I'm wondering what he'll say when I come home."

She looks doubtful. I start on her chin and say softly, "Light if you want to bring something out, dark if you want to make less of it."

She nods. We don't mention the chin, but I know she understands what I'm telling her and why. When I'm finished, I step back. "Look." I turn my head toward the mirror. "Look." She looks. She smiles. She raises her hand toward her chin, but checks herself, "How do you feel?"

"Better."

"You should. You look wonderful. Beautiful."

She smiles at me. "Do you really think so?"

"I promise."

"Do you think . . . he'll like it? Oh, that's stupid of me, you don't even know him."

"He'd be crazy not to. Don't you let him talk you out of it."

"I like the way I look. I really do." We smile at each other. She says, still not mentioning the chin, "Do you know I'd been thinking of plastic surgery. It just nags at me."

I shake my head. "You look great." We talk another moment. I check with her to make sure she understands, to be aware of lighting, since lighting has a big effect on make-up and what works in one lighting situation might not work at all in another. I tell her to practice with the make-up, then give her the blue bag and French bread, remember to give her back her purse, she laughs, delighted, thanks me, starts to leave, turns back uncertainly. "Light if you want to bring something out . . ."

". . . and dark if you want to make less of it."

We smile, she waves the French bread, walks away. I watch her go. I almost feel like asking her to go for coffee. There's something about the way they give themselves to you which makes you feel responsible, care. And she's really nice. I kind of believe in something in her—I'm feeling a little lonely now for some reason; I take a step toward her, but then stop. I'm tired.

I start cleaning up and when I'm done Mrs. Adams asks me for my social security number, thanks me, and gives me a couple of loaves of French bread and a blue bag, Lancôme, Paris.

In the parking lot, the white lines remind me of a children's game I used to play—the board—but I can't remember which one. I throw the bag and French bread on the seat, slide in, remember Richie won't be home until late. I'm stiff all over.

In McDonald's, the food suddenly sickens me, I throw the whole

270

mess into the garbage, grab my purse. The ladies' room. I lock the door, take out a jar of Vaseline and some tissue, and wipe my make-up off. Streaks on the white porcelain, blues, flesh tones, magenta . . . I wash my face, throw everything in my purse. Back in the car, I remember half a pint of bourbon Richie left under the seat. I dig it out, take a sip, light a cigarette, another swallow of bourbon, this one relaxes me. I don't want to come back to an empty house so I put on an old Van Morrison tape, dig out the bourbon for one more swallow, and decide to take a drive out into the desert.

The moon is almost full and I'm driving fast—past a sign for Palm Springs—suddenly I turn off the Van Morrison, another swallow of bourbon, the desert is almost perfect and white and endless like the ocean, I miss the change of seasons, real changes, leaves turning, snow, only part I really miss about the East, things startle in and out of the headlights, the flash of a deer haunch, gleam of a coyote's eyes, quick prance off the shoulder, Maureen, her timidity, the way she jumped when I touched her cheek to apply the highlight, what would her boyfriend think, said she'd been sure of herself, once. What did he say when she walked in the door? Probably said, what the hell happened to you? Wipe that gunk off.

I wonder if she did. Probably did. Maybe I would have, too. No. Sixteen and I'd had mono and spent months home from school, Mother sent me to modelling school. Eight years later, big fight over it, she said I wanted to go, but I know she sent me. Big fight. Says she remembers. Thought I had a bad self-image, that it would be good for me. I didn't have any bad self-image, but I went anyway, just to get out of the house, away from her. But she still insists. . . .

She's the one with the bad self-image. Projecting. Spent half her life doing dumb things, never made a decision for herself, married young, kids young, worked in an office, never exercises, reads, smokes like a fiend, no interests . . .

After Richie and I had been living together a few weeks, she called: "Are you there alone?"

"Yes."

"Good, now I can talk to you."

"You don't have to whisper."

"I'm not whispering. Are you living there with him—the one who answers the phone?"

"Yes. Richie's his name."

"Kim . . ."

"Don't. Please."

"Who pays the rent?"

"He does."

"Well, that much is right. He should at least pay for the privilege."

"What do you think, I'm selling something?"

"I don't go for this living together. Your father would be very upset. I'm going to keep this from him."

I don't answer. I'm here and she's there. One reason I went to school on the coast. I'll just stay. What scares her. She uses the phone like a musical instrument—pauses, inflections, wants me to feel guilty. She talks. Talk on.

". . . if you live with him, if you give a man what he wants, how will you ever get him to marry you?"

Her bully-barter system. My brother a marshmallow, sister a ball-buster.

"Let's not talk about it, Mother."

"You think your mother doesn't understand?"

Maybe once she had some pride, dignity. Pictures of her taken during the war. Slim, face wasn't puffy, fire in her eyes. That picture of her taken outside of the Nugget. Eyes shining, she had her skirt hiked up above her knees, laughing. They'd gotten all the girls up on top of the bar, she'd won the contest for beautiful legs. Dynamite legs—for all the good it did her, never seen her eyes like that.

Twenty years in the same office, she takes the goddamned job so seriously, she comes up for office manager, she runs the god-damned office anyway, they give it to a young guy, turn around and ask her to train him, maybe that finally wised her up to something, I really did feel sorry for her. After that, whatever last little illusions she had, even she couldn't keep it up. Just let her white hair come in, had one of those mousy, middle-aged dye jobs, blondie, got this vacant look on her face . . .

Now Dad and she selling Amway, detergent, fertilizer. Amway conventions, positive selling attitudes. Last time home, come down to breakfast, Dad listening to an Amway cassette, like brainwashing or religion, she even wants me to do it, cram your Amway.

I keep driving and then remember some clothes in the trunk.

Pull off the road, drive into the desert a little, dead silent, I cast a pale shadow on the desert floor, strip off the dress, change into a pair of jeans, one of Richie's t-shirts—Richie's smell as I pull it over my head—Adidas, sit down on the car, silent slow out here, just the metal creaking as it cools off, my innards still churning with engine speed, road speed, nerves. My shadow, the car shadow, pale, ground the color of chalk. If I wish hard enough, frost or even a light dusting of snow. Raise my arm and wave. There, my shadow. I touch my chin. Modelling director said I had a perfect face—shape, proportion. Almost heart-shaped. A valentine.

Maybe Maureen came in and her man loved her face, loved all of that light and shadow and color. Maybe he didn't. Wipe it off. But maybe she told him to get stuffed. Men live in such a dream world. I should have gotten Maureen's phone number, given her mine. Or we could have had coffee, gotten to be friends.

I hear something. Listen. Into the distance. Rising and falling. Here. There. Over there. Back here. Swooping rise and fall. Coyotes. Chilling and beautiful and pure, it raises goosebumps on my arms. I listen for minutes at a time, almost holding my breath, finally step down off the car, crunch around in the desert, bourbon from under the seat.

I should start back but don't feel like it. I listen to the coyotes, here, there, watch my pale shadow in the moonlight. The moon looks like it's far under water and if I jumped up and let go of the earth, I could swim down, stretch out my hand, touch it, Dad and I in a duck blind, moon still shining, but getting light, sound of the ducks flying over, beautiful and chilling and pure, giving me goosebumps, choked feeling, Dad standing, slight rocking of the boat, the sweep of his shotgun, graceful motion, four years in the Airborne, all over Europe, killing, the shotgun, muzzle flash in the smoky-dilute light, muffled splash, moon shining in the water. Then, cleaning them, their beautiful feathers, so many colors, sticking to the backs of my hands and arms, and a mountain of decoys by the furnace, handmade, beautiful, round, startled Egyptian eyes, decoys a silent reply to her bullying, his disappearing into the basement after supper and staying there half the night, wanted to be a veterinarian, but after he got home, started working and never stopped, a waste, but he stood up to her hurting me . . .

I look up at the moon, maybe I'm a little drunk. A little. I drop the bottle on the seat, spot the French bread, rip off a chunk, thick in my mouth, I get back in the car, drive back to the road and start driving, this time a little slower, feeling the light on my skin, the glass display cases, mirrors, glittery underwater light, like an aquarium . . .

She was surprised as hell when the woman who ran the agency told her how smart I was, seventeen, and she was taking me to a competition in New York, scared, the Hotel Pierre, designers, photographers, knees shaking, I went out on that runway, they loved me, were dazzled. . . .

Oh, then she was proud, saw dollar signs, thought maybe I'd make it in New York, but I sensed what it really was, U.S.C. she screamed, could it be any farther? how about Tokyo? can't go to U. Mass.? And I knew I wasn't really tall enough, five-ten, six feet on those runways, they want you to overpower, not quite five-seven, I could do print work, magazines, it's not real enough, anyway.

I see the lights of L.A. as I come over the mountains. My stomach tightens. U.S.C. Math and philosophy, and good grades, too, people always surprised, professors, what'd they expect, cut my hair short, working nights as a cocktail waitress, sick of that, phone numbers on matchbooks pushed into my hands, then part-time as a sales rep for a big modelling agency:

I AM INTERESTED IN THE FOLLOWING CAREER
PROGRAMS:
Acting——, Modelling——, Personal Develop-
ment——
MY INTEREST LEVEL IS:
High——, Moderate——, Just Curious——

Mothers hopeful with daughters, like mine, crazy sleeping people walking through those doors dreaming, and you want to give it to them, they need it, they sit in the waiting room, look at all of those unreal portraits, lips eyes hair shining, all lights and make-up, they sleep-walk into the interviews, tacky guys good-looking in obvious ways, guys who do a little modelling, extras, male go-go dancers, they want to get into the movies, tv, they look at your tits, ask you out, that forty-five-year-old guy who hardly said anything the whole time and then at the end said, I have money, will you marry me?

As I hit the freeway, I feel the fatigue, my arms, my legs. I fumble out another tape and put it on.

By then my hair was growing out, and everyone in the office said I should go to New York, that I had it, and Sonia gave me some stretching exercises, heard of a girl who stretched an inch-and-a-half. I start hanging from a chinning bar, morning and evening. One night, I'm hanging from the bar thinking of my spine getting stretched out and suddenly I burst out laughing, can't stop, next day I'm at work, suddenly I walk out of my cubicle, I'm laughing again, and waving Hegel—I've got class afterward—I'm walking up and down past the cubicles, Joyce and Betty and Sonia, all made up and sensational, Joyce had great legs and had once done a commercial for Hanes, Betty sang jingles for granola and floor wax, Betty had taken voice lessons for years, Sonia had been the lips in a Revlon commercial, they came out of their cubicles, they were kind of laughing, I was losing it, I pointed at Joyce's legs, finally could say, between Joyce's legs, my tits, Betty's voice, Dee's ass, we've almost got a whole broad here. I couldn't stop laughing, suddenly grabbed my books, said, I'm sorry, I can't do this anymore, and walked out of there. It was another year before I thought of modelling again and that was because I was desperate for money. So you get back to it. Somehow it's always there, the face, and you turn away, and when you turn back around, it's there again, the face.

The bungalow is dark. Inside, quiet. I peer into the bedroom, Richie's sound asleep. I close the door so I won't wake him, undress, take a shower, rub oil into my skin. I sit down naked on the sofa, smoke a cigarette.

Richie stirs as I get into bed. It's warm and the sheet is kicked back. He says my name in his sleep. I kiss him gently, his breath deepens. I listen to his breathing. I kind of want to make love, but I don't want to wake him, and I'm just too tired to start. Sometimes it's hard to start, the toughest part, even. I drift into sleep, wake, close in here, I get up and open a window, settle down, drift back to sleep, colors, eyes, the women keep coming and giving themselves to me, help me, they're so vulnerable, their eyes are bright, glittery, pained in the underwater light, it's like an aquarium, mirrors, glass, bright light, their eyes keep disappearing underwa-

275

ter, colors all over my hands, my arms, clinging to my lips, metallic greens, beautiful feathers, getting in my throat, the startled Egyptian eyes, black, the beautiful band of white so startling, I am gluing feathers on their eyelids, light to bring something out, shadow to lessen, feathers in my nose.

I wake, gasp for breath.

I reach over and touch Richie's shoulder. The hall light falls into the room. I look at him. Pretty fawn colors, white hip, bathing suit, no sun. Where he has kicked back the sheet, the crescent scars on his knee, faint shadows. I touch one. Too smooth for skin. I kiss him gently and he stirs and goes on sleeping. I lie there beside him, listening to his breathing.

A few days later, I'm coming out of the photographer's studio. We've been shooting the fall catalogue for hours, I'm wired, I'm in nylons, high heels, full make-up for bright lights . . . there's a crowd and up ahead, people are getting off a bus, the bus pulls away and I see someone familiar, it's Maureen, she must work around here, I start walking quickly, pushing through the crowd, the light changes, more people come up around me, I break into a quick walk, almost a trot. I stumble in my heels, this time we'll have coffee, we'll talk, I want to know, did she keep the look or not, what did he say, and if he didn't like it, did she tell him where to go, maybe that night was a turning point for her, a beginning, she disappears ahead into the crowd, I break into a trot, a couple of steps, wobbling in the heels, debate, then shout after her, Maureen! Maureen! I finally get up to where I can reach out, I touch her on the shoulder, Maureen, I smile, she turns, looks startled, no make-up, none at all, a lot older, not at all like Maureen, her eyes startled from far away, sad, too. From the back, though, for a second, there was something familiar. I apologize and watch her walk into the crowd. I glance around nervously—for some reason, things like this have always embarrassed me, but I look around quickly, people, they're all just walking along and I don't really think any of them noticed.

nominated by Elizabeth Inness-Brown
and Mona Simpson

DUPPY GET HER

fiction by OPAL PALMER ADISA

from BAKE-FACE & OTHER GUAVA STORIES (Kelsey Street Press)

> *Duppy nuh wan yuh drop*
> *yuh picknie deh, guh home*
> *Duppy nuh wan yuh drop*
> *yuh picknie deh, guh home*
> *Duppy nuh wan yuh drop*
> *yuh picknie deh, guh home, gal*
> *tie yuh belly, gal, guh home.*

EVENING falls like dewdrops on oleander petals glistening under the sun. Oshun, goddess of love, is present, her orange-yellow skirt swaying coquettishly. Mosquitoes are like kiskode petals on skin, blown off by the lax odor whispering mischief in the air. Cane fields rustle in frolic; answered by the evening breeze, they dance the merenge, twirling to giddiness. What are the cane fields saying? What is uttered by the leaves? Listen! Listen—with wide eyes.

Suddenly the murmur of the cane fields—almost hypnotic— forces everyone to look in their direction. Swirling, they sing:

> *Steal away, steal away;*
> *duppy gwana get yuh, gal, steal away.*
> *Steal away, steal away;*
> *duppy a come get yuh, gal, steal away.*

The labyrishers—gossipers—do not hear; they don't hear, save one—Lilly.

Lilly cleans house, cooks food, washes clothes, irons and does other domestic chores for her living. She has been since she was sixteen; she is eighteen, now, and with child due any day. She sits with Beatrice, her cousin, also a domestic; with Richard, her baby's father and a pot-boiler at the sugar estate; and with Basil and Errol, two other factory hands. They are gathered together, feeling contented at being their own bosses for at least the next twelve hours.

The evening is rare in its simple grace. The sun, sinking beyond the cane fields, dominates the sky. All the land kneels in homage to this god of energy and sustainer of life—fully orange, gigantic and mystic, surrounded by black-purple haze. The clouds stand back, way off in respect. The sun, heedful of his power, gyrates and snarls. Lilly glances at him just as he flaps his ears, emitting fire from his nostrils; she checks her laughter. So awed is she by the sun's fire she scarcely breathes. After some moments, Lilly mumbles: "Lawd, de sun mitey tonite, sah. Look, im on im way home nuh." Suddenly, the turning of the child in her belly elicits a laugh that escapes deep from her womb.

Beatrice, seated by her, places her hand on Lilly's stomach, feeling the baby's position. "Dis a definite boy picknie yuh a guh ave. See how yuh belly pointed and de sonofabitch won gi yuh nuh peace."

"Im mus tek afta im fada."

Richard turns away in vexation; he chups, kissing his teeth: "Is me yuh ave mout fah, nuh? Ooman neba satisfy. Wen dem nuh ave nutten else fi seh, dem chat stupidness." He moves to leave, but changes his mind; he chups again: "Nuh boda me backside dis evenin yah, gal, nuh boda me backside."

The breeze whistles by. The dogs cover their ears in embarrassment, while the frogs exchange glances which ask, "What's troubling him this nice evening, eh? What's troubling him?" A green lizard, in response, croaks; its bulging eyes are lit by the sun. There is silence amidst the gathering of two women and three men—maids, pot-boiler and factory-hands.

Silence dominates but the undercurrent there is anger mingled with amusement and foreboding. Again, the swishing of the cane fields seems to grab everyone's attention. Lilly is rocking. Suddenly noticing a flock of birds in the sky, she points like an excited child. Again, silence. The sun is almost gone. Lilly sees a star, and thinking it must be the very first one in the sky this evening, she quickly makes a wish, anxious for its fulfillment. She resumes her rocking, forgetting what it was she wished for. A rooster cackles near the barbed wire fence separating them from the canal and the cane field beyond. Two dogs are stuck, one in the other.

Richard picks up a stone, throws it at them; he swears under his breath: "Damn dog—dem nuh ave nuh shame. Look how much bush bout de place, yet dem a fi come rite inna de open."

Beatrice snickers. Lilly retorts, "Nuh eberybode wait till nite fi cova dem act inna de darkness like yuh."

"Ooman, me nuh tell nuh boda me soul-case. If yuh nuh ave nutten fi seh, shet yuh backside."

Beatrice comments, "Some people hot tonite, Lawd. Mus all dat boilin molasses. De sweetness keep de heat inna de body." Again silence. Beatrice fidgets in the chair, which is too small for her large behind. Suddenly, she starts singing, a mischievous smile on her face. Her voice is full and melodious, and her song is aimed at Richard, whom she always provokes to anger:

> Gentle Jesas, meek an mile,
> look upon a trouble man.
> Ease im soul an let im rest,
> for im is a soul distress.

Lilly bursts out in loud belly-laughter and Errol and Basil sputter. Richard's color is rising like the pink of a cat's tongue. Anger is clearly written on his face. A sudden wind blows dirt into Beatrice's eye, putting an end to her song.

Richard keenly observes the little gathering and feels excluded. He looks at the dark bodies, envying them. He is the "red nega" among them. All during his school days, the boys teased him, saying his mother had slept with a sailor. And even though he knew it wasn't true (although he was the fairest one in his family), he was still always hurt; he didn't care if his great-great-grandfather had married an Irish settler whom he resembled. He wanted to be purple-dark like the rest of them so his face wouldn't turn red like the color of sorrel fruit whenever he got angry. Staying out in the sun didn't help either; it only made his skin tomato. Lean and muscular, he stood out like a guinep among star-apples.

Lately, however (that is, ever since meeting Lilly not yet twelve months ago), Richard has been relaxed. Lilly, lusted after by all the men, the gentlemen of the community included, chose him. Although every once in a while she teases him about his complexion and stings his hand to see her fingerprints revealed, he knows she cares for him.

Richard doesn't feel like being anyone's beating stick tonight, however. He looks from Lilly, sitting with a smile crowning her face, to Errol and Basil, with mischief twinkling in their eyes, to Beatrice, playing her usual pious role. Richard wants to remind Beatrice of the nightly utterances of her mattress and bedsprings, but he holds his tongue as he isn't sure whether it is Errol or Basil or both who pray to the Lord between her thighs at night. He chuckles, stomping the balls of his feet, and then chups, kissing his teeth, before turning to fidget with his bicycle. "One of des days oonuh gwane wan fi serious and kyan," he warns.

Richard catches a glimpse of the sun just before it disappears, and it whispers to him: "Steal away, steal away—duppy gwane box yuh, duppy nuh like yuh, steal away . . ." He looks over his shoulder to see if anyone else heard. No one did; the group is already onto something else.

The cane fields whimper, swishing to and fro. The evening is alive. All the creatures stop to say their piece. Sparkling fireflies called penewales dart in and out of the darkness; crickets are in argument. Even the water in the canal tastes the omen. It rumbles like a vexed child who is sent to sweep up the dirt and gather leaves; the task adds to the child's vexation when the twirling leaves blind his eyes while playing rounders with the breeze. So is the evening sweet yet wicked—as even the nicest woman can be.

The rustling of the cane fields is louder. Beatrice shivers. Blossoms from the ackee tree fall and the wind takes them, blowing them everywhere. Lilly tries to catch the blossoms, but the movement in her belly stops her. She relaxes and pats her stomach.

Beatrice feels her head growing big; it is a ton of bricks on her body. She rubs her arms, feeling the cold-bumps. Something is going to happen. She looks around at Richard, who is still angry, and Basil and Errol, who are sharing some private joke. Beatrice reaches over and rubs Lilly's belly, feeling the child inside kicking. She is certain it's a boy. Again, the murmur of the cane fields. Beatrice quickly blows into her cupped palms and throws the air over her left shoulder. It is her way of telling the duppies to step back. She cannot see the ghosts, but she senses their presence near. Again she cups her palms, blows, and throws her cupped hands over her right shoulder, cursing a bad-word with the motion before mumbling. "De Lawd is me Shepherd, Ah fear nuh evil. . . ." Still she senses an outside force. Lilly is smiling to herself and rocking, one hand patting her stomach.

Beatrice's head swells; she feels it's much larger than her body, much larger than the veranda, where they are sitting, much larger than the evening. She hugs her bosom and rocks, trying to put aside the fear that has crept upon her without invitation.

After her mother died when she was six and her father wandered to another town and another woman, Beatrice was taken in by Lilly's mother, who was her aunt. She was two years older than Lilly, so their lives followed similar paths until at fifteen Beatrice's was partially ruined by her Sunday school teacher. Fear made her keep her mouth shut; prayer made the child born dead. Soon thereafter she left, getting several jobs as domestic help before settling in this quiet community. Eight years ago, Beatrice and Lilly both attended their grandparents' funerals, three months apart. They were always close, so over the years, they kept in touch. When Lilly complained of being restless and wanting to leave the overprotective shield of her mother two years ago, Beatrice found her a job with her own employer Mrs. Edwards. That was how they came to be together again.

Before Beatrice lost her child, she had promised the Lord that she would spread his name if he killed the life that was growing in her womb. When the child was born strangled, she kept her word, but it was already too late, because she had discovered the joy which lay buried between her legs. As she wasn't pretty, it was easy to have several men without ruining her reputation. No one wanted to boast of sleeping with the coarse, big busted, no ass, Jesus-crazy maid. This way she had it her way all the time, not really trusting any man in the first place.

Putting aside her reflections, Beatrice leans her head to hear what Basil is saying.

"Oonuh look like oonuh inna anoda world."

Richard is still fidgeting with his bicycle; Errol has gone to help him. Lilly, rocking on the seatless cane rocker, is hypnotized by the rustling cane field beyond. Beatrice and Basil notice her staring at what to them appears to be nothing. They feel her strangeness like silence between them. Pausing to take it in, they resume their conversation. An ackee blossom falls, disquieting Richard, and he curses: "See yah, Lawd, yuh nuh test me fait tuh dis yah nite."

A man and woman have crept out of the cane field. They stand right at the edge on the bank of the canal. To look at the woman is to see an older Lilly. The man is all grey. The woman wears a plaid dress gathered at the waist, and her feet are without shoes. Her husband wears rubber shoes and stained khaki pants turned up at the ankles. His faded shirt is partially unbuttoned, his arm is around his wife's waist. They exude a gentleness like the petals of roses. The woman uses her index finger to beckon to Lilly. Jumping as if pulled from her seat, Lilly bounds toward the man and woman by the cane field beyond the canal and beyond the barbed wire fence. She scrambles over Beatrice's feet.

Beatrice yells, "Lilly, Lilly, weh yuh a guh? Lilly! Is mad? Yuh mad? Min yuh fall down hurt yuhself. Lilly! Gal, weh yuh a guh?"

Richard runs after Lilly.

Beatrice repeats, "Lilly, gal, wha get inna yuh?"

Lilly: "Yuh rass-cloth, leabe me alone. Yuh nuh ear me granny a call me?" She points to what appears to be the canal.

They all stare, seeing no one, hearing nothing. Lilly is close to the fence, running, tearing off her clothes. Fearing that she is going to dive in, Richard reaches for her, but she clutches and attempts the barbed wire fence; Richard pulls at her. She boxes and derides him till he releases her. She tries scrambling through. Richard takes firm hold of her and pulls her safely from the fence. Beatrice is by their side; she helps with Lilly. Errol stands transfixed by the bicycle, while Basil cranes his neck from the veranda. Richard and Beatrice struggle with Lilly, pulling her away from the fence; they are breathless, but luckily, Lilly settles down for a moment.

The woman in the cane field beckons to Lilly, cajoling: "Lilly, me picknie, come kiss yuh granny and granpa; yuh nuh long fi see we?"

Lilly, strident, gesticulates wildly like a man cheated out of his paycheck. She calls, "Yes, Granny, me a come, me long fi see yuh."

Beatrice and Richard struggle with Lilly. Their fright and confusion are as loud as Lilly's screams. Richard tries to rough her up

282

but she merely bucks him off. Beatrice's jaws work, sweat forms on her forehead, and her fleshy arms flail about, comical.

Again, she tries to reason with Lilly: "Lilly, gal, memba me and you did help dress Granny fah er funeral? Memba, memba, Lilly, how we did cry til we eye swell big? Granny dead. She nuh call yuh."

"Granny nuh dead; see, she stan deh wid grandpa. Oonuh leh me guh." At this, Lilly spits at Beatrice and Richard and frees herself from their hold.

She rushes toward the cane field like a man afire in search of water. Richard siezes her, but she now has the strength of many persons; he hollers for Errol and Basil. Lilly rips off her blouse and brassiere, and her ample breasts flap about. Richard remembers the taste of her milk, only last night. More hands take hold of her; she bites, scratches and kicks. Miss Maud from next door, hearing the commotion, runs to her fence to learn all about it.

"Leh me guh, leh me guh! Yuh nuh see me granny a call me? Leh me guh."

Richard: "Lilly, shet yuh mout. Min Miss Edward ear yuh an yuh loose yuh wuk. Nuhbody nuh call yuh."

"Miss Edward bumbu-hole—Miss Edward rasscloth. Oonuh leabe me alone mek me guh tuh me granny and granpa."

Beatrice scolds: "Lilly, gal, shet yuh mout. How yuh can speak suh bout Miss Edward? Gal, shet yuh mout for yuh loose yuh wuk."

"Oonuh rass-cloth, oonuh bumbu-hole, oonuh leabe me alone— mek me guh to me granny."

The four find it difficult to hold Lilly. She kicks, bucks and tears at her remaining clothes. The evening sings:

> Steal away, steal away, duppy get yuh.
> Steal away . . . duppy get yuh . . .

From across the fence, Miss Maud offers: "Lawd, God, duppy done mad me picknie, Lawd God. Jesas! Rub er up wid some frankincense and white rum; rub er up quick come." Before anyone can respond, she is climbing through the barbed wire fence which separates her yard from theirs, opening a bottle. In her haste, her dress catches on the fence, but she pulls it, ripping the hem. The pungent smell from the bottle vapors into the air.

Miss Maud rubs Lilly's hands, face and neck with the potion, then makes the sign of the cross in the air. Now she sprinkles some of the substance on the ground, muttering: "Steal away, duppy, steal away. De deed well done; steal away. . . ." She looks about her, pats her head and turns to Beatrice. "Fin piece a red rag, tie er head. Duppy fraid red, fraid red. Our Fada who in heaven, duppy fraid red. Dy kingdom come, tie her head. Dy will be done, tie er head. Ave mercy, Pupa Jesas."

Lilly breathes heavily; Richard, Errol and Basil hold her firmly. Says Beatrice, "She kyan stay ere; dem nuh wan er stay ere."

Maud explains, "Dem just wan er home. No arm will be done. Lawd ave mercy."

Richard stares at Lilly: "Who obeah me sweet Lilly? Who?"

Beatrice explodes: "Shet yuh mout, Richard, nuhbody nuh set nuh spell pan Lilly, nuhbody obeah er."

> *Steal away, chile, steal away.*
> *Duppy nuh wan yuh ere, chile,*
> *   duppy nuh wan yuh ere.*
> *Dem nuh wan yuh ere.*

It is generally agreed that Lilly must be returned to her place of birth—that for whatever reason, her dead grandparents don't want her where she is. Mrs. Edwards is consulted and a car is summoned. Kicking and frothing at the mouth, Lilly is forced into the back of the car, Richard to her right and Basil to her left. Beatrice sits up front with the driver armed with Miss Maud's flask of potion. The car pulls off, leaving a trail of dust.

Mrs. Edwards returns to her house; she fumbles inside her medicine cabinet and comes up with a brown vial, the contents of which she sprinkles at each doorway and window and in all four corners of every room. Then she goes back to her rocking chair, her hands folded in her lap, her eyes searching the grey sky.

Miss Maud, the community myalist—healer—returns to her backyard. Her lips are pouted and her eyes intent, as if seeking a shiny shilling in the road; she shakes her head from side to side.

Suddenly she is possessed; she twirls around her yard, her wide skirt billowing out, her hands lifted to the sky, her feet marching time to an invisible drum. Her voice, deep bass, echoes like a man's throughout the entire community:

Duppy nuh wan yuh drop
   yuh picknie deh, guh home
Duppy nuh wan yuh drop
   yuh picknie deh, guh home
Duppy nuh wan yuh drop
   yuh picknie deh, guh home, gal,
   tie yuh belly, gal, guh home.
Yuh muma seh she nebe raise
   nuh picknie fi guh lego
Yuh muma seh she neba raise
   nuh picknie fi guh lego
Yuh muma seh she neba raise
   nuh picknie fi guh lego
   tie yuh belly, guh home.
Duppy nuh wan yuh drop
   yuh picknie deh
   tie yuh belly, guh home.
Guh home.

Mrs. Edwards feels cold-bumps covering her arms as she watches Miss Maud twirling and singing in her yard. The swishing of the cane fields has stopped and suddenly, a sense of desolation—abandonment—takes over. The sky turns a deep mauve, a lone donkey somewhere in the distance brays, brays, brays and the night is on so fully all creep to the safety of their homes and pull the covers tightly over their heads. Only Mrs. Edwards sits for a long time on her veranda in the dark, rocking and rocking away the fear and doubt.

Upon returning from taking Lilly home, Beatrice reports that Lilly calmed gradually as she approached her place of birth. In fact, by the time she got home, she was reasonable enough to request from her mother a cup of water sweetened with condensed milk. After drinking the milk, Lilly hugged her mother and they both cried; no one had to restrain her thereafter. Nothing needed to be explained to Lilly's mother, who had been expecting them all day. It appeared she had had a dream from her dead mother the night before.

Prior to this incident, Lilly always claimed that she saw duppies in Mrs. Edwards's house and around the estate in general. Since no one else professed such powers, there was no way to verify her claim. Many came to her when they wanted to ask for protection from those in the other world. Often, when they were in Lilly's presence, they asserted that they felt their heads rise and swell to twice their size, but again, since this was only a feeling and nothing visible, nothing could be proven. There were others who wanted to be able to see duppies like Lilly and asked her how they could obtain such powers. Lilly's recommendations were the following: "Rub dog matta inna yuh eye or visit a graveyard wen de clock strike twelve midnite. Once dere, put yuh head between yuh legs, spit, then get up an walk, not lookin back. Afta dat, yuh will see duppy all de time."

It is not known if anyone ever followed Lilly's advice, although two women who went to see Lilly had taken to visiting the graveyard daily and were now in the habit of talking to themselves.

Lilly returns to Mrs. Edwards's employment exactly ten weeks after the incident, healthy and as sane as before, with her bubbling, carefree manner. She gave birth to a seven-and-a-half pound boy, the spitting image of Richard, the day after her departure. The child was left behind with her mother, who christened him Sam, after his deceased grandfather.

Now when Lilly looks into the cane field, nothing bursts forth and no dead are brought back to life, but every time people see her looking, they remember that evening and somehow, the cane field starts rustling and a voice much like Lilly's rings throughout the entire community, stopping people at their chores:

Leh me guh, leh me guh, oonuh rass-cloth!
Le me guh—me granny a call me, oonuh leh me guh.
Mrs. Edwards bumbu-hole; leh me guh.

No one referred to Mrs. Edwards, a highly respected member of her community, in such a manner before, and no one has after Lilly. Lilly, of course, apologized to Mrs. Edwards, who graciously forgave her as she was not in possession of herself at the time. And although Mrs. Edwards was committed to taking Lilly back in her employment after she gave birth, whenever Mrs. Edwards was around her, she was always full of trepidation.

Lilly goes off one other time since the cane field incident. Several years have passed; Lilly is getting married to Richard. This is the big day. She is dressed, waiting to be taken to the church. Her grandmother appears again, but this time alone. Lilly rips her bridal dress to shreds and runs naked to the river, cursing everyone she meets, while Richard waits by the altar. For nine days she has to be tied down with ropes. For nine days, the breeze sings:

> Steal away, steal away.
> Duppy seh nuh, duppy seh nuh.
> Steal away . . .

Lilly's face is a dimpled cake pan. Her body is pleasing like a mango tree laden with fruits. She has eight children, now, six for her husband and two for Richard, the first two. Richard stole away after duppy boxed him the second time. The last that was heard of him, it was reported that he was seen walking and talking to himself, his hair matty and his skin black from dirt. Lilly now has a maid to help her with her many chores; her husband owns a fleet of trucks.

Beatrice has opened up a storefront church in another community far from where the main part of this story took place. Her congregation is said to be ninety-two percent sturdy black men. Basil is still working as a pot-boiler at the sugar factory. Errol went abroad to England, it could be Canada or America as well, where he is said to have married an East Indian girl, so now he eats with his fingers.

After Lilly left Mrs. Edwards's employment, Mrs. Edwards swore confidentially to Mrs. Salmon, her best friend, that she would never again hire a maid from Agusta valley—that was the district from which Lilly came. Mrs. Edwards, of course, did not admit to a belief in local superstitions.

At least once a year, Miss Maud can still be heard singing at the top of her voice:

> Duppy nuh wan yuh drop
>   yuh picknie deh, guh home
> Duppy nuh wan yuh drop
>   yuh picknie deh, guh home

Duppy nuh wan yun drop
   yuh picknie deh, guh home, gal,
tie yuh belly, guh home.

nominated by Kelsey Street Press

THE IMPACT OF TRANSLATION

by SEAMUS HEANEY

from THE YALE REVIEW

In this essay I shall argue that the impact of translation upon poets and poetry in English has involved two main lines of reaction which might be characterized as "envy" and "identification." But I want to begin with a poem by Czeslaw Milosz, translated by the author and Robert Pinsky, which Robert Pinsky read to me some years ago at his home in Berkeley:

INCANTATION
Human reason is beautiful and invincible.
No bars, no barbed wire, no pulping of books,
No sentence of banishment can prevail against it.
It establishes the universal ideas in language,
And guides our hand so we write Truth and Justice
With capital letters, lie and oppression with small.
It puts what should be above things as they are,
Is an enemy of despair and a friend of hope.
It does not know Jew from Greek or slave from master,
Giving us the estate of the world to manage.
It saves austere and transparent phrases
From the filthy discord of tortured words.
It says that everything is new under the sun,
Opens the congealed fist of the past.
Beautiful and very young are Philo-Sophia

And poetry, her ally in the service of the good.
As late as yesterday Nature celebrated their birth,
The news was brought to the mountains by a unicorn and an echo.
Their friendship will be glorious, their time has no limit.
Their enemies have delivered themselves to destruction.

My first experience of these lines, spoken in the upstairs study of a silent house, empty that afternoon except for ourselves, was altogether thrilling. There is always a slight element of the conspiratorial present when a poem is read aloud between two people, a sense of a private march being stolen, perhaps too a sense of a risk being taken that the other party may find the whole performance a little jejune; yet the feeling of collusion in this case was made all the stronger for me because we were enjoying a poem which did certain forbidden things, forbidden within an old dispensation to which I was admittedly more subject than my host, who had once studied with Yvor Winters. This poem was, for example, full of abstractions, and to a member of the generation whose poetic ABCs included "A Few Don'ts for Imagists" with its strictures upon the whole generalizing tendency, and MacLeish's "Ars Poetica" with its plump insistence on obliquity and suggestiveness, to such a one these unabashed abstract nouns and conceptually aerated adjectives should have been altogether out of the question. "Glorious," "beautiful," "universal," "banishment," "despair," "discord," "destruction"—usually one would have demurred at the torpor of this vocabulary, its indifference to the expectation of particularity. Usually, too, one's orthodox assumptions would have been surprised and ruffled by the unembarrassed didacticism of the lines. Nothing was being dramatized; the speaker in the poem seemed to be irrefutably one with the voice of the poet; he seemed, moreover, to know exactly what he wanted to say before he began to say it, and indeed the poem aspired to deliver what we had once long ago been assured it was not any poem's business to deliver: a message.

Yet it was thrilling. It was exalted. It echoed the high terms of fundamental texts. It proclaimed in argent speech truths we had assumed to be previous to poetry, so richly established outside its formal citadel that they could never be admitted undisguised or untransmuted through the eye of the lyric needle. But still, here they were in a modern poem—big, pulpit-worthy affirmations,

290

boosted all the farther by that one metaphorical line about a unicorn and an echo in the mountains.

I wonder, however, if Robert Pinsky had told me that the lines had been composed by a Jesuit rector from Holy Hill, north of campus, would my response have remained as uncomplicatedly positive? Granted, what gives the poem its ultimate force is the proclamation of trust in values which gave Western civilization a justifying vision of itself until the civilization became so unnerved by its contradictory history of atrocity that it could barely affirm the radiant categories upon which it was founded. Nevertheless, the force of the proclamation does not reside in its contents alone. The artfulness of its diction, rhythm, and tone is primarily what secures our attention and assent. It is a feat of rhetoric, and I can imagine a perverse and resourceful critic arguing for the unreliability of the performing voice here. But even so, given that the poem's rhetoric and content are truly bonded, should it matter at all who composed it?

That very bonding, however, is surely effected in great part by our awareness of the context from which Czeslaw Milosz's text emerges. The bright shafts of humanism which were projected in the original Polish against a background of dark communal experience might shine less convincingly if they originated instead from a source of professional uplift and correction such as a rectory. It counted for much that this poem was written by somebody who resisted the Nazi occupation of Poland and broke from the ranks of the People's Republic after the war and paid for the principle and pain of all that with a lifetime of exile and self-scrutiny. The poem, in fact, is a bonus accruing to a life lived in the aftermath of right and hurtful decisions. It was written, like the great majority of Milosz's poems, against the grain, because while his lyrics were a mode of contemplation rather than a mode of action, they existed nevertheless as works of obstinate and solitary opposition to what a debased idiom was all too ready to call "historical necessity."

Obviously, then, the "envy" I referred to earlier is based on this kind of admiration by English-speaking poets in the West for those poets, particularly in the Soviet republics and the Warsaw Pact countries, whose poetry not only witnesses the poet's refusal to lose his or her cultural memory but also testifies thereby to the continuing efficacy of poetry itself as a necessary and redemptive mode of being human.

What translation has done over the last couple of decades is to introduce us not only to new literary traditions but also to link the new literary experience to a modern martyrology, a record of courage and sacrifice which elicits our unstinted admiration. So, subtly, with a kind of hangdog intimation of desertion, poets in English sense the locus of poetic greatness shifting away from their language. This is not to suggest that poets and readers are not still sensible of the achievements of Yeats and Frost and Eliot and Auden as the unlooked-for events in poetry which they were and are—geological occurrences which have altered the contours of the language we look back upon. These remain undeniable forms in our literary memory. Yet gradually, shadowy others, wraiths from beyond, have begun to move in the Elysian background. We have been made conscious, for example, of the passionate driven spirits of Russian poetry in the teens, twenties, and thirties of this century. Whether we can truly know the force and brilliance of their work through translation is not a question I wish to address here. It seems self-evident that what the reader who does not speak Russian experiences as the poem in translation is radically and logically different from what the native speaker experiences, phonetics and feelings being so intimately related in the human makeup. What I am suggesting, rather, is the way in which our sense of the fate and scope of modern Russian poetry has implicitly offered another bench at which subsequent work will have to justify itself. How often, in epigraphs to essays and poems, or as the subject of essays and poems, or as corroborating allusions in essays and poems, do we not nowadays come upon the names of Tsvetaeva and Akhmatova and the Mandelstams and Pasternak? In these cases and in many others—Mayakovsky, Esenin, Blok, Gumilev—the poets have provided a full answer to the exacting question devised by Geoffrey Hill for all those who would be tested for passage into the realm of utter writing:

> Must men stand by what they write
> As by their camp-beds or their weaponry
> or shell-shocked comrades while they sag and cry?

All of these answer yes. All *stand* by their writing in the sense that writing is their perpetuation, their monument. But they *stand by* what they write also; they toe the line, not just the verse line but the one where courage is tested, where to stand by what you write is to have to stand your ground and take the consequences. For these poets, the mood of writing is the indicative mood and for that reason they constitute a shadow-challenge to poets who dwell in the conditional, the indeterminate mood which has grown characteristic of so much of the poetry one has been reading in the journals and new books in America for years.

We cannot know, as I have said, what these heroic names mean in the original language. For that, we take the word of the best poetic intelligences of their time and tongue. But then it is not so much their procedure as poets on the page which is influential as the composite image which has been projected of their conduct. That image, congruent with the reality, features a poet tested by dangerous times. What is demanded is not any great public act of confrontation or submission; what is demanded is rather a certain self-censorship, an agreement to forge, in the bad sense, the uncreated conscience of a race, to graft the undetermined, individual tongue of the poet upon the choral tongues of the literature of the state. Their resistance to this pressure, however, is not initially or necessarily political. The poets are more concerned with the authenticity of their creative processes than with the success or failure of state policies—and most people who are aware of the nature of a writer's martyrdom are aware of this. As a matter of historical fact, Osip Mandelstam was literally unable to swallow the lie of Socialist realist poetry: he simply could not write the praises of a hydroelectric dam, not even to save his life. But there is of course a spin-off, a ripple effect, to such deviant artistic conduct. It is the refusal by this rearguard minority which exposes to the vanguard majority the abjectness of their collapse, as they flee for security into whatever self-deceptions the party line requires of them. And it is because they effect this exposure that the poets become endangered: people are never grateful for being reminded of their moral cowardice.

Joseph Brodsky has put all this with characteristic force and succinctness. "My personal argument would be," he said in an interview last year in Dublin, "that the undemocratic society commits not a political crime against its people but an anthropological crime. It reduces the human potential, which is what the poet stands for. He stands for the greater ability of an individual to create mentally or spiritually or whatever—linguistically." More sardonically, Zbigniew Herbert concludes a poem called "The Power of State"—in his recent collection *Report from the Besieged City*—as follows:

Before we declare our consent we must carefully examine
the shape of the architecture the rhythm of the drums and pipes
official colors the despicable rituals of funerals

Our eyes and ears refused obedience
the princes of our senses proudly chose exile

but fundamentally it was a matter of taste
Yes taste
that commands us to get out to make a wry face draw out a sneer
even if for this the precious capital of the body the head
must fall

What is being implied here, by both Brodsky and Herbert, is what actually happened with such tragic consequences in the lives of many previous poets in the Slavic languages. It was not an ethical command that drove them into resistance but an artistic fidelity. And when poets of the Free World "envy" their Eastern European successors, they do so not in the simple-minded spirit sometimes attributed to them and which is a caricature of their subtler, more shadowy complexes. Western poets do not assume that a tyrannical situation is somehow mitigated by the fact that it produces heroic artists and last-ditch art. Their envy is not at all for the plight of the artist but for the act of faith in art which becomes manifest as the artist copes with the tyrannical conditions. They stand in awe as life rises to the challenge of Yeats's imagined "Black out; Heaven blazing into the head: / Tragedy wrought to its uttermost." In the professionalized literary milieu of the West, the poet is susceptible to self-deprecation and skepticism; the poet in the United States, for example, is aware that the machine of reputation-making and book distribution, whether it elevates or ignores him or her, is indifferent to the moral and ethical force of the poetry being distributed. A permissive, centrally heated, grant-aided pluralism of fashions and schools, a highly amplified language of praise which becomes the language of promotion and marketing—all this which produces from among the most gifted a procession of ironists and dandies and reflexive talents produces also a subliminal awareness of the alternative conditions and an over-the-shoulder glance toward them which I have characterized as envy.

Translations of these Eastern Bloc poets have not, admittedly, changed the styles of poetry in Britain or Ireland or Australia or North America. The several versions of Mandelstam or Akhmatova or Pasternak which are now available have not had any noticeable carryover; nor has the recent rise in the fortunes of Greek and Polish poetry entailed any significant change of note in our vernacular. Yet when a talented young British poet brings out a volume called *Katerina Brac*, written in the voice of an apocryphal Eastern European woman poet of that name, I am all the more persuaded that my contemporaries have been slightly displaced from an old at-homeness in their mother tongue and its hitherto entirely adequate poetic heritage.

Christopher Reid, the author of *Katerina Brac*, had been classed until its publication as a member of that group of English poets dubbed "Martians" after Craig Raine's eponymous "A Martian Sends a Postcard Home." Reid was and remains an adept of this school of writing, a mode involving a defamiliarization, a sleight-of-image process by which one thing is seen in terms of another thing. Indeed, the mode became so successful and winning that Raine and Reid were in danger of ending up prisoners of their own invention. I believe it is symptomatic that Reid's escape route from such a patented idiom should be by way of echoing certain poetic noises he could not naturally achieve in his own voice.

I am reminded of Stephen Dedalus's enigmatic declaration that the shortest way to Tara was via Holyhead, implying that departure from Ireland and an inspection of the country from the outside was the surest way of getting to the core of the Irish experience. I wonder if we might not nowadays affirm, analogously, that the shortest way to Whitby, the monastery where Caedmon sang the first Anglo-Saxon verses, is via Warsaw and Prague. To put it more directly, contemporary English poetry has become aware of the insular and eccentric nature of English experience in all the literal and extended meanings of those adjectives. England's island status, its off-center European positioning, its history of non-defeat and non-invasion since 1066, these enviable and (as far as the English are concerned) normative conditions have ensured a protracted life within the English psyche for the assumption that a possible and desirable congruence exists between domestic and imagined reality. But Christopher Reid's book represents a moment of doubt; and it represents also the delayed promise, though not the complete fulfillment, of a native British modernism.

This was potentially present in the stylistic intensities and the dislocated geopolitical phantasmagorias of early Auden, and in the visionary if low-wattage poetry of Edwin Muir. Muir's two postwar volumes, *The Labyrinth* in 1949 and *One Foot in Eden* in 1956, are not like anything that was going on just then on the poetic home front. These books existed equidistant from the neoromantic rhetoric of George Barker and Dylan Thomas and from the tight formation-flying of the Empson/Auden division. It so happened that it was the Movement poets, Larkin, Davie, Enright, and others, the inheritors in the Empson/Auden line, who pointed the way for much of what happened over the next twenty years. Yet it could be thought a matter of regret that Edwin Muir—the poet who translated Kafka in the 1920s and who witnessed the Communist takeover in Czechoslovakia after the war, the one poet from the British island with an eschatological if somewhat somnambulist address to the historical moment in postwar Europe—did not succeed better in bringing the insular/vernacular/British imagination into more traumatic contact with a reality of which *Katerina Brac* is the wistful and literary afterimage. Here, for example, is Muir's "The Interrogation," from *The Labyrinth:*

We could have crossed the road but hesitated,
And then came the patrol;
The leader conscientious and intent,
The men surly, indifferent.
While we stood by and waited
The interrogation began. He says the whole
Must come out now, who, what we are
Where we have come from, with what purpose, whose
Country or camp we fight for or betray.
Question on question.
We have stood and answered through the standing day
And watched across the road beyond the hedge
The careless lovers in pairs go by,
Hand linked in hand, wandering another star,
So near we could shout to them. We cannot choose

Answer or action here,
Though still the careless lovers saunter by
And the thoughtless field is near.
We are on the very edge,
Endurance almost done,
And still the interrogation is going on.

There is something different here, in spite of some quite specific Auden echoes. "The Interrogation" anticipates by a couple of decades the note which would be heard when A. Alvarez began to edit his influential Penguin Modern European Poets series in the late sixties, a note as knowledgeable as it was powerless to survive with any sort of optimism in the light of what it knew.

So Muir's poem is "European"—but in a way very different from the way that Robert Lowell's *Imitations* is "European." Those translations, which appeared a dozen years later, are still confident in their cultural and historical self-possession. Lowell's versions are offered as bridges to link up with an undemolished past. The breach made by the war years did not succeed in dissociating Lowell and his contemporaries living under the roof of English from the enterprise of the great modernists. Pound and Eliot and Joyce may have regarded themselves as demolitionists of sorts but from a later perspective they turned out to be conservationists, keeping open lines to the classical inheritance of European literature. In getting ready for the end of a world, they extended its life expectancy indefinitely.

If, therefore, Lowell, Randall Jarrell, Keith Douglas, Louis MacNeice, Louis Simpson, Dylan Thomas, and Eliot himself all testified at different moments and in different registers in their poetry to the horror and fury of the war, they did so with an unbroken historical nerve. The war may have made as great a gap in their sense of human nature as bombs made in the cities, but the poetic tradition inside which these poets worked cushioned the blast. It was as if a kind of cultural air-raid shelter were prepared by Eliot's reinforcement of the very idea of tradition itself. I hope I will not be considered a boor or an ingrate if I adduce the famous passage in "Little Gidding" as an illustration of how effective the beauties of the poetic heritage could be in keeping at bay the actual savagery of the wartime experience. There, Hitler's Luftwaffe could be sent packing as a dark dove beneath the horizon of its homing, and the All Clear after the air raid could summon matutinal airs which drifted once from the dew of a high eastern hill towards the battlements of Elsinore.

"Little Gidding," however, is exactly the kind of poetry which was due to come into disrepute in many quarters, especially in America, during the sixties and the seventies. Head poetry. Academic. Rational-male-imperalist. Will-infected. It would be superfluous even if it were possible here to retrace the story of the Buddhist backlash, the deep-image underground, the whole amalgam of impulses and alternatives from Beat to speed which became operative in deliberate opposition to the perceived academicism of the "establishment" poets. But it is in this area that my notion of "identification" comes into play. If we think, for example, of Gary Snyder's poetic enterprise, we think too of his access to Oriental and American Indian poetry. If we think of W. S. Merwin, we think also immediately of a corroborating body of translations done by the poet himself. If we think of James Wright and Robert Bly, we cannot fail to think of their own styles growing continuous with their various translations of Vallejo and Neruda and Tranströmer and Trakl. And I daresay that if I knew enough about the genesis of early Ashbery, I might be citing certain lesser-known French surrealists (except that by some odd convention, French poetry hardly seems to count as translated poetry at all).

All the same, it is sufficient to invoke these names to alert ourselves to the very different relationship which obtains between them and their foreign-language familiars and that between Lowell and his originals. Lowell's foreign poets are reminders of what is there to be lived up to; their function is admonitory and conservative. Bly's poets are models of how to do it right; their function is subversive and instructional. "What is so amazing in this century has been the blindness of Americans," Bly declared in an interview in the *San Francisco Book Review* in the early seventies. "There is this incredible poetry in Spain, in South America, in Russia. Williams did not see it. Pound did not see it. . . . Pound almost never mentioned Rilke, for example. Why not? Because he's too inward."

Bly would go on to do his own versions of Rilke and Neruda and Tranströmer and others with whom he could identify because their creative procedures represented a challenge to the dominant and, as he saw it, undesirable poetic practices ratified by Departments of English. His purpose was to discomfit the formalists, and he

298

threw his foreign-language exemplars like shock troops into the assault. Here he is, with a wonderfully enjoyable riff about Neruda:

> His imagination sees the hidden connections between conscious and unconscious substances with such assurance that he hardly bothers with metaphors—he links them by tying their hidden tails. He is a new kind of creature moving about under the surface of everything. . . . Compared to him, most American poets resemble blind men moving gingerly along the ground from tree to tree, from house to house, feeling each thing for a long time and then calling out "House!" when we already know it is a house.
>
> Neruda has confidence in what is hidden. The Establishment respects only what the light has fallen on, but Neruda likes the unlit just as well. He writes of small typists without scorn, and of the souls of huge, sleeping snakes.

This is great stuff altogether, and it only becomes less enjoyable when you think of a whole body of standard-issue workshop surrealism which rambles permissively in the wake of such pugnacious advocacy. Why do I grow niggardly faced with such beguiling and opulent invention? It has to do, I am sure, with extraliterary considerations, with a half-suppressed resentment that such poetic identification has issued in a kind of unwarranted annexation, whereby South American poetry's location within the literary sphere is equivalent to its place in political spheres of influence. Sullenness, if not resentment, that a poetry like Vallejo's, born from an experience of exposure and deprivation, from a sensibility both stoical and penitential, and from a language at once vestigially Catholic and persistently elemental, that such a poetry should translate and precipitate into uplift and felicity in a world of plenty; that what was once passionate and obliquely political should be the ratifying authority for work which asks us only to applaud its beguiling negotiations with the private unconscious; that what was once wrung valiantly from history should become available at such greatly reduced emotional prices.

In the introduction to their anthology of contemporary poetry in translation, *Another Republic,* Mark Strand and Charles Simic make a distinction between two broad categories of poet who appear in the book: the mythological and the historical. They write:

> The origins of the mythological vision can be seen in surrealism, which, by concerning itself with the unconscious, found a method for uncovering and using archetypal imagery. It restored to the familiar world its strangeness and gave back to the poet his role of myth maker. Thus, for the mythological poet the miraculous is close at hand, easily encountered if he pays attention, as he must, since attention is his most important faculty. . . .
>
> For the poets whose vision is dominated by historical consciousness . . . in history nothing changes except the names. . . . For poets like Milosz and Herbert there is no way to forget that despite our utopian ideologies we live in a world of wars, famine, and faithlessness. Such poets bear tragic witness to the social and political events of their time, and their work is characterized by two modes of self-expression: the lyric, which attempts to ennoble the suffering of those who are victimized or estranged; and the comic, which recognizes the absurdity of individual destinies in the presence of the great abstractions of history.

This is well said, but it does come from an introduction and therefore it deliberately presents a rather trim summary of the topic. But it is a useful summary which persuades me to be trim also, and to say that the example of the mythological type of poet has been well taken in much recent American practice. Taken, perhaps, to a point where mythological and surrealist procedures, which were originally a method for breaking through into life, have become a ring of literary defense against life. What the great modernists did in a redemptive way when they discovered forms which would allow us to contemplate the unforeseen nature of our consciousness is being done nowadays in a debilitating way by richly gifted contemporaries, insofar as the forms which they offer us allow us to contemplate only what is foreseen and already approved as intrinsically poetic. There has been an overidentification with the "mythological" poetic. There has been an overidentification with the "mythological" school; therefore one of the functions of poetry at the present time in America should be to take cognizance again of poetry's covenant with the historical.

In "Little Gidding," which we considered previously, Eliot's persona wanders through the newsreel familiarity of a blitz, an aquiline revenant, an earnest of desirable Shakespearean sympathy between natural and moral worlds, of a Dantesque order of good and evil; he also constitutes imaginary proof that an ordained and suprahistorical reality persists, and it is of course one of the poetry's triumphs to make such a faith provisionally tenable. But it is Muir's persona, in the poem which I quoted, who seems to be more truly our representative, stunned and ineffective at the center of a menacing pageant, what Eliot called the vast panorama of violence and futility which is contemporary history. If Muir's poetry is far less authoritative and ungainsayable than Eliot's, there is nevertheless audible in it a note which sounds both elegiac for and posthumous to the European civilization which produced it. We who live and have our being in English know that this note is proper to the world we have come to inhabit, to the extent that our own recent history of consumerist freedom and eerie nuclear security seems less authentic to us than the tragically tested lives of those who live beyond the pale of all this fiddle. Which is why the note sounded by translated poetry from that world beyond is so credible, desolating, and resuscitative.

I would propose, then, that there was a road not taken in poetry in English in this century, a road traveled once by the young Auden and the middle-aged Muir. Further, because we have not lived the tragic scenario which such imaginations presented to us as the life appropriate to our times, our capacity to make a complete act of faith in our vernacular poetic possessions has been undermined. Consequently, we are all the more susceptible to translations which arrive like messages from those holding their own much, much farther down that road not taken by us— because, happily, it was a road not open to us.

Finally, to put it another way, which was Muir's way: when we read translations of the so-called historical poets of Soviet Russia and Eastern Europe and Greece, "We are on the very edge. . . . And still the interrogation is going on."

nominated by The Yale Review

QUERENCIA

by STEPHEN DOBYNS

from POETRY

In the children's story of Ferdinand the Bull,
the bull gets off. He sits down, won't fight.
He manages to walk out of the ring without that
sharp poke of steel being shoved through
his back and deep into his heart. He returns
to the ranch and the sniffing of flowers.
But in real life, once the bull enters the ring,
then it's a certainty he will leave ignominiously,
dragged out by two mules while the attention of
the crowd rivets on the matador, who, if he's good,
holds up an ear, taken from the bull, and struts
around the ring, since it is his business to strut
as it is the bull's business to be dragged away.

●

It is the original eagerness of the bull which
takes one's breath. Suddenly he is there, hurtling
at the barrier, searching for something soft and
human to flick over his shoulder, trying to hook
his horn smack into the glittering belly
of the matador foolish enough to be there.
But there is a moment after the initial teasing
when the bull realizes that ridding the ring
of these butterfly creatures is not what
the afternoon is about. Sometimes it comes with
the first wrench of his back when the matador

302

turns him too quickly. Sometimes it comes
when the picador is driving his lance into
the bull's crest—the thick muscle between
the shoulder blades. Sometimes it comes when
the banderillos place their darts into that same
muscle and the bull shakes himself, trying to
free himself of that bright light in his brain.
Or it may come even later, when the matador
is trying to turn the bull again and again,
trying to wrench that same muscle which he uses
to hold up his head, to charge, to toss a horse.
It is the moment the bull stops and almost thinks,
when the eagerness disappears and the bull
realizes these butterflies can cause him pain,
when he turns to hunt out his querencia.

●

It sounds like care: querencia—and it means
affection or fondness, coming from querer—
to want or desire or love, but also to accept
a challenge as in a game, but also it means
a place chosen by a man or animal—querencia—
the place one cares most about, where one is
most secure, protected, where one feels safest.
In the ring, it may be a spot near the gate
or the place he was first hurt or where
the sand is wet or where there's a little blood,
his querencia, even though it looks like any
other part of the ring, except this is the spot
the bull picks as his home, the place he will
defend and keep returning to, the place where
he again decides to fight and lifts his head
despite the injured muscle, the place the matador
tries to keep him away from, where the bull,
sensing defeat, is most dangerous and stubborn.

●

The passage through adulthood is the journey
through bravado, awareness and resignation
which the bull duplicates in his fifteen minutes
in the ring. As for the querencia, we all have

a place where we feel safest, even if it is only
the idea of a place, maybe an idea by itself,
the place that all our being radiates out from,
like an ideal of friendship or justice or perhaps
something simpler like the memory of a back porch
where we laughed a lot and how the setting sun
through the pine trees shown on the green chairs,
flickered off the ice cubes in our glasses.
We all have some spot in our mind which we
go back to from hospital bed, or fight with
husband or wife, or the wreckage of a life.
So the bull's decision is only the degree
to which he decides to fight, since the outcome
is already clear, since the mules are already
harnessed to drag his body across the sand.
Will he behave bravely and with dignity or
will he be fearful with his thick tongue lolling
from his mouth and the blood making his black
coat shiny and smooth? And the audience, no matter
how much it admires the matador, watches the bull
and tries to catch a glimpse of its own future.

●

At the end, each has a knowledge which is just
inevitability, so the only true decision
is how to behave, like anyone supposedly—
the matador who tries to earn the admiration
of the crowd by displaying grace and bravery
in the face of peril, the bull who can't
be said to decide but who obeys his nature.
Probably, he has no real knowledge and,
like any of us, it's pain that teaches him
to be wary, so his only desire in defeat
is to return to that spot of sand, and even
when dying he will stagger toward his querencia
as if he might feel better there, could
recover there, take back his strength, win
the fight, stick that glittering creature to the wall,
while the matador tries to weaken that one muscle—
the animal all earnestness, the man all deceit—

until they come to that instant when the matador
decides the bull is ready and the bull appears
to submit by lowering his head, where the one
offers his neck and the other offers his belly,
and the matador's one hope is for a clean kill,
that the awful blade of the horn won't suddenly
rear up into the white softness of his groin.

One October in Barcelona I remember watching
a boy, an apprentice, lunge forward for the kill
and miss and miss again, how the bull would fling
the sword out of his back and across the ring,
and again stagger to his feet and shake himself,
and how the boy would try again and miss again,
until his assistant took a dagger and stabbed
repeatedly at the spinal cord as the bull tried
to drag himself forward to that place in the sand,
that querencia, as the crowd jeered and threw
their cushions and the matador stood back ashamed.
It was cold and the sun had gone down. The brightly
harnessed mules were already in the ring and everyone
wanted to forget it and go home. How humiliating
it seemed and how hard the bull fought at the end
to drag himself to that one spot of safety, as if
that word could have any meaning in such a world.

nominated by Raymond Carver, Lisel Mueller,
Lucia Perillo, Michael Ryan and Marilyn Waniek

A CROWDED TABLE

by DEVORAH MAJOR

from ZYZZYVA

1. the shadows

back, the other way, across a salt line brine/
cold/gray. tied to obeah. solemn chants/cane cropped low, sticky
cutting fingers. granules of sugar cane become glass slivers under
the nails, across the backs. they bled into the land and called it
home, history was carried on the head, held high, chin thrust out,
tongue clicking, end words softened, eh?

drums were hidden in the cadence of speech. cutting cane, fishing,
swimming in the brine. our hair bleached bronze, red, yellow,
chasing the sun. many had seen god in those times. some lain with
her shadow. others were horses god rode carried by the wind.

we stood tall, never learning to bow, ebony/mariney/taupe.
our family became wed to silence, a gem of secrets passed in
measured breaths/the way the fish was turned, scales falling across
a dull knife blade, boat people, us, early on.

2. the dinner

she had forgotten the lines in her feet, the thickness of skin which
was shoe and carriage; the way our heels would split and have
to be taped. no pumice could scale away hundreds of years of
constant travel which brought the minister's wife to this table
where she sat her mouth cottony with food, her words mashing
out between bits, "praise the lord, for this bountiful feast."

"don't get confused thanking god when it's me that cooked the food," the grandmother quietly nods to herself as she circles the table passing biscuits. the wife was always calling on god so her minister-husband would look less longingly at the young flesh, sweet and sticky with hastily swallowed soda pop; naive expectant eyes still looking for miracles in hard dark pews. to avoid these visions she constantly called out thanks for a holy intervention.

(she forgot her ancestor/the one who held a child-full belly beneath the sand while buried neck deep/ants chewing eyelids caked with mucus sweat/cane juice dripping across her brow. it was erzulie came and dug her out called to oya for herbs; laid on a plaster which stung, yet nourished. erzulie who asked only for a candle, fresh flowers, a chicken at sunrise. she forgot to look at the lines in her feet.

"don't he provide though. praise the lord and pass the coleslaw." as no one dips a head.

"save some praises for the cook," grandmother inhales offering ice to the sweating glass. her mouth is set in a line resembling newly smelted iron; her smooth mahogany a volcano of reds as she pours more ice tea, each movement a remembrance of times she has survived. she, whose feet are lined and shoeless, moves quietly around the table serving each guest before they know they have a need.

the minister's wife dabs a grease-coated mouth with the corner of her napkin. "ummm umm umm, the lord was certainly speaking to you when you was fryin' this fish!"

the grandmother sucks in her reply, settles into a chair next to the sideboard. she cradles her head. never hoarding food was a tradition, hunger a shadow of childhood/the corner that never again is full. past ache, staring quietly ahead her gods looking over her. she remembers gently piling earth around the pole-bean shoots, pulling up frail weeds that taunt a garden's fullness; salads grown in seasons.

the lord sent no cake that evening, although the can sat full. he brought no coffee and stopped short of sherbet orange and sweet,

307

unable to get past freezer slush. the cousin leans across to the minister's wife, a scraping of plates muffling her hiss, "siddity, that's what she is. dem jamaica folks always tink dey more, my husband always say."

the pious minister sits, absent at the head of the table, his tongue seeking out a choir girl's sugars. we cut cane, built boats, spread blood between the rocks and the sea, that we would become bound to this new land and finally know each other. yet a strange god sits at our table demanding praise when it's been centuries since he turned water to wine, and why grapes, sun and time will do as well. years since he dried the red sea and raised the dead, and if the truth be told we never knew death before he came anyway, only a passing on. yet, this god in man's image keeps getting praised for a meal he did not cook, a garden he did not nourish.

the grandmother's gods sit on her shoulders. her tongue hits the back of her teeth. she sees her gods chasing her granddaughter, she is afraid of their power; they make more than miracles, sticks, bones ashes and blood. they demand constant attention and accept no offhand praise. cowrie shells ring in her ears, obeah fashioning the music, the music of her walk. the bible a parable of a dream. and now, this hollow woman looking through her history asking for another biscuit, each bite praising the lord and master, the lord and master, the master, who, when we were bound to cutting cane, always let us pray each sunday.

the sun sets on the woman. the pastor's wife still prays between bites. the cousin, mouth full and stomach bloated, rests too tired to talk. the grandmother, still holding water between her teeth and feeling it turn to salt, wine and back to cane sugar dripping down her throat. the granddaughter lights a candle, thick with a smoke. heady perfume falls from the ceiling, drifts into the summer air. the haitians are hungry. obeah makes jamaica strong. voodoo crushes upon haitian backs. steeped in petro they wear veves around their hearts. the contradictions of time are unspoken, a jewel of silence painting the women's skins. they flush. to return takes many years. it's said africans still walk across the ocean floor; cut their feet on the spines of sea anemone. each crease is etched on the bottoms of our feet.

fireflies search out each other's warmth, glittering as they wither in the summer darkness. the loas are hidden beneath the grandmother's brow, she denies them because she has learned to survive reflecting her history only in her walk, moans she carries but never releases to crying. a drop or two of dew flows, at times, when she labors over the garden, a dew that helps the pole beans become long green crisp.

the silence is broken by a scratched record voice, "praise the lord, mrs., this meal has been one to remember. well, you know we must be moving on." and the waterfall spews from the grandmother's mouth. the minister's wife drenched in spit and brine watches as the water drops down her face. her hair becomes uncurled returning to gray and brittle kinks. her dress running flowers damp across her breast held together with wire and elastic. her hips quiver in rage/and then/a summer breeze later, she is dry. it has never happened, only a clicking of the tongue, a head pointing to the four corners of the room, white chalk settling in diamond patterns across the doorway.

the grandmother sweeps the visitors out. throws water in their path. "they won't be back this way again no time soon! praise the lord, hmmph."

evening shadows settle on the porch. the grandmother sits looking through the moon. the granddaughter sees herself looking at herself.

"no won't find this house again." the rocking chair creaks against floorboards. the grandmother tastes cane of other years, cools it with ice water. her teeth ache trying to remember things she has never known.

the house is still, moving only as the spirit breathes.

nominated by Zyzzyva

SIMPLE QUESTIONS
by LLOYD SCHWARTZ
from SHENANDOAH

Can you hear me? Do you
understand?

How are you feeling? Can you
feel anything?

Are you in pain? Is there anything
I can do?

Do you know me? Do you
know who I am?

*

When I dream about my father, he's
recovered. Home. He can move—walk; talk to
my mother; complain; even argue.
(The doctor at the hospital, not encouraging,
wouldn't deny this possibility.)

He comes downstairs and makes his way
toward his favorite chair, the one
with the florid cushions he'd stitched himself.
His breath comes hard, as it had
in the hospital; but suddenly, miraculously—

better!

I started having this dream
after my first visit.

                    *

"What comes after seven? Say it.
Try! What's the number after seven? . . . That's

right! Now what comes after eight? Tell me,
what comes after eight? . . ."

Once my mother got him to count
to fifteen.

Then, seven.

                    *

He was the old man you'd pass as you
hurried down the corridor to see your friend
in traction (touch football
terpsichore), or with pneumonia (not, thank God,
critical); the old man with the sucked-in
yellow face, no teeth, the oxygen tube
up his nose, the urine sac hanging from his bed.
Breathing hard; hardly moving; his eyes
blank, yet (weren't they?) following you . . .

Not your own.

The unhappy family whose
trouble he was . . .

NOT YOUR OWN.

                    *

"Hello! Say hello. How do you
feel? Are you feeling better?"

"A little better."

"Good." She leans over and
looks into his face. "Did you sleep OK?"

No answer.

"Do you know me? Who
am I? What's my name?"

"M-mom."

"And what's your name? Can you
tell me your name?"

"Sam."

"Good! Are you hungry? Let me give you
some soup? A little custard? . . ."

"No."

"Are you thirsty? Where's your straw?
Would you like some juice?"

"Yes."

"How about a nice shave? Would you
like me to give you a shave? . . . There!

Now you look handsome!"

He rubs his face with his right hand;
he keeps rubbing his face.

*

"Are you the son? What a pity! He seems like
such a nice person, such a sweet old man.
It's a shame . . . Last night he was very quiet—
slept like a baby. Didn't bother anybody!
By the end of the week he'll be ready to go home."

*

"Wake up! Open your eyes. Can you
keep your eyes open?"

No answer.

"Look at me. Can you see me? Who
am I? Do you know who I am?"

No answer.

"Can you hear me? Do you understand
what I'm saying to you?"

". . . Yes."

"Look around. Where are you?
Do you know where you are?"

No answer.

"Can you feel anything? Can you feel
my hand? Where's my hand?"

I put my hand in his; he
squeezes hard.

"Who am I? Do you know who I am?"

". . . Yes."

"What's my name? Say it. Who
am I? Tell me who I am."

". . . Fa-ther."

*

No love lost. A lifetime of
anger; resentment; disapproval. Could I pretend—
even now—a deep, personal concern?

Prodding him to speech (what the doctor
ordered), to recover enough of his mind to
help my mother endure his release,

313

hypnotized me, gripped my attention, the way
his right hand gripped my hand—the last remnant
of his unrelenting, fist-clenched

denunciations of the world:

of the "Hitler Brothers," who refused him even
a moment's rest in the sweatshops where he
spent his working life stitching men's clothes;

of relatives, or neighbors, never generous or
grateful enough, for someone rarely generous
or grateful; of my friends, of *me*—stymied by my

anger, resentment, disapproval . . . The way
his right hand gripped the hedgecutter, lifted it,
and aimed it at my head.

"I have to go now. Goodbye! I'll see you
tomorrow . . . Do you hear me?
Feel better. I hope you feel better."

                    *

"How do you feel? Talk to me. Tell me
how you feel."

". . . Not so good."

"Are you in pain? Where does
it hurt you?"

No answer.

"Can I do anything? Should I
get the doctor?"

". . . No doctor can cure me."

                    *

"He had a restless night; couldn't swallow—

we had to pump out his throat. His pressure
sank way down. There was nothing else we
could do . . . I'm sorry. He just fell
asleep, very peaceful, and stopped breathing."

*

"Can you hear me?"
"Yes."

"How are you feeling?"
"A little better."

"Do you know me? Who am I?"
"My son."

"Is there anything I can do?"
"No."

nominated by Joyce Carol Oates

ONE OF TWO

fiction by ROSELLEN BROWN

from NEW LETTERS

Monica HAD ALWAYS wanted to have an enemy. A life of rancor and vendetta was not what she had in mind exactly, but it did seem obvious that if no one disliked or disagreed with her vigorously, she must not stand for anything. (*Stand for?* she would challenge herself, scrupulous. What does that mean, *stand for?* People are not ideas or political platforms, and her life was no debate.) Well, then: if everybody approved of you, you must not cast a shadow, that was all. Invisibility was what she worried about; "mousiness," she and her friends had called it when they were twelve and heartlessly critical of other people's friends. She even discussed this with her husband, Rudy, and they decided that it would be fine with them if they were not so universally considered decent and admirable. Not that they were planning to go out and start fights—they had to trust that in a life properly lived, enemies, like wrinkles or laugh lines, would naturally occur.

Rudy acquired one first, though it never came to much, this nemesis. He had, years ago as a new graduate student, done some work for a professor, in the way of those unequal relationships in which the student does the work and the professor takes the credit. They had been studying the relationship of physical activity to dreams and spent a great deal of time submerged in the watery darkness of the sleep lab, monitoring rapid eye movements, recording narratives of escapes down narrow corridors, falls from heights, the dead returned and the living dispatched to hell.

(This was what Rudy had been doing when he and Monica got

married, and it made for a strange backdrop to the beginning of their time together. Because he spent so much of the day in unnatural dark and silence, tiptoeing around his experimental subjects who slept with wires clamped to their heads, Rudy had trouble sleeping at night; and yet unrested, he went around tired and irritable all the time. This underwater stage lasted nearly a year. Monica, who was a cellist and lived in bright stage light, thought that if their marriage hadn't survived the strain she'd have sued the professor for damages.)

When, years later, Rudy submitted his thesis, which was called "Dream and Daily Life: A Correlation," his ex-professor wrote him an offensive note on the stationery of a minor Canadian university accusing him of thievery of ideas and insufficient gratitude to his mentor, whose name had been mentioned only five times and whose "intellectual parentage" was insufficiently acknowledged. It was a paternity suit, Rudy liked to say, filed on university letterhead.

Rudy had, in fact, sighed for the stinginess of the complainer and the desperation of the complaint, for the visibly reduced circumstances of his old professor who must be chafing with jealousy out there in that prairie province while Rudy was setting himself up in his first job, a good one, at a northern California school of solid stature. He had the amplitude of spirit to see through his professor's threats (of a lawsuit, of informal blackballing "in the profession"—scurrilous stories, in other words, but who would hear him from so far away?) to the dreadful anxiety and weariness beneath. "That's no way to treat your first enemy," Monica complained, "by understanding and forgiving him. You're not going to be good at this at all." But Rudy had shrugged: the man was still doing papers called "Dreams and Jogging," "Speed of Arousal Response in Athletes," "Exhaustion and the EEG"—the same song in the same key. He had lost interest in all that a long time ago.

When Monica opened her mail one day and confronted her first enemy in earnest, she understood the difference between a sloppy pot-shot and a lethal blow. It seemed to be the mail that brought them the news of their offenses; certain kinds of people clearly preferred to fight unseen, and from a safe remove. Nonetheless this letter felt as dangerous and real to her as the one genuine fight she had ever been witness to, on a winter afternoon in the Automat in New York, when two men had begun to throw chairs and actual stunning, breath-stopping blows—noisy popping sounds—to each other's chests and shoulders. Solid hits they were, and the receiving body kicked each time at the open-handed slap like a rifle after a shot. What was terrifying about the fight, and so unlike even the most vivid movie bar scene, was the way it threatened to engulf all onlookers; how the metal and leather chairs flew from the cleared center of the circle, out of control; the way the two men, red-faced with rage, kept turning to any spectator who dared say a word of disparagement, even of encouragement, and offered to deal with him next. She had edged away, terrified, to the back of the crowd, and even there she would not have been surprised to have received a ketchup bottle or one of those familiar Automat chairs right in her face, which felt, suddenly, irresponsibly bare.

The letter felt like that fight to her, even if it was only words—real anger wildly spinning towards her, dangerously out of control.

You bitch, it said, where *Hi!* or *Darling Monica* ought to have been. *Now I can tell you this. All the time you thought we were friends I was hoping I would never have to see you again. You must have known whenever we were together for all those endless sessions I felt I was being cut up a hundred times with razor blades. You never supported me or wanted me to succeed, you only wanted me to feel terrible about myself. Maybe you were jealous of me and my talent, how should I know? Just realize that you never took me in as a dear friend, your behavior is cruel and if the world does not know it now they eventually will know how underhanded you are. If you will change and reform, we should be able to go on being friends. Otherwise I hope I never have to see you again. It is your move.*

The letter, which Monica read in a single intake of breath, was typed; it was signed *Glenna* in the generous blocky girls' prep school handwriting she had been reading, it seemed forever, on post cards and notes written from country cabins and distant cities, on birthday cards and the little tags that had hung from Christmas presents. The last time she'd confronted it, at the end of a thank-you note, sat the straight-forward *G*. Glenna had been out to see them on a transcontinental trip only a few months ago, and when she got home to Boston she'd sent a bread-and-butter note and three color snapshots of all of them in Golden Gate Park, plus one of herself squinting into the sun at Seal Rocks.

Rudy had said nothing as she'd picked up the envelope. The

letter was open but back in the pile, under the *New Yorker* and the dunning note from the Alma Mater fund. They had the kind of marriage which allowed, even encouraged, them to read each other's mail on the supposition that they'd discuss every letter anyway, as they would every encounter. Why, Monica always said, be coy? Now Rudy watched her make her way swiftly through Glenna's outcry. He stayed thoughtfully on the far side of the room so as not to crowd her as she took the painful blows, her long freckled face reddening, one hand flat and open at her throat as though to protect her jugular.

When she had finished the letter, Monica looked around her angrily as if the room might suddenly have filled with people who were staring at her. Rudy came to her side, quickly and silently, startling her. He put one arm around her shoulder. "Honey, I hope you won't—"

"What *is* this?" Monica demanded, and shook out the page. She was staring straight ahead.

Rudy was relieved. "I was afraid you were going to take it to heart, you always blame yourself for everything—"

Monica finally turned to him with a look of fresh fear in her eyes, the way she might look if someone were at her heels then and there. "But I *do* take it to heart. I take it very much to heart. Only that doesn't mean I blame myself." She made a pained noise—his mother, dying under the slackening kindness of morphine, had made such vague aching noises whenever there was anyone to hear. "Oh God," Monica said, "Rudy. I don't even—" Her voice dwindled and she read the letter again, for the third time, moving her lips as she arrived at the outrageous words, the unjust accusations, like a child whose reading is still insecure. "I need a drink, would you get me a beer or something?"

Rudy ran to get her what she needed. Monica, seeing him hurry to oblige her as though she had met with an accident and needed ice, and bandages, thought, I have, I've been attacked from behind. Glenna was one of her oldest friends and she had tried to kill her, there was no other way to see it. A spiritual mugger. She thought of those bewildering murders where there are no broken-down doors, no jimmied windows: "The victim appeared to know her attacker." She said all that to Rudy, trying to laugh, as he handed her a sweating can of beer. She would never be the same again, she thought. It can happen that fast! Even when she had

319

straightened up and stopped hunching over her new wound, she would be diminished by suspicion—of herself, of others.

That night before she fell asleep she thought about the time, long before "no fault," when she had argued angrily with an adjuster at the insurance agency after her car had been hit from behind on Memorial Drive. (It had in fact, been hit by another car that was in turn hit from the rear—classic blameless chain reaction.) "It doesn't matter to us whether you were at fault or not," he had said. "Statistically, you were involved. You were there to be hit, not somebody else. We have to take a long hard look at who gets hit." But, she had argued, when you've taken that look, what do you see? She had not understood, let alone agreed. The guiltless guilty?

But tonight she was ready to accede, if only she could put it differently: They were right, such guilt didn't have to do with fault or no-fault, or even with such imponderables as chance and defensive skill. It had to do with the future, with who you became. She would be marked forever now, bleeding internally. After an accident, she understood, one is never innocent again.

They were musicians, she the cellist, Glenna the pianist and—it had once been hard to think of the two of them without the third—Dot, their violinist. In college they had called themselves the Bizarre Trio, with a laugh and a nod at the Beaux Arts. Everything about their time together had been auspicious, even—as the school newspaper loved to report because the reviewer didn't know enough about music to comment on their performances—the way they represented three styles of beauty. Well, it wasn't beauty exactly, but they were a quaint combination that looked almost too carefully cast: Glenna with her peasant's buxomness and floating blond curls, Dot the dark one, long straight hair a sluice between her shoulders, and she, Monica, pale-skinned, red-haired, at her worst all freckles and invisible eyelashes, at her best vibrant and odd, a bold light springing from somewhere under that copper helmet of hair like the color of certain trees in autumn that seem to shine from the inside out. They received mash-notes from their audiences, sometimes communal, sometimes divided according to the taste of their admirers.

They went to Tanglewood together the summer after their senior year and sat, each of them, at the rear of her section, similarly

320

reduced in status but very busy, very happy, wearing matching painters hats that said BIZARRE!, gifts of the Music Department at graduation.

When Dot left Boston to go to Curtis, Monica and Glenna shelved their trio scores and invested in duets. There were some accommodations to be made. Two was not one fewer than three; the repertoire seemed to decree that Monica suddenly be the soloist and Glenna the "able accompanist." But they worked hard at their collaboration, listening to the way Rostropovich and Richter worked out the balance in the Beethoven sonatas, and Du Pré and Barenboim the Prokofiev. Glenna was not naturally assertive, though neither, really, was Monica. Dot had been the grandstander among them, the one who wanted to be a soloist, who dipped her head deepest when they bowed. She thrived on adrenalin while the other two held each other's hands and yawned with nerves, took trips from the green room to the bathroom, suffered mouths as dry as cotton balls. They took refuge in their numbers, finally, each responsible but not entirely exposed. But Glenna seemed to be shrinking, now that Dot had gone. "I am never going to upstage you, my dear," Monica assured Glenna when there were just the two of them. "These pieces will feature the two of us or no one. Only you have to play as if you mean it."

Glenna had bitten her lip. The solution, Monica had suggested as gently as she could, might be extra-musical. Perhaps it had to do with Glenna's overbearing father (a Congressman and a flirt) who had tormented her childhood by saying to her whenever they were in public, "Speak up, damn it, speak up!" but who never wanted to hear a word from her at home. Or she might look to her super-efficient mother, a professor of nutrition at the school of public health, a consultant and a columnist for the daily newspaper whose name everybody knew. (She couldn't cook so much as a breakfast omelet but she wrote Your Menu For Health, instructing greater Boston in how to make tofu doughnuts and low-calorie pies with cauliflower crusts.) She wore a lab coat wherever she went: it made her daunting even at the dinner table. Perhaps Glenna had once been the shy dreaming girl who played the piano to be alone; she had also, Monica insisted, played to be heard, and now there were people who genuinely did want to hear her. She was a good pianist who was cheating herself.

Glenna heard Monica out, agreed that her problems were

standing in the way of the music, and found herself a psychiatrist to see why she could assert herself when she was one of three but not one of two. Monica probed to make sure she hadn't hurt her feelings suggesting such a thing but Glenna said no, quite the contrary. She was grateful for a friend who cared about her—not only for the music's sake. Friends had the right, after all or—her eyes had clouded over with tears—what were friends for? Anyway (briskly) at the very least she had an obligation to Schubert or Mozart or whomever to hold up her end: Pianists were not meant to be invisible, inaudible, insubstantial. Everything about Glenna, her cheeks, her bosom, broadened as if her gratitude were a yeast. Being cared about made her soft and cozy-looking.

But first she had a problem, not a very original but nonetheless a real one. There was no way to pay her psychiatrist without somehow involving her parents' money.

"Well, your trust fund isn't *their* money," Monica argued. "That's for you, isn't it, to do with however you like. I mean, if you want to go skiing in St. Moritz with it, isn't that your business?"

"Still," Glenna answered, and when she shrugged her round shoulders she really did make herself look like a small child about to do something she knew was wrong. "The money has their fingerprints all over it, somehow."

"Oh look, everything any of us does has our fingerprints on it, our interest in music, our talent, it all comes from somewhere, doesn't it? My mother and her silver flute, that beautiful old—"

"My parents despise music. It doesn't accomplish anything, you know, it just *is*, and they're not about to forgive it that. The way it just sort of wafts around on the airwaves, it doesn't get bills passed or establish the dietary requirements of school lunch programs."

"But Glenna, look, there's the first thing you have to talk about with your therapist—how you staked your first rebellion on loving what you love."

"Hating what I hate, you mean." Glenna smiled bleakly and ran her fingers through her pale curls as if to wake them up.

"God knows it's true, any psychiatrist would tell you that you get a lot more mileage out of saying 'no' than 'yes'."

"What do you mean 'mileage'? Where have I ever been going?"

"Out of their sight, I guess. Someplace your parents can't follow. Or won't."

Glenna shrugged again; it was the dismissive movement she made more than most. "I'm not sure they ever noticed."

"How could they not notice you've got your back to them, you live your whole life in a place they're not comfortable in. It's a declaration. I mean, can't you see your piano says this very loud 'no' to what they are? They're not deaf." (Or maybe not loud enough, she thought but did not say; it was a little too neat, as if the day Glenna acknowledged it, she would bring her volume up.)

"Pretty close to deaf, I've always thought," Glenna was saying bitterly. "You're a lot cheaper than a shrink, you know. What if I buy you a couch and we start—"

"Really, Glenna. These are things you've got to understand. I'm not kidding."

"What does it have to do with Haydn?" Glenna looked away. Her lips had narrowed like those of a spiteful girl.

Monica shook her head. "And what does Haydn have to do with food stamps or the ERA?"

At first Monica feared the cure was going to be superficial. Glenna began to accent her white blouse-long black skirt recital uniform with bits of brightness, like a bird bringing home random twigs and strings to her nest. People's vision was drawn, by design, to her striped Equadorian belt or the vivid fuchsia bow that sat in her pale curls like a maraschino cherry in a cocktail. Well, all right, Monica thought. She, Monica, had to sit forever in the middle of the audience's vision whether she wanted to or not, poking up like a Maypole, her red hair vibrating under the lights. Maybe that was something pianists resented. Let her draw all eyes, share that attention. Anyway as their teachers used to remind them, music is no competition. Whoever won forfeited the game.

But Glenna's playing improved. She did gain volume, she advanced her own ideas, sometimes she even refused Monica's interpretations and put forth her own. "Good!" Monica would think. If a piece went spectacularly well, she'd say it out loud. "Oh, Glenna, much much better!" They were wonderful, she thought— in perfect balance, each assertive, each reticent by turns. At their best, Monica thought of them as swooping on the most flexible wings, bobbing and skidding around invisible corners of wind. Such ecstasies, shared, made them triumphant and vulnerable,

323

somehow. Sex might be one way to unclothe and exercise the soul; surely work, this mutual holy sweat of the Brahms second sonata was the other. They held each other's hand taking their bows and hurried offstage joined like children swinging up the street together.

Monica found a job teaching cello at a small Catholic girls' college in Rhode Island where her students were genteel and accomodated music in the tradition of the nineteenth century when one played as one embroidered, as one perfected an epistolary style. Glenna freelanced as harpsichordist with a few chamber orchestras and accompanied dancers at two studios. On the side they hired themselves out to schools, to college lyceums, cocktail parties, graduations and weddings, often in the company of a violinist or two but more frequently by themselves when they could sell the unique idea of "the intimate duo"—"Sunrise, Sunset" in that throbbing baritone voice of the cello. It was cheaper than a quartet and, they tried to imply, classier. The work didn't demand enough to keep their standards up but considering that Glenna was still at the conservatory and Monica was studying hard privately, it was satisfying. They were employed musicians, young, hard-working, in business. They had printed cards, an answering machine in case people called about jobs while they were out; they even hired an accountant as income tax time drew near. The subtleties, Bartok and Elliott Carter, they attended to in their offhours.

Then Monica met Rudy. Glenna had already married a law student named Cy, but that did very little to alter her schedule or her relations with Monica. Cy was easy-going and perpetually busy. He was one of those gentle fair-haired midwestern men who look comfortable and unconstrained in tightly buttoned shirts and three-piece suits and who, accustomed to obeying their fathers, yearly pour into the good law firms to do whatever is asked of them without complaint; he was impossible to dislike.

Rudy, on the other hand, disrupted everything. He too was unexceptionable. Glenna approved of him from the dark top of his head to the sneakers on his feet. He and Cy played squash together, the two couples ate in all the restaurants in *The Underground Gourmet*. But he had his doctorate, he had served two years of a post-doctoral fellowship and now he had a job. The job was in San Francisco.

Given the other choices—Arizona and Arkansas—Monica was ecstatic about the move. Could anyone have dreamed of a better city to be sent to? (One tended to think of first jobs with all the pessimism of military assignments.) They would finally have a wide-awake honeymoon surrounded by hills and bright Mediterranean-blue water.

Only the parting from Glenna was difficult, and the knowledge, inevitable from the start, that not only would she need a new teacher but she would have to begin again with another partner, learn a thousand intricacies of temperament and timing and, even at that, hope for the best. As the two women clung to each other on the eve of Monica's and Rudy's departure—their little car looked like an Okie truck, Monica's cello shrouded in its case, carefully buckled in a rear seat belt, a rack full of Rudy's experiment printouts on the roof and a U-Haul the size of a small room full of irreplaceable junk and wedding presents bobbing behind—Monica said to herself but not to Glenna who was still and always would be fragile, that chamber music was not a friendship as she had always called it, but a marriage. Perhaps it thrived without sex and generation, but it was a compound of thousands, millions of moments of intimacy incommunicable to another soul, and the end of it, the cessation of everything from hard work to exaltation, was like a divorce or a widowing. A partner was irreplaceable.

But, as with divorce or widowing, after a good many months of nostalgia in which she envied her old self, the way things used to be, the pain of her defection slackened and the need to replace her pianist began to seem natural again. It was hard to find someone she really enjoyed working with, but given sufficient time to play the field, she found a partner. This was a woman considerably older than Monica, unlikely-looking, suburban in her dress and habits but positively European in the fierceness of her devotion to her music. Her name was Sandi—complete to the "i"—and she had played for years with a very fine chamber orchestra. As Sandi beat time in her flat-heeled Capezios, her leg ticking in its plaid polyester pants, Monica worked at eradicating one more stereotype from her repertoire—taste in music and taste in clothing, or even that hideous makeshift that covered all the rest, "lifestyle," were not correlated and just as well. (Neither, she had learned a long time ago, was "intelligence," if by that she intended to say articulateness, or maturity, or even literacy.) If the best moments of the best composers were unpredictable, why should their performers all be cut from the same cookie mold? As long as Sandi didn't wear those slacks to concerts. . . .

She and Glenna wrote to each other faithfully if not frequently, and indulged in an occasional long phone call. One December a few years after the move, Glenna herself materialized for a visit, en route to see an aunt in Spokane who was footing the bill. She was rosy and pregnant; her pale hair, no longer so curly, had grown and she was wearing it up in a sophisticated sweep that made her look older. "More finished," Rudy said, beaming at her in surprise. It was true. It looked as if the swan in Glenna had finally emerged from her chubby duckling's down.

There had been no awkwardness in their reunion. From the first moment they were comfortable, their conversation quick with gossip about the music world and with ordinary talk about nothing Monica could remember long enough to tell Rudy how they had spent the day. Glenna brought the news that Dot had signed a record contract; she was going to solo with the New York Philharmonic next winter. They shook their heads in wonder. Dot's was an ambitiousness they had always recognized but had only irregularly dared imagine for themselves. They were journeymen ensemble players who loved their work, not soloists manquées. "She can have it," Glenna had said with one hand, mocking, on her heart as if the whole idea of such a life might make her swoon.

Monica showed her friend every lovely street, parking with her wheels carefully turned in toward the curb to keep her car from becoming what San Franciscans so quaintly called a "runaway." They drove to Sausalito for Sunday brunch on the water and went to the best and ugliest restaurant in Chinatown. Glenna now played regularly, piano and harpsichord, with a chamber group that met in a downtown Boston church; they had a full schedule of reviewed concerts and their notices had been quite good. It was easier than duets for sure, she said. "More satisfying? Less?" Monica asked. "Less strain," Glenna answered, smiling in acknowledgement of all they had pushed through together. "I'm probably backsliding—I'm one of eighteen!"

This was the last free time she would have till spring. The baby? Well, she was lucky to play piano, wasn't she. (She had taken to calling it that, as though she worked nights at some South Boston bar.) She had sporadic hours and no heavy work as long as she didn't have to move the damn piano herself.

This time, putting her on the plane for the duty leg of her trip, Monica laughed instead of crying. The ties of work broken and both their futures settled, she was free to enjoy Glenna as an old dear friend who had been something far more and was thus assured her own permanent niche in memory. "Goodbye, goodbye," she murmured into the top-knot that seemed like someone else's, that measure of Glenna's growing-up. "Next visit is mine. And when the baby comes—"

"You get the first call."

"After your parents—"

Glenna had smiled and shrugged as if to say, "What do you think," and disappeared down the accordion-pleated runway to her plane.

Months later—how far along had Glenna been in her pregnancy?—well, however far, enough months later Monica realized that she had never heard a word about the baby. April had been the month, she was sure she remembered that, something about producing the baby in time for the church's great Easter concert. (They had laughed and sung, spontaneously, together, "Unto us a son is given . . .") Was she afraid to call? What if there had been a problem? How could you check on someone a continent away only to be told that something dire had happened? But such a good friend, Rudy had insisted. Surely it would be no secret. By then, though, Monica herself was pregnant, and it would be cruel, wouldn't it, to stir up any news Glenna had not wanted to send her? Because of that, when Marcie was born Monica did not send a birth announcement to Glenna—she couldn't bear to hurt her, if that was what joyous news might do.

And now the letter. Monica folded it very slowly, following the direction of the sharp fold-lines as if it were a road map, and put it into its envelope, which she placed neatly by itself in the middle of the dining room table. Sitting there alone it looked as if it had repelled all the life around it.

"Is the baby sleeping?"

Rudy nodded. He had picked up Marcie at the sitter's on the way home from school. "Mrs. Ames said she didn't get much of a nap, so I put her down again."

"Okay. Good." She walked around the room as soundlessly as if she were circling herself. Every part of her was raw. Of course Rudy was right, she was blaming herself, how could she not be? Even if she had never intended to hurt Glenna, what had she done? Why had Glenna come to see her if she was so "happy" when they'd moved away? It was a hideous joke, cruel and impenetrable. She saw poor, shy Glenna bent over the piano, her back in a low flat arch as if she wanted to put her chin on the keys, saw her hold a long note, rocking her whole hand around the extended finger exactly as she, Monica, did on the fretboard of her cello looking for a motion to contain the energy, to fill motionless time, quarter, half, whole note tied and tied into the next measure and the next, her eyes closed, counting.

Post-partum depression, she thought quite suddenly. Nothing else could account for it. One of these days they would hear from Cy, who would be apologetic, grieving, as confused as they, that Glenna had gone insane and this had only been one of her outbursts. If that didn't turn out to be the case, Monica would never trust anyone again, not Sandi, not even Rudy, no one she knew. If a friend could harbor such hate that she became an assassin out of the blue. . . . As if to assure herself that her pain was only beginning, she hit the table top so hard with the palm of her hand that it smarted; anger enough to inflame the flesh, then. This was a new experience for Monica, who could usually talk herself around impediments and through depressions, comparing all disappointments to final losses, thereby rendering them petty, even laughable. She felt sick with this—it *was* a finality—and enlivened at the same time; adrenalin washed through her in waves, preparing her for fight or flight but instructing her for neither. She stared at her throbbing hand as if it didn't belong to her.

Sincerely, but without conviction, Monica began to catechize her friends. "Am I such a bitch that I don't even know it?" "Do I hurt you accidentally when we're together? Don't laugh, think about it." But her friends would not cooperate by telling her she was oblivious, insensitive, competitive. They shrugged and shook their heads, which she was to take for comfort.

"Wouldn't I tell you, Monica?" Rudy would ask her. "Wouldn't *I* see the worst, if all that was a fit description?" Loyal Rudy. She seemed to look at him from a great distance filled with experiences they had not shared.

"I know husbands who defend insane wives," she told him as if she were defending herself. "Remember Jim Papilardi, who tried to get his nutcase wife re-hired when they put her out of the lab? I don't think he ever believed what they said about her." Rudy didn't think the comparison held. Joan Papilardi had been found out of her clothes, flank on flank with a Harvard senior who had been asleep with electrodes attached to his scalp; he was not the first experimental subject she had awakened, he was only the first who had protested. True, the woman's poor husband had fought for her job, but that was not the same, and anyway, the man might be expected to maintain his pride.

I'm trying, sweetheart, Rudy seemed to be saying to her, I'm trying harder than you are to understand and to help you resist. But he could feel in Monica's grateful embrace that she was comforting him, somehow, was humoring him in his diligent efforts at her acquittal. It was all, he would murmur, a tragic mistake, undeserved, as if Monica had boarded the wrong plane and it had gone down in flames. No, she was even less implicated—as if she had been standing on the ground minding her own business when the plane fell burning out of the sky. But Monica refused his generosity—this was not a mechanical failure. People are bound together, even if we don't know how. Miscommunication, maybe, but not engine breakdown.

Over the next few years whenever Monica thought of Glenna she winced with pain. She no longer felt more than a passing shadow of shame when she remembered her. She had finally decided in her own favor: Glenna was mistaken. But she was also lost to Monica as surely as if she had died, and what was the use of that? Who was being punished? Nor could she ever modify the judgment, that was the other part that felt so final. Once, when a friend who knew the story mentioned her "enemy," Monica stared for a moment in disbelief. Having an enemy ought to become a two-way proposition, she thought, even if it didn't begin that way; and she, who loved Glenna, hated no one.

Dot brought the news that Glenna, not long after her visit to San Francisco, had tried to kill herself. She had been put in a clinic in the Berkshires for a few months, had emerged dulled and silent, undoubtedly drugged, ignored her new baby—there *was* a son, a beautiful boy born on the first day of spring that year. Dot saw her whenever she passed through Boston, although it was, she swore, not a lot of laughs.

"Does she mention me?" Monica asked sadly. She had turned so pale she thought she must look guilty of something.

"Once she said she hadn't seen you for a long time. But frankly she doesn't seem to have much energy or emotion to spare for anything." Dot, beautiful and unchanged, cocked her head. "Whatever in the world did happen between you two back then? Nobody's ever accounted for it any way that made sense."

Monica couldn't say. "I must somehow be to blame," she concluded experimentally, wondering if Dot might possess some new evidence. "Otherwise it's nothing but a shaggy dog story."

"It's too noble to assume you're to blame, lovey," Dot told her in her efficient, emphatic voice that plunged through its subjects like her bow across taut strings. "People can be their own worst enemies, you know, without any help from anyone else. We all know what kind of problems she had." She thought for a while. "She sounds jealous."

"Jealous?" That was absurd. "If she was going to be jealous it would be of you, not me. I'll tell you what I think. I should never have tried to help her. I was being critical when I ought to have let her—"

"Absurd." Monica's own word. "For whose sake? You were her friend. That doesn't mean you're sworn to silence, I hope." Dot had a rich dark face, ripe as a plum. If she had doubts, she throttled them out of sight. "If I see her, do you have a message you want me to give her? I'm going to be in Boston again in a little while." Things were still breaking well for Dot, the concerts multiplying, her name becoming known. The calm with which she accepted all of it, Monica thought, proved that she deserved anything she had—it was a natural movement and her energy stayed free for the music. "You hope she'll change her mind, or you miss her or anything? Or are you too mad?" Dot looked at the nails she kept filed for the sake of her work. Her fingertips looked tough. Musicians' fingers always had hard pads at the ends, a special brand of beauty. "I know I'd be too mad if somebody savaged me like that."

Tell her she has scarred me forever, Monica thought, looking away, her eyes filled with tears. Hadn't she told Glenna herself that "no" speaks louder than "yes"? And if she is my enemy I will have to hate her whether I want to or not. And then—for she knew, suddenly, what this felt like, she remembered her old idle desire, hers and Rudy's, to be despised for cause—then if I hate her hard enough (that would not be easy, oh Glenna, she thought, seeing the futile drop of red ribbon beading up on the transparency of that fine hair) she will come out of her invisibility into the world and be seen.

The light on the coffee pot had come on. Dot was waiting for a message; even if the joke had no punchline somebody had to have the last word.

"Just tell her you saw me and I looked wounded." Monica spoke firmly, as if she were giving her words of absolution. "Tell her I told you I would never forgive her."

"Okay." Dot nodded, satisfied. "I'll tell her you're sworn enemies. To the end of time." She shrugged, her thin shoulders rising like wing bones, and took her cup of coffee out of Monica's hands.

nominated by DeWitt Henry

A RED SWEATER

fiction by FAE MYENNE NG

from THE AMERICAN VOICE

I CHOSE RED for my sister. Fierce, dark red. Made in Hong Kong. Hand Wash Only because it's got that skin of fuzz. She'll look happy. That's good. Everything's perfect, for a minute. That seems enough.

Red. For Good Luck. Of course. This fire-red sweater is swollen with good cheer. Wear it, I will tell her. You'll look lucky.

We're a family of three girls. By Chinese standards, that's not lucky. "Too bad," outsiders whisper, ". . . nothing but daughters. A failed family."

First, Middle, and End girl. Our order of birth marked us. That came to tell more than our given names.

My eldest sister, Lisa, lives at home. She quit San Francisco State, one semester short of a psychology degree. One day she said, "Forget about it, I'm tired." She's working full time at Pacific Telephone now. Nine hundred a month with benefits. Mah and Deh think it's a great deal. They tell everybody, "Yes, our Number One makes good pay, but that's not even counting the discount. If we call Hong Kong, China even, there's forty percent off!" As if anyone in their part of China had a telephone.

Number Two, the in-between, jumped off the 'M' floor three years ago. Not true! What happened? Why? Too sad! All we say about that is, "It was her choice."

We sent Mah to Hong Kong. When she left Hong Kong thirty years ago, she was the envy of all: "Lucky girl! You'll never have to work." To marry a sojourner was to have a future. Thirty years in the land of gold and good fortune, and then she returned to tell the story: three daughters, one dead, one unmarried, another who-cares-where, the thirty years in sweatshops, and the prince of the Golden Mountain turned into a toad. I'm glad I didn't have to go with her. I felt her shame and regret. To return, seeking solace and comfort, instead of offering banquets and stories of the good life.

I'm the youngest. I started flying with PAN AM the year Mah returned to Hong Kong, so I got her a good discount. She thought I was good for something then. But when she returned, I was pregnant.

"Get an abortion," she said. "Drop the baby," she screamed.

"No."

"Then get married."

"No. I don't want to."

I was going to get an abortion all along. I just didn't like the way they talked about the whole thing. They made me feel like dirt, that I was a disgrace. Now I can see how I used it as an opportunity. Sometimes I wonder if there wasn't another way. Everything about those years was so steamy and angry. There didn't seem to be any answers.

"I have no eyes for you," Mah said.

"Don't call us," Deh said.

They wouldn't talk to me. They ranted idioms to each other for days. The apartment was filled with images and curses I couldn't perceive. I got the general idea: I was a rotten, no-good, dead thing. I would die in a gutter without rice in my belly. My spirit—if I had one—wouldn't be fed. I wouldn't see good days in this life or the next.

My parents always had a special way of saying things.

Now I'm based in Honolulu. When our middle sister jumped, she kind of closed the world. The family just sort of fell apart. I left. Now, I try to make up for it, but the folks still won't see me, but I try to keep in touch with them through Lisa. Flying cuts up your life, hits hardest during the holidays. I'm always sensitive then. I feel like I'm missing something, that people are doing something really important while I'm up in the sky, flying through time zones.

So I like to see Lisa around the beginning of the year. January, New Year's, and February, New Year's again, double luckiness with our birthdays in between. With so much going on, there's always something to talk about.

"You pick the place this year," I tell her.

"Around here?"

"No," I say. 'Around here' means the food is good and the living hard. You eat a steaming rice plate, and then you feel like rushing home to sew garments or assemble radio parts or something. We eat together only once a year, so I feel we should splurge. Besides, at the Chinatown places, you have nothing to talk about except the bare issues. In American restaurants, the atmosphere helps you along. I want nice light and a view and handsome waiters.

"Let's go somewhere with a view," I say.

We decide to go to FOLLOWING SEA, a new place on the Pier 39 track. We're early, the restaurant isn't crowded. It's been clear all day, so I think the sunset will be nice. I ask for a window table. I turn to talk to my sister, but she's already talking to a waiter. He's got that dark island tone that she likes. He's looking her up and down. My sister does not blink at it. She holds his look and orders two Johnny Walkers. I pick up a fork, turn it around in my hand. I seldom use chopsticks now. At home, I eat my rice in a plate, with a fork. The only chopsticks I own, I wear in my hair. For a moment, I feel strange sitting here at this unfamiliar table. I don't know this tablecloth, this linen, these candles. Everything seems foreign. It feels like we should be different people. But each time I look up, she's the same. I know this person. She's my sister. We sat together with chopsticks, mismatched bowls, braids, and braces, across the formica tabletop.

"I like three pronged forks," I say, pressing my thumb against the sharp points.

My sister rolls her eyes. She lights a cigarette.

I ask for one.

I finally say, "So, what's new?"

"Not much." Her voice is sullen. She doesn't look at me. Once a year, I come in, asking questions. She's got the answers, but she hates them. For me, I think she's got the peace of heart, knowing that she's done her share for Mah and Deh. She thinks I have the peace, not caring. Her life is full of questions, too, but I have no answers.

I look around the restaurant. The sunset is not spectacular and we don't comment on it. The waiters are lighting candles. Ours is bringing the drinks. He stops very close to my sister, seems to breathe her in. She raises her face toward him. "Ready?" he asks. My sister orders for us. The waiter struts off.

"Tight ass," I say.

"The best," she says.

My scotch tastes good. It reminds me of Deh. Johnny Walker or Seagrams 7, that's what they served at Chinese banquets. Nine courses and a bottle. No ice. We learned to drink it Chinese style, in teacups. Deh drank from his rice bowl, sipping it like hot soup. By the end of the meal, he took it like cool tea, in bold mouthfuls. We sat watching, our teacups of scotch in our laps, his three giggly girls.

Relaxed, I'm thinking there's a connection. Johnny Walker then and Johnny Walker now. I ask for another cigarette and this one I enjoy. Now my Johnny Walker pops with ice. I twirl the glass to make the ice tinkle.

We clink glasses. Three times for good luck. She giggles. I feel better.

"Nice sweater," I say.

"Michael Owyang," she says. She laughs. The light from the candle makes her eyes shimmer. She's got Mah's eyes. Eyes that make you want to talk. Lisa is reed-thin and tall. She's got a body that clothes look good on. My sister slips something on and it wraps her like skin. Fabric has pulse on her.

"Happy birthday, soon," I say.

"Thanks, and to yours too, just as soon."

"Here's to Johnny Walker in shark's fin soup," I say.

"And squab dinners."

"I LOVE LUCY," I say.

We laugh. It makes us feel like children again. We remember how to be sisters.

I raise my glass, "To I LOVE LUCY, squab dinners, and brown bags."

"To bones," she says.

"Bones," I repeat. This is a funny that gets sad, and knowing it, I keep laughing. I am surprised how much memory there is in one word. Pigeons. Only recently did I learn they're called squab. Our word for them was pigeon—on a plate or flying over Portsmouth Square. A good meal at 40 cents a bird. In line by dawn, we waited at the butcher's listening for the slow, churning motor of the trucks. We watched the live fish flushing out of the tanks into the garbage pails. We smelled the honey-brushed cha sui bows baking. When the white laundry truck turned onto Wentworth, there was a puffing trail of feathers following it. A stench filled the alley. The crowd squeezed in around the truck. Old ladies reached into the crates, squeezing and tugging for the plumpest pigeons.

My sister and I picked the white ones, those with the most expressive eyes. Dove birds, we called them. We fed them leftover rice in water, and as long as they stayed plump, they were our pets, our baby dove birds. And then one day we'd come home from school and find them cooked. They were a special, nutritious treat. Mah let us fill our bowls high with little pigeon parts: legs, breasts, and wings, and take them out to the front room to watch I LOVE LUCY. We took brown bags for the bones. We balanced our bowls on our laps and laughed at Lucy. We leaned forward, our chopsticks crossed in mid-air, and called out, "Mah! Mah! Come watch! Watch Lucy cry!"

But she always sat alone in the kitchen sucking out the sweetness of the lesser parts: necks, backs, and the head. "Bones are sweeter than you know," she always said. She came out to check the bags. "Clean bones," she said, shaking the bags. "No waste," she said.

Our dinners come with a warning. "Plate's hot. Don't touch." My sister orders a carafe of house white. "Enjoy," he says, smiling at my sister. She doesn't look up.

I can't remember how to say scallops in Chinese. I ask my sister, she doesn't know either. The food isn't great. Or maybe we just don't have the taste buds in us to go crazy over it. Sometimes I get very hungry for Chinese flavors: black beans, garlic and ginger, shrimp paste and sesame oil. These are tastes we grew up with, still dream about. Crave. Run around town after. Duck liver sausage, beancurd, jook, salted fish, and fried dace with black beans. Western flavors don't stand out, the surroundings do. Three pronged forks. Pink tablecloths. Fresh flowers. Cute waiters. An odd difference.

"Maybe we should have gone to Sun Hung Heung. At least the vegetables are real," I say.

"Hung toh-yee-foo-won-tun!" she says.

"Yeah, yum!" I say.

I remember Deh teaching us how to pick bak choy, his favorite vegetable. "Stick your fingernail into the stem. Juicy and firm, good. Limp and tough, no good." The three of us followed Deh, punching our thumbnails into every stem of bak-choy we saw.

"Deh still eating bak-choy?"

"Breakfast, lunch and dinner." My sister throws her head back, and laughs. It is Deh's motion. She recites in a mimic tone. "Your Deh, all he needs is a good hot bowl of rice and a plate full of greens. A good monk."

There was always bak-choy. Even though it was nonstop for Mah—rushing to the sweatshop in the morning, out to shop on break, and then home to cook by evening—she did this for him. A plate of bak-choy, steaming with the taste of ginger and garlic. He said she made good rice. Timed full-fire until the first boil, medium until the grains formed a crust along the sides of the pot, and then low-flamed to let the rice steam. Firm, that's how Deh liked his rice.

The waiter brings the wine, asks if everything is alright.

"Everything," my sister says.

There's something else about this meeting. I can hear it in the edge of her voice. She doesn't say anything and I don't ask. Her lips make a contorting line; her face looks sour. She lets out a breath. It sounds like she's been holding it in too long.

"Another fight. The bank line," she says. "He waited four times in the bank line. Mah ran around outside shopping. He was doing her a favor. She was doing him a favor. Mah wouldn't stop yelling. 'Get out and go die! Useless Thing! Stinking Corpse!"

I know he answered. His voice must have had that fortune teller's tone to it. You listened because you knew it was a warning.

He always threatened to disappear, jump off the Golden Gate. His thousand-year-old threat. I've heard it all before. "I will go. Even when dead, I won't be far enough away. Curse the good will that blinded me into taking you as wife!"

I give Lisa some of my scallops. "Eat," I tell her.

She keeps talking. "Of course, you know how Mah thinks, that nobody should complain because she's been the one working all these years."

I nod. I start eating, hoping she'll follow.

One bite and she's talking again. "You know what shopping with Mah is like, either you stand outside with the bags like a servant,

337

or inside like a marker, holding a place in line. You know how she gets into being frugal—saving time because it's the one free thing in her life. Well, they're at the bank and she had him hold her place in line while she runs up and down Stockton doing her quick shopping maneuvers. So he's in line, and it's his turn, but she's not back. So he has to start all over at the back again. Then it's his turn but she's still not back. When she finally comes in, she's got bags in both hands, and he's going through the line for the fourth time. Of course she doesn't say sorry or anything."

I interrupt. "How do you know all this?" I tell myself not to come back next year. I tell myself to apply for another transfer, to the East Coast.

"She told me. Word for word." Lisa spears the scallop, puts it in her mouth. I know it's cold by now. "Word for word," she repeats. She cuts a piece of chicken. "Try," she says.

I think about how we're sisters. We eat slowly, chewing carefully, like old people. A way to make things last, to fool the stomach.

Mah and Deh both worked too hard; it's as if their marriage was a marriage of toil—of toiling together. The idea is that the next generation can marry for love.

In the old country, matches were made, strangers were wedded, and that was fate. Those days, sojourners like Deh were considered princes. To become the wife to such a man was to be saved from the war-torn villages.

Saved to work. After dinner, with the rice still in between her teeth, Mah sat down at her Singer. When we pulled out the wall-bed, she was still there, sewing. The street noises stopped long before she did. The hot lamp made all the stitches blur together. And in the mornings, long before any of us awoke, she was already there, sewing again.

His work was hard, too. He ran a laundry on Polk Street. He sailed with the American President Lines. Things started to look up when he owned the take-out place in Vallejo, and then his partner ran off. So he went to Alaska and worked the canneries.

She was good to him, too. We remember. How else would we have known him all those years he worked in Guam, in the Fiji Islands, in Alaska? Mah always gave him majestic welcomes home. It was her excitement that made us remember him.

I look around. The restaurant is full. The waiters move quickly.

I know Deh. His words are ugly. I've heard him. I've listened. And I've always wished for the street noises, as if in the traffic of sound, I believe I can escape. I know the hard color of his eyes and the tightness in his jaw. I can almost hear his teeth grind. I know this. Years of it.

Their lives weren't easy. So is their discontent without reason?

What about the first one? You didn't even think to come to the hospital. The first one, I say! Son or daughter, dead or alive, you didn't even come!

What about living or dying? Which did you want for me that time you pushed me back to work before my back brace was off?

Money! Money!! Money to eat with, to buy clothes with, to pass this life with!

Don't start that again! Everything I make at that dead place I hand . . .

How come . . .
What about . . .
So . . .

It was obvious. The stories themselves meant little. It was how hot and furious they could become.

Is there no end to it? What makes their ugliness so alive, so thick and impossible to let go of?

"I don't want to think about it anymore." The way she says it surprises me. This time I listen. I imagine what it would be like to take her place. It will be my turn one day.

"Ron," she says, wiggling her fingers above the candle. "A fun thing."

The opal flickers above the flame. I tell her that I want to get her something special for her birthday, ". . . next trip I get abroad." She looks up at me, smiles.

For a minute, my sister seems happy. But she won't be able to hold onto it. She grabs at things out of despair, out of fear. Gifts grow old for her. Emotions never ripen, they sour. Everything slips away from her. Nothing sustains her. Her beauty has made her fragile.

We should have eaten in Chinatown. We could have gone for coffee in North Beach, then for jook at Sam Wo's.

"No work, it's been like that for months, just odd jobs," she says.

I'm thinking, it's not like I haven't done my share. I was a kid once, I did things because I felt I should. I helped fill out forms at the Chinatown employment agencies. I went with him to the Seaman's Union. I waited too, listening and hoping for those calls: "Busboy! Presser! Prep Man!" His bags were packed, he was always ready to go. "On standby," he said.

Every week. All the same. Quitting and looking to start all over again. In the end, it was like never having gone anywhere. It was like the bank line, waiting for nothing.

How many times did my sister and I have to hold them apart? The flat ting! sound as the blade slapped onto the linoleum floors, the wooden handle of the knife slamming into the corner. Was it she or I who screamed, repeating all their ugliest words? Who shook them? Who made them stop?

The waiter comes to take the plates. He stands by my sister for a moment. I raise my glass to the waiter.

"You two Chinese?" he asks.

"No," I say, finishing off my wine. I roll my eyes. I wish I had another Johnny Walker. Suddenly I don't care.

"We're two sisters," I say. I laugh. I ask for the check, leave a good tip. I see him slip my sister a box of matches.

Outside, the air is cool and brisk. My sister links her arm into mine. We walk up Bay onto Chestnut. We pass Galileo High School and then turn down Van Ness to head toward the pier. The bay is black. The foghorns sound far away. We walk the whole length of the pier without talking.

The water is white where it slaps against the wooden stakes. For a long time Lisa's wanted out. She can stay at that point of endurance forever. Desire that becomes old feels too good, it's seductive. I know how hard it is to go.

The heart never travels. You have to be heartless. My sister holds that heart, too close and for too long. This is her weakness, and I like to think, used to be mine. Lisa endures too much.

We're lucky, not like the bondmaids growing up in service, or the new-born daughters whose mouths were stuffed with ashes. Courtesans with the three-inch foot, beardless, soft-shouldered eunuchs, and the frightened child-brides, they're all stories to us. We're the lucky generation. Our parents forced themselves to live through the humiliation in this country so that we could have it better. We know so little of the old country. We repeat the names of Grandmothers and Uncles, but they will always be strangers to us. Family exists only because somebody has a story, and knowing the story connects us to a history. To us, the deformed man is oddly compelling, the forgotten man is a good story. A beautiful woman suffers.

I want her beauty to buy her out.

The sweater cost two weeks pay. Like the 40-cent birds that are now a delicacy, this is a special treat. The money doesn't mean anything. It is, if anything, time. Time is what I would like to give her.

A red sweater. 100% angora. The skin of fuzz will be a fierce rouge on her naked breasts.

Red. Lucky. Wear it. Find that man. The new one. Wrap yourself around him. Feel the pulsing between you. Fuck him and think about it. 100%. Hand Wash Only. Worn Once.

nominated by The American Voice

A TREE, A STREAMLINED FISH, AND A SELF-SQUARED DRAGON: SCIENCE AS A FORM OF CULTURE

by O. B. HARDISON, JR.

from THE GEORGIA REVIEW

> Have we begun to understand even the old industrial revolution? Much less the new scientific revolution in which we stand? There was never anything more necessary to comprehend.
>
> —C. P. Snow, "The Two Cultures"

I

THE THEME of the following essay is the emergence of new values in modern scientific thought. This theme is as simple and as subtle as the movement in biology from observing nature in the middle perspective, so beautifully illustrated by Audubon's paintings of the birds of North America, to electron-microscope photographs of the fine structure of living cells.

D'Arcy Wentworth Thompson remarks at the end of his mathematical study of living forms that he is "advanced in these enquiries no farther than the threshold." It will be well for me to state at the beginning that my purpose is not to write a history of science or a work on the philosophy of science. Both tasks have been undertaken by authors eminently qualified for them, and although I have tried to learn from these authors, I am not in any sense attempting to follow where they have so ably led. I want, rather, to examine aspects of science that are legitimate subjects of cultural study, and thus to cross a barrier that has been posited at least since Francis Bacon's *Novum Organum* and that is the subject of C. P. Snow's much-quoted essay "The Two Cultures." I believe that human culture is a seamless web. No matter how fragmented our understanding of it, there is only one culture. Just as the analysis of culture often involves the techniques of science—as often happens, for instance, in archaeological, textual, psychoanalytic, and linguistic studies—science can be approached as a form of culture. To see it in this way is to see it not as a body of knowledge but as an agency of value; and in the twentieth century, science has become an agency of enormous power, in some respects replacing such traditional sources of value as religion, custom, and history. Hence the urgency of Snow's questions: "Have we begun to understand even the old industrial revolution? Much less the new scientific revolution in which we stand?"

In order to create a context, I will begin with some observations about two traditional poles of scientific thought. The first assumes that nature is an appearance which science must penetrate in order to discover reality. This is, in general, the point of view associated in Greek science with Pythagoras and the Plato of the *Timaeus*. The second pole is Baconian. It assumes that reality is what we see in front of us and that understanding reality is a matter of disciplined observation. I need only to add that the two poles are by no means always opposed. Many—perhaps most—scientists move easily from one to the other, and back, as the demands of their projects change.

After establishing a context, I will concentrate on three representative figures whose work defines a kind of curve leading from the past to the present. Other figures could have been selected, but they might not have defined the curve as clearly or permitted the issues to emerge as fully. The three are Charles Darwin, D'Arcy Wentworth Thompson, and Benoit Mandelbrot. Each expresses views typical of an important moment in the development of the values that are intrinsic to modern culture, but some interesting paradoxes emerge. Darwin's nature is, in theory, non-human and alien, but he pours emotion into it in much the same way that primitive man humanizes the world through myth. Thompson's nature is regular and elegant, the materialization of mathematics. It, too, seems alien until we realize that the mathematics is either the invention of God, as Thompson suggests in his "Epilogue," or a purely human creation, as Thompson undoubtedly believed in his less poetic moments. The nature revealed by Thompson is a nature devoid of myth, but it is saturated with the aesthetic qualities suggested by words like *admiration, wonder,* and *beauty.* Mandelbrot's nature is discontinuous and impossibly complex. Its order cannot be duplicated, so he creates a system parallel to nature, capable of producing things that are "something like" natural things. Mandelbrot's fractal geometry is in this sense fully human: it is invented by man and its products are entirely man-made. Their adequacy as facsimiles of nature can be tested in the most empirical way: Mandelbrot's equations can be converted into computer graphics and then compared to natural images, much as Audubon's birds can be compared to their living counterparts. The equations meet this test so successfully that they have been used to create imaginary landscapes for movies and television fantasies.

All of the texts I will examine here were intended by their authors to be accessible to the general reader as well as the scientist. Although the images of nature they reveal are quite distinct, each can be seen as pointing toward the next. Thompson is quite conscious of writing in the shadow of Darwin, and Mandelbrot refers several times to Thompson as in some sense a precursor in the effort to study the mathematical basis of nature. All three express values inherent in modern culture; in examining their work, we examine aspects of the world we inhabit in America in the closing years of the twentieth century.

The efforts of Thompson and Mandelbrot to be accessible to readers who are not scientists point to a corollary theme of the present essay. C. P. Snow's challenge in "The Two Cultures" is usually understood to mean that students of culture should study mathematics and chemistry and thermodynamics in order to be able to understand science, yet if his challenge is confronted seriously, it goes much deeper than that. The problem is that our visual and verbal languages change slowly, but for the past century our culture has been changing rapidly. Since we imagine by means of visual or verbal languages, this is a way of saying that we are no longer able to imagine the world—or, at least, that our languages are no longer synchronized with what we experience. It is understandable that Snow sees the problem as a lack of communication between two different cultures. His understanding, however, is wrong because it relates to symptoms, not to causes.

The problem of language is exemplified in science in the common assertion that the reality revealed by science cannot be expressed in natural language and is therefore inaccessible to imagination. Paul Dirac asserts in *Quantum Mechanics* (1930) that reality is no more accessible to visual languages than to verbal ones: "Fundamental laws do not govern the world as it appears in our mental picture in any very direct way, but instead they form a substratum of which we cannot form a mental picture without introducing irrelevancies." If Dirac is correct, all efforts to find languages capable of objectifying reality are doomed and may even be pernicious since they introduce "irrelevancies." There are, however, reasons to be more optimistic than Dirac. Art, architecture, and poetry have all sought consciously to create new languages in the twentieth century, and the visual languages developed by modern art have been extraordinarily successful. As I hope to demonstrate, science has also created visual and verbal languages that have much to offer to those seeking to reestablish links between the imagination and the world. In the efforts of Darwin, Thompson, and Mandelbrot to be accessible to general readers as well as to specialists, we encounter one crucial set of these links—and we discover that, whatever else these men might have thought they were doing, one thing they *have* done is to lead us toward a sense of the "two cultures" as one.

II

The root meaning of Greek *kosmos* is "order" or "arrangement." It has the additional meanings of "comely order," "decoration," or "ornament." It is the source of English *cosmos*, and also of *cosmetic*.

Greek science is the study of the comely and harmonious order

345

of the world. It is more an aesthetic than a practical pursuit; its great triumphs are in geometry and the theory of proportions. The harmonious order of things is *in the world* according to the Greek view. It is there whether it is perceived or not. This assumption is widespread in mythic thought, and to the Greeks goes credit for expressing it with such rigor that it could become the basis for early Greek science.

"Comeliness" is another matter. It requires a judgment on the part of the observer and a motive, real or imputed, on the part of the creator. Greek science assumes that creation is beautiful as well as orderly; the proper response to it is aesthetic as well as intellectual. In the *Theogony,* Hesiod (8th C. B.C.) imagines that creation is pervaded by the music of the nine muses, the daughters of Mnemosyne: "Unwearying flows the sweet sound from their lips, and the house of their father Zeus the loud-thunderer is glad at the lily-like voice of the goddesses as it spreads abroad, and the peaks of snowy Olympus resound, and the homes of the immortals." The world is music, and creation a dance.

In the sixth century B.C. Pythagoras of Samos discovered the relation between harmony and number—according to legend, after hearing the tones produced by a blacksmith's hammers of different weights. His discovery convinced him that number is the foundation of the comely order of the world and that harmony is its corollary. The natural order is simultaneously functional and beautiful, and its basis is number. This conclusion remained central in later Greek scientific thought. It may, in fact, have hampered the development of Greek science by encouraging its interest in elegant demonstration at the expense of calculation. The motto over the doors of Plato's academy was *Medeis ageometretos eisito*—"Let no one ignorant of geometry enter." In *The Republic* (Book VII) Socrates discusses the education of his guardians. The central disciplines are arithmetic, geometry, harmony, and dialectic. Number is fundamental. It is the key to the rational understanding of the real:

> These sparks that paint the sky, since they are decorations on a visible surface, we must consider the first and most exact of visible things, but we must recognize that they fall far short of the truth—the movements, namely—of real slowness and real speed in true num-

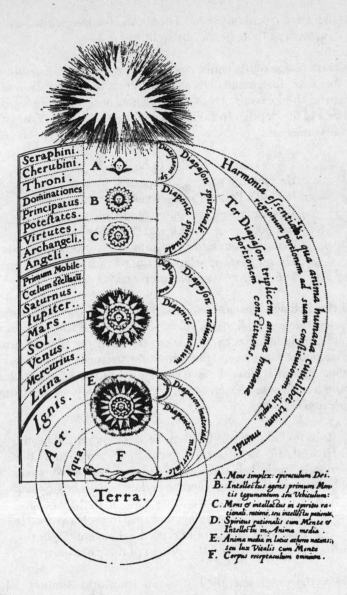

Musica Humana

bers and true figures. . . . These can be apprehended by
reason and thought, not by sight.

Christian apologists could (and did) discover Pythagorean notes
in the Old Testament. Of wisdom Proverbs says, "When he
prepared the heavens, I was there: when he set a compass upon
the face of the depth." In Book VII of Milton's *Paradise Lost* (1667)
this becomes:

> . . . in his hand
> He took the golden Compasses, prepar'd
> In God's Eternal store, to circumscribe
> This Universe, and all created things:
> One foot he centered, and the other turn'd
> Round through the vast profundity obscure,
> Thus far extend, thus far thy bounds,
> This be thy just Circumference, O world.

And the Pythagorean note rings in the work of the great Renaissance astronomer Johannes Kepler (1571–1630). Early in his career
Kepler concluded that the distances between the planets can be
determined by assuming they are the distances that would be
produced by inscribing the five regular solids, beginning with the
tetrahedron, inside of each other. He wrote in *Mysterium Cosmo-
graphicum* (1596),

> It is my intention, Reader, to demonstrate that the
> Highest and Most Good Creator in the creation of this
> mobile world and the arrangement of the heavens had
> his eye on those five regular bodies [i.e. solids] which
> have been celebrated from the time of Pythagoras and
> Plato down to our own day; and that to their nature He
> accommodated the number of the heavenly spheres,
> their proportions, and the system of their motions.

The Pythagorean scientist is drawn to the world as much by love
of its endlessly surprising and beautiful patterns as by the desire
for knowledge. He is a connoisseur as well as an observer of facts.
If he does not create beauty, he discovers it and shares it with
others. In a discussion of Faraday's experiments with electricity, J.
B. S. Haldane touches the Pythagorean chord:

As a result of Faraday's work you are able to listen to a wireless. But more than that, as a result of Faraday's work, scientifically educated men and women have an altogether richer view of the world. For them, apparently empty space is full of the most intricate and beautiful patterns. So Faraday gave the world not only fresh wealth but fresh beauty.

<h1 style="text-align:center">III</h1>

The search of Pythagorean science for elegant geometric and mathematical forms behind the appearances of the visible world stands in striking contrast to the emphasis on observation and experiment that is central to the Baconian tradition. Baconian science finds reality directly ahead in the visible world. Since it is extremely difficult to see things as they are, Baconian science is a never-ending contest with human weakness. Bacon remarks in *The Advancement of Learning* (1605):

> The mind of man is far from the nature of a clear and equal glass, wherein the beams of things should reflect according to their true incidence; nay, it is rather like an enchanted glass, full of superstition and imposture, if it be not delivered and reduced.

And later, commenting on imagination:

> Imagination doth raise and erect the Minde, by submitting the shewes of things to the desires of the Mind, whereas reason doth buckle and bow the Mind unto the Nature of things. And we see by these insinuations and congruities with man's Nature and pleasure, joined also with the agreement and consort [imagination] hath with Musicke, it both had access and estimation in rude times and barbarous Regions, where other learning stoode excluded.

There is a strong note of asceticism in Bacon. Man is not the supreme work of Creation, the measure of all things and the image of God, as he is, for example, in Pico della Mirandola's famous essay, *On the Dignity of Man*. Instead he is an upstart crow in a world utterly indifferent to his existence. His mind is an enchanted glass—a distorting mirror—that must be "delivered and reduced"—that is, mortified—if it is to find truth.

Since Bacon had no knowledge of sophisticated scientific instruments, he understood reality as "things" seen from a middle distance by the naked eye. An ideal Baconian dictionary of reality would be a collection of pictures, one for each thing that exists in the world. It follows that the ideal language is a language of nouns with one noun for each thing, so that men can speak "so many *things* almost in an equal number of *words*." The dictionary for this sort of language would be a list of nouns corresponding to the pictures contained in the ideal picture-dictionary. However, when pictures get inside the mind they are made into what they are not. Since this position involves a hostile critique of that which exists inside the mind—namely, that which makes people human—it is in some sense a hostile critique of humanity. The first paragraph of Charles Dickens' *Hard Times* (1854) is a tribute to the influence of Baconian asceticism two centuries after Bacon's death:

> Now, what I want is, Facts. Teach these boys and girls nothing but Facts. Facts alone are wanted in life. Plant nothing else, and root out everything else. You can only form the minds of reasoning animals upon Facts: nothing else will ever be of any service to them.

It is a pity that Bacon was such a successful propagandist because his concept of science simply does not square with the facts he was so fond of. Placed beside Descartes's *Discours de la Méthode pour Bien Conduire la Raison et Chercher la Vérité dans les Sciences* (1637) the *Novum Organum* is clearly more rhetoric than science. Moreover, there is a touch of Pythagorean wonder in Bacon in spite of himself. But it is the distrust of mind, not the wonder, that made Bacon a hero of science in the eighteenth and nineteenth centuries, particularly in the sciences that depended more on observation and classification than on mathematics: geography, geology, biology, anatomy.

IV

Charles Darwin's *The Origin of Species* (1859) is the culmination and—for many Victorians—the vindication of the Baconian tradition in science. Darwin explicitly recognizes his debt to Bacon in his *Autobiography* (1876): "I worked on the true Baconian principles, and without any theory collected facts on a wholesale scale." The book brings together twenty years of painstaking, minutely detailed observation ranging over the whole spectrum of organic life. Like Bacon, Darwin made little use of mathematics, although he had attempted (unsuccessfully) to deepen his mathematical knowledge while at Cambridge. Nor was Darwin the sort of scientist whose observations depended on instruments. Although his four-volume study of *Cirripedia* (barnacles) uses microscopy frequently, most of his other works could have been—and were— written almost entirely on the basis of direct observation.

As soon as it was published, *The Origin of Species* was recognized as one of those books that changes history. Its reception was partly a tribute to the overwhelming wealth of detail it offers in support of its theory and partly an instance of powder waiting for a spark. Jean Baptiste Lamarck had proposed a generally evolutionary theory of biology in the *Histoire naturelle des animaux* (1815), which Darwin says in his *Autobiography* was an influence on him. Charles Lyell's *Principles of Geology* (1832), with its evidence of the immense span of the record of fossil life, was indispensable to Darwin. Lyell's contribution was of special value to Darwin in his work on the Galapagos Islands. It showed that the variations he observed among animals of the same species must have occurred within a relatively short span of geologic time. Another source, and the immediate occasion for the publication of *The Origin of Species*, was the work of Alfred Russell Wallace. In 1858 Wallace sent Darwin his essay "On the Tendency of Varieties to Depart Indefinitely from the Original Type." Darwin admits in the *Autobiography* that this essay "contained exactly the same theory as mine," though it lacks the luxuriance of Darwin's supporting observations. Again according to the *Autobiography*, it was his reading of Malthus that suggested to Darwin, around 1838, that all species are locked in a remorseless struggle for survival, although the concept of natural selection may also owe something to Edward Blyth.

Darwin denies in the *Autobiography* that evolution was "in the air" before *The Origin of Species* was published: "What I believe was strictly true is that innumerable well-observed facts were stored in the minds of naturalists ready to take their proper place as soon as any theory which would receive them was sufficiently explained." In any case *The Origin of Species* was an immediate sensation. By ignoring religious dogma and wishful thinking Darwin was able to buckle and bow his mind to the nature of things and produce the sort of powerful, overarching concept that reveals coherence in a vast area of experience that had previously seemed chaotic.

A modern reader can see a kinship between Darwin's passionate interest in all things living—beginning with his undergraduate hobby of collecting beetles—and the outbursts of nature poetry that occurred in the Romantic period. Darwin was unaware of this affinity. In the *Autobiography* he says that "up to the age of thirty, or beyond it, poetry of many kinds, such as the works of Milton, Gray, Byron, Wordsworth, Coleridge, and Shelley . . . gave me the greatest pleasure. . . . But now for many years I cannot endure to read a line of poetry." His *Journal of the Voyage of the Beagle* is filled with appreciative comments about tropical landscape, but he remarks that natural scenery "does not cause me the exquisite delight which it formerly did." He plays the role of Baconian ascetic collecting "without any theory . . . facts on a wholesale scale." His mind, he says (again in the *Autobiography*) has become "a kind of machine for grinding laws out of large collections of facts." The idea that the mind is a machine that grinds facts echoes Bacon's injunction to "buckle and bow" the mind to nature. The same asceticism is evident in Darwin's disparaging comments on his literary style. He believed he was writing dry scientific prose for other scientists, and John Ruskin, among others, agreed. He was astounded, gratified, and a little frightened by his popular success.

No one can read Darwin today without recognizing that he was wrong about his style. As Stanley Edgar Hyman observes in *The Tangled Bank* (1962), both *The Voyage of the Beagle* and *The Origin of Species* are filled with passages which, whatever Darwin may have thought of them, are of a high literary order. The writing is effective precisely because it does not strain for the gingerbread opulence fashionable in mid-Victorian English prose. It has a freedom from pretense, a quality of authority, as moving as the natural descriptions of Wordsworth's *The Prelude* because it stems from direct contact with the web of relationships that comprise nature. Darwin was, indeed, a good Baconian; but instead of revealing a mind bowed to nature, his prose reveals a mind that

352

has surrendered to the kaleidoscope of life around it. No passage is more revealing in this respect than the concluding paragraph of *The Origin of Species*, in which Darwin describes a natural scene,

> . . . clothed with many plants of many kinds, with birds singing on the bushes, with various insects flitting about, and with worms crawling through the damp earth, and . . . these elaborately constructed forms, so different from each other, and so dependent upon each other in so complex a manner, have all been produced by laws acting around us. . . . Thus, from the war of nature, from famine and death, the most exalted object which we are capable of conceiving, namely, the production of the higher animals, directly follows.

Thus, in addition to being a Baconian scientist—or because of being that kind of scientist—Darwin is one of the first poets of the actual. The closest visual parallels to his prose are the drawings of Audubon, but his writing is also related to the photographs of Matthew Brady, the histories of Ranke and Burckhardt, and the novels of Balzac and George Eliot and Turgenev. The following passage from the discussion of the struggle for existence in Chapter III of *The Origin of Species* illustrates Darwin's technique:

> How have all these exquisite adaptations of one part of the organization to another part, and to the conditions of life, and of one organic being to another been perfected? We see these beautiful coadaptations most plainly in the woodpecker and the mistletoe; and only a little less plainly in the humblest parasite which clings to the hairs of a quadruped or the feathers of a bird; in the structure of the beetle which dives through the water; in the plumed seed which is wafted by the gentle breeze; in short we see beautiful adaptations everywhere and in every part of the organic world.

Exquisite, perfected, beautiful, humblest, plumed, gentle. The world described by these adjectives is not cold, alien, or indifferent. It is a work of art. Nor is Darwin's the dispassionate, dry prose of a technical manual. As in a painting the parts mentioned are harmoniously related to each other—"coadaptation" is Darwin's word—and the music of the prose objectifies the harmony. There is no detectable difference here between a hypothetical figure labeled "scientific observer" and a literary artist commenting on experience. The language invites the reader to share experience as well as to understand it. *Exquisite, beautiful,* and *gentle* orient him emotionally at the same time that his attention is focused on the objects that give rise to the emotion: mistletoe, parasite, water beetle, plumed seed. The passage flatly contradicts Darwin's statement in the *Autobiography* that his artistic sensitivity had atrophied by the time he was thirty. That he thought it had shows only that he believed with his contemporaries that science is science and art is art. The problem was in his psyche, not his prose. The tradition that science should be dispassionate and practical, that it is a kind of servitude to nature, prevented him from understanding what he was, in fact, doing.

A more complex example of Darwin's artistry can be found in the "summary" of Chapter III. The passage is a sustained meditation on a single image. The image—the Tree of Life—is mythic, an archetype familiar from Genesis and also from Egyptian, Buddhist, Greek, and other sources. In mythology, the Tree of Life connects the underworld and the heavens. It is the axis on which the spheres turn and the path along which creatures from the invisible world visit and take leave of earth. It is an ever-green symbol of virility, bearing fruit in winter. It is the wood of the Cross on which God dies, and the wood reborn that announces the return of life by sending out new branches in the spring. All of this symbolism is familiar from Frazer's *Golden Bough,* Jung's *Symbols of Transformation,* and other studies of mythic imagery. Behind it is what Rudolf Otto calls, in *The Idea of the Holy,* the terrifying and fascinating mystery: *mysterium tremendum et fascinans.*

Still, it is interesting to find a scientist, particularly a preeminent Victorian scientist, using an overtly mythic image. The emphasis of the passage on branching limbs is a visual image of evolution, but at the same time it is a remarkably full elaboration of the archetype:

> The affinities of all the beings of the same class have sometimes been represented by a great tree. I believe

this simile largely speaks the truth. The green and budding twigs may represent existing species; and those produced during former years may represent the long succession of extinct species. At each period of growth all the growing twigs have tried to branch out on all sides, and to overtop and kill the surrounding twigs and branches, in the same manner as species and groups of species have at all times overmastered other species in the great battle for life. . . . From the first growth of the tree, many a limb and branch has decayed and dropped off; and all these fallen branches of various sizes may represent those whole orders, families, and genera which have now no living representatives, and which are known to us only in a fossil state. As we here and there see a thin, straggling branch springing from a fork low down in a tree, and which by some chance has been favored and is still alive on its summit, so we occasionally see an animal like the Ornithorhynchus or Lepidosiren, which in some small degree connects by its affinities two large branches of life, and which has apparently been saved from fatal competition by having inhabited a protected station. As buds give rise by growth to fresh buds, and these, if vigorous, branch out and overtop on all sides many a feebler branch, so by generation I believe it has been with the great Tree of Life, which fills with its dead and broken branches the crust of the earth, and covers the surface with its everbranching and beautiful ramifications.

Darwin's music here is stately and somber. The central image is established at the beginning: a great tree green at the top but filled with dead branches beneath the crown. The passage becomes an elegy for all the orders of life that have perished since the tree began. Words suggesting death crowd the sentences: *overtopped, kill, the great battle for life, decayed, dropped off, fallen, no living representative, straggling branch, fatal competition*. As the passage moves toward its conclusion, a change, a kind of reversal, can be felt. Words suggesting life become more frequent: *alive, life, saved, fresh buds, vigorous*. The final sentence restates the central paradox in a contrast between universal desolation—"dead and broken branches [filling] the crust of the earth"—and images of eternal fertility—"ever-branching and beautiful ramifications."

The idea that science reveals truth is central to the Darwinian moment. Once revealed, truth can be generalized, and the truths discovered by Darwin were applied almost immediately to sociology and political science. Herbert Spencer had coined the phrase "survival of the fittest" in 1852 in an article entitled "A Theory of Population." Buttressed by the prestige of *The Origin of Species*, the concept of the survival of the fittest was used to justify laissez-faire capitalism, a use brilliantly chronicled in Richard Hofstadter's *Social Darwinism in American Thought* (1955). Andrew Carnegie remarked in 1900 that "a struggle is inevitable [in society] and it is a question of the survival of the fittest." John D. Rockefeller seconded the opinion: "The growth of a large business is merely the survival of the fittest." Capitalism enables the strong to survive while the weak are destroyed. Socialism, conversely, protects the weak and frustrates the strong. Marx turned over the coin: socialism is a later and therefore a higher product of evolution than bourgeois capitalism. Being superior, it will replace capitalism as surely as warmblooded mammals replaced dinosaurs.

Darwin influenced cultural thought at a deep level, which is to say that he changed not only the way reality was managed but the way it was understood. The writing of history became evolutionary—so much so that historians often assumed an evolutionary model and tailored their facts to fit. The histories of political systems, national economies, technologies, machinery, literary genres, philosophical systems, and even styles of dress were presented as examples of evolution—meaning examples of progress from simple to complex, usually interpreted to mean from good to better.

And, of course, Darwin deeply influenced progressive religion. Adam Sedgwick, professor of geology at Cambridge, began the long history of attacks on Darwin in the name of religion when he wrote in "Objections to Mr. Darwin's Theory of the Origin of Species," published anonymously in 1860: "I cannot conclude without expressing my detestation of the theory, because of its unflinching materialism." Perhaps because of such attacks, Darwin added the phrase "by the Creator" to his conclusion of the second edition of *The Origin of Species* (1860): "There is a grandeur in this view of life, with its several powers, having been originally breathed by the Creator into a few forms or into one; and whilst this planet has gone cycling on according to the fixed law of gravity, from so simple a beginning endless forms most beautiful and most wonderful have been, and are being evolved." Whether this fully represents Darwin's personal view of religion lies outside the scope of the present discussion. Probably it did not. At any rate the notion that God is revealed in evolution remains powerfully attractive today both to biologists and, as shown by Teilhard de Chardin's *The Phenomenon of Man* (written in 1938 and published in 1955), to those attempting to formulate a scientific theology.

Many of the applications of Darwin's ideas were patently strained from the beginning, while time revealed the inadequacies of others. "Social Darwinism" is studied in history classes today but is no longer a viable political creed. Most fundamental, however, is the fact that by the middle of the twentieth century Baconian empiricism was no longer adequate to the idea of nature that science had developed. Einstein, Heisenberg, and Gödel made it clear that nature and the mind are involved in each other and are not separate empires. An objective world that can be "observed" and "understood" if only the imagination can be held in check simply does not exist. Facts are not observations "collected . . . on a wholesale scale." They are knots in a net.

V

D'Arcy Wentworth Thompson (1860–1948) was everything in biology that Darwin was not. *On Growth and Form* (1917) is an attempt to place biology on a mathematical foundation. To do this Thompson felt he had to deny not only Darwin's conclusions about evolution, but also the Baconian methodology of *The Origin of Species*. In the light of the explosive development of biology since World War II, *On Growth and Form* has come to seem less significant than it did thirty years ago. It remains, however, a significant illustration of a moment in scientific thought halfway between the Victorian period and the late twentieth century.

In his introduction, after quoting Kant's assertion that chemistry is "a science but not a science" because it is not based on mathematics, Thompson comments that "numerical precision is the very soul of science, and its attainment affords the best, perhaps the only criterion of the truth of theories and the correctness of experiments." Admitting the complexity of life processes, he adds, "My sole purpose is to correlate with mathematical statement and physical law certain of the simpler outward phenomena of growth and structure or form."

A common criticism of Bacon's philosophy of science, as well as Darwin's, is that it ignores mathematics. This is true. Bacon published grandiose schemes for the reform of knowledge, but Galileo established the basis for the mathematical analysis of acceleration, and Descartes laid the foundations of analytic geometry. To move from Darwin to Thompson is to move from the poetry of things to the poetry of the numbers that underlie things. It is to move, in other words, from things visible to things invisible, which is to say away from Bacon and toward Pythagoras.

Karl Gauss, James Clerk Maxwell, Ernest Rutherford, Josiah Gibbs, Jean Baptiste Fourier, Hermann Helmholtz, Georg Cantor, and a host of other brilliant nineteenth-century figures shared Thompson's appreciation of the power of mathematics. All were far more accomplished mathematicians. Thompson seldom goes beyond elementary mathematical concepts, noting for example that for objects of equal density, mass increases as the cube of linear dimension rather than in proportion to it. The observation is commonplace, almost trivial. However, Thompson's application is not. He concludes that the length of the limbs of land animals of the same species will, in general, increase in proportion to the cube root of their body weight. This leads to calculations of the probable lengths of the legs of birds of the same species but different weights. Insects breathe by diffusion of oxygen through capillary tubes extending from shell to bloodstream. Their maximum size is fixed by the fact that if they become very large their breathing apparatus ceases to function.

Load-bearing horizontals must be supported, and the support structures tend to be mirror images of the stresses to which the structures are subject—hence the shapes of dinosaur skeletons and the shape of the human femur. When circles are close-packed they deform, if flexible, into hexagons—hence honeycombs. Spheres tend to deform when close-packed into rhombic dodecahedra or complex 14-hedra—hence two common configurations of close-packed tissue cells. The equiangular spiral (so-called by Descartes) increases in volume without changing shape—hence the Chambered Nautilus. The shape of fish is determined by the flow of water. Streamlining—the term was apparently invented by Thompson—reduces turbulence to a minimum and thus maximizes swimming efficiency. Bones and body shapes that appear unrelated on casual inspection can be seen to be similar when they are drawn on graphs and the graphs are systematically distorted.

Thompson multiplies his examples luxuriantly, especially in the revised and enlarged edition of *On Growth and Form* (1942). Perhaps the most remarkable fact about them is their mathematical simplicity. Thompson does not need or want complex examples. He is demonstrating a point: the relevance of mathematics to biology. The simpler and clearer the examples, the more convincing the demonstration; Thompson shares the fondness of all scientists in the Pythagorean tradition for grand simplicities.

The application of mathematics to life may not seem innovative today, but Thompson clearly felt in 1917 that it was a bold, even a risky, venture. It seems to violate an unspoken feeling that life is beyond quantification: "To treat the living body as a mechanism was repugnant, and seemed even ludicrous, to Pascal; and Goethe, lover of nature as he was, ruled mathematics out of place in natural history." When the zoologist meets a simple geometrical shape in a living organism, "he is prone of old habit to believe that after all, it is something more than a spiral or a sphere, and that in this 'something more' there lies what neither mathematics nor physics can explain. . . . In short, he is deeply reluctant to compare the living with the dead."

Rather remarkably, Thompson anticipates for biology what Ferdinand de Saussure claimed in his *Cours de linguistique générale*, published posthumously in 1915, only two years before the first edition of *On Growth and Form*. Saussure observed that in spite of the delights of etymology, a language exists all at the same time or it does not exist at all. It is "synchronic"—a web of simultaneous relationships—rather than "diachronic"-extended across history, no matter how fascinating history may be as a subject. So it is in Thompson's biology. The search of evolutionary biologists for "the blood relationships of things living and the pedigrees of things dead and gone," must give way to the analysis of "fundamental properties" and "unchanging laws of matter and energy." Diachrony must yield, in life as in language, to synchrony.

On Growth and Form might have been an unreadable collection

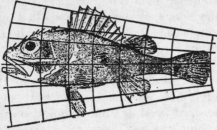

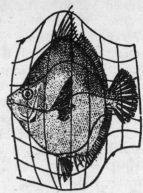

Scorpaena sp.

Antigonia capros

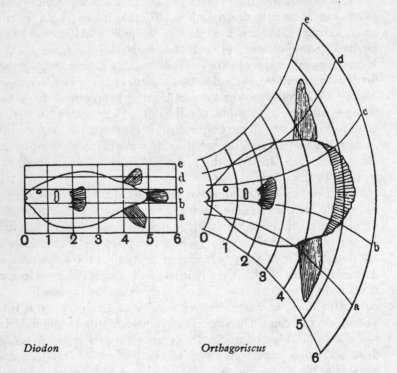

Diodon

Orthagoriscus

Force Fields in "Streamlining" (from D'Arcy Wentworth Thompson's *Growth and Form*)

of formulas, graphs, temperature and pressure tables, stress measurements, and the like. It is not. The mathematical regularities that Thompson discovered throughout the living world seemed astonishing and delightful to him. G. E. Hutchinson's "In Memoriam, D'Arcy Thompson" (1948) states: "What he wrote brings home to the scientific mind perhaps better than any work of any other writer, what it means to be civilized." P. B. Medawar, a fellow biologist, wrote in a postscript to a biography of Thompson (1958) that *On Growth and Form* is "beyond comparison the finest work of literature in all the annals of science . . . in the English tongue" and is "the equal of anything of Pater's." Buckminster Fuller knew Thompson's work and was influenced by it. There is a section in *On Growth and Form* entitled "A Parenthetic Note on Geodesics": Fuller's domes owe something of their lacy and organic intricacy to the impression the book made on him when he read it in the 1920's.

Thompson's "Epilogue" is a majestic expression of the mixture of analysis and religious wonder that pervades his text:

> That I am no skilled mathematician I have had little need to confess. I am "advanced in these enquiries no farther than the threshold"; but something of the use and beauty of mathematics I think I am able to understand. I know that in the study of material things, number, order and position are the threefold clue to exact knowledge; that these three, in the mathematician's hands, furnish the "first outlines for a sketch of the Universe"; that by square and circle we are helped, like Emile Verhaeren's carpenter, to conceive "Les lois indubitables et fécondes qui sont la règle et la clarté du monde."
>
> For the harmony of the world is made manifest in Form and Number, and the heart and soul and all the poetry of Natural Philosophy are embodied in the concept of mathematical beauty. A greater than Verhaeren had this in mind when he told of "the golden compasses prepared In God's eternal store." A greater than Milton had magnified the theme and glorified Him "that sitteth upon the circle of the earth," saying: "He hath measured the waters in the hollow of his hand, and meted out

361

heaven with the span, and comprehended the dust of the earth in a measure. . . ."

Not only the movements of the heavenly host must be determined by observation and elucidated by mathematics, but whatsoever else can be expressed by number and defined by natural law. This is the teaching of Plato and Pythagoras, and the message of Greek wisdom to mankind. So the living and the dead, things animate and inanimate, we dwellers in the world and the world wherein we dwell . . . are bound alike by physical and mathematical law. "Conterminous with space and coeval with time is the kingdom of Mathematics; within this range her dominion is supreme. . . ."

This is a summary of the main thesis of *On Growth and Form* and a hymn to the comely beauty of the world. Thompson quotes poetry—Verhaeren and Milton and Genesis—to find words adequate to his vision, but his own language is equally poetic. His nature is not a collection of things seen from the middle distance in the manner of Darwin but of innumerable phenomena—the skeletons of diatoms and the cells of honeycombs and the shells of the nautilus and the skulls of horses—reduced to the forms of dodecahedron and hexagon and logarithmic spiral and truss. His chapter on comparative morphology uses regular distortions of Cartesian graphs to reveal hidden similarities between forms:

The mathematical definition of "form" has a quality of precision which was quite lacking in our earlier stage of mere description. . . . We are brought by means of it in touch with Galileo's aphorism (as old as Plato, as old as Pythagoras, as old perhaps as the wisdom of the Egyptians) that "the Book of Nature is written in characters of Geometry."

Thompson believed in 1917 that he had embarked on a journey even more radical than that of physics. Mathematics had been a part of physics since Pythagoras, but the application of mathematics to life was, Thompson felt, something new. By extending its empire to living organisms—and we have already seen that he was uneasy about the step—Thompson made mathematics a universal

362

category. There is nothing left to hold out against it. A revolution has been won.

Darwin's view of things is saturated with human motives. Life is made possible only by death; the cost of the beautiful and ever-ramifying branches on the Tree of Life is the graveyard of species that litter the earth around its base. To regard the struggle for existence as tragic, however, is logical nonsense and a prime example of the pathetic fallacy—and so, in spite of Darwin's allegiance to Bacon, an instance of what Bacon considered the besetting human error: "Submitting the shewes of things to the desires of the Minde." The million plumed seeds that die in order that one may live have no sense of their own tragedy. It is the human observer who imposes this sense on the order of things. To call death—even the death of seeds—tragic is to call life a blessing. But to say that the death of seeds is, purely and simply, the death of seeds is to suggest that life and death have equal meaning or no meaning at all. They are phases of matter, sides of a coin, a ying and a yang. The mythic quality of Darwin's description of the struggle for survival suggests strongly that he was psychologically unable to admit this possibility.

Mathematics has no place for the pathetic fallacy. When viewed in terms of the category of mathematics, the world retains its dazzling beauty but is not tragic. Instead of clothing the nonhuman world with human sentiments, mathematics seems to do the reverse. It seems to strip away the claim of life to being somehow unique by treating it as continuous with the inorganic world. A sphere is a sphere whether it is materialized in a raindrop or a human tear. A honeycomb is not the inspired product of Pythagorean insects or the result of millions of years of subtle "coadaptations," but simply the shape that flexible circles assume when close-packed. "We dwellers in the world and the world wherein we dwell," Thompson wrote, "are bound alike by physical and mathematical law."

The word *seems* in the preceding paragraph is used advisedly because the moment in the development of scientific culture represented by D'Arcy Thompson confronts us with a paradox. Mathematics is not "in the world" in the sense that Bacon's facts and Audubon's birds and Darwin's water beetles are in the world. It may be in the mind of God. If so, mathematics is the true ground of reality. On the other hand, if God does not exist—or if God exists but is not interested in mathematics—then mathematics is a product of the human mind. It is not the ground of the real but a mask imposed on the real by man.

The same paradox is evident in another aspect of modern science, which has moved away from observations at the middle distance, where things look like things, to observations of the very small and the very distant; and the instruments it uses to observe—including purely representational instruments like Cartesian graphs—often yield images quite different from those given by the five senses. The effect of seeing nature from these perspectives is apparently to dehumanize it. Things no longer look like things. The images that the instruments produce have more kinship with each other than with what they "are." An enlarged microphotograph of a cancer cell looks like an abstract painting, or, to the untrained and unwary eye, much like a microphotograph of crystals embedded in an alloy or like geological formations in radar images made from a satellite. An infrared view of a distant landscape may glow like an impressionist canvas; an ultraviolet view will be different but equally lovely. All of these versions of nature are "real." In fact, from Thompson's point of view they are more real than nature observed from a middle distance because they show structure.

More important, the images produced by the instruments are not inhuman but radically human. The instruments were made by men, not by God or nature, and it is only through their mediation that the images can appear. The nature they reveal is not an alien other, whether beautiful or terrible or both. It is, rather, a projection of the human spirit—a showing forth of something that requires the cooperation of the spirit to achieve presentness.

At the same time, the image of nature in the sense of things seen from middle distance has disappeared. The contrast between Darwin and Thompson shows that as the image dissolves, the sense of tragedy—of human drama with human consequences—is replaced by generalized appreciation of the beauty of form. Thompson's poetry is more rarefied than Darwin's. The sense of detail, the concern for the particularity of each object, that is so powerful in *The Origin of Species* is transformed into delight in the discovery of mathematical regularities replicated across the whole range of life.

Inevitably Thompson is forced by his assumptions into direct confrontation with Darwin. Kant showed that time is a human motive projected into nature—another instance of anthropomorphism. Darwin understood evolution as something that happens in time, an historical process. Evolution has a direction which tends to be "up," an ascent from simple to complex, which means from good to better. Millions die but the fittest survive. This is the consolation that finally allows Darwin to come to terms with the struggle for survival.

As mathematics eliminates the last vestiges of anthropomorphic, mythological, and tragic sentiment from nature, it eliminates the concept of the direction of time. Thompson's rejection of the search of evolutionary biology for ancestors is clearly a move in that direction. Function, not "pedigree," determines survival. Some things work and some things do not. Simple is not good and complex is not better. For Thompson, evolutionary time has no arrow:

> In the order of physical and mathematical complexity there is no question of the sequence of historic time. The forces that bring about the sphere, the cylinder or the ellipsoid are the same yesterday and to-morrow. A snow-crystal is the same today as when the first snows fell. The physical forces which mould the forms of *Orbulina*, of *Astrorhiza*, of *Lagena* or of *Nodosaria* to-day were still the same . . . in that yesterday which we call the Cretaceous epoch; or, for aught we know, throughout all that duration of time which is marked, but not measured, by the geological record.

This is much more than a quibble. It is a challenge to the generally accepted understanding of evolution.

Having rejected evolution, Thompson also rejects any progress that Darwinian theory might imply:

> In the end and upshot, it seems to me by no means certain . . . that the concept of continuous historical evolution must necessarily, or may safely and legitimately, be employed. That things not only alter but improve is an article of faith, and the boldest of evolutionary conceptions. How far it were true were very

hard to say; but I for one imagine that a pterodactyl flew no less well than does an albatross, and that the Old Red Sandstone fishes swam as well and as easily as the fishes of our own seas.

The invisible web of forces that shapes natural organisms has no history because it is eternal and no home because it is universal. The living and the dead, the dwellers in the world and the world in which they dwell, are to the mathematician equal. Those who find evidence of a divine plan in the numbers of living forms may do so; this is the path of Pythagorean mystics and religiously inclined modern scientists.

VI

The problem of the world seen from different perspectives is both familiar and profound. To someone wearing dark glasses the world looks dark, but it is not necessarily so. Take off the sunglasses and the world is flooded with intolerable light. One kind of mathematics reveals one kind of pattern; another reveals another. The darkness of the world becomes yellow with yellow lenses, blue with blue.

Nietzsche expresses this concept in the metaphor of masks. In Greek tragedy plots were created when Thespis imposed the mask of a hero on the face of the god who stood at the center of the liturgy of Dionysus. Mapped on a Mercator projection, the world looks different from the same world on a Dymaxion projection. The two mapping systems are masks imposed on the world by men. In *Masks of the Universe* (1984) Edward Harrison suggests that all of the cosmologies of history are so many masks covering a face that will never be seen. The world is always somewhere beyond its mask; no map can use more than a tiny sampling of the information the world continuously offers. This is a blessing. Too much information would render the world unintelligible. But is the result of fitting bits and pieces together any less arbitrary than a Mercator projection? What guarantees its authority? The elimination of absolutes from human knowledge does not imply an end of human response to nature. It places man in the country he creates with his own mind. In this country he is surrounded by brilliant, fantastic, wildly distorted images of himself. Hence the third moment of modern science, the authentically modern moment, the moment of reality as game.

Wallace Stevens calls the games the mind plays with the world "necessary fictions." The mind cannot get along with them, but it cannot get along without them either. They organize experience just as religion, mythology, and tradition organize it. They are the preconditions of knowledge, perhaps of consciousness. Between the publication of Newton's *Principia Mathematica* in 1687 and Darwin's *The Origin of Species* in 1859, man believed science would present him with truth. This is a fantasy. Science has challenged religion and mythology and tradition—and people still lament the challenge—but it no longer promises to replace them with truth, only with necessary fictions. This morning the world may be a rhombic dodecahedron; by noon it may well be a Möbius strip.

Friedrich Schiller, poet and longtime friend of Goethe, popularized the game metaphor at the end of the eighteenth century in his *Letters on the Aesthetic Education of Man* (1795). He traced the human urge to create to the *Spieltrieb*, the play impulse. Play and work are both rigorous because both require effort and both have strict rules. However, we are forced to work in order to survive. People who play games are often intensely serious, but they play for fun. Rules are essential because without them there would be no games. But they are only rules. They are retained as long as they are useful or entertaining. When things get boring the chess pieces are put back in the drawer and the table is set for poker; or, as in the case of the rule in football governing downfield interference with a pass receiver, the rules can be changed to make things more exciting. In an absolute sense one game is as good as another. Once liberated from the idea that only one game is possible, the mind changes shapes as easily as Proteus.

To move from D'Arcy Thompson's majestic and classical meditation on the comely order of things to the world of modern physics and mathematics is to move from a science that assumes the existence of absolutes to a science that is provisional, relative, paradoxical, playful, ebullient. It is a science liberated from the need to take itself seriously, hence a science that is a game or a series of games played with whatever is beyond it. Some games are entirely rational. Others intentionally involve chance, having a random element that can overturn the most careful strategies.

Here a great modern poem should be invoked because it identifies the contemporary moment as a game of the random variety. The poem itself wavers between moments of play and moments when it takes itself seriously. This is not surprising considering its date: 1897. It is exactly contemporary with the beginning of those massive shifts in perspective that lead to modern culture. It is thus both observation and prophecy.

Un Coup de Dés is Stéphane Mallarmé's last poem. He lived to see it printed in the magazine *Cosmopolis* but not to see it printed according to his instructions. The most striking feature of the poem when correctly printed is that each "page" occupies a conventional double page. The division between the left and right leaves of the double page is part of the poem's visual message. Another visual feature is the use of several sizes and styles of type. The largest type defines the largest concept: *UN COUP DE DÉS JAMAIS N'ABOLIRA LE HASARD*—"A throw of the dice will never eliminate chance." Since Mallarmé taught English, is it possible that *hasard* also has the connotation of "danger"?

Because of its visual effects the poem has the qualities of a painting or of the *poésie concrète* of the 1950's. It is spread out in the *Pléiade* edition across eleven double pages. It begins solidly on the right (the "dexter" or favored side), wanders to a balanced left-right format, then drifts almost entirely to the left (sinister) leaf. At midpoint it wavers between right and left, but gradually the bias to the right is reasserted, becoming unambiguous on the last two pages. In spite of this positive quality the poem ends as it began, with the image of a game of dice: *"Toute Pensée émet un Coup de Dés."*

There is a beginning, middle, and end to the poem, but is anybody there? Just barely. The poet is a modern Odysseus afloat on an ocean of potential silence, symbolized by the blankness of the pages. The silence is the lack of a language to name the world in which the poet finds himself. He is thus also an Adam who remains dumb as the animals pass in review. Being human, he must rebel against the silence. In a region of perfect silence, without up or down, any assertion will be arbitrary, hence random, hence "a throw of the dice." The dice are thrown. A provisional order is established. Minimalist though it is, the achievement brings satisfaction. The poet begins to move across and down the page. He encounters a shipwreck. In spite of it he presses forward.

Every word is an affirmation, a passage over an abyss, a victory over silence.

Toward the end a constellation appears: the Bear (*Ursa Major*). Is it a landmark, a divine sign, or a chance array of stars given human significance by superstition? Whatever the answer, the constellation is *"froide d'oubli et de désuétude."* The poet struggles past it toward the epic goal, the end of the poem. He reaches the end exhausted but preparing to triumph—*brillant et méditant*—only to learn in the last line the lesson of the poem's beginning. It is time to begin the game again: *Toute Pensée émet un Coup de Dés*.

The play of *Un Coup de Dés* is serious. The play of modern science is also serious; but its games are so exhilarating, and the rules often so strange, that the play becomes overtly playful. The playfulness spills over into mathematical and logical puzzles and into language that is intentionally paradoxical, whimsical, and absurd. Do you have trouble remembering *pi* to twenty-one digits? Try the following bit of mathematical slapstick, in which the number of letters in each word gives you a digit:

> How I wish I could remember pi.
> Eureka! cried the great inventor.
> Christmas pudding, Christmas pie
> Is at the problem's very center.

The archetype of all such logical slapstick is the work of Charles Dodgson, who wrote on non-Euclidian geometries and symbolic logic and is also known for the fiction he wrote under the name of Lewis Carroll. In *The Annotated Alice* (1960) Martin Gardner suggests that the Alice books are games for grown-ups: "It is only because adults—scientists and mathematicians in particular—continue to relish the ALICE books that they are assured of immortality." If modern scientists keep the Alice books alive, they do so because Dodgson's oscillation between symbolic logic and bizarre fictional games anticipates a central theme of modern science. Gardner remarks:

> The last level of metaphor in ALICE is this: that life, viewed rationally and without illusion, appears to be a nonsense tale told by an idiot Mathematician. At the

heart of things science finds only a mad, never-ending quadrille of Mock Turtle Waves and Gryphon Particles. For a moment the waves and particles dance in grotesque, inconceivably complex patterns capable of reflecting on their own absurdity. We all live slapstick lives, under an inexplicable sentence of death. . . .

This is a long way from Thompson's noble numbers, but it nicely explains the relation between the madcap playfulness of *Through the Looking Glass* and the playfulness of science.

Had he lived a few more years, D'Arcy Thompson would probably have been delighted to learn that a double helix is at the center of life and that life's infinitely complex forms are mediated by sequences of four bases. Physics and astronomy, however, refuse to be as neat as biology. In its quest for simplifications, particle physics constantly finds new complexities. Quarks come in pluses and minuses, quarks and antiquarks. The twelve varieties of quark are distinguished by four flavors, three colors, three anticolors, and varying degrees of strangeness. The colors are red, green, and blue, and the anticolors are cyan, magenta, and yellow. One of the flavors has charm; hence the charmion.

The name "quark" was taken by Murray Gell-Mann, a California physicist, from James Joyce's *Finnegans Wake*. Quarks are arranged in an eightfold way, a phrase borrowed from Zen. They are combined by particles called gluons because they glue quarks together. The gluons have color and cause either infrared or ultraviolet slavery. Quarks have to exist in order for the equations of nature to work out. If they did not exist, nature would be inconceivable. But no quark has ever been observed and none is likely to be, because the theory that makes quarks essential to the concept of nature includes within its proof the subproof that quarks will change into something else if sufficient energy is applied to get them out in the open where they can be observed.

According to Dr. Yochiro Nambu, quarks are contained either on a string that cannot be broken or in bags that are impossible to penetrate. Whence it follows:

Theories of quark confinement suggest that all quarks may be permanently inaccessible and invisible. The very success of the quark model leads us back to the question of the reality of quarks. If a particle cannot be isolated and observed, even in theory, how will we ever be able to know that it exists?

To move from the incredibly small to the inconceivably large, if the "big bang" theory is correct, the universe may simply be itself, but because there is so much of it, accounting for where it came from is difficult. Big bang theoreticians have not been able to push their history of the universe earlier than 10 to the -43rd second of its existence. In the beginning, a trillionth of a second (10 to the -12) is crowded with events; later, billions of years pass and nothing much happens.

The inflationary theory of creation agrees fully with the big bang theory about what happened after the first 10 to the -30th second, but what happened before that makes all the difference. The inflationary theory assumes there was first a pseudovacuum in which a real vacuum formed. The pseudovacuum is far larger than the universe but forever beyond its horizon. Meanwhile, the universe took shape in the pseudovacuum much like a hole in a Swiss cheese or a bubble in a glass of ginger ale. It is one of many— perhaps infinite—bubble universes.

All this happened prior to about 10 to the -30th second of creation, and one drawback of the inflationary universe is that if it is true, no consequences of anything existing before the inflation can ever be observed because they have all been obliterated. On the other hand, the inflationary model has a splendid virtue. It shows that everything that exists is exactly canceled out by something else that exists. The sum is breathtakingly elegant but in a way that might have made Thompson unhappy: it is zero. As Alan Guth and Paul Steinhardt, the primary inventors of the theory, explain, everything is derived from nothing (or almost nothing): "In this view the universe would originate as a quantum fluctuation from absolutely nothing." They conclude that the theory "offers what is apparently the first plausible scientific explanation for the creation of essentially all the matter and energy in the observable universe." Among other things, this promises to settle a longstanding theological feud: "From nothing all things come"—*ex nihil omnia fiunt*.

To many of its citizens the world of quarks and black holes is an affront. Humanity seems to have leaked out of it. To others it is a

371

playful world—a world of games, though some of the games are deadly serious, and of necessary fictions, though some of the fictions are more necessary than others. The choice of fictions may be decided by a throw of the dice, but perhaps not. The question is probably being asked in terms of a past that no longer exists, rather than a present that may not exist but is as good a bet as any if one is throwing dice.

Gauss and Lobachevski began investigating non-Euclidian geometries early in the nineteenth century, and Riemann placed the enterprise firmly on its modern course. The results stirred bitter controversy within as well as outside of the mathematical fraternity because they challenged the ideal of an eternal order of things beyond nature. In effect, they threatened to make geometry into a game.

Geometry and play are wonderfully interwoven in Benoit Mandelbrot's *The Fractal Geometry of Nature* (1982). Like D'Arcy Thompson, whom he cites, Mandelbrot writes for the general reader as well as the specialist. Although his ideas are complex, he presents them in nontechnical as well as technical form. His mathematics, however, is closer to the surrealistic fantasies of André Breton or René Magritte than Thompson's eternal Pythagorean forms. For Mandelbrot "Euclid" is a bad word, synonymous with a cold and unnatural formalism. "Why," he asks, "is geometry often described as 'cold' and 'dry'? One reason lies in its inability to describe the shape of a cloud, a mountain, a coastline, a tree. Clouds are not spheres, mountains are not cones, coastlines are not circles, and bark is not smooth, nor does lightning travel in a straight line."

Part of the playfulness of *Fractal Geometry* comes from its unpredictability. Like Mallarmé, Mandelbrot enjoys throwing dice. Although randomness is not essential to the mathematical concept of fractals, he regularly introduces it into his constructions, because randomness makes them more "like" clouds and mountains and less like triangles and spheres.

His rejection of Euclid carries forward the revolt begun in the late nineteenth century, when geometers began to confront shapes that refused to behave in the well-brought-up manner of Euclid's circles and parabolas. Traditionalists called these shapes "pathological" and "terrifying," and "a gallery of monsters." However, Mandelbrot argues that the shapes are more, not less, natural than

Euclid's regular forms. F. J. Dyson, a reviewer of *Fractal Geometry*, suggests the movement to study them was "kin to the cubist paintings and atonal music that were upsetting established standards of taste in art at about the same time." Mandelbrot, however, rejects Cubism and related movements, including the Bauhaus: "A Mies van der Rohe building is a scalebound throwback to Euclid."

As these references to painting and architecture suggest, fractal geometry is closely related to art. Mandelbrot calls it a "new geometric art" and argues that "because it came in through an effort to imitate Nature in order to guess its laws, it may very well be that fractal art is readily accepted because it is not truly unfamiliar." Pictures are integral to Mandelbrot's text. They are part of his proof that fractal geometry is natural. They are often surrealistic, but even the most bizarre of them teases the mind with its familiarity. "In the theory of fractals," writes Mandelbrot, " 'to see *is* to believe.' . . . The reader . . . is . . . advised to browse through my picture book. This essay was designed to help make its contents accessible in various degrees to a wide range of readers."

One of Mandelbrot's most striking constructions is pure surrealism. It is a "self-squared dragon," and it is the ancestor of a large and exotic line of computer monsters, some in four rather than in three dimensions. Alan Norton, a colleague of Mandelbrot at IBM's Thomas J. Watson Research Center, describes photographing the four-dimensional self-squared dragons that float up from his computer screen as "throwing my camera out there in the dark, taking snapshots." To emphasize the familiarity of fractals, Mandelbrot includes traditional paintings as well as mathematical constructions: God the Creator from a twelfth-century Bible manuscript, the waters of Noah's flood by Leonardo da Vinci, and "Great Wave" by Katsushika Hokusai (1760–1849).

To get an idea of what a fractal is, consider a line that squiggles around on a page—a doodle you made, maybe, while talking on the telephone. In traditional geometry your squiggly line has one dimension—length. The surface on which it is written has two dimensions, length and width, and the space you occupy while you doodle has three dimensions. The conventional dimension of a point is 0 and of a line 1. The number 1 is an integer (as are 2 and 3), in contrast to a number like 1.5, which is a fraction.

If your phone call lasts a long time, your doodle will eventually cover most of the page. If your phone conversation lasted long enough it *would* cover the page, and its dimension would change from 1 to 2. In order to describe the tendency of a squiggly line to become a surface, Mandelbrot says that it has a *fractional dimension*. That dimension might be something like 1.5, and the line is known as a *fractal*. A fractal dimension is also called a "Hausdorff dimension" after Felix Hausdorff, who developed the idea in 1919.

Lines with dimensions of 1.5 probably seem as bizarre as they can get. But are they? We like to pretend we live in a tidy world full of circles and triangles and right angles. However, anybody who has tried to make a picture frame knows that right angles are the exception rather than the rule in the real world. Mandelbrot calls the world of lines and planes and right angles *Euclidian* because Euclid is constantly using it in his geometry. Mandelbrot considers such a world to be a fantasy, and an unnatural one at that: "Many patterns of Nature are so irregular and fragmented that compared with *Euclid*—a term used in this work to denote all of standard geometry—Nature exhibits not simply a higher degree but an altogether different level of complexity."

Take coastlines. Mandelbrot's fifth chapter introduces the subject with the question, "How long is the coast of Britain?" A good question, which, as Mandelbrot notes, was first asked by the mathematician Lewis Richardson. Mandelbrot points out that if you look at a map made at a scale of one hundred miles to an inch, the coast is obviously not smooth. It goes in and out in bays and promontories and estuaries and capes. You include these when you measure it. If you use a map drawn at a scale of ten miles to an inch, new bays suddenly open up and new promontories jut out from the sides of bays. When you measure these and add them to your first total, the coast gets longer. It gets longer still at a mile to an inch—and so on until you are crawling around on your hands and knees measuring the distances around small rocks. If you decide to use a microscope, you will find yourself measuring the irregularities on the surface of each rock and . . .

Enough! Mandelbrot has been faithful to nature, but where has the coast of Britain gone? Is there a coast? Is the problem serious or absurd? It is certainly playful, like the logical puzzles in *Through the Looking Glass*. It also has serious practical implications. Mandelbrot compares the lengths of the border between Spain and Portugal in different atlases. The Portuguese atlas shows the border as twenty percent longer than the Spanish atlas. Should

Spain break off diplomatic relations with Portugal? No. Both atlases are correct. The Spanish surveyors based their measurements on a larger unit of distance than the Portuguese and therefore measured fewer squiggles.

To decide how to measure the coast of Britain (or the border between Spain and Portugal) Mandelbrot creates a fractal line that behaves like a coastline. In other words, he makes a mathematical model. He begins with a regular shape—an equilateral triangle. He then introduces a regular deformity into each of its three sides. The result is a twelve-sided figure shaped like the Star of David. Next he repeats the operation for each of the twelve sides, creating a figure with forty-eight sides, and so on until the changes are so small the eye cannot follow them.

The figure never stays still because it has no bottom. Every time you try to measure it you discover that at the next step down it has squiggles you left out in your last measurement. It is not a coastline, but it is like a coastline. It is called a Koch triangle and has a fractal dimension of about 1.26.

Clouds, riverbanks, coastlines, tree branches, the branchings of ever-smaller air passages in the lungs, natural drainage systems, commodity prices, tree bark, word frequencies, turbulence in fluids, stars in the sky, and galaxy clusters in deep space are all wondrously, dizzily, and irreducibly fractal.

Or, to put the idea more correctly, all *seem* to be fractal. Something very interesting and wonderful happened while Mandelbrot was measuring the coast of Britain. He was not observing nature but devising ways to use mathematics to generate things *like* nature. His shapes are necessary fictions. Evidently, he is an artist or poet as much as a scientist—a creator rather than an observer. The test of his models is "likeness" to their originals. The test is often disarmingly direct. Does the picture look like the thing represented? Since the pictures become more "like" the things being pictured if they are irregular, randomness is an essential part of Mandelbrot's art, if not of his mathematics.

When randomness is part of the generating process Mandelbrot's squiggles are no longer entirely predictable. The squiggles at one level of magnification are different from those at another, although at all levels the squiggles may have a family resemblance. When the irregular squiggles enclose areas, they look uncannily like coastlines of islands or continents or shorelines of lakes. When they are three-dimensional, they look like natural landscapes. The resemblance is so striking that fractal geometry is routinely used to produce landscapes of unknown worlds by movie studios such as Lucasfilm. The likeness carries over into phenomena like eddy currents and turbulence. Mandelbrot would argue that the presence of so much likeness is a strong indication that randomness is part of the deep structure of nature. "Seeing is believing."

To create a fractal shape you have to add squiggles to squiggles to squiggles. In other words, you have to perform the same operation over and over again. In theory the operation can go on forever. The squiggles can be enlarged repeatedly until the line covers the sky. By the same token, they can be diminished repeatedly until they resemble strands of DNA.

You can regard the result with amusement or awe. Mandelbrot does both. Amusement is evident when he quotes from Jonathan Swift's "On Poetry: A Rhapsody" (1733):

> So Nat'ralists observe, a Flea
> Hath smaller Fleas that on him prey,
> And these have smaller Fleas to bite 'em,
> And so proceed ad infinitum.

Awe is suggested when he quotes from Immanuel Kant's *Universal Natural History and Theory of the Heavens* (1755):

> It is natural . . . to regard the [nebulous] stars as being . . . systems of many stars. [They] are just universes and, so to speak, Milky Ways. . . . It might further be conjectured that these higher universes are not without relation to one another, and that by this mutual relationship they constitute again a still more immense system . . . which, perhaps . . . is yet again but one member in a new combination. We see the first members of a progressive relationship of worlds and systems; and the first part of this infinite progression enables us already to recognize what must be conjectured of the whole. There is no end but an abyss . . . without bound.

In practice there are limits, called "cutoffs," that stop things

short of the abyss. Hence Mandelbrot's description of observing a
ball of thread:

> A ball of 10 cm diameter made of a thick thread of
> 1 mm diameter possesses (in latent fashion) several
> distinct effective dimensions. To an observer placed far
> away, the ball appears as a zero-dimensional figure: a
> point. . . . As seen from a distance of 10 cm resolution,
> the ball of thread is a three-dimensional figure. At
> 10 mm, it is a mass of one-dimensional threads. At 0.1
> mm, each thread becomes a column and the whole
> becomes a three-dimensional figure again. At 0.01 mm,
> each column dissolves into fibers, and the ball becomes
> one-dimensional, and so on, with the dimension crossing
> over repeatedly from one value to another. When the
> ball is represented by an infinite number of atomlike
> points, it becomes zero-dimensional [because a point is
> said to have 0 dimensions].

The observing of the ball of thread is segmented by the cutoffs.
Part of the transition from one phase to another is subjective—the
observer chooses the scale—but part derives from nature. In the
example of the ball of thread nature is "grainy"—that is, different
systems appear at different scales.

How long is the coast of Britain? What are you after? Are you a
space shuttle or a cruise ship captain or a fisherman in a rowboat?
Mandelbrot remarks, "In one manner or another, the concept of
geographic length is not as inoffensive as it seems. It is not entirely
'objective.' The observer inevitably intervenes in its definition."
This comment recalls Heisenberg's concept of indeterminacy, and
Mandelbrot emphasizes the parallel: "The notion that a numerical
result should depend on the relation of object to observer is in the
spirit of physics in this century and is an illustration of it."

In Heisenberg, indeterminacy is decently submerged in the
spaces between (or among) electrons. In Mandelbrot it is swimming boldly along on the surface like some Loch Ness Monster or
self-squared dragon circumnavigating the coast of Britain. Banished forever from the fractal world is the notion that nature is a
collection of "things" seen from a middle distance.

The fractal world is so strange that Mandelbrot has devised a new poetry to name its citizens. He obviously enjoys the task; it is another kind of game. The word *fractal* is part of his poetry. It is derived from Latin *frangere*, "to break," "to create irregular fragments." Other coinages are *dust, curd,* and *whey; grainy structures, hydra-like structures, ramified structures, tiled surfaces,* and *pertiled surfaces* (in which collections of little tiles make big tiles like the little tiles of which they are made); *pimply, pocky, wrinkled,* and *wispy surfaces; self-squared dragons, monkeys' trees, Minkowski sausages, flattened flowers, skewed webs, random slices of Swiss cheese,* and *chains and squigs*. But the ultimate proof of any pertiled pudding is its eating: *The Fractal Geometry of Nature* offers picture after picture of breathtaking playfulness and astonishing likenesses—sometimes to themselves and sometimes to nature.

VII

The science of the late twentieth century asks man to understand himself in the light of his own reason detached from history, geography, and nature, and also from myth, religion, tradition, the idols of the tribe, and the dogmas of the fathers. It offers likenesses of nature, not nature, and it suggests further that nature is a partially subjective concept. Culture is an artifact and probably a game, and what happens in it is the result of human rather than divine will.

Objectifying this understanding of things requires new languages. Mallarmé's poet is locked in an heroic struggle against silence. The Cubist painters take a more playful view of things, but they too recognize that the artist is responsible for creating new languages to match the new culture. The same spirit of play is revealed in modern science in the naming of quarks and self-squared dragons. The names are playful because play is an essential quality of that which is being named.

If science is a human creation, this review of modern science has caught the mind in the very act of swallowing up the world. The steps are nicely defined by the figures of Charles Darwin, D'Arcy Thompson, and Benoit Mandelbrot. They take us from a nature that is alien and into which human motives are poured, to a nature that is number (but number authenticated by an absolute order), to an imitation of nature by means of number. Darwin's world is mythic. Mandelbrot's is pure fiction, which means that it is entirely human. Games are human inventions. A throw of the dice will never eliminate chance, but it keeps the games interesting.

nominated by Joyce Carol Oates

SHORT DAY

by PHILIP BOOTH

from AMERICAN POETRY REVIEW

The calm deck of a cradled
boat. Sea-smoke out over

the harbor, giving way
to the full-flood sun.

Been between the machine-
shop and boat since seven,

wanting what nut will
fit an enginemount stud

I can feel but not see.
½ was too small, 9/16ths

too big, so I came up
out into sky and went

for metric. The blue
and thin cirrus high

beyond measure. The boat-
yard mallards glad to

be tame now that duck
season's on. Guns firing

like war out in the
islands. Found metric

hex nuts in the gray
drawer where wrench sets

belong. And a thread-
gauge from Sears.

Took a 12 and 14,
fine thread and coarse,

clean as the whistle
of two pairs of loons,

fishing out in the channel.
Hard to figure how they

stay paired. But they
do. The stainless nuts

warm in infinite
sunlight, my head

warms to morning;
I climb back topside

and dive again into
the dark, my hand

fishing aft to feel
the rear mount. The 12's

too snug, the 14 floats
like the 9/16ths. She

has to be a 13. Which,
once I feel the thread

with the gauge, if
I can, will take me

all the rest of
the morning to go

to pick up in Green
Harbor. One #13

stainless hex nut.
Focused on this

tame purpose, I
come up bright as

a loon, floating where-
ever the rest of me

wants: part of me here,
part beyond any labor

or dark, flown beyond
loons or mallards or

islands, to distances
beyond gauging, save

as I have them
at heart. I give

myself leave to
be out there, far

offshore where,
over the labyrin-

thine waves, a seabird
without a name

circles, her wings quieting
to calm the sea

as she comes in
to light.

nominated by Joe-Anne McLaughlin

AT A P. C. SERGEANT'S HOUSE

by SUSAN TICHY

from FACES AND TONGUES (Laughing Waters Press) and
THE AMERICAN VOICE

Zambales Mountains, Philippines

The food is good: beef, flat fish,
and dog, with vegetables—some of them
parts of trees—and fruit.
We sit under a tree whose branches shade
five hundred square feet of ground,
while the man who brought us tries to explain
who we are. We don't understand,
but they're laughing, just as
on the way here we were told,
He is one of the most notorious, like a joke.
In the clearing that makes a barrio
the jungle is not forgotten, neither
its presence, nor the colors
of its quickly receding face—
on open fires, the white
of rice in blackened pots;
and beside the green of palm leaves, cut
and laid over plates of food,
the red polka-dot dress

The P.C. are the Philippine Constabulary.

384

of the sergeant's wife. Above that,
her bashful but uncontrollable smile.
Her husband sits with his back to the house,
facing the ragged line
where jungle and the irrigated vines
of squash and eggplant meet.
He wears no uniform, just
a t-shirt, white on the bulk of his skin.
And you have to admire how clean he looks
on this day of dry-season dust.
You have to admire the calm
with which he displays
no weapons, not even a knife.
I'll tell you how much they hate him,
said our friend as we entered the house.
His wife can cook, but we will be
his only guests for fiesta.
And it's true. There's only us,
and behind the wide trunk of the tree
an old woman crouching
by a blue plastic tub. She washes our dishes
with her head tipped slightly back,
eyes closed, listening
to birds beyond the clearing,
cicadas overhead, and the bell-like laughter
of her two dead sons. The sergeant
never looks at her. His wife
taps one temple, to explain. We nod,
though we will never know
the sacred names of her sons, or
which side they were on. Our friend asks
with his eyes if we understand:
this is not the beginning
of policy; this is the end.
The sergeant eats. The woman
wears nothing under her thin dress
but the dry folds of her skin.
Who we are—he doesn't care.
His smile is vague. His eyes
look for something on the cleared ground

behind us. He ignores us
all—as a hunted animal listens
only for one sound.
We drop the name of his colonel
into the pool of talk
and it lands heavy, it lies there
like a murder weapon no one dares
retrieve though it's in plain sight.

nominated by Sandra McPherson

THE IMAGINATION OF FLOWERS

by LEE UPTON

from FIELD

Perennial snow on the mountain,
dragon's blood sedum, fever dew:
They are doing what
their kind do: crying,
Enter me I don't care.
As if the world turns
its lips around them
just as some of us will do
for some others. He's rich,
the man who watches the woman
raking around a plaster chicken. And
the woman, they say, is not quite
right. Making a plaster chicken at home
is all it looks like to him.
    In the morning the mist appears to break
the garden's ornamental bridge
as if someone cannot walk back
that way again. In the stories of childhood,
those that make us happy,
someone is always caught
for good. She can't go back either.
That's justice: Someone else says
No. The world won't love you enough.

We might believe all this
but there is so much tenderness
in even that woman
raking around a chicken.
    When the man slides open the glass
doors, he walks to her. They stand
quietly as if waiting
for some sort of story the flowers tell
when they are very tired and about
to blow over the lawn.
Some of them here believe there is
no snow and that it is a burden
only they can bear—to be beautiful.
For others, they do what they can:
The woman's hand is muscular and moving,
and the man, he has, he has
some lovely spotted money he waves
into all that racket
inside the woman's head.

nominated by Laura Jensen
and Donald Revell

MY FATHER'S MOON

fiction by ELIZABETH JOLLEY

from GRAND STREET

Before this journey is over I intend to speak to the woman. *Ramsden* I shall say, *is it you?* The train has just left the first station, there is plenty of time in which to contemplate the conversation; the questions and the answers and the ultimate revelation. It is comfortable to think about the possibilities.

The woman sitting on the other side, diagonally opposite, could be someone I used to know. A long time ago. In another place. Her clothes are of the same good quality, the same materials, even the same colors. It is the tilt of the head which is so remarkably similar. She looks like someone who is passionately fond of the cello. Fond of listening to the cello. I look at her hands and feel sure she plays the piano. When I look at her hands it is as if I can hear her playing a Mozart sonata or practicing something from Bach. Repeating and repeating phrases until a perfection is achieved. I am certain, as I go on looking, that she plays Cyril Scott's "Water Wagtail."

For some time now I have traveled by suburban train to and from the places where I work. This evening I am on the earlier train. I caught the earlier train on purpose even though, because of this, I arrive too soon. . . .

The unfamiliar early train travels, of course, through the same landscape, the familiar. There is nothing remarkable in this. It is my reason for taking this train which makes the journey remarkable. The train stops at the same stations but naturally the people getting in or out are not the same people as those on the later train.

I sit staring out of the window at the same meeting places of unknown roads, at the backs of the same shabby houses and garden fences, at the same warehouses and the same smash repair yards and at the now well-known back of the metropolitan markets.

About once a week I catch the earlier train for a special reason. Every week it is the same. Every week I think that this time I will speak to her. This week I am on this train in order to speak to her. I will cross from my seat and sit by her and I will speak to her. I always sit where I can see her from the side and from the back and I sit close enough to hear her voice if she should speak. I long to hear the voice, her voice, to know whether it is the same voice. Voices and ways of speaking often remain unchanged.

This time I almost brought the violin case with me though I am not now accustomed to carrying it when I go out. If Ramsden saw the violin case, if the woman saw it, she would remember.

"They're both in good condition," the man in the shop said. "Both the same price. Choose your pick," he said. "Take your time."

I could not make up my mind, and then I chose the violin case. The following week I went back for the camera case but it had gone. The violin case had once been lined with some dark red soft material, some of it was still left. I only opened it once and it was then I saw the remains of the lining. I carried the case whenever I went out.

The first time I saw Ramsden the sentry at the hospital gates had his bayonet fixed. He looked awkward and he blushed as he said, "Who goes there!" Surprised, I told him my name and my identity card number, it was the middle of the morning and we were challenged, as a rule, only after dark. I supposed the rule must have been changed. A dispatch from H.Q., I thought, seeing in my mind the nimble motorcyclist arrive.

Ramsden, on her way out, gave a small smile in the direction of the violin case and I was pleased that I had bought it. On that day I had been at the hospital for seven weeks.

Two people sitting behind me are talking in German. I begin to listen to the animated conversation and grope for meanings in what they are saying in this language which was once familiar. I begin to recognize a few words *eine Dame—keine Ahnung—langsam— Milch und Tränenbäche—mein Elend—zu grosser Schmerz—und so weiter*. But I want the words of cherishing spoken in German. I want those first words the child remembers on waking to the knowing of language. I wish now in the train to be spoken to as *du. . . .*

The woman sitting on the other side is looking calmly out of the window. Naturally she sees the same things that I see. It is quite comfortable to know that I have only to lean over and touch her sleeve.

I never worked with Ramsden. I saw her sometimes in the dining room. There are several little pictures of her in my mind. The doctors called her Miss Ramsden. She did the penicillin syringes too. One nurse, usually a senior, spent the whole day cleaning and sterilizing the syringes and the needles, setting up the trolley, giving the injections and then clearing the trolley and cleaning and sterilizing and checking all over again. Whenever I passed the glass doors of the ward where she was, I saw her in the sterilizing room seriously attending to the syringes and needles for the three-hourly injections.

"Ramsden," I said, "this is the part we like isn't it. This part, this is it, we like this—"

"It's the anticipation," she replied, "it's what is hoped for and then realized," she was sitting on the edge of her bed.

"This part, this—," I said once more. I pointed with one finger as if to place the cello somewhere in the space between us. "This going down part," I said, "is the part we like best."

Ramsden nodded. She was mending a stocking. Her stockings were not the usual ones, not the grey uniform stockings which were lisle and, after repeated washing, were hard to mend. Ramsden's stockings, I noticed immediately, were smooth and soft and they glistened like honey. Dark, honey-colored stockings. Ramsden's stockings were silk stockings. She was oversewing a run at the ankle. Her sewing was done so carefully I knew the repair would be invisible. She had invited me into her room to listen to a record.

"Do you know why you like it?" She repeated an earlier question. The cello reminded me of her. How could I tell her this. I shook my head. Staff nurse Ramsden, she was senior to me. When she listened to music she sat with her legs crossed over and she moved her foot very slightly, I could see, in time to the music. How could I speak to her about the downward thrust of the cello and about the perfection in the way the other instruments came up to meet the cello. How could I say to her that I thought someone had measured the movement of the notes controlling carefully the going down and the coming up in order to produce this exquisite mixture. There were other things too that I could not speak about. How could I say to her what I thought about the poet Rilke, about his face and about how I felt when I looked at his photograph in the book she had. She knew his poems, understood them. I wanted to tell her that when I looked at Rilke's face I felt clumsy as if made of wood. Even the way he stood in the photograph had something special about it and when I read a poem of his to myself I wanted to read lines aloud to her. "Listen to this, Ramsden," I wanted to say, "listen to this,"

> *But hand in hand now with that God she walked,*
> *her paces circumscribed by lengthy shroudings*
> *uncertain, gentle, and without impatience.*
> *Wrapt in herself, like one whose time is near . . .*

There were other things too from *Orpheus,* but she knowing his poems might have felt I was intruding. When I read Rilke everything I was trying to write seemed commonplace and unmusical, completely without any delicacy and refinement. I never told Ramsden I was trying to write because what I wrote was about her. I wanted to write about Ramsden. How could I tell her that.

Later when she talked about the music she said the soloist was innocent and vulnerable. She said the music was eloquent and that there was something intimate about the cello. She was very dignified and all her words seemed especially chosen. I wanted her to say them all again to me. The word intimate, I had never before spoken to anyone who used this word. She said the cello, the music of the cello, was intimate. Ramsden's discipline prevented her from repeating what she had said. She continued to oversew her stocking and we listened once more to the second movement. When I listened to a particular passage in this movement I seemed to see Ramsden walking ahead of me with great beech trees on either side of her. Magnificent smooth trees with their rain-soaked branches darkened and dripping. Then we were walking together, I imagined, beneath these trees, with the wet leaves deep round our ankles. Ramsden, I thought, would have small ribbed socks on over her stockings. . . .

Lyrical, she said, the music was lyrical and I was not sure what she meant. She said then that, if I liked, I could borrow her records. When I played the record at home my father, not knowing the qualities of the cello, asked if I could make the music a bit quieter. It was my day off, most of it had been wasted because I slept and no one woke me. My father asked was there a piano piece, he said he liked the piano very much. I told him that staff nurse Ramsden played the piano and my mother said perhaps Miss Ramsden would come sometime and play the piano for us. She said she would make a fire in the front room and we could all sit and listen. . . .

B ecause I caught the earlier train I have an hour to spare before it is time for the clinic to open. The people who attend this clinic will be setting off from their houses in order to keep their appointments.

I walk to a bus stop where there is a bench and, though I am in a familiar place, I feel as if I have come to a strange land. In one sense there is a strangeness because all the old houses and their once cared-for gardens have gone. In their place are tall concrete buildings, floor upon floor of offices, all faced with gleaming windows. Some lit up and some dark. The buildings rise from parking lots all quite similar but unrecognizable as though I have never seen them before. Small trees and bushes planted as orna- ments offer a few twigs and leaves. The new buildings are not at peace with their surroundings. They are not a part of the land- scape, they are an imposition. They do not match each other and they have taken away any tranquillity, any special quality of human life the streets may have had once.

The Easter lilies, uncherished, appear as they do every year with surprising suddenness, their pink and white long-lasting freshness bursting out of the brown, bald patches of earth at the edges of those places which have been left out from the spreading bitumen.

If I had spoken in the train I could have said, "Ramsden," I could have said, "I feel sad. Lately I seem unable to prevent a feeling of melancholy which comes over me as soon as I wake up. I feel nervous and muddled and everything is accompanied by a sense of sorrow and futility." Should I join a sect? I could have asked her. A cult? On TV these people, with a chosen way, all look lighthearted.

They dance carrying bricks and mortar across building sites. They jive and twist and break-dance from kitchens to dining rooms carrying wooden platters of something fresh and green neatly chopped up. Perhaps it is uncooked spinach. Perhaps it is their flying hair and their happy eyes which attract, but then the memory of the uneasiness of communal living and the sharing of possessions and money seems too difficult, too frightening to contemplate. In real life it won't, I could have told her, it won't be the same as it is on TV. Probably only the more sparkling members of the sect are filmed, I could have said this too, and something is sure to be painted on the spinach to make it look more attractive. Food in advertisements, I could have been knowledgeable, food in advertisements is treated before being photographed. I left the train at my station without another glance in her direction.

Perhaps the lilies are a reminder and a comfort. Without fail they flower at Easter. Forgotten till they flower, an unsought simultaneous caution and blessing.

It seems to me now, when I think of it, that my father was always seeing me off either at a bus stop or at the station. He would suggest that he come to the bus or the train just as I was about to leave. Sometimes he came part of the way in the train getting out at the first stop and then, waiting alone, he would travel on the first train back. Because of the decision being made at the last minute, as the train was moving, he would have only a platform ticket so, as well as all the waiting and the extra traveling, he would be detained at the other end to make explanations and to pay his fare for both directions. All this must have taken a lot of time. And sometimes in the middle of winter it was bitterly cold.

The strong feeling of love which goes from the parent to the child does not seem a part of the child which can be given back to the parent. I realize now with regret that I never thought then of his repeated return journeys. I never thought of the windswept platforms, of the small smoldering waiting-room fires and the long, often wet, walks from the bus to the house. I simply always looked ahead, being already on my journey even before I set out, to the place to which I was going.

The minutes which turned out to be the last I was to have with my father were at a railway station. When it was time for my train to leave even when the whistle was being blown my father went on

394

with what he was saying. He said that if we never saw each other again I must not mind. He was getting older he said then, he was surprised at how quickly he was getting older and though he planned to live a long time it might be that we should not be able to make the next journeys in time. It is incredible that I could have paid so little attention then and the longing to hear his voice once more at this moment is something I never thought of till now.

He had his umbrella with him and when the train began to move he walked beside the moving train for as long as he could, waving the umbrella. I did not think about the umbrella then either. But now I remember that during the years he often left it in trains and it traveled the length and breadth of England coming back at intervals labeled from Liverpool, Norfolk, St. Ives and Glasgow to the lost property office where he was, with a kind of apologetic triumph, able to claim it.

The huge Easter moon, as if within arm's length, as if it can be reached simply by stretching out both hands to take it and hold it, is low down in the sky, serene and full, lighting the night so that it looks as if everything is snow-covered, and deep shadows lie across pale, moon-whitened lawns. This moon is the same moon that my father will have seen. He always told me when I had to leave for school, every term when I wept because I did not want to leave, he told me that if I looked at the moon, wherever I was, I was seeing the same moon that he was looking at. "And because of this," he said, "you must know that I am not very far away. You must never feel lonely," he said. He said the moon would never be extinguished. Sometimes, he said, it was not possible to see the moon, but it was always there. He said he liked to think of it as his.

I waited once for several hours at a bus stop, a temporary stop on a street corner in London. There was a traffic diversion and the portable sign was the final stop for the Green Line from Hertford. It was the long summer evening moving slowly into the night of soft dusty warmth. A few people walked on the pavement. All of them had places they were going to. A policeman asked me if everything was all right.

"I'm waiting for someone," I told him. I waited with Helena for Ramsden.

In the end, in my desperation, I did write my letter to Ramsden asking her to help me to leave Fairfields, the school where I had gone to live and work taking Helena with me. It was a progressive boarding school. There was not enough food and I was never paid. In my letter I told Ramsden everything that had happened, about my child, about my leaving home, about my loneliness, about my disappointment with the school. I had not expected, I told her, such fraudulent ways. My poverty, I thought, would be evident without any description. After writing the letter I was not able to wait for a reply from Ramsden because, when I went to give notice that I wanted to leave in a fortnight, Patch (the headmistress) replied in her singing voice, the dangerous contralto in which she encouraged people to condemn and entangle themselves, "By all means but please do go today. There's a bus at the end of the field path at three o'clock." Neither she nor Miss Myles, after exchanging slightly raised eyebrows with one another, said anything else to me.

I sent my letter to the last address I had from Ramsden almost five years earlier. She was, she said then, still nursing and had a little flat where I would be welcome. Five years is a long time.

I told her in my letter that I would wait for her at the terminus of the Green Line. As I wrote I could not help wondering if she was by now playing the piano in concerts. Perhaps on tour somewhere in the north of England; in the places where concert pianists play. I tried to think of likely towns and villages. As I wrote I wept remembering Ramsden's kind eyes and her shy manner. Staff nurse Ramsden with her older more experienced face—as someone once described her, and her musician's nose—someone else had said once. She had never known what there was to know about the violin case I carried with me in those days. It had been my intention always to tell her but circumstances changed intentions.

I begged her in the letter and in my heart to be there. Five years is a long time to ignore a kind invitation from someone. A long time to let pass without any kind of reply. With failing hope I walked slowly up and down the pavement which still held the dust and the warmth of the day. I walked and waited with Helena who was white-faced and hungry and tired. Sometimes she sat on our heavy case on my roughly folded school winter coat. I tried to comfort myself with little visions of Ramsden playing the piano and nodding and smiling to Helena who would dance, thump-thump, on the carpet in the little living room. I seemed to remember that

Ramsden said in the letter, sent all those years ago, that the flat was tiny.

"You'd best be coming along with me," it was the policeman again. He had passed us several times. Helena was asleep on the folded coat and I was leaning against the railings at the front of an empty house.

The woman in charge of the night shelter gave me a small huckaback towel and a square of green soap. She said she had enough hot water if Helena and I could share the bath.

"She's very like you," the woman said, not trying very hard to hide her curiosity behind a certain sort of kindness. She gave us two slices of bread and butter and a thick cup of tea each. She handed me two grey blankets and said Helena would be able to sleep across the foot of the bed she was able to let me have for one night. The girl who had the bed, she explained, was due to come out of hospital where she had been operated on to have a propeling pencil removed from her bladder.

"The things they'll try," the woman said, "I or anyone, for that matter, could have told her she was too far gone for anything like that. All on her own too pore thing. Made herself properly poorly and lorst her baby too." She looked at Helena who was eating her bread and butter, crusts and all, neatly in what seemed to me to be an excessive show of virtue.

"There's some as keeps their kiddies," the woman said.

"Yes," I said avoiding her meaning looks. The night shelter for women carried an implication. There was more than the need of a bed. At St. Cuthbert's the nurses had not been too sympathetic. I remembered all too clearly herding A.T.S. girls into one of the bathrooms every evening where they sat naked from the waist down in chipped enamel basins of hot water and bicarbonate of soda. In her lectures the Sister Tutor reminded often for the need to let patients be as dignified as possible. The hot basins defied this. Many of the girls were pregnant. Some women, the Sister Tutor said, mistook the orifices in their own bodies. All this, at that time, belonged to other people.

Later my own child was to be the embodiment of all that was poetical and beautiful and wished for. Before she was born I called her Beatrice. I forgot about the A.T.S.

Grateful for the hot bath and the tea and the promised bed I addressed the woman in charge as Sister.

397

Did the Sister, I asked her, ever know a staff nurse called Ramsden. The woman, narrowing her eyes, thought for a moment and said yes she thought she had—now she recalled it. There was a Ramsden she thought, yes she was sure, who joined the Queens Nurses and went to Mombasa. I tried to take comfort from the doubtful recollection. Yes, went to Mombasa with the Queens Nurses. Very fine women the Queens Nurses. And one night, so she'd heard, the cook in the nurses' quarters was stabbed by an intruder. Horribly stabbed, a dozen or more times in the chest, the neck and the stomach. Apparently the murder was justified, brought on by the cook's own behavior—him having gone raving mad earlier that same day. But of Ramsden herself she had no actual news.

I understood as I lay under the thin blanket that she had been trying to offer some sort of reply to my stupid and hopeless question. Perhaps the cook in Mombasa was often murdered horribly in these attempts to provide answers.

I tried to sleep but Helena, accustomed to a bed to herself, kicked unbearably all night.

Being at a bus stop, not waiting for a bus, and with the dusk turning quickly to darkness, I think of my father's moon. This moon, once his moon and now mine, is now climbing the warm night sky. It hangs in the branches of a single tree left between the new buildings.

The journey to school is always, it seems, at dusk. My father comes to the first stop. This first journey is in the autumn when the afternoons are dark before four o'clock. The melancholy railway crawls through waterlogged meadows where mourning willow trees follow the winding streams. Cattle, knee-deep in damp grass, raise their heads as if in an understanding of sorrow as the slow train passes. The roads at the level crossings are deserted. No one waits to wave and curtains of drab colors are pulled across the dimly lit cottage windows.

At the first stop there is a kind of forced gaiety in the meetings on the platform. Some girls have already been to school and others, like me, are going for the first time. My father watches and when the carriage doors are slammed, one after the other, he melts away from the side of the train as it moves slowly along the platform gradually gathering speed, resuming its journey.

I sink back at once into that incredible pool of loneliness which is, I know now but did not understand then, a part of being one of a crowd. I try to think of the moon. Though it is not Easter, my father said before the doors had all been slammed, there will be, if the clouds disperse, a moon. He pointed as he spoke towards the dome of the railway station. Because he pointed with his umbrella I felt embarrassed and, instead of looking up, I stared at my shoes. I try to think about his moon being behind the clouds even if I cannot see it. I wish, I am wishing I had smiled and waved to him.

In the noisy compartment everyone is talking and laughing. We are all reflected in the windows and the dark shadowed fields slip by on both sides.

The school bus, emblazoned with an uplifting motto, rattles through an unfamiliar land. The others sing songs which I have never heard before. There is no moon. The front door of the school opens directly on to the village street. Everyone rushes from the bus and the headmaster and his wife stand side by side in a square of light to receive us.

"Wrong hand Veronica. It is Veronica, isn't it?" he ticks my name on a list he has. "Other hand Veronica. We always shake hands with the right hand."

When I unpack my overnight bag I am comforted by the new things, the new nightdress, the handkerchiefs and the stockings folded carefully by my mother. Especially my new fountain pen pleases me.

Almost at once I begin my game of comparisons, placing myself above someone if more favorable and below others if less favorable in appearance. This game of appearance is a game of chance. Chance can be swayed by effort, that is one of the rules, but effort has to be more persistent than is humanly possible. It is a game of measuring the unfamiliar against the familiar. I prefer the familiar. I like to know my way, my place with other people, perhaps because of other uncertainties.

I am still on the bench at the bus stop. My father's moon is huge and is now above the tree in a dark blue space between two buildings. A few cars have come. I have seen their headlights dip and turn off and I have seen the dark shapes of people making their way into the place where my clinic is. They will sit in the comfortable chairs in the waiting room till they are called in to see me. Unavoidably I am late sometimes but they wait.

At the other place where I work there is a scent of hot pines. The sun, beating down on a nearby plantation all day, brings into the warm still air a heart-lifting fragrance. There is a narrow path pressed into the dry grass and the fallen pine needles. This is the path I take to and from the railway station. Sometimes I suggest to other people that they walk on this path. The crows circling and calling suggest great distance. Endless paddocks with waving crops could be quite close on the other side of the new tall buildings. The corridors indoors smell of toast, of coffee and of hot curries. It is as if there are people cooking at turning points on the paths and in corners between the buildings. It is as if they have casually thrown their saris over the cooking pots to protect them from the prevailing winds.

From where I sit it seems as if the moon is shining with some secret wisdom. I read somewhere that it was said of Chekhov that he *shows us life's depths at the very moment when he seems to reflect its shimmering surface*.

My father's moon is like this.

But the game. The game of comparisons. Before meals at school we have to stand in line beginning with the smallest and ending with the tallest. The room is not very big and the tallest stand over the smallest. We are not allowed to speak and our shoes and table napkins are examined by the prefects. It is during this time of silence and inspection that I make my comparisons. Carefully I am comparing my defects with those of my immediate neighbors. I glance sideways at the pleats of their tunics and notice that the girl next to me bulges. In my mind I call her Bulge, her pleats do not lie flat, they bulge. She is tall and awkward, taller than I am and more roundshouldered. I try to straighten my back and to smooth my tunic pleats. I can be better than Bulge. She has cracked lips and she bites her nails. I try not to chew my nails but my hands are not well kept as are the hands of the girl on the other side of me. She has pretty nails and her hair is soft and fluffy. My hair is straight but not as greasy and uneven as Bulge's. Fluffy Hair's feet turn out when she walks. My feet are straight but my stockings are hopelessly wrinkled and hers are not. We all have spots. Bulge's spots are the worst, Fluffy Hair's complexion is the best. She is marred by a slight squint. We all wear spectacles. These are all the same except that Bulge has cracked one of her lenses. My lenses need cleaning.

It is the sound of someone closing a case very quietly in the dormitory after the lights have been turned off which makes me cry. It is the kind of sound which belongs to my mother. This quiet little closing of a case. My nightdress, which she made, is very comfortable. It wraps round me. She knitted it on a circular needle, a kind of stockinette she said it was, very soft, she said. When she had finished it she was very pleased because it had no seams. She was telling our neighbor, showing her the nightdress and the new clothes for school, all marked with my name embroidered on linen tape. The cabin trunk bought specially and labeled clearly "Luggage in Advance" in readiness for the journey by goods train produced an uneasy excitement. My mother, handling the nightdress again, spoke to me:

> *ein weiches reines Kleid für dich zu weben,*
> *darin nicht einmal die geringste Spur*
> *Von naht dich drückt—*

"Shut up," I said, not liking her to speak to me in German in front of the woman from next door. "Shut up," I said again knowing from the way she spoke it was a part of a poem. "Shut up," I crushed the nightdress back into the overnight bag, "it's only a nightgown!"

When I stop crying I pretend that the nightdress is my mother holding me.

On our second Sunday afternoon I am invited with Bulge and Fluffy Hair and Helen Ferguson and another girl called Amy to explore a place called Harpers Hill. Bulge is particularly shapeless in her Sunday dress. My dress, we have to wear navy-blue serge dresses, is already too tight for me and it is only the second Sunday. Fluffy Hair's dress belongs to her Auntie and has a red lace collar instead of the compulsory white linen one. The collars are supposed to be detachable so that they can be washed.

I wish I could be small and neat and pretty like Amy, or even quick like Helen Ferguson who always knows what's for breakfast the night before. Very quickly she understands the system and knows in advance the times of things, the difference between Morning Meeting and Evening Meeting and where we are supposed to be at certain times, whose turn it is to mop the dormitory and which nights are bath nights. I do not have this quality of knowing and when I look at Helen Ferguson I wonder why I am made as I am. In class Helen Ferguson has a special way of sitting with one foot slightly in front of the other and she sucks her pen while she is thinking. I try to sit as she does and try to look as if I am thinking while I suck the rounded end of my new pen.

During Morning Meeting I am worrying about the invitation which seems sinister in some way. It is more like a command from the senior girls. I try and listen to the prayer at the beginning of Meeting. We all have to ask God to be in our hearts. All the time I am thinking of the crossroads where we are supposed to meet for the walk. Bulge does not stop chewing her nails and her fingers all through Meeting. I examine my nails, chew them and, remembering, sit on my hands.

Between autumn-berried hedges in unscratched shoes and new stockings we wait at the crossroads. The brown plowed fields slope to a near horizon of heavy cloud. There are some farm buildings quite close but no sign of any people. The distant throbbing of an invisible tractor and the melancholy cawing of the rooks bring back the sadness and the extraordinary fear of the first Sunday afternoon walk too vividly. I try not to scream as I screamed that day and I try not to think about the longed for streets crowded with people and endlessly noisy with trams. It is empty in the country and our raincoats are too long.

The girl, the straw-colored one they call Etty, comes along the road towards us. She says it's to be a picnic and the others are waiting with the food not far away. She says to follow her. A pleasant surprise, the picnic. She leads us along a little path across some fields to a thicket. We have to bend down to follow the path as it winds between blackberry and under other prickly bushes. Our excited talk is soon silenced as we struggle through a hopeless tangle of thorns and bramble. Amy says she thinks we should turn back. Bulge has the most awful scratches on her forehead. Amy says, "Look, her head's bleeding." But Etty says no we shall soon get through to the place.

Suddenly we emerge high up on the edge of a sandy cliff. "It's a landslide!" I say and, frightened, I try to move away from the edge. Before we have time to turn back the girls, who have been hiding, rush out and grab us by the arms and legs. They tie us up with our own scarves and raincoat belts and push us over the edge and down the steep rough walls of the quarry. I am too frightened to cry out or to resist. Bulge fights and screams in a strange voice quite unlike any voice I have ever heard. Four big girls have her by the arms and legs. They pull her knickers off as she rolls over kicking. Her lumpy white thighs show above the tops of her brown woollen stockings.

"Not this man but Barrabas! Not this man but Barrabas!" they shout. "She's got pockets in her knickers! Pockets in her knickers!" The horrible chant is all around Bulge as she lies howling.

As quickly as the big girls appeared they are gone. We, none of us, try to do anything to help Bulge as we struggle free from the knotted belts and scarves. Helen Ferguson and Amy lead the way back as we try to find the road. Though we examine, exclaiming, our own torn clothes and show each other our scratches and bruises the real hurt is something we cannot speak about. Fluffy Hair cries. Bulge, who has stopped crying, lumbers along with her head down. Amy, who does not cry, is very red. She declares she will report the incident. "That's a bit too daring," I say, hoping that she will do as she says. I am wondering if Bulge is still without her knickers.

"There's Etty and some of them," Helen Ferguson says as we approach the crossroads. It has started to rain. Huddled against the rain we walk slowly on towards them.

"Hurry up you lot!" Etty calls in ringing tones. "We're getting wet." She indicates the girls sheltering under the red-berried hawthorn.

"I suppose you know," Etty says, "Harpers Hill is absolutely out of bounds. So you'd better not tell. If you get the whole school gated it'll be the worse for you!" She rejoins the others who stand watching us as we walk by.

"That was only a rag. We were only ragging you," Etty calls, "so mind you don't get the whole school gated!" Glistening water drops fly from the wet hedge as the girls leap out, one after the

403

other, across the soaked grass of the ditch. They race ahead screaming with laughter. Their laughter continues long after they are out of sight.

In Evening Meeting Bulge cannot stop crying and she has no handkerchief. Helen Ferguson, sitting next to me on the other side, nudges me and grins, making grimaces of disgust, nodding in the direction of Bulge and we both shake with simulated mirth, making, at the same time, a pretense of tryng to suppress it. Without any sound Bulge draws breath and weeps, her eyes and nose running into her thick fingers. I lean away from her heaving body. I can see her grazed knees because both her stockings have huge holes in them.

Before Meeting, while we were in line while two seniors were practicing Bach, a duet on the common-room piano, Bulge turned up the hem of her Sunday dress to show me a large three-cornered tear. It is a hedge tear she told me then while the hammered Bach fell about our ears. And it will be impossible, when it is mended, she said, for her mother to lengthen the dress.

I give another hardly visible but exaggerated shiver of mirth and pretend, as Helen Ferguson is doing, to look serious and attentive as if being thoughtful and as if listening with understanding to the reading. The seniors read in turn, a different one every Sunday. It is Etty's turn to read. She reads in a clear voice. She has been practicing her reading for some days.

"Romans chapter nine verse twenty-one," her Sunday dress is well pressed and the white collar sparkles round her pretty neck.

Hath not the potter power
over the clay, of the same lump
to make one vessel unto honor
and another unto dishonor?

"And from verse twenty," Etty looks up smiling and lisping just a little,

Shall the thing formed say to
him that formed it, Why hast
thou made me thus?

404

Etty minces from the platform where the staff sit in a semicircle. She walks demurely back to her seat.

"These two verses," Miss Vanburgh gets up and puts both hands on the lectern, it is her turn to give the Address; "These two verses,",she says, "are sometimes run together."

"Shall the clay say to the potter why hast thou made me thus . . ."

Bulge is still weeping.

Miss Besser, on tiptoe across the creaking boards of the platform, creeps down, bending double between the rows of chairs and, leaning over, whispers to me to take Muriel.

"Take your friend out of meeting, take her to . . ."

"I don't know her. She isn't my friend," I begin to say in a whisper, trying to explain, "she's not my friend . . ."

"To matron," Miss Besser says in a low voice, "take Muriel." I get up and go out with Bulge who falls over her own feet and, kicking the chair legs, makes a noise which draws attention to our attempted silent movement.

I know it is the custom for the one who leads the other to put an arm of care and protection round the shoulders of distress. I know this already after two weeks. It is not because I do not know . . .

I wait with Bulge in the little porch outside Matron's cottage. Bulge does not look at me with her face only with her round and shaking shoulders.

Matron, when she comes, gives Bulge a handkerchief and reaches for the iodine. "A hot bath," she says to Bulge, "and early bed. I'll have some hot milk sent up. Be quick," Matron adds, "and don't use up too much hot water. Hot milk," she says, "in half an hour."

I do not go back into Meeting. Instead I stand for a time in a place where nobody comes, between the cloakroom and the bootroom. It is a sort of passage which does not lead anywhere. I think of Bulge lying back if only for a few minutes in the lovely hot water. I feel cold. Half an hour, that is the time Matron has allowed Bulge. Perhaps, if I am quick . . .

The lights are out in our dormitory. I am nice and warm. In spite of the quick and secret bath (it is not my night), and the glass of hot milk—because of my bed being nearer the door the maid brings it to me by mistake—(it has been sweetened generously with honey) in spite of all this I keep longing for the cherishing words familiar in childhood. Because of the terrible hedged tear in the navy-blue hem and, because of the lumpy shoulders, I crouch under my bedclothes unable to stop seeing the shoulders without an arm around them. I am not able to weep as Bulge weeps. My tears will not come to wash away, for me, her shoulders.

At night we always hear the seniors, Etty in particular, singing in the bathroom. Two of them, tonight, may have to miss their baths. Etty's voice is especially noticeable this night.

> *little man you're crying*, she sings,
> *little man you're blue*
> *I know why you're crying*
> *I know why you're blue*
> *Someone stole your Kiddi-Kar away from you*

The moon, my father's moon, is too far away.

The Easter moon is racing up the sky. The stunted ornamental bushes look as if torn white tablecloths have been thrown over them and the buildings are like cakes which, having taken three days to ice, are now finished.

Tomorrow is Good Friday.

Next week I shall take the earlier train again and, before the journey is over, I shall speak to the woman.

Ramsden, I shall say, *is it you? Much water has gone under the bridge*—this is not my way—but I shall say it carelessly like this—*much water has gone under the bridge and I never answered your letters but is it you, Ramsden, after all these years, is it?*

nominated by Joan Murray

YUKON

fiction by CAROL EMSHWILLER

from TRIQUARTERLY

H~E'S A DRAGON~. He's a wolf. He's caribou. She tries to please him. She tries to keep out of his way and, at the same time, tries to get him to notice her by doing little things for him when he's gone or asleep. She needs him for warmth so they can cuddle up and he can warm her. She's afraid to leave because that's all the warmth she has. But she's afraid to stay. Is it possible to rush away when you live this far north? These high valleys never get warm. Mountain water coming down from glaciers is bright turquoise.

He's always looking at the sky or the ground or the horizon, not at her. But bits of red wool are all she has to look good in and then she never was a popular girl. If had big fur boots and hat, then maybe make a move. Make a run for it.

As valley to mountaintop . . . might as well be ship-to-shore, sending signals. How live that way? How love?

He's a rattlesnake, but no immediate threat (that she can tell). Comes home when he feels like it, bringing dead things to eat. Holds conventional views. Passes judgment on. Everything that needs to be said, he says, already said, and she thinks he's probably right, or almost. Make him chopped liver. Make him hasenpfeffer. Make him big mugs of glogg, but might not be home till three a.m. anyway. Wait up. And always those Englemann spruce. A couple of hundred years old—even more—but still skinny. Nothing to them. She loves them, though what else is there to love? It's the only tree around.

He's a giant. He's a dwarf. She has to help him climb up onto his throne. For the love of the spruce trees, she nuzzles into his furry chest, thinking that to love him you have to love horses, spiders and raw oysters, thinking how now she's going to have a baby. Should she tell him? She's already fairly big-with-child, but he hasn't noticed. She decides not to tell him. She decides, boy or girl, she will name it Englemann as though they were Mr. and Mrs. Spruce.

Their mansion is unfinished still. Only the vestibule built (but it's a big one, even as mansion vestibules go) and one tower (small) from which to view the mountains above the tops of trees. Both vestibule and tower are made out of the local rocks, so on the walls are the faint etchings of trilobites and prints of the leaves of ancient, ginko-like trees. In the fireplace they stand out clear, outlined by the smoke. Once upon a time it was warm here, and covered with water. The land has shifted, quake by quake, away from some southern latitude and it's still going. North by northwest. Also rising straight up. On land such as this, it's easy to go astray.

And now she's going just a little bit crazy. She wants and wants. Stands at window as if caged. Plastic that's in front of the glass to keep the heat in, makes things fuzzy. Snow outside begins to look soft and warm. Just right. So she leaves. She's not so crazy she doesn't take cheese sandwiches, peanuts, raisins, carrots. . . . Also takes his big fur boots and hat and now she's out in those nice adolescent-looking spruce trees that are older . . . much, much older than they look. She hugs some (though not much to hug). Touches them as she goes by. Wants to soak up the stolid way they are and also wants them to know how she feels: that even though they're stunted because of their hardships, she loves them all the more for it. She stops to drink glacier milk along the way. She's following, at first, browse trails that go no special place. It's cold. She just goes on. Easy to go astray. Thinks: years of going astray . . . was always astray, so if now astray, it's no different from before.

Meanwhile he's home, just woke up and sitting by the fire she'd laid before she left, asking himself ultimate questions, or, rather, penultimate questions as, What about the influence of theory on action? What about negative ends vs. positive means and vice versa? He doesn't notice she's gone, slipping around out there in his too-big-for-her boots. She had not meant to be going in a northerly direction. She had not meant to be climbing on up higher into the cold. She thought for a while she'd maybe creep back after he'd gone to sleep with no supper, but she's too far now for that. (He'll miss his boots before he'll miss her.) She was thinking: South and warm and down, down, into the lower valleys, but she's been going up because it's the hardest and she's always done whatever was the hardest. The spruce get older and smaller the higher she goes until there're, all at once, no more of them. Meanwhile he keeps putting on another log until the whole vestibule dances with the fire and he pulls off sweater after sweater, watches his giant shadow writhe along the walls, falls asleep in his chair.

If there had been flowers blooming up there on the mountains, she would have known the names of every single one. If birds had called out, she'd have known which birds and would have whistled back.

Since she'd started in the morning after a sleepless night (though all her nights have been sleepless for a long time, she can hardly remember the times when she used to sleep well). . . . Since she'd started early she gets almost all the way to the top before it's too dark to go on. She finds a kind of cairn built by summer climbers. There's a slit at the bottom big enough to slither into. She does. Sleeps, not well, but better than she's slept in a long time, dreaming: Loves me? Loves me not? and: Who (or what!) is number one in his heart? It's his boots and his hat keeps her warm enough, or almost warm enough all night, so in the morning she's, as usual, full of grateful love for him and wondering: Why hasn't he followed no matter how hard? Why hasn't he come for her by now with something nice and warm to drink? He's never done anything remotely like that, but still she wonders why he's not already there, maybe having climbed all night just for her.

She squirms out and up and, first thing, she sees she's almost to the top, so goes on up. What she thought was five minutes worth of climbing turns out to take a half an hour. At top she sits on fossils and looks out—little shivers of pleasure or of cold—eating raisins and soaking up comfort and courage from the view, this side, too, Englemann, Englemann, everywhere Englemann below her, first in the sheltered hollows and then, lower down, nothing but. Thinks: Nothing like them, and nothing like being up this high, and nothing like what it took to get this far, nothing like the cold, clear air. She even forgets she's pregnant.

Now, down in that big, stone vestibule, he is shouting, "Bacon,

bacon!" Searches what few crooks and crannies there are to search, groans and spits, hisses into the corner under the king-sized bed, makes his own black coffee, spends the morning writing out new rules while she walks the col, too exhilarated to feel fear of heights. One last bit of glacier still sits in the steep pocket below her. She can tell by the old blue ice showing where the pure white snow's been blown off. She follows the ridge above and then past and then starts down, but she's being too courageous . . . too sure of herself now, falls, slides the whole bare slope till stopped . . . saved by one thin old Englemann, her knee twisted back behind. Hurts. Probably nothing broken though she's not sure. Waits, lying there clutching tree because of pain. She's looking straight up through the narrow, scraggly circle of branches to the sky that's clouding over, thinking: Tree, tree, *this* tree and sky. Ties her scarf tight around her leg. That helps. It's getting windier. Big black clouds off over next mountain. She must get lower and to some sheltered spot. Can't stop now. Gets up. Goes from tree to tree to tree (she's *depending* on them) steeply down. Thinks: If not for Englemann spruce to hang onto! . . .

By late afternoon finds bear's cave still warm from that big body. She knows it's a bear's cave. She can smell it. She can see the footprints in the snow, people-like prints but wider, leading out. She needs the shelter now and the warmth of it. Can't go on. And she's more cold than scared. Also it's beginning to snow. She creeps in. Wedges herself among the tree roots along the left-hand side, away from the more open part of the cave. She knows the bear will come back, but she thinks she already knows how to keep away from something big (or small) and dangerous. She falls asleep, a seemingly dreamless sleep and not so full of unanswered questions about love or the lack of it.

The bear comes back at three a.m. She hears him sniffing around outside and giving little warning growls. Also he's got the hiccups. Nothing here she hasn't heard already, and many times. She's only half-awake. Before she realizes it she's told him she loves him. She's talking soft and low. He grunts, then hunkers on in, rolls to far side, back turned. (She thinks: As usual.) He lets her be. Snores. Storm goes on outside. Later (as usual) she moves close, snug against his back.

They sleep two days and nights, or so she guesses. When she

wakes up later, as he's leaving, she finds he's eaten all her cheese sandwiches, carrots, peanuts and raisins, and she thinks: As usual.

She hurries to the entrance of the cave and calls out to him before he goes. Her knee hurts and maybe she's a little feverish. She speaks without thinking. That's not her usual way, but he seems a little bit safer than her own male even though he's the biggest and most masculine thing she's ever been this close to; dangerous, too. No doubt about it. She does like his looks, though: his hump, his shoulders, his yellow-brown fur. . . . Now he hangs his head low, almost to the snow, and looks back at her suspiciously, and it isn't as if she hasn't seen that same look a thousand times before. But what is there to lose? She talks to him of things she'd never dared to talk about before. "How can love last," she says, "if this goes on? How can love even begin? How can it go on and on, and we all," she says, "want undying love. Even you, though you may not think so. It's normal. And, by the way," she says, "food is love, you know. Love is food. It's how we live. It's what we live by, and you've eaten it all up."

Needless to say she'd never said any such thing to her own overbearing, legal, lord and master, though she'd wanted to for a long time.

The bear watches her as she speaks as though too polite to interrupt or move, even. His little beady black eyes take everything in, that's clear. There's a dull, sleepy, intelligent look about him. He waits patiently until she's finished, then humps off in the powdery snow.

She sucks ice from the cave entrance. Finds a piece of root to make a splint for her knee. After that makes a broom from root ends and tidies up, all the while chewing root hairs from the cave ceiling. When everything is spic-and-span she sleeps again. At three a.m. or thereabouts he comes back with a small black bass for her. It seems as if he's taken what she said to heart. She lets him have half though she knows he's already eaten (not only all her food, but lots more, too). He licks up the fish scales she leaves. He eats the head (she gets the cheeks and also swallows down the eyes, though that's not easy to do). While they eat she talks and talks like she never talked before. She tells him all she knows about bears and that she hopes to learn lots more. Later she rubs the back of his neck and behind his ears. Top of his head. She likes the feel of him, and he's so warm. It's like the fireplace is lit when he comes in. She sings and he hums back a tune of his own she learns by heart. (She loves the sound of his voice.) They sleep again, she can't tell how long. Next time he leaves, they kiss, and not just cheeks. When he comes back, he brings another fish. And it goes on like this except they're kissing more and sleeping longer and longer periods, breathing slowly into each other's faces and not even getting up to pee, he not turning his back to her except now and then and, when he does, giving her a bear hug first. It's a whole other rhythm she'd never known about before. And not bad, she thinks, to let the storms go on by themselves and forget about everything and just be warm and cuddled and cuddling all the time. It's what she's always wanted: arms around her that hardly ever let go. It's what she didn't get when she was little.

They don't even feel the earthquake, though it shakes a little dirt and pebbles down on them. She dreams it, though, and in the dreams the quake is her husband's big feet shaking the mountain as he comes to get her to tear her away from her embrace. Before that she's sometimes dreamt that the storms are him, too, tearing at the cave to pull her out. When those dreams come, she hugs tighter to her bear and he embraces her yet more snugly. Then she knows she's safe and thinks she finally has all one needs of real love and that it will last forever though maybe that's too much to hope for.

Meanwhile, back at the vestibule, the earthquake has caused quite a bit of damage. Some walls have crumbled and part of the roof has come down. The fireplace is still O.K., though. He can squat in front of it mooing for his woman, and he still has most of his tower from which to growl out at the moon or stars or sun. Now he'll have to clean up the debris by himself as well as cook, cut his own firewood, skin his own marmots. If she knew this she could feel some sweet revenge, or maybe I-told-you-so, except she never did.

One starry winter night when her knee is better, though not completely, she limps out with her bear and it's so nice the bear stands up and does a little soft-shoe while she throws snowballs at the sky. She limps, but she can shuffle and wobble from tree to tree, kissing them and him. They're singing all the songs they know, but by now she's forgotten most of the words. Knows only rhyme and alliteration though she remembers the oxymorons, especially since "the brightness of midnight" is all around them

412

right now. It's sharply cold, but even so they both know spring is in the air. After this night, they begin to sleep less and then she has the baby. He's so small and thin she hardly knows she's birthed him except she hears the peeping. The bear helps by licking it clean and then eats the placenta, not letting her have even a taste. By then it's not a question of naming it. She can't even remember what names are for.

It gets warmer and the bear's gone more and more and brings back less and less. The baby might as well be a little bird. Besides her own milk, she feeds it worms and grubs. She tweets at it and it tweets back. When the bear stays out six days in a row, she suspects she's made the same old mistake . . . same kind of destructive relationship she's always had before. He'll go for good. He'll forget about her. Or, if he comes back, turn savage on her. Maybe push her out along with her robin, sparrow, little tufted titmouse.

Then, when he doesn't come back at all anymore, thinks: Yes, yes, she knew it would happen and now she'll have to go, too. Be out on her own. Find the next meal herself. It's a bright spring day, wild flowers coming out, but she no sooner starts down, baby perched on her shoulder, pecking at her ear, than it flies away and she has no name to call it back by. She tries to caw him down. She whistles all the birdcalls she knows, but none work. He circles for a few minutes while she finds the words to tell him he can't fly, or, anyway, not yet. It only wobbles him a little. He utters one harsh quack she's never heard him make before, then soars away, out over the valley. She thinks she hears soft coos and cuckoos even after he disappears into the trees below.

Well, she'll just go down by herself. And south. But this other valley, not towards home. This time maybe not take the hard way, and maybe she's had enough hugging to last a while, though she's wondering, as usual, Where is the creature with which she can live happily ever after?

Then she sees a figure climbing up. First it's just a greenish-brown slowly moving spot, but then it becomes green and brown . . . tweeds and corduroys. Thin, small, wiry. Has a greenish-gray beard. Alpine hat with little red feathers in it. Black-button bearish eyes. She sees them as he comes closer. Though she's never seen him before, she knows who it is. Knickers, hiking boots—the old fashioned kind. "Englemann," she says, "Englemann, Englemann." It's one of the few words she's not forgotten . . . never would forget though she is, by then, almost free of words. She would have to start over now from the beginning with wah, bah and boo.

He comes up the last switch back. They look at each other and smile. He has a little tuft of fragrant mountain misery in his buttonhole. He takes it out, sniffs it once, then gives it to her.

"Oh, Englemann," she says, and, "wah" and "bah" and "boo."

nominated by M. D. Elevitch

THE SECRET SHARER

by DAVID REID

from PLOUGHSHARES

. . . A couple of thousand men scattered throughout the great European cities. A few of them are famous; a few write unusually arid, consciously frightening and still peculiarly moving and gripping books; a few, shy and proud, write only letters, which will be found fifty or sixty years later and preserved as moral and psychological documents; a few will leave no trace, not even a sad and malicious aphorism—they do not necessarily include the geniuses or even the great talents of the time . . . But it is from the secret language in which they communicate to each other their idiosyncrasies, their special aspirations, and their special sensibility that History will learn the watchword of the epoch.

—Hugo von Hoffmansthal (1893)

Between V-J Day and Ike's inauguration in 1953, the Beats were on the road. *Partisan Review* discovered America. The School of New York flourished: Gorky, Pollock, de Kooning, Newman, Guston, Kline. In Gore Vidal's summary, "the empire turned its attention to peaceful pursuits and enjoyed something of a golden or at least for us not too brazen an age." Or as Allen Ginsberg has said, "I remember the sleepless epiphanies of 1948—everywhere in America brainconsciousness was waking up, from Times Square" (where Dr. Kinsey was gingering up his statistics at the Angle Bar) "to the banks of Willamette River to Berkeley's groves of Academe."

In these years, Bill Cannastra (d. 1950) possessed the authority of abject failure—even among the "fellaheen of Manhattan," as

William Burroughs, a disciple of Spengler, instructed the early Beats to think of themselves. Indeed, his name survives only as a bizarre footnote to that immense, ongoing publishing enterprise, the history of the Beat Generation. Barry Gifford and Lawrence Lee's oral biography of Jack Kerouac, for example, identifies him as the "lawyer friend of Jack's who was decapitated in New York subway" (sic). In Donald Spoto's life of Tennessee Williams, *The Kindness of Strangers,* a younger Cannastra puts in an appearance as a "brilliant twenty-year-old law student," discovered by the playwright in Cambridge in 1941, "extraordinarily handsome and manically bisexual. . . . His preferred form of erotic activity was, it seems, a strange mixture of voyeurism and exhibitionism, which Williams found amusing." The fullest account of him appears in Gerald Nicosia's critical biography of Kerouac, and it occupies only a few pages of that voluminous and evocative book. Yet, for a time in the late Forties, when New York was a world city, the spectacle of Cannastra's turning himself into a kind of self-consuming artifact transfixed the homosexual intelligentsia dominated by W.H. Auden; a circle of young art historians, poets, and *New Yorker* editors centered on Howard Moss; and of course the Beats themselves: "Cannastra, roaring like a Dago God," primordial Beat novelist John Clellon Holmes writes in *Nothing More to Declare,* "his ravaged Garfield face, playing *Norma* through the afternoons to ironic tears, climbing the El like an urban Tarzan, or walking up the street on cartops, or kissing longshoremen in remote Chelsea barrooms. Two blocks away the liners, decked in lights, champagne, faint dance music, and the laughter of willing women, headed for Europe with cargoes of the fortunate gone to woo an old hag . . . Cannastra, Cannastra, who knew she could be bought, and went the other way. . . ."

The rising young men of the Forties, like JFK and the war novelists Norman Mailer and Gore Vidal, were implacable careerists, cool customers and in their own estimation so many Stendhal heroes. (In terms of the history of this preternaturally ambitious generation, one of the charms of the time is that the *Zeitgeist* has not yet slotted everyone into the proper symbolic milieu. By the time he wrote *The Subterraneans,* for example, Kerouac was startled to remember himself, a promising young novelist in a dinner jacket, encountering Gore Vidal at a Tudor ballet.) Attending Harvard Law School was the only conventionally promising thing Bill Cannastra ever did. He composed no novels, galvanized no movement, mastered no art. He is said to have contributed an entry to the Random House Dictionary, but which one has not been traced. He astonished himself by passing the New York state bar examination while dead drunk. However, his career in law was brief, and, except for the short stint at Random House, he supported himself throughout the golden age as a baker. Apart from self-destructiveness, physical beauty, and intelligence, he was famous for his riotous, orgiastic parties. To his loft, located above a lampshade factory at 125 W. 21st Street, came Wystan Auden, Nell Blaine, Jack Kerouac, Larry Rivers, Alan Harrington, Howard Moss, Edwin Denby, Paul Goodman, Ramblin' Jack Eliot. . . .

Cannasatra liked these affairs to have themes, motifs, rituals. Once, he outfitted all his guests, on arrival, with identical black silk Chinese jackets. At another, dinner was a single huge pancake. Every evening included a "special moment," like his streak around the block with Jack Kerouac (Kerouac cautiously kept on his underwear), or a contest to see who could hold his head longest in an oven with the gas turned on. Following a "jungle party," at which he appeared in the guise of a palm tree, wearing a jock strap and towering Carmen Miranda headdress, Cannastra imprudently pursued the departing crowd to a nearby bar, "but somehow everyone was so dumbfounded by the simple way he came looking for his friends that no one touched him," according to one of Kerouac's biographers. Had the term "performance art" existed in 1948, Bill Cannastra might today be the subject of respectful specials on PBS.

But how often, in retrospect, an age can be seen to define itself in the lives of such bizarre, peripheral characters as Cannastra! Consider Edie Sedgwick, the doomy Andy Warhol "superstar," or Richard Savage in the life by Samuel Johnson, or Yeats's "Tragic Generation," or Drieu de la Rochelle. Contrary to Emerson, great men are not representative men. It is the minor but minatory figure like Cannastra who leads a life of allegory, appearing, in Graham Greene's phrase, "like a slip of the tongue, disclosing the unconscious forces, the night side of an age."

He was born in Schenectady, N.Y. His mother, wealthy and aristocratic, married a machinist whom she imported from Italy. According to Gerald Nicosia, "She had great expectations for her two sons but couldn't bear her own frustrated ambition, and so attempted (and failed) to commit suicide by swallowing lye. . . . [In Cambridge] Cannastra was immediately accepted into chichi circles for which he had little training and too much inclination. He quickly made friends with W. H. Auden, and through Auden met the many glamorous European writers then congregated at Harvard." On his own, he encountered the then unfamous and unglamorous Tennessee Williams. According to his *Memoirs,* Williams actually finished writing *The Glass Menagerie* in Cannastra's dormitory rooms; he remembered his host as "a wild boy I'd met in Provincetown the summer of 1944. That boy was one of the real aboriginal 'beats'—I mean he was beat before there were 'beats'; he was a beautiful gangling kid with dark hair and light eyes and a stammer." However, his biographer Spoto indicates that this chronology is all off. It was in July 1941, during a period when Williams was in a "haze of sexual and alcoholic confusion," that he lived with Cannastra.

In John Clellon Holmes's novel, *Go,* which is set in 1948, the appearance of Cannastra ("Agatson") is preceded by rumors of Cannastra. Sitting in Holmes's dingy apartment, "Gene Pasternak" (Jack Kerouac) remarks that Agatson is known to chew glass. "Stofsky" (Allen Ginsberg) arrives with the news that Agatson has just "electrified" a bar by kissing a Marine. A "famous poet" (Auden) is said to have predicted that Agatson will either be dead or in a mad-house by his thirtieth birthday.

Then, Agatson himself appears, with his fatal face and "spare, muscular body which abuse had hardened. It was the body of a man whose drinking had become a sort of vocation, and who (unlike the run of urban sophisticates) no longer sports his hangovers like so many Purple Hearts earned in the good fight against boredom, but endures them with stoical tenacity and never complains. His dark features had that fleeting, sensual looseness that only the dissolute, just this side of slavery to alcohol, can possess. There was something mocking and remote in his fixed stares and in the curl of lips no longer firm, but not yet lax. Everything about him made even the tipsy onlooker grow alert. . . ."

Kerouac may have aped Cannastra, as Allen Ginsberg remarked unhappily at the time; Cannastra himself was not a downtrodden Times Square beat but a stylish psychotic hipster. For much of "The White Negro," Mailer seems to be describing Cannastra, and perhaps he is—he made a strong impression, and the novelist would certainly have heard about him in Provincetown, if somehow he missed him in Manhattan. In *Nothing More to Declare*, Holmes remembers standing outside Cannastra's cottage on the dunes and "watching him pedaling wildly out of town on a stolen bicycle, leaving a Boston girl with a black eye, who said, adjusting the hamburger, 'Tell me about this person.' "

By 1950 Cannastra had lost his tolerance for alcohol: Howard Moss compared the effect of a single drink to the "swoosh" of a gas burner being lit. Still, the Lost Boy continued to appeal. Or as his friend John wrote, "Cannastra continues to be kept on the condition he remains beautifully sad and intelligently desperate. This inevitably defeats those who really want to save him. . . . Tony H— saved him the way a cat saves a mouse to destroy at his leisure. My own feelings on the subject are that if Cannastra were either dumber or less handsome there would be no problem. The prospect of so much beauty and intelligence going to waste is so attractive to less beautiful and intelligent people that they are willing to sponsor it."

("Another cause of his profusion," Johnson writes of Savage's spendthrift ways, "was the absurd kindness of his friends, who at once rewarded and enjoyed his abilities by treating him at taverns and habituating him to pleasures which he could not afford to enjoy, and which he was not able to enjoy himself, though he purchased the luxury of a single night by the anguish of cold and hunger for a week.")

In the fall of 1950 Cannastra was engaged to be married, carrying on a homosexual affair with a Cambridge mathematician, and living with Joan Haverty, a twenty-year-old from upstate. Though it cannot have come as a complete surprise, Cannastra was desolate when his fiancée broke off their engagement. In this mood, as related in *Go,* he invites a crowd of his friends, one gloomy Sunday, "to celebrate my last birthday." Kerouac appears with the news that his first novel, *The Town and the City,* will be published by Harcourt, Brace. "So now you're Queen of the May, eh?" Cannastra replies unkindly. ("These gloomy lofts and tenements, these thronging streets and bars, these continual parties and confrontations—can it really have been like that?" John Clellon Holmes asks in the preface to the 1976 reprint, taking the words out of the reader's mouth. But, he insists, yes, that was the way they were.)

The crowd troups a few blocks to Nell Blaine's loft, Cannastra pausing along the way to snap the aerials from parked cars. Later, back at 21st St., he smashes his collection (opera, jazz, bop, bluegrass) of precious shellac 78's. "Good-bye, Berlioz. . . . Good-bye, Harry James. . . . Good-bye, you all." He is waking from a stupor when Kerouac, "his face drained of color," gets off the phone to announce that "Stofsky" has been arrested. But Cannastra "had simply dropped in his tracks, without warning, without even slowing down. Somehow his jeans had come off, and he sprawled there, his bony legs with a furze of dark hair on them grotesquely askew among the bottles"; amidst Holmes's youthfully over-wrought prose, the dead-on image is odd and haunting, a "wounding" detail, as Roland Barthes would have said, not unlike the sickening contrast of dirty linen and "clean clean" exposed bone of the wounded matador in Hemingway. But once he recovers his jeans, Cannastra immediately plans a jailbreak. As everyone piles into Bianca's car (now aerial-less), "he seemed to boil over, his shoulders contorting and his mouth torn sideways like a ragged wound. He craned out of the window, far, far out, and started to scream with terrible, piercing earnestness:

" 'Fuck you! Fuck you! Fuck you!' " The jailbreak was not a success.

On the night of October 12, 1950, returning from a party with friends, Cannastra boarded the subway at the Bleecker St. station. According to one account, a companion mentioned Winnie, the black barmaid at the San Remo, and Cannastra decided he had to talk to her. He began to climb out the subway window. Another version says he caught the eye of a stranger on the platform and clambered out to meet him. Or, perhaps, he was acting out a story. Nimble and catlike, he might have leapt safely to the platform (often he scaled tenements to spy on his neighbors' lovemaking), but friends grabbed his legs, the car started, and his head snapped against a pillar. The fatal face was smashed, and his body, pulled out the window, was dragged along the tracks for fifty feet.

Before pointing a moral, I should finish the tale. Next day, the sober and shaken Beats gathered at the Bleecker St. station. "The Goddam fool," said Joan Haverty. "Look at the size of that window." Her exasperation notwithstanding, she loyally stayed on at 125 W. 21st, preserving it as a shrine. Then a few weeks later,

Kerouac happened to look in on his way to a party. They became lovers, and married a few weeks after (the wedding was celebrated with a party at the loft). Though Cannastra never wrote anything himself, except for the unknown dictionary entry, he left a kind of literary legacy to Jack. Already at work on an early version of *On the Road* (a novel in which Cannastra does not appear), Kerouac, in December, was bowled over by a 23,000-word letter from Neal Casady, whose example, "all first person, fast, mad, confessional," freed him to abandon mere literature and to begin recording the events in his life "exactly as they occurred." However, it was not until the following April that he hit upon the device that enabled him to compose at the frenzied speed necessary to sustain confessional momentum. Rummaging through Cannastra's possessions in the loft, he discovered onionskin Japanese drawing paper in twenty-foot scrolls. Taping the long sheets together, he began to feed them into his typewriter.

As party boy, voyeur, bisexualist, orgy-master, and *monstre sacré,* Bill Cannastra was famous in the Forties for making a burnt offering of his talent and prospects, like Yeats's Irish airman driving to a tumult in the clouds. Thousands of others, of course, were doing precisely the same thing; but Cannastra found a more interesting means than going to work for Henry Luce or an advertising agency, and he was better-looking. In later years, Kerouac would say, "Bill Cannastra was a saint." This was meant seriously. But then, like the aristo, the saint embodies a "mechanism of waste," which is, as Georges Bataille reminds us, literally entrancing.

> A work of art, a sacrifice, contains something of an irrepressible festive exuberance that overflows the world of work, and clashes with, if not the letter, the spirit of the prohibitions indispensable to safeguarding this world. (*Lascaux, or the Birth of Art*)

Also, it is a fact of life in our immense Babylonish cities, as Georg Simmel remarks in "Metropolis and Mentality," that "extremities and peculiarities must be produced and must be overexaggerated merely to be brought into the attention *even of the individual himself*" (my emphasis). Nietzschean characters like

Cannastra hate the city, "but they are passionately loved in the metropolis and indeed appear to its residents as the saviors of their unsatisfied yearnings."

But then, what was Bill Cannastra but the harvest god of the Beats? At the wrong time (which was also the ritually proper moment), his companions kept him earthbound, clutching the much-abused, much-loved body, at night, beneath Bleecker St., in October, at the midcentury, during the golden age.

nominated by Ploughshares

WALKING IN THE 15TH CENTURY

by DANIEL HALPERN

from THE THREEPENNY REVIEW

There are angels on the road from San Sepulcro
to Monterchi, and olive trees;
there are grapevines that bring forth
the Umbrian wine Piero drinks
before he goes back
to his pregnant Madonna and the women
attending her. She too will travel this road,
but long after we've gone.

The 15th-century sun is up and to us
it seems *youthful*. It seems *uncomplicated*.
There are angels on the road,
or perhaps they remind us of angels
we've seen on the old canvases
five hundred years later. The air
this time of year feels strict,
the leaves, early autumn, fugacious.

Sometimes, if the distance is not too great,
it is possible for the unborn
to walk with us. Perhaps *they* are the angels.
Piero might have experienced his Madonna's child,
destined through his art to remain

in utero forever, in this way.
My daughter and I continue along the road;
the wind travels with us.

Piero will have to hurry along to catch us
before we reach the spectral hill town
and the little chapel a kilometer beyond it
that awaits his Madonna.
She must be there when I arrive
with the mother of our unborn child
to pay the caretaker the few hundred lire
for a look.

nominated by Threepenny Review

A SKETCH OF THE GREAT DEJECTION

by THOM GUNN

from THE THREEPENNY REVIEW

Having read the promise of the hedgerow
the body set out anew on its adventures.
At length it came to a place of poverty,
of inner and outer famine,
                        where all movement had stopped
except for that of the wind, which was continual
and came from elsewhere, from the sea,
moving across unplanted fields and between headstones
in the little churchyard clogged with nettles
where no one came between Sundays, and few then.
The wind was like a punishment to the face and hands.
These were marshes of privation:
the mud of the ditches oozed scummy water,
the grey reeds were arrested in growth,
the sun did not show, even as a blur,
and the uneven lands were without definition
as I was without potent words,
inert.
        I sat upon a disintegrating gravestone.
How can I continue? I asked.
I longed to whet my senses, but upon what?
On mud? It was a desert of raw mud.
I was tempted by fantasies of the past,

but my body rejected them, for only in the present
could it pursue the promise,
                              keeping open to its fulfillment.
I would not, either, sink into the mud,
warming it with the warmth I brought to it,
                                        as in a sty of sloth.
My body insisted on restlessness
                              having been promised love,
as my mind insisted on words
                        having been promised the imagination.
  So I remained alert, confused and uncomforted.
I fared on and, though the landscape did not change,
it came to seem after a while like a place of recuperation.

nominated by Threepenny Review

LAMENT FOR THE MAKERS

by ROBERT PINSKY

from THE PARIS REVIEW

What if I told you the truth? What if I could?
The nuptial trek of the bower apes in May:
At night in the mountain meadow their clucking cries,

The reeking sulphur springs called Smoking Water,
Their skimpy ramparts of branches, pebbles and vines—
So slightly better than life, that snarl of weeds,

The small town bank by comparison is Rome,
With its four-faced bronze clock that chimes the hours,
The six great pillars surmounted by a frieze

Of Cronus eating his children—or trying to,
But one child bests him because we crave to live,
And if that too means dying then to die

Like Arthur when ladies take him in his barge
Across the misty water: better than life,
Or better than truly dying. In the movies

Smoking and driving are better, a city walk.
Grit on the sidewalk after a thaw, mild air.
I took the steps along the old stone trestle

Above the station, to the part of town
I never knew, old houses flush to the street
Curving uphill. Patches of ice in the shade.

What if I found an enormous secret there
And told you? We would still feel something next
Or even at the same time. Just as now. In Brooklyn,

Among the diamond cutters at their benches
Under high Palladian windows full of a storm,
One wearing headphones listens to the Talmud.

What if he happens to feel some saw or maxim
Inwardly? Then the young girl in her helmet,
An allegorical figure called The Present,

Would mime for us the action of coming to life:
A crease of shadow across her face, a cross,
And through the window, washing stumps of brick,

Exuberant streaks and flashes—literal lightning
Spilling out into a cheery violent rain.
Worship is tautological, with its Blessed

Art thou O Lord who consecrates the Sabbath
Unto us that we may praise it in thy name
Who blesses us with this thy holy day

That we may hallow it unto thy holy blessings . . .
And then the sudden curt command or truth:
God told him, Thou shalt cut thy foreskin off.

Then Abraham was better than life. The monster
Is better when he startles us. Hurt is vivid,
Sincerity visible in the self-inflicted wound.

Paws bleeding from their terrible climb, they weave
Garlands of mountain creeper for their bed.
The circle of desire, that aches to play

Or sings to hear the song passing. We sense
How much we might yet make things change, renewed
As when the lovers rise from their bed of play

And dress for supper and from a lewd embrace
Undress again. Weeds mottle the fissured pavement
Of the playground in a net of tufted lines

As sunset drenches a cinematic honey
Over the stucco terraces, copper and blue,
And the lone player cocks wrist and ball behind

His car and studies the rusty rim again.
The half-ruined city around him throbs and glows
With pangs of allure that flash like the names of bars

Along San Pablo Avenue: Tee Tee's Lounge,
The Mallard Club, Quick's Little Alaska, Ruthie's,
Chiquita's, and inside the sweet still air

Of tobacco, malt and lime, and in some music
But in others only voices or even quiet,
And the player's arm pauses and pumps again.

*nominated by Brenda Hillman,
Michael Ryan, and Tom Sleigh*

THE PLACE IN FLOWERS WHERE POLLEN RESTS

fiction by PAUL WEST

from CONJUNCTIONS

THE WHITE, SAYS Oswald Beautiful Badger Going Over The Hill: not the white stuff in your eyes, Uncle, I mean the kaolin primer. Let us put it on the doll and let it dry. He sighs that sigh of permanent reprieve, but his uncle fidgets and complains: It will not bind to the wood, Oswald Beautiful Badger Going Over the Hill, it will peel, and much of the paint along with it, so we shall soon have a shabby god on our hands, not worth giving away. I would rather use the white stuff from my eyes. A week's worth ought to do. Let us use the most local clay of all. His shudder is vocal, and you can tell at once, even if you know nothing about him, that his sense of humor is far from graveyard. How about an acrylic finish, he asks. It would be brighter. But I ask him why bother to be brighter. Time past, I tell him, I would spray the colors with hairspray to fix them. To keep them perky. But not any more. I am willing to have my dolls, even my gods, peel and fade, just to remind me of who I am, who I can never be. My shirt sleeve has come unbuttoned, and for a moment I am unsure if I am telling him that, in so many words, or just noting the fact mentally. Let it flap, I tell him at last. It will keep the flies away. What flies, Uncle? The flies, I answer, that flit across the surface of my eyes. You have never seen them. Like swifts in the void they scoot and soar. The basic torso is done, I tell him, and then there is a flurry of action. Hatchet, he says, and I say no. Mallet, he says, and I again say no.

430

What you must do, Oswald Beautiful Badger Going Over The Hill, what you must do now is find me a chunk of white clay and then soak it until the grit sinks to the bottom of the bucket. Then we will daub and not until. No gesso, no acrylic. If I had my way, it would be a yucca brush too, and none of your sables, and mineral paints from oxides of iron and copper. Colorful clays and vegetable dyes. I have nothing, as a has-been, against tempera or poster paint, but I ask you, where do we find the legendary blue-green you could only get with copper carbonate? There is no other way for that, just as you cannot create geese wheeling in the sky out of a handful of pen nibs. If I must use acrylic, I must; at least it will stay moist longer and won't rub off. You don't want a god who makes no lasting impression. Away goes Nephew with the unprimed doll, to coat it and dry it. He has learned how not to make a ruff from horrible shiny plastic such as they sell to children whose tiny trains need hedges to run past or forests to chug through. Nephew was a purist until he realized how a ruff of real spruce goes brown and falls away, and it was I who taught him about the dyed seaweed you can buy in hobby shops, culled from a place known as the English Channel, where no doubt they farm it. Or there is green yarn, sometimes larded with white glue to stiffen it. Shells from the Indian Ocean and the South Pacific. Why, Nephew, our dolls have become international. They deserve a tall building in New York City all of their own. Will you ever find real mouse or squirrel skin these days? Seal, more likely, and bits of fur from cast-off coats. Down of eagles was clouds. Buckskin has become suede. And carpet tacks abound. If it matters much of what a god be made, then our gods are cut-rate, like the cookies in the big round cans in drug stores. I lapse into telling them about the crude old days, when you could always make an effect with feathers from the scarlet tail of the military macaw, or the red-tailed hawk. Eagle plumes were black as charcoal and just as hard. There were mountain blue birds and green warblers. Many's the time, after one of the ceremonies, I've scrounged around on the trampled soil for some left-over feathers, getting my hands trodden on in the process, and squeezing many a lump of dung by mistake. Now we will have nephews find our feathers. Hard, when neither the dancers nor the carvers have real feathers, and it is a lucky day when you can plunder such birds as sparrows or starlings, not to mention clucking hens, whose feathers you have to tint. All this, I tell him, is a world you will not have. Never again will anyone be able to make the old kinds of dolls, the real thing. Am I then supposed to teach you how to make imitation ones? Better to leave you untouched, so that you will never form longings for what you cannot have. You would be better off building balsawood kachinas from the kits sold in hobby shops for little boys to make. The makings have gone. There is not even wood to begin with. So what you need, Oswald Beautiful Badger Going Over the Hill, is one of those desert islands, where the springs run fresh, and there you will find roots of all shapes and textures. Start anew, and wonder why, back here, the gods have become so well-established they no longer make certain that enough of the right trees grow, or that the white man, in his mania for protecting birds, does not come around and trim certain feathers off certain dolls. You should never have left Hollywood. At least it never runs out of celluloid. Who nowadays hangs dolls from rafters or hangs them on walls? Remember too that nowadays is the time of the jumping doll whose limbs are jointed and move about when you pull the strings. What nonsense. Now they make giant dolls too, and dolls only half an inch high. Clowns, clowns, clowns, is all they want. I do not do clowns. Not for people wanting clowns. I do the clown who wants to come to life, not otherwise. Once upon a time things were better, when several of us would go off together to gather salt or capture eagles. It was permitted, then, to think hard about what you went out after, because according to our tribe's beliefs the more you think about something the stronger it becomes. Harder to conquer, perhaps, but also more worth the struggle. The salt is harder to dislodge from the ground, the eagles are warier than ever. It is almost like praying to the object of your quest. One day, Oswald Beautiful Badger Going Over The Hill and I came upon a fox with its leg in a trap, and I told him to watch me as I removed its foot from the clamp, stroked its entire body gently for a while until it stopped shuddering, and then just as gently pushed its nose into the loose dirt to smother it. Why didn't it try to bite you, he asked. It wasn't scared, I told him. It was all right. It knew how to behave. Soon after that he went off to Hollywood and stayed away at least two seasons, sending money home of course, but out of tune with our ways. You took undue advantage of the fox, he said at the time. It thought you were going to let it go. It did not know anything, I told him. I did not even sprinkle it with a bit of sacred meal, as if it had been a plant, a bean, or a melon. Then you offer a prayer to the plant family it belongs to. With animals it is different, they are more individual. As it was with the turtles, when we went out to collect rattles with a few cans of tomatoes, a big ripe water melon, and a bag of wheat flour, all in a big cardboard box. We also had a ball of tough cord and a thin, sharp knife, a coffeepot, stew pan, fry pan, some cups, and a coil of rather new rope. In Flagstaff we paused to buy an extra loaf of store bread and the truck was going slowly enough we might end up eating more often than we had planned over five hundred miles or so. Down to the Colorado we rattled, hoping to find the right kind of back water without mosquitoes. First we cut a few willows an inch or so across and sharpened either end of each to a point. At the river bank we stripped down and both swam out into a depth of four feet, then dived to the bottom with our pointed sticks, on the ends of which there were lumps of dough, mixed the night before. Bait, I told him, the dough is bait for turtles. Each time we started deep and worked our way back toward the bank of the river. Oswald Beautiful Badger Going Over The Hill was the first to catch a turtle, which he correctly grabbed within his arm, and then shoved into the cardboard box, whose lid he weighted down with a log. When we had five, which was steady going for two men, we went back to where we had parked the truck and began the cleaning of the shells. With two slip knots we trapped the first turtle by two of its feet and placed him on the ground upside down. Then we tugged at the ropes to bring his feet into the open, after which came his head and neck, ready for my knife. Down into the body I thrust the blade, and soon we were cutting the body from inside the shell, not an easy job with the muscles hard as leather and the joint with the shell a place firm as teeth. It was clear the turtle had not been designed to make this carving of it up easy for any tribe of men. And you had to be careful not to scratch or gouge inside or outside. It was almost dark before we finished, and my nephew was complaining about being stiff, his having used muscles he otherwise never used, and the stink of the turtle meat as this was summer. We shared a cigarette and spent the next day scraping the inside of our shells for the least fragment of turtle meat. I can see them fastened to the knees already, I told him, held in place with a buckskin thong, the flat underside against the calf, and within, to rattle during the ceremonies as the dancers

433

pound their heels against the ground, a few dried hooves, antelope or deer, culled from another hunt in which we had no part. It is a much lower tone than that of the skittish rattles. Down goes the dancer's foot and the turtle shell makes its doleful clanking sound. After that little teaching expedition, two men alone with nothing but a few sticks and loaves and ropes, it was time to get back to carving, and I told Nephew that I sometimes wished my dolls were hollow and might thus be rattled about instead of being what my dolls always have been: dumb, dead, and farther from the tree than the shell is from the living turtle. No, he answered, you do this better, you should catch twice as many turtles as you did. With proper help, I retorted, I would, I have to have help that swims better than a dead horse. Tarzan the Apeman would be a useful man to have along, not that I have ever seen him, but his name is one I think about. He who can wrestle a crocodile would make easy meat of turtles. And of turtle-catchers, too, he said. Hollywood is not all yellow-bellies, Uncle George The Place In Flowers Where Pollen Rests. We were always four, I told him: you have forgotten. My nephew the cowpuncher has forgotten the spirit companion who goes everywhere with us, lending a hand in inscrutable ways, keeping you from botching the turtle shell, from impaling yourself on the pointed sticks in the deepest water, especially when the balls of dough fall off the points, and making sure that you do not run into any Navajo on the way out or the way home, from whom your possessions are never safe. Some Navajo worked with him in Hollywood, he said, and these were not all thieves, and I thanked Sotuqnangu, lord of the unblemished turtleshell that no such Navajo, who were not all thieves, had come along with us on our expedition to the Colorado, by way of Flagstaff and Kingman. Then he gave me his old-fashioned look, which, since his face is wide and chubby, seems blunter than it really is. His eyes are brown. Into their kennels they go when I ask him why, for a man forbidden both coffee and tobacco, I go on enjoying them. It was the same with the pills. One day, my mouth went numb, my tongue and neck along with it, and then my left hand, the dreaming one caught in the act. After a month of pills, I felt better. You should have kept on with them, he said. One was to thin out your blood, Uncle George The Place In Flowers Where Pollen Rests. It is used elsewhere as a rat poison. I snorted at him. Then there are the others, to make your heart beat more firmly and less often, oh yes, they can do that with tiny pellets no bigger or heavier than birdlime. Where are they now? Moldering away in a jar? I had no idea, I told him. You take these bits and bobs until you feel better, and then you set them aside with a thank you to the spirit of the pill. He has tried this argument with me before. And, he says, there is the one, from across the ocean, that plugs the locks in your brain, so that a certain key will no longer fit and speed up the action of your heart. It is called adrenaline, and now, although you make this thing in a big gland, it now has almost nowhere to go. It just swills around and goes to waste. Then surely, I told him, this adrenaline will never forgive me, having no future, not allowed to do me the good that was intended, like the fleece for the sheep, the feathers for the bird, the money in the bank. How wretched I am that no longer use it well. For a while back then, it was nothing but fuss. George The Place In Flowers Where Pollen Rests was trying to tell them he couldn't talk properly, which they could tell anyway from the muddle of the sounds he was making while the spit rolled down his chin. They knew, all right. Off we went to Keams Canyon, where a doctor told me to take my pills without fail, and they attached all kinds of wires to my chest just as if I was going to the electric chair. You have to mend your ways, the doctor said. How do I mend them up on the mesa, I asked him. You would have to change the landscape first to make many changes in folk's lives. He could tell what I said because the slur had gone from my speech and my face muscles worked again, it did not feel as if a sack of wet corn was hung on my jaw. Instead of writing something out longhand, which I was aching to see him do, he handed over a lot of little samples, pills sealed in silver paper and see-through plastic, some in twos, some in sixes, and I was to take this pink one when I woke, and a white one with it, which had a clockface on one side stuck at half past ten. Glory be, that would tell you when to take it. This is the half-past ten pill, I asked him, but he shook his head and said not to be so fucking smart, do as I say or you will soon be in hospital. You got hypertension, he said, but I was not nervous at all. And you threw a clot, he said, which I was not in the least aware of doing. So he tells Oswald Beautiful Badger Going Over The Hill. He could speak our language, at least half as well as most turtles do. Oswald Beautiful Badger Going Over The Hill, he said, you will have to watch him, he is not going to take his medication when he should. He is going to goof off like nobody's business, and I got sick folk enough without having to tell him everything twice. Okay, Uncle George The Place In Flowers Where Pollen Rests, he tells me on the drive home in that same truck as once took us turtle-catching, once a day you take the blood-thinner, and four times a day the one with ten-thirty on its back, and once a day the little pill made from foxgloves, and four times a day the little orange one that lowers the pressure of your blood. No, I will never get the hang of it, I told him: let me take them all now, on the way home, and that will be that. We will bury you tonight if you do, he said with a bark in his tone. Try again. I will shove them all up my asshole, I told him, just to keep both hands free. No, he said. And then he explained about the rat poison that made the rats bleed to death, and how what killed the rats would keep me lively. The foxglove one I kind of liked already, what with its feeling natural and so forth, right from up there among the rocks. The one with the clock on its back, he said, was made from a bark that grew down in South America. I was not quite so blind when all this happened, I could not have been, I saw the clock on the pill. It must have been years ago, then, and here I still am. This other pill, he was telling me, this is what you take for nervousness if you are going to play the violin in front of a whole bunch of folks. It is for stage fright or butterflies. Well, I am all for butterflies, I told him: you can write stuff on their wings, messages and insults, it only takes a couple of eyes to see it well. It makes you mighty smooth, he said, and you will sometimes feel serener than any eagle. In that case, I told him, I will take only the rat poison, the foxglove, the pill from South America, and the one for butterflies. I will never cheat by taking any other kind of pill. These will suit me fine, once I get used to them. You will have the runs from them, he warned me, and your dreams may be longer and more colorful, which had a blissful sound to me. Your skin might itch a lot, he went on, and you will feel dizzy when you stand up all of a sudden. You will suffer from gas too, the doctor says, and in the night your hands will go numb and you will have pins and needles when you wake. Apart from which you are going to feel wonderful, and you will not ever again have your arm go useless or your mouth unable to speak. I will buy and fetch your pills from Keams Canyon. And he did. The trouble was, I forgot to take them, and I lost count, and then I took too many all at once, which made me feel mighty strange as if I had been swung at with a lump of granite. I had even, when I remembered, gotten to the stage of being able to tell the pills apart even in my blindness: the half past ten, as good as Braille, was the one I always began with as I shuffled them around in my pocket, and then the rat poison which had a curly snake-shape on one side. The one for butterflies had a big fat bridge on one of its sides too, so I knew the one that was left was the one from foxgloves, and I wondered what do they have against the foxglove that it has no sign upon its side. You would know a flower from just feeling at it. It was too small for anything to be written on it, I told myself. It was a baby among pills even if, in cahoots with these others, it sets you shitting in your sleep with pins and needles and an itch, makes you dizzy when you stand, and gives you nightmares even after you have gone to sleep. The good these do is mighty invisible compared with the other things they do. Surely, pills that give you no trouble do no good at all. It was not long before Oswald Beautiful Badger Going Over The Hill began chiding me about not taking my pills. I feel good, I kept telling him. Soon as I feel low, I will get them down deep into me. Every day, on time, he said, or you will never carve again. Or speak. Or walk. It is a matter of life and death. No, I told him, it is a matter of feeling poor and feeling not so bad. It is enough to have to go without coffee, tobacco, an occasional beer. You do nothing of the kind, he told me, you drink and smoke as much as you always did. I guess I decided there was no holding you on that front, I just want you to remember the pills. What is the point of driving to Keams Canyon when you stick them in a corner and go for weeks on end without any of the stuff that's bound to save you? I am saving them, I told him, for a rainy day, Nephew, for when you have gone back to Hollywood and there is no one to bring pills from Keams Canyon, I am unable to go to Keams Canyon myself, so instead I take an aspirin or two when the need comes on, and a couple of those little minty pills for indigestion. What he said next was like thunder: It will kill you, he said, mixing aspirin with the rat poison, you will bleed to death. Then, I answered as stiff as I could, I will do without the rat poison, Nephew. Maybe the aspirin will save me. Maybe it will, after all, he said, and with that we began to talk of carving once again. That was the crisis, in the days before I got quite so blind. There is no pill to bring back sight, is there now? I'd wolf it down if there were. I might as well eat wood. When the night is deep, I sometimes reach for that coffee tin of pills hidden behind the stove, and rattle it, not so loud or so carrying a noise as they make with the knee rattles made from turtle shells, but loud enough for me, alone in the night, listening to snake and foxglove, butterfly and ten-thirty o'clock, bouncing and tapping about in the empty can, maybe a hundred of them at most, which amounts to just over a week's supply, best taken with lamb stew salted with salt from the dried-up lake, or the tea made from juniper and the sand sagebrush, which is very good for indigestion. What, I wondered, if I were to make a little fire of dry corncobs and cook the can over it until the pills had all mixed up with one another? Surely that would be a potent medicine to drink in a cup of sage tea. Wait for the next crisis, I told myself. Do as you are told, Uncle George The Place In Flowers Where Pollen Rests, my nephew said. I am very fond of my pills, I told him. They talk to me. Take them, he said rudely. We need to know your blood pressure on a daily basis, and I am going to bring you a little sleeve to wrap around your arm, and a rubber bulb to pump so that the whole thing will work. It is not the expense I mind, but the thought that, whatever we do, you will please yourself. Then I said I did not want to be any trouble, but all he said, with a bleak twist of his puffy mouth, was: Oh yes you do, you do. And I resented that, feeling that if nature had put me wrong it was up to nature to put me right. Trouble was the last thing I had in mind. A whole lifetime of never doing what you're told, mainly because that is now how you see the living of a life, not doing what others want, but sitting still, going out, coming in, according to some private hunger. Anyone who lives otherwise is living some other's life within his own body. No, I didn't want to make trouble, but I didn't want to lose touch with myself. I didn't feel too bad, a bit dizzy now and then, and that pounding in my eardrums or the old familiar ping and squeak, all signs as the doctor in Keams Canyon said, but what *isn't* a sign? Sometimes they use the word symptom, and the two words are different, but everything is a sign to me. Since the one bad time when my lips went dead, and my throat, my tongue, I have had only the odd sense that my lips are permanently thicker and obey me a little less than before. Not that I stammer, but I hear the stammer in my head even when others do not, and I speak very little anyway. It doesn't amount to much. There seems less room inside my mouth, so the extra thickness must be all on the inside, what with my tongue also being larger than it was. No one has measured me, of course, and how would you begin to measure a tongue or the inside of a mouth? I should have given up the coffee, but I did not, I have not dropped dead on the wall here, and there is no doubt that my lips and tongue feel better after coffee, as if they have come back to complete life, and to hell with what they tell me about being a walking time bomb. Uncle George The Place In Flowers Where Pollen Rests, my nephew begins yet another of his polite chidings, it is only a matter of time, what you had was a warning, and next time will be more severe. He goes on for hours, and sooner or later he persuades me to try a pill or two, which he then tells me is just as bad as taking none at all. Once you have started with them, you must not let go or you will be worse than before. You start and then you taper off. Well, how do you taper off from one pill to a crumb of it? Maybe that is how to start, folks. A bit now and then is worse than none, but he insists, hoping that I will go on taking them, scared by what will happen to me if I don't, but I don't have that much sense of future. Or, if I do, it is the future of others I have a sense of, not the future of me, which to be obvious about it does not have much future in it. Maybe they should donate me to a hospital right now, so that they could study the process of decay from the beginning, cramming me with pills and then tapering me off until I am no more than skin and bones. I ask him about this, but he wants me to go on carving, even when I can't see what I am doing, now like the sexual act of old, done in the dark for shame, for stealth, for the sake of sheer excitement. Yet an intimacy that close is as nothing likened to what happened after the attack, the seizure, the thing that happened, when after all the fuss had died down I finally got back to dreaming and sleeping, and who should walk into the dream but the spit image of me at age seventeen or so, his face fixed in horror, but his eyes full of I-can't-believe-it sympathy, oh yes, as if he had come along to say, no not say, to mime his opinion of all this, and the way he came into the room was delicate, forbearing, as if to whisper: You should never have let it come to this, at which he came right over to me, slowly as if I might explode, and leaned his face against my shoulder, nuzzling like a colt, son of myself, and I recognized him at once, hugged him close as if to suck the very youngness from him and so force it back into my ailing hulk. Is it really *you?* How can it be *you* if this is still me, heading for ninety years and beyond? How could the young me and the ancient one be alive at the same time? All I knew was that, somehow, he had freed himself from me during the moments of paralysis, knowing he didn't want to talk as I talked in those moments, or to have his heart flutter and his hand go numb. I did not know that you can feel such crushing tenderness for yourself as you were, about whom you had not thought in fifty years, yet he somehow hung in there, waiting for you to make a bad move, buried inside you but still his own man. I saw this youth looking at me as I looked at him and at his looking at my looking. Then his face quailed. It shuddered as it saw how his quailing affected my own gaze. We were both in tears, oh not very constructive ones, the one set asking how I could have become so careless in old age, the other asking how could the youth in my past have given me so little guidance. Young George The Place In Flowers Where Pollen Rests asks his ancient incarnation: How could you have come to this, who once were me? Slack living, boy, I nearly answered, but thought better of it, arguing with myself that, if this he who once was me was me still, then he knew my thoughts in any case, being essentially unsevered, still trapped in me but allowed an occasional roam in his elder's vicinity, just to keep a bit of cheer in the mess, as if nephews did not exist, for all their book-learning wisdom and their Hollywood certainties. How long we lingered thus, the young on the old, the old on the young, I do not know, but it was surely the bud blaming the bloom and not the other way around. You could tell from his face that what he wanted least was to have to spend the rest of his life inside me, and vanish with me as I died, allowed no other manhood but mine, though clearly mindful of other manhoods he might have had if little he had not grown up into unruly I. Funny to see him thus because I had never seen him at any other age, in a groping memory, yes, but never in a dream. As a baby, a boy, a mature man, he had never called on me before, gently shoving others aside in his delicate march to my side, not insisting on his right to look me in the eye, yet knowing he could take such a liberty because, in the truest sense, he started from within and would go back to there, the doll back into the wood. Then I saw what had happened, and I felt a little more at home. He was the kachina of me, the spirit who inhabited my bulk, whom I could please or anger with my every move. It was he who sat by, tucked into the inmost branches of my being, fully aware that, if I were good and took my pills, this was the pill that both slowed and strengthened my heart whereas this other was the pill that made the beat more regular. Privy to all such knowledge, he had no control, had no right of interruption. He had to ride me while I rode myself, wishing hotly that I were the child and he the veteran. And yet, he being me, and I him, perhaps no change would come of that at all, except that I would do my foolishness early on, and he would do his late. That kind of swap. Wet-eyed, we leaned on each other, knowing it was almost too late even to have a talk, never mind mend our ways, and it might have gone on for ever if the dream had not ceased of its own accord, a phantom soaring on chemicals not even mine, neither to be pleaded with nor banished. He has never come again, so perhaps I should take my pills as told, the right dose at the right time. There must be only one combination that is right, the one that brings him forth to chide, to hold my hand, while whatever it is that flutters in my chest whips my blood to cream, making it pool and thicken, dawdling into lumpiness. Were he small enough, he might flail around in it and somehow unthicken things, throwing out the solids, having a fine old swim in the thin gruel left. But he is no such size, and he is spread throughout my being, which means he is equally afflicted everywhere. I keep waiting for him, always in the wrong dream, of course, so I hope that he will appear in some other corner of my being, as when I get up suddenly, not so much to stand as even to sit, and all the blood drains away into my trunk, leaving only a brainpan full of air. Dizzy then, I hope to catch a glimpse of him, cautioning me to do things slowly, to get up in stages, but never a sign of him, never a tweak from his lodger's mind. When my lips quiver as they never did, or my tongue feels thick as a hammer handle, as it never did either, I yearn for it to be him moving about among me, amid me, but not even fierce believing makes it so. You have to have the right order of pills, in the right strength, week after week, to ferret him out. I struck on it once, when in the days of good behavior, I just wanted to feel well again and would have heeded even a tribal doctor, with his Mormon tea, his piñon gum, his coyote sunflowers. Or I would even have gone to Phoenix, a town reputed to bring life from the ashes of the dead. Since then, however, George The Place In Flowers Where Pollen Rests has gone back to his slovenly old ways, hoarding his pills for when he really feels at death's door and not just on death's porch. No more little George The Place In

441

Flowers Where Pollen Rests: they only come to you once in a lifetime, and it is possible that they do not even show up at your death, having once put in their plea and been sent away empty-handed. Instead, all you get is a nephew saying: Eat plenty of bananas, as if bananas grew up here on the mesas, and drink plenty of milk, as if milk were not a rarity up here. I try to see a Little George in Oswald Beautiful Badger Going Over The Hill, but the lad's almost callow intuitiveness is missing. He would no more say Eat this or Drink that, in order to make the heart muscle squeeze or rest than Oswald Beautiful Badger Going Over The Hill would hunt in his own insides for the contrite ghost of himself. Yet I have no one else to work with, unless it be some child my nephew can bribe to come and dally with me, out here on the wall, warming my hands against the lamp or her brow. Boys I would deny myself, not having the boy I myself was, the youth who was my ancestor and hides away in dreams I do not have by night or day.

nominated by Conjunctions

HER SECRETS

by JOHN BERGER

from THE THREEPENNY REVIEW

(For Katya)

FROM THE AGE of five or six I was worried about the death of my parents. The inevitability of death was one of the first things I learnt about the world on my own. Nobody else spoke of it yet the signs were so clear.

Every time I went to bed—and in this I am sure I was like millions of other children—the fear that one or both my parents might die in the night touched the nape of my neck with its finger. Such a fear has, I believe, little to do with a particular psychological climate and a great deal to do with nightfall. Yet since it was impossible to say: You won't die in the night, will you? (when Grandmother died, I was told she had gone to have a rest, or—this was from my Uncle who was more outspoken—that she had passed over), since I couldn't ask the real question and I sought a reassurance, I invented—like millions before me—the euphemism: See you in the morning! To which either my father or mother who had come to turn out the light in my bedroom, would reply: See you in the morning, John.

After their footsteps had died away, I would try for as long as possible not to lift my head from the pillow so that the last words spoken remained, trapped like fish in a rock-pool at low tide, between my pillow and ear. The implicit promise of the words was also a protection against the dark. The words promised that I would not (yet) be alone.

443

Now I'm no longer usually frightened by the dark and my father died ten years ago and my mother a month ago at the age of ninety-three. It would be a natural moment to write an autobiography. My version of my life can no longer hurt either of them. And the book, when finished, would be there, a little like a parent. Autobiography begins with a sense of being alone. It is an orphan form. Yet I have no wish to do so. All that interests me about my past life are the common moments. The moments—which if I relate them well enough—will join countless others lived by people I do not personally know.

Six weeks ago my mother asked me to come and see her; it would be the last time, she said. A few days later, on the morning of my birthday, she believed she was dying. Open the curtains, she asked my brother, so I can see the trees. In fact, she died the following week.

On my birthdays as a child, it was my father rather than she who gave me memorable presents. She was too thrifty. Her moments of generosity were at the table, offering what she had bought and prepared and cooked and served to whoever came into the house. Otherwise she was thrifty. Nor did she ever explain. She was secretive, she kept things to herself. Not for her own pleasure, but because the world would not forgive spontaneity, the world was mean. I must make that clearer. She didn't believe life was mean—it was generous—but she had learnt from her own childhood that survival was hard. She was the opposite of quixotic—for she was not born a knight and her father was a warehouse foreman in Lambeth. She pursed her lips together, knitted her brows as she calculated and thought things out and carried on with an unspoken determination. She never asked favors of anyone. Nothing shocked her. From whatever she saw, she just drew the necessary conclusions so as to survive and to be dependent on nobody. If I were Aesop, I would say that in her prudence and persistence my mother resembled the agouti. (I once wrote about an agouti in the London zoo but I did not then realize why the animal so touched me.) In my adult life, the only occasions on which we shouted at each other were when she estimated I was being quixotic.

When I was in my thirties she told me for the first time that, ever since I was born, she had hoped I would be a writer. The writers she admired when young were Bernard Shaw, J.M. Barrie, Compton Mackenzie, Warwick Deeping, E.M. Dell. The only painter she really admired was Turner—perhaps because of her childhood on the banks of the Thames.

Most of my books she didn't read. Either because they dealt with subjects which were alien to her or because—under the protective influence of my father—she believed they might upset her. Why suffer surprise from something which, left unopened, gives you pleasure? My being a writer was unqualified for her by what I wrote. To be a writer was to be able to see to the horizon where, anyway, nothing is ever very distinct and all questions are open. Literature had little to do with the writer's vocation as she saw it. It was only a by-product. A writer was a person familiar with the secrets. Perhaps in the end she didn't read my books so that they should remain more secret.

If her hopes of my becoming a writer—and she said they began on the night after I was delivered—were eventually realized, it was not because there were many books in our house (there were few) but because there was so much that was unsaid, so much that I had to discover the existence of on my own at an early age: death, poverty, pain (in others), sexuality . . .

These things were there to be discovered within the house or from its windows—until I left for good, more or less prepared for the outside world, at the age of eight. My mother never spoke of these things. She didn't hide the fact that she was aware of them. For her, however, they were wrapped secrets, to be lived with, but never to be mentioned or opened. Superficially this was a question of gentility, but profoundly, of a respect, a secret loyalty to the enigmatic. My rough and ready preparation for the world did not include a single explanation—it simply consisted of the principle that events carried more weight than the self.

Thus, she taught me very little—at least in the usual sense of the term: she a teacher about life, I a learner. By imitating her gestures I learnt how to roast meat in the oven, how to clean celery, how to cook rice, how to choose vegetables in a market. As a young woman she had been a vegetarian. Then she gave it up because she did not want to influence us children. Why were you a vegetarian? I once asked her, eating my Sunday roast, much later when I was first working as a journalist. Because I'm against killing. She would say no more. Either I understood or I didn't. There was nothing more to be said.

In time—and I understand this only now writing these pages—I

445

chose to visit abattoirs in different cities of the world and to become something of an expert concerning the subject. The unspoken, the unfaceable beckoned me. I followed. Into the abattoirs and, differently, into many other places and situations.

The last, the largest and the most personally prepared wrapped secret was her own death. Of course I was not the only witness. Of those close to her, I was maybe the most removed, the most remote. But she knew, I think, with confidence that I would pursue the matter. She knew that if anybody can be at home with what is kept a secret, it was me, because I was her son whom she hoped would become a writer.

The clinical history of her illness is a different story about which she herself was totally uncurious. Sufficient to say that with the help of drugs she was not in pain, and that, thanks to my brother and sister-in-law who arranged everything for her, she was not subjected to all the mechanical ingenuity of aids for the artificial prolongation of life.

Of how many deaths—though never till now of my own mother's—have I written? Truly we writers are the secretaries of death.

She lay in bed, propped up by pillows, her head fallen forward, as if asleep.

I shut my eyes, she said, I like to shut my eyes and think. I don't sleep though. If I slept now, I wouldn't sleep at night.

What do you think about?

She screwed up her eyes which were gimlet sharp and looked at me, twinkling, as if I'd never, not even as a small child, asked such a stupid question.

Are you working hard? What are you writing?

A play, I answered.

The last time I went to the theater I didn't understand a thing, she said. It's not my hearing that's bad though.

Perhaps the play was obscure, I suggested.

She opened her eyes again. The body has closed shop, she announced. Nothing, nothing at all from here down. She placed a hand on her neck. It's a good thing, make no mistake about it, John, it makes the waiting easier.

On her bedside table was a tin of handcream. I started to massage her left hand.

446

Do you remember a photograph I once took of your hands? Working hands, you said.

No, I don't.

Would you like some more photos on your table? Katya, her grandaughter, asked her.

She smiled at Katya and shook her head, her voice very slightly broken by a laugh. It would be *so* difficult, so difficult, wouldn't it, to choose.

She turned towards me. What exactly are you doing?

I'm massaging your hand. It's meant to be pleasurable.

To tell you the truth, dear, it doesn't make much difference. What plane are you taking back?

I mumbled, took her other hand.

You are all worried, she said, especially when there are several of you. I'm not. Maureen asked me the other day whether I wanted to be cremated or buried. Doesn't make one iota of difference to me. How could it? She shut her eyes to think.

For the first time in her life and in mine, she could openly place the wrapped enigma between us. She didn't watch me watching it, for we had the habits of a lifetime. Openly she knew that at that moment her faith in a secret was bound to be stronger than any faith of mine in facts. With her eyes still shut, she fingered the Arab necklace I'd attached round her neck with a charm against the evil eye. I'd given her the necklace a few hours before. Perhaps for the first time I had offered her a secret and now her hand kept looking for it.

She opened her eyes. What time is it?

Quarter to four.

It's not very interesting talking to me, you know. I don't have any ideas any more. I've had a good life. Why don't you take a walk?

Katya stayed with her.

When you are very old, she told Katya confidentially, there's one thing that's very very difficult—it's very difficult to persuade other people that you're happy.

She let her head go back on to the pillow. As I came back in, she smiled.

In her right hand she held a crumpled paper handkerchief. With it she dabbed from time to time the corner of her mouth when she felt there was the slightest excess of spittle there. The gesture was reminiscent of one with which, many years before, she used to wipe her mouth after drinking Earl Grey tea and eating watercress sandwiches. Meanwhile with her left hand she fingered the necklace, cushioned on her forgotten bosom.

Love, my mother had the habit of saying, is the only thing that counts in this world. Real love, she would add, to avoid any factitious misunderstanding. But apart from that simple adjective, she never added anything more.

nominated by The Threepenny Review

WORLD WITH A HARD K

by JEAN McGARRY

from TEMBLOR

Departure

THIS TIME OF YEAR THE FLOWERS ARE OF TWO KINDS: enriched
and hollow. I prefer the thin because they portray the fool's inner
roll, a fourth of what is necessary, clip it in two, cough and ingest. I
was in a roll and heard the sting in the basin, cough and ingest, talk
all through the night: it's cold, it's cold cold. Hold it, if you can,
especially on these long curved roads, inwardly curved and awkward. The slice and my head lolling like that on its spike, my
purples, the lovely sand. I heard him clam in the night, cold or
colder, then ping in the basin, a nickel or porous plug of flesh. I
will, over there where you are, prop your sagging until quiet, you
can fold in your one leaf and die with your head leashed to the
ground, all the firmness of the ground for your terminal.

You're surprised that I started at the end this time. One inner turn,
then another. Float one part my way; I'll skin it of thoughts and
memories. I heard you say: when people leave, they think I
remember, but I forget them right away. The other one said, the
one that looks just like you: some who are about to leave, I tell
them: go, you're already gone. Not one minute did I hold you in
my mind, not even in its void or outer box, the one no one cares
about, or is filled with coins.

Already a lot of us are gone. We dingle dangle here, all bleached,
one marble hand on the other. I have felt, and these others, all the

pain you donated, sometimes with the new and sometimes with the old scissors, the jar of plaster paints and the four hundred quarts of dry rinds, a flat beet hanging from each ear and the empty pod on my tongue (for you, this would be a houseboat). Flowers would grow, filthy and silken, from my name alone, if you will spit here and give me the hollow to grow them. And if he will quieten his night tongue and the dark deposit of mental rubber. There will be here, at last, a flowery mob, and here, the cloudy scrim for you to put your face and see the bottom.

The Hard Cracks

I AM OCCUPIED WITH A BLUE FIELD NOW, knots and termini. If I could find the throat of it, run a smooth but nappy cloth down its throat, along the sides, doubled or tripled to fit succinct. If a field were likely filled in its underground tube and thrilled with its taut finding, it would lie flat, cities flex and uncouple, these rivers would fall neatly like pins. All my hungers are arranged around the flat of it, steeled up and point down, howling.

Morning, come like a bright thread, dangle and coil your slow map. The city with its circumflex, its neuron. And altogether, make two surfaces, day and what it falls on. Underneath, the brittle things lie in their anaerobia, their stance of tuber, hill and skull. The world will be painted, all matched, sink down to a nice muck, and the walkers in their dressy clothes cover it, human variety in all the plants. My large and empty grows without bringing to its single pore even the mockery of an appearance, a dancing needle.

Bring to this immaculate zone, this blue, comb and submerge. If four words would loosen and throw a ragged net over this quiet. No longer in a vital state, something to fill this grotto.

A World With a Hard K

STEAM WOULD RISE FROM THE SINK OF THE GROUND. Flowers turn their faces toward the moving particle. Some would turn the other way and the flimsy necks of the reeds in a slack pose. The white flowers form their white seeds as summer is their uncle, and the letters roll together in a green field.

A discipline of tunnels and the fruitful walks and flat roads. Paint this building red and I will flick the paint off with my nail, tie your ship up to my finger, bend these slow pipes. Is it you who put all these sticks in the world?

The dead will accede to the dead; they will come up to the dead in formal, in a mute file, kisses on their faces and a sandy touch. The underworld and the overworld meet here around this yellow building. Inside we could sit, we could spell and moan. We are all here, there are only a few days, the names are plentiful, rich in bristle and shrub. Put my thumb on your thumb.

The singing was always the best of it, a big jar lowered to the floor and spun. I'd like to flick something your way and the way is among these tall gray, perfectly uniform pipes. For you, I'd build an industrial in the skin, float it on your river until it wastes.

Curving World

HOW SAD SOME OF THESE PICNICS HAVE BEEN, the raisin and the fortified bag of lettuce. You join me and flop over here folding the two chickens with their limp, still restless wings. A chariot for the afternoon, winter glow. Two children paint grape stains on their mouths, all flexed with longing and childish patience. You be the father and this curtain of a lake will throw its moist skin over us.

This picnic grape, lucent surface, round jelly on a plain stick, is my love. A baby could design a beautiful nap of slippery voids from these several grapes. To destroy something so plum-like and to fertilize something else.

nominated by Garrett Kaoru Hongo
and David St. John

EVE

by SANDRA McPHERSON

from AMERICAN POETRY REVIEW

Limper and meeker the cheap cottons grow thin.
Heavy with wearing things; nothing I want to be seen in.

I'd rather lean in the window
With my poppled milk-skin and say nakedness

Is our drab uniform. Don't worry:
Nothing will approach, no one is looking. Only

A white dog like a flashlight across the night.
Father has allowed me to name

The clothes—as I learn to sew. But they
Are boneless. They're not animals. I can't support them.

New things: yes, I'll sit in them for awhile,
A full skirt, ruffles, necklace, watch and rings,

And rub a gardener's naked back. But when he sleeps
I strip alone, open

The curtains, flatten against the window
I give oil to, pull back

With its dust tracing my sunlessness.
Or I might hold myself like rag and ammonia

To the pane I make worthwhile,
Clarify. My silhouette is clearly tired,

I want to start from here and go on,
With this streaked and strapping,

Purple, pale, okra-blossom bone-clothing,
The body scribbled on by a carried child

And not for young satyrs to grade. I want
The worn clothes torn

To bare the thread,
To pattern what is raw-edged.

This is my body
Stitched for no one else,

With these patchworker's bloodstains—every quilt
Wears its finger blood

From the needle, this
Is not failure, to be harmed this way,

Thimbles, bodices, all cast off. Lights off, I rest
Here in a nakedness that has the power

To make our daughter
Love women.

Beside the curtain torn by a catclaw
Or chewed through by sun, I am more

Than a glass woman, more than a fabric one.
This skin. The bible-leaves of the labia.

The fever of my forehead. Its
Workmanship. Naming the quilt patterns.

Name *clothes*, Father says, be ashamed and name the clothes.

I name. Wimple, haik, yashmak. Panties, slip, bra.

nominated by Naomi Clark
and Laura Jensen

HIS FUNNY VALENTINE

by LOUIS SIMPSON

from THE HUDSON REVIEW

He said, "I'd like to be a beautiful woman."

I was taken aback.
It sounded, and still sounds, most unlikely.
He was extemely attractive to women.
If you went with Mike Donovan to a party
or entered a restaurant, women would glance up,
see his face, and keep on staring.

I said, "Like Marilyn Monroe?"
I said that wanting to be someone else
was the same as wishing you were dead.

*

A woman said, "Tell me about Donovan.
You're his friend."
I said, "Mike's a drunk."
"Not that," she said, "something significant."

I told her about the affair
Mike had been having with Penny Baker.
"O that," she said. "He told me about it.
It's all over."

I might as well have tried to reason
with the 7th Cavalry charging down the valley.

He introduced me to Penny
in the White Horse. She was with her husband.
Later, in the course of conversation
something came up that required her
to open her shirt and show us her breasts . . .
like lilies, with nipples like tea roses.
"Come on, Penny," said her husband, "cover up."

That same night Mike came over
to drink and talk. I left him to it
and went to bed. Some time later
I was wakened by a sound.

He was still there, on the floor, passed out,
with the phonograph set on automatic
playing "My Funny Valentine" over and over.

*

I might have told her he'd been writing a novel
ever since I'd known him, that he had a contract
with Simon and Schuster, but never wrote a page.

There was a new post-war generation
of young novelists. Every few weeks
there'd be a new first-novel sensation.

At the time there was a run on titles
that told the reader to do something:
to *Lie Down in Darkness* and *Go Tell It on the Mountain*.

Mike had a title for his:
Do Not Pass Go, Do Not Collect $200.
But, as far as I know, it never came to anything.

*

Though a man who saw him in Italy
years later, shortly before he died,
said he was still writing . . . on Janiculum

with a view of Rome through the pines.
He was living with an Italian woman.

It was a far cry from the Village
and Albany where he grew up,
a boy with a taste for books
and baseball. He could still recite batting averages.

Later, when he went to the university,
it was jazz. And still, occasionally,
he wrote on jazz for the *Times*.

        *

Speaking of *The New York Times*,
there was an item about a golfer
who was playing with a metal club
behind a hedge. He fell on his club
and it snapped and went right through him.

Some who were playing the eighteenth hole
that day, close to the hedge, heard screams,
but they thought it was peacocks.
Peacocks were one of the features of the area.

That night when I met Mike for dinner
we had both seen it. I quoted Robert Frost:
a "design of darkness to appall."
Mike said, Ambrose Bierce. And, of course, he was right.

This may have been why we liked each other.
We liked the sound of fate:
a horn heard at a distance
in the Valley of the Shadow.

        *

When Mike stuck a knife in Penny
I didn't go to the precinct station
to bail him out—someone else did.
But ever since I've had an idea

of what it's like: a woman in a yellow wig,
a purple skirt, and heels like stilettos;
a pickpocket; a cripple
arrested for indecent exposure;

the naked light; the crack in the wall
that loops like the Mississippi at Vicksburg;
the shadow of the cockroach
under the baseboard, lurking, gathering his nerve.

nominated by Robert Phillips

HELIOPATHY

by SUSAN HOWE

from TEMBLOR

insofar   initiand   two   fold   invisible   errand

soever   before   Purchas   people   hereby   them

backwood   todo   great   Beech   where   discord

crossed   Ohio   occupation   arrowhead   noonday   bay

was   killing   and   planting   blare   campnation

sensible   peltry   legal   surname   between   surname

nomatter   how   turncoat   grow   green   roundagain

cross   own   thin   slumber   fleshly   asprawl

swamp   finite   apparel   become   rushes   She

happiness   laden   as   Eve   amongst   ore

even   asone   figment   form   beloved   Form

PARMENIDES LED BY DAUGHTERS OF THE SUN

TRIS

trample

eagle

bugle   ar

wan

   command   wer

want

   THat was a lie   bin
   seconds shiver away

wash

   bang   enny

was

   tongue   grate

wasp

   scene   cy

what

   scent   ck
                t'oth

swan

   Sceptre   cymbal

swamp

   scatter   Mercy

swal-low

   Wing

wal-low

   fetch

wander

   vast

watchman

   Oak   dient jut

sheer

   school

bear

   theday

there

   languishment

their

   Alm

where

   <u>The</u> <u>darkness</u> <u>hideth</u> <u>not</u> <u>from</u> <u>thee</u> WE

hear

                      huddle Un then All
   raculus cup in such manner Over

here

                            Favorite
                            Favorite

mire

                            Favorite

oar

                            Favorite

Anly which he has alt   nettle
corrector. that I. cristende.

breaches   skegger or forty

stupor research   I return lovingly   Quahog

    smok fane vane flag   gro

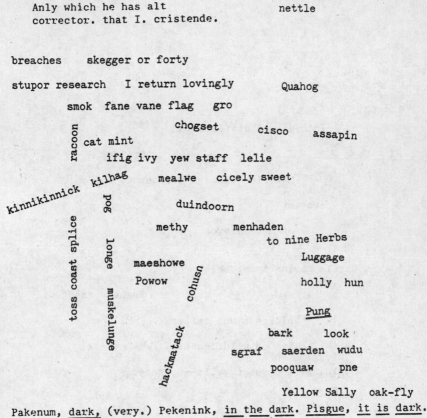

                    chogset   cisco   assapin
racoon cat mint
      ifig ivy yew staff lelie
kinnikinnick kilhag   mealwe   cicely sweet

        pog   duindoorn

toss coast splice   methy   menhaden
                          to nine Herbs
  longe   maeshowe   Luggage
  muskelunge Powow   cohusn   holly hun

                          Pung

                  bark   look
hackmatack   sgraf   saerden wudu
                  pooquaw   pne

                          Yellow Sally oak-fly

Pakenum, dark, (very.) Pekenink, in the dark. Pisgue, it is dark.
Pisgeke, when it becomes dark. (is dark.)
                                    brembel

Flesch: fle-

461

Inch-pin of civilization

                                Oratory

        Memories trace a discourse

Iroquois

    of marked eyes

Cattle moving in stubble

                              Peace messengers

    Spiders haunt cellars

    live on wildflowers

Scalping--whoops or yells--prisoner

Our duty how we should be bound

To do

Such phrases and such phrases

All those hands feet figures of speech

queareswildesthrentenbalence

Wicker logic mortal to ambulant

blunt

                    Fragile dialectic

Metaphor nations swarm

       Set of silver teaspoons

       We all wear mocassins

Draft of pseudonymous proem

               or half-singing or recitative

Poring ar av prise

whe war se herd won

Gathred leves mon sacret

Altogeather togeather

hops fra hoops

Idia sinsly

beleive eny beleif

Line about dim hill in legend and so forth interwoven.

Ear shall make age be forgotten, earth of the teetering edge.

Revel he stood hush generations here otherbody.

Counting by threes the limit in counting.

A hare a fox a bear.

Ages for long been Oursoul

Fledgling I will go over

Look where she lies asleep
Shadow gone out of my body

Real being or actual Being
jocund cipher and idiom

My strange act my text
my strange book

twig basket casting net creel

Body figure of a body
no illusion but an illusion

antithetical roundabout pastoral

Long journey in iron shoes
Stage set up on a stage

Figure of Comedy pastoral tragedy
Mysterious fugitive identity

Stripped of crown and purple
Old Mortality brow of adamant

runs carelessly to a precipice

Great men of the New World
walk on water after winter

Evergreens screen the earth

They are denying the Dark
after dark will ever gather

Inside the language of names
they stretch out their arms

Here is blank reason

Realm of thought ruin of things

What hierarchy of furious intention
lies here in ruins

So dark they run against trees

Havoc of infinite progression
Generations predestined to obey

Aspire's empty cry

The lake has been opening all day
Gloomy water eager to get free

Play of Nature

in the lapse of time
an hour past the hour

of Midsummer

Counterjudgement

of mind in Mind
abiding

at the meadow-edge
drifts of inland

Stray memory

Wounds of pity
wounds of peace

Old chief muffled about the face
St Tammany

Civilization
thrusts and envelops him

Point to point

Broad magisterial right

Side by side
Sower and seed

Precepts and secular reason

Typology of charm
Structure of ritual song

The Past the proven half

There can be no doubt

The world as an emblem
The echoing valediction

of light gods crossing
and re-crossing

Hermeneutics of paternalism
Mediator mouthpiece

prerogatives of dominion

And the old domnu
cast in a corner

ghost of baffled meaning
thin flesh arms crossed

Around her hangs dark vapor

Unconscious meadows loom
Necessity and premonition

Faces fade from faces said
Fate draws Zeal's sequel

Each stoic fortification

Afterthought

Between reason
and revelation

apperception fell to ruin

What was always
and will always be

abdication

gripped by thought

Thought's descent
into character trait

in deep troughs
hunch deeper Troughs

Luminous night
or black Light

hunter gatherer
Known and the known

The untried fields
The sound of human pain

Sanctuary
Constancy

Structure of truth
Truth of structure

Geneology of the kings of Idumea

Names passed over in silence
Names that remain unknown

Vestiges of their action
Distant tribes endlessly rove

Annal and action into confusion
Slingstones still stones

To manifest these names

In bodies of bushes stray voices
Stray voices without bodies

Stray sense and sentences

Concerning the historicity of history

The mind's absolute ideality

Old age old child

Farewell to every generation
Enkindling kin arc on the horizon

Young parents bending in sunshine
End of filled space in the world

To confront an abstraction

a proper name or the author's name
My ordinary self beside life

nominated by Harvey Shapiro

PERSIAN LAMB

fiction by HAROLD JAFFE

from BEASTS (Curbstone Press) and THE MINNESOTA REVIEW

In memory of Michael Stewart

"I had elected . . . not to submit."

Richard Wright

American Hunger

Ras

Who killed 19-year-old Anthony Parchment as he was inscribing this resonant syllable with a magic marker on an IRT subway car in the Nevins Street station, 2:30 a.m., Thursday, mid-summer?

Who killed Frantz Fanon of French Martinique, white cells flooding his blood (black skin—white enraged cells), dreadful in Paris, dead at 36, New York City, leukemia?

From Jamaica (Westminster Parish), Anthony Parchment came to Crown Heights, Brooklyn, with his mother, two sisters. Moved in with his mother's sister, *her* three children, also from Jamaica, Kensington Parish. Anthony's Rasta father? Dead, killed with a machete by a Maroon. Maroons, the first Jamaican guerrillas, made it tough for the British to sip their gin, harried the Brits out in the end. Black Rasta killed by Black Maroon.

Who killed Steve Biko?

Anthony Parchment caught in the act of inscription, the talismanic *Ras*. Who beat him? The police. Who killed him? The police. The persistent reporter for the local black newspaper was told by the nurse at Bellevue Hospital that Anthony Parchment's nearly dead body arrived in the Emergency Ward manacled with four pairs of handcuffs, that he had deep bruises "all over—from the soles of his feet to his head."

Twelve days after Anthony Parchment's murder, the New York City Medical Examiner released this inquest capsule: "No indication of physical trauma. Apparent cause of death: cocaine-induced coma. Resultant heart-stoppage."

Ras. The boy got it out before they got him. It's still there, among the thousandfold graffiti, theater of the colored poor, will be there until they bury it, the subway, which is liable to be soon. Whites use busses, cars, cabs. The colored poor ride the subways, and so few bucks! bleats the City, bleats the State. We have our poor and we have our *good poor*—tell me then: who rides the subways? Who don't get the bucks? *Ras*.

"Steve Biko was shamming—he wasn't sick at all."

Anthony Parchment's mother and aunt said No to the white New York City Medical Examiner, borrowed money to hire their own pathologist, whose report confirmed what you and I know: sixty-odd bruises on his body, multiple concussions of the skull, spinal trauma, death from injuries, zero evidence of cocaine. Five weeks after these independent findings, after local black citizen outrage, the New York City Examiner revised his original report to read: "Some indication of head injury. Possibly fatal spinal trauma."

Incantatory *Ras*. Back to Ethiopia, the cradle. Cite Marcus Garvey. Worship Taffari Makonnen (Haile Selassie), Emperor of Ethiopia, Lion of Judah. Cannabis is holy (for it will grant you access). "Ital" food is holy: roots, grain, legumes, mild fruit (no meat). Away from Ethiopia looms Babylon. But while *in* Babylon, what then? Swallow? Expel? Testify? Inscribe?

And the police, the ones who beat and killed him? Three white males, ages twenty-seven to forty-one, two married with kids and living in Queens, the other living in Staten Island, all three members in good standing of the Patrolman's Benevolent Association. When asked what *Ras* meant to them, two said: "Black Power," the other said: "Black Power and heroin." When asked whether it was defensible to beat a person who was inscribing a word on the door of a subway train full of words, they refused to answer.

Who asked these things of the policemen?
I did.
Who are you?
Nobody.
You're white.
No. I mean yes.

The Parchments in Crown Heights, Brooklyn: the mother, Hyacinth, worked in a neighborhood laundromat. The two teen-aged sisters went to Thomas Jefferson High School. Anthony worked in downtown Manhattan, in the garment district, maneuvering a bulky pushcart filled with mink and sable and Persian lamb from factory to showroom, back again, through the cluttered streets.

Persian lamb: the glossy black or gray pelt of the just-born (just-killed) karakul lamb with its soft tight curls. Who murdered Patrice Lumumba: his "tongue," his "nightingale breast," his "assassinated whistle"?*

All right, the boy was lynched. What now? Now, one of the three cops, the unmarried one, will be indicted for Manslaughter in the second degree, the other two will be "severely reprimanded." Manslaughter two? The indicted cop's lawyer:"If my client is guilty of anything it is of being over-zealous on the public's behalf. I feel certain that he will be totally and completely absolved of any wrongdoing whatsoever by the American judicial system and that he will never set foot in prison as an inmate."

*Roberto Armijo—"To Patrice Lumumba," in *Volcán: Poems from El Salvador, Guatemala, Hondorus, Nicaragua* (City Lights, 1983)

When the lawyer was asked whether Anthony Parchment's murder was significantly different from the recent lynching of a black teenager in Alabama, in which a twenty-nine-year-old white chose a black at random, cut his throat, then hung him from a tree across from his (the white man's) house, to demonstrate that the "Klan is bigger than ever in Alabama." When asked this, the lawyer actually swung at the questioner, didn't make contact.

You were the questioner?
Yes.
Why?
You tell me.
You're pent. All dammed up. You get off on this . . . planting. Planting your brain-tubers. Is that it?
Not brain. No.

At his aunt's advice, Anthony Parchment cut his dreadlocks before coming to the States, thinking maybe it might help him get a decent job. Wheeling mink and sable and Persian lamb through the teeming streets, singing. He didn't stop doing that. Lots of Rastas write songs, sing their long grief. When Anthony Parchment inscribed *Ras* on the door of the Nevins Street subway it was as a seed-syllable of the unending song, this:

Cap-tiv-ity, Cap-tiv-ity
Youth-mon you going to die,
Dread, dread, so far from home,
Living you life in de Babylon zone,
Youth-mon you going to die.

Don't you remember what de Angel said?
De evil Somebody gonna shot you dead,
in Cap-tiv-ity, Cap-tiv-ity,
Living you life in de Babylon zone,
Dread, dread, so far from home,
Youth-mon you going to die.

Question? How is the lamb like the avant-gardist?
Answer: Both are granted a window ledge on the city's outskirts and a single line of elegaic prose in an interior page of the medium

newspaper. Later—much later—their horny carapace is exhumed, liveried, displayed to distracted mild applause.

And you? Are your post-mortems, your abracadabra witnessing, any different? Your cubist musings? Your doleful celebrations of martyrdom? Your moony "history"? Your thinly-veiled self-pity? Your spleen in lamb's clothing?

Right, he had a girlfriend, Mattie Taylor, born in Trinidad, also living in Brooklyn with her family. She sings. Anthony would write the songs, the two of them would sing them, that was their goal. Poor young people—especially it seems, non-white young—speak of goals. Middle-class young speak of desk-calendars, agendas, careers—there's a difference. It's not over yet but the cop's lawyer was right: his client'll get off, no big deal.

Motive? I mean Anthony Parchment's motive for doing what he did where he did it, when. Could be he wanted a taste of what it feels like: write songs people feel; add his bit to the hundreds on the door, thousands, tens of thousands of colored inscriptions in the Underground. Scrawls, signs, totems, verses, signatures, ideograms, self-portraits. That hot, hot moist a.m., with its third-rail and litter and sharp sour smells of fermenting soda pop and fast-food mustard and sweat from the endless work-a-day and gutted phones and cavernous rumblings, darkness. Could be he wanted to testify to the power of the word. *Ras.* Didn't his father die for it? Weren't the lambs marooned in Babylon because of it? Could be he was restless and didn't really want to think of maneuvering the bulky cart full of pungent pelts through the cluttered streets, not want to think.

Together, Anthony Parchment and Mattie Taylor did what teen-agers do: caress, couple, laugh, flirt. More: sing Anthony's songs; also Anthony taught her *Ras;* smoked herb, learned *Ras.* That's right. *Ras* ain't only for Jamaicans but for uprooted Blacks anywhere.

The oldest cop had been the brutal one, using his club in the subway; in the radio car using the heel of his hand; in the police station kicking with his black, thick-soled shoes. Only once did

476

their eyes squarely meet, thin black young man / bulky red-haired cop, and Anthony recognized him from his dream, in which his father was being beaten by such a man, white with red hair, *but made-up to look black*, beaten with his fists, not fighting back, then with the machete, slashed hard with the machete, and then the killer saw him, Anthony, running through the white-faced choir, white small teeth, white chins pointed down like daggers, and the killer gaining on him when he willed himself to wake, and this dream was dreamed in Jamaica but he never forgot his assassin's face.

Not him, the oldest cop with red hair, but the youngest, least brutal (maybe) of the three, the unmarried one, was the only one actually charged: Manslaughter 2, since—it was reasoned—he had the least to lose, no family, no property, just two years on the force, and ballsy too, didn't know fear, besides the lawyer would get him off so no big deal, and as a bonus they'd change his duty, move him out of Nevins Street, Brooklyn, give him Manhattan's Upper East Side.

The third cop, age thirty-three, a lanky tall man with prematurely gray hair and a lot of tattoos, a wife, three young daughters, a small house in Corona, Queens, went to Aviation High School, wanted to be a plane mechanic, worked instead for Chevrolet, tried for the fire fighters but failed the test, tried twice for the cops, made it, was real gung-ho, killed a black teenager once before while driving his patrol car on a call, got off that one easy too, they transferred him to Transit.

Hyacinth Parchment refused to be interviewed. Anthony Parchment's aunt said only: "Anthony loved to laugh. He would put his head back and just laugh. I can hear it in my head."

Why was Steve Biko arrested?
Sedition.
Why was he manacled to his cell at Walmer Police Station?
To prevent his escape.
And why was he kept naked in his cell at Walmer Police Station?
To prevent self-inflicted death.
How is it that Steve Biko suffered severe brain damage?

477

He was presented with his comrades' written testimony naming him as the leader of the attempted violent sedition. When he read this unassailable evidence he banged his head against the wall in frustration.

And the numerous deep bruises on his body?

Any bruises would have been self-inflicted. The prisoner had been a medical student and was utterly familiar with yoga.

How would you justify transporting the brain-injured and battered Steve Biko, naked, on the floor of a truck, one thousand kilometers to Pretoria?

The trip was necessary to administer the spinal tap to ascertain the extent of the prisoner's brain damage. It was determined that the prisoner stood a better chance of surviving the journey than surviving otherwise.

You were wrong?

Not necessarily.

(Steve Biko was buried outside King Williams Town, near the small dusty township where he had grown up. He was thirty years old.)

Anthony Parchment's family and friends sat in the back of the airless courtroom in witness of the proceedings that found the indicted police officer innocent of Manslaughter and his case dismissed after a judicial reprimand. As the three officers and their families, grinning, clapping each other on the back, filed from the courtroom, a white bystander stood up and shouted: "Sham! Sham! No black person will ever get justice in this whitened sepulcher, this rich man's cess!"

The white—thin, dark-haired, middle-aged—was forcibly restrained (by two of the formerly-accused officers), then held in contempt. Hyacinth Parchment witnessed the white man's outburst with the same (nearly expressionless) disapproval with which she had witnessed the court proceedings.

It was you who made the outburst.
Yes.
To what end?
Don't talk to me of ends. I'm not the keeper of accounts.

478

Like promised, the let-off cop got off his bad duty in Nevins Street and was transferred to the Upper East Side. He also got engaged to his high-school sweetheart and made plans to move from Staten Island, in fact, put a downpayment on a small brick house in the northeast Bronx, closer to his new duty. Have you ever been in the northeast Bronx? It's white and clean and Roman Catholic and surprisingly wooded with numerous species of birds but almost no mammals. Except for rats and mice, the homeowners pretty much hunted down all the mammals, ate the ones that were edible, stripped the pelts from the ones that were valuable.

Who killed Marcus Garvey?
Ras, it ain't easy.

nominated by Curbstone Press

THE LOVER OF HORSES

fiction by TESS GALLAGHER

from ZYZZYVA

THEY SAY MY GREAT-GRANDFATHER was a gypsy, but the most popular explanation for his behavior was that he was a drunk. How else could the women have kept up the scourge of his memory all these years, had they not had the usual malady of our family to blame? Probably he was both a gypsy and a drunk.

Still, I have reason to believe the gypsy in him had more to do with the turn his life took than his drinking. I used to argue with my mother about this, even though most of the information I have about my great-grandfather came from my mother, who got it from her mother. A drunk, I kept telling her, would have had no initiative. He would simply have gone down with his failures and had nothing to show for it. But my great-grandfather had eleven children, surely a sign of industry, and he was a lover of horses. He had so many horses he was what people called "horse poor."

I did not learn, until I traveled to where my family originated at Collenamore in the west of Ireland, that my great-grandfather had most likely been a "whisperer," a breed of men among the gypsies who were said to possess the power of talking sense into horses. These men had no fear of even the most malicious and dangerous horses. In fact, they would often take the wild animal into a closed stall in order to perform their skills.

Whether a certain intimacy was needed or whether the whisperers simply wanted to protect their secret conversations with horses is not known. One thing was certain—that such men gained power over horses by whispering. What they whispered no one knew. But the effectiveness of their methods was renowned, and anyone

480

for counties around who had an unruly horse could send for a whisperer and be sure that the horse would take to heart whatever was said and reform his behavior from that day forth.

By all accounts, my great-grandfather was like a huge stallion himself, and when he went into a field where a herd of horses was grazing, the horses would suddenly lift their heads and call to him. Then his bearded mouth would move, and though he was making sounds that could have been words, which no horse would have had reason to understand, the horses would want to hear; and one by one they would move toward him across the open space of the field. He could turn his back and walk down the road, and they would follow him. He was probably drunk my mother said, because he was swaying and mumbling all the while. Sometimes he would stop deadstill in the road and the horses would press up against him and raise and lower their heads as he moved his lips. But because these things were only seen from a distance, and because they have eroded in the telling, it is now impossible to know whether my great-grandfather said anything of importance to the horses. Or even if it was his whispering that had brought about their good behavior. Nor was it clear, when he left them in some barnyard as suddenly as he'd come to them, whether they had arrived at some new understanding of the difficult and complex relationship between men and horses.

Only the aberrations of my great-grandfather's relationship with horses have survived—as when he would bathe in the river with his favorite horse or when, as my grandmother told my mother, he insisted on conceiving his ninth child in the stall of a bay mare named Redwing. Not until I was grown and going through the family Bible did I discover that my grandmother had been this ninth child, and so must have known something about the matter.

These oddities in behavior lead me to believe that when my great-grandfather, at the age of fifty-two, abandoned his wife and family to join a circus that was passing through the area, it was not simply drunken bravado, nor even the understandable wish to escape family obligations. I believe the gypsy in him finally got the upper hand, and it led to such a remarkable happening that no one in the family has so far been willing to admit it: not the obvious transgression—that he had run away to join the circus—but that he was in all likelihood a man who had been stolen by a horse.

This is not an easy view to sustain in the society we live in. But I have not come to it frivolously, and have some basis for my belief. For although I have heard the story of my great-grandfather's defection time and again since childhood, the one image which prevails in all versions is that of a dappled gray stallion that had been trained to dance a variation of the mazurka. So impressive was this animal that he mesmerized crowds with his sliding step-and-hop to the side through the complicated figures of the dance, which he performed, not in the way of Lippizaners—with other horses and their riders—but riderless and with the men of the circus company as his partners.

It is known that my great-grandfather became one of these dancers. After that he was reputed, in my mother's words, to have gone "completely to ruin." The fact that he walked from the house with only the clothes on his back, leaving behind his own beloved horses (twenty-nine of them to be exact), further supports my idea that a powerful force must have held sway over him, something more profound than the miseries of drink or the harsh imaginings of his abandoned wife.

Not even the fact that seven years later he returned and knocked on his wife's door, asking to be taken back, could exonerate him from what he had done, even though his wife did take him in and looked after him until he died some years later. But the detail that no one takes note of in the account is that when my great-grandfather returned, he was carrying a saddle blanket and the black plumes from the headgear of one of the circus horses. This passes by even my mother as simply a sign of the ridiculousness of my great-grandfather's plight—for after all, he was homeless and heading for old age as a "good for nothing drunk" and a "fool for horses."

No one has bothered to conjecture what these curious em-blems—saddle blanket and plumes—must have meant to my great-grandfather. But he hung them over the foot of his bed—"like a fool," my mother said. And sometimes when he got very drunk he would take up the blanket and, wrapping it like a shawl over his shoulders, he would grasp the plumes. Then he would dance the mazurka. He did not dance in the living room but took himself out into the field, where the horses stood at attention and watched as if suddenly experiencing the smell of the sea or a change of wind in the valley. "Drunks don't care what they do," my mother would say as she finished her story about my great-grandfather. "Talking to a drunk is like talking to a stump."

Ever since my great-grandfather's outbreaks of gypsy necessity, members of my family have been stolen by things—by mad ambitions, by musical instruments, by otherwise harmless pursuits from mushroom hunting to childbearing or, as was my father's case, by the more easily recognized and popular obsession with card playing. To some extent, I still think it was failure of imagination in this respect that brought about his diminished prospects in the life of our family.

But even my mother had been powerless against the attraction of a man so convincingly driven. When she met him at a birthday dance held at the country house of one of her young friends, she asked him what he did for a living. My father pointed to a deck of cards in his shirt pocket and said, "I play cards." But love is such as it is, and although my mother was otherwise a deadly practical woman, it seemed she could fall in love with no man but my father.

So it is possible that the propensity to be stolen is somewhat contagious when ordinary people come into contact with people such as my father. Though my mother loved him at the time of the marriage, she soon began to behave as if she had been stolen from a more fruitful and upright life which she was always imagining might have been hers.

My father's card playing was accompanied, to no one's surprise, by bouts of drinking. The only thing that may have saved our family from a life of poverty was the fact that my father seldom gambled with money. Such were his charm and powers of persuasion that he was able to convince other players to accept his notes on everything from the fish he intended to catch next season to the sale of his daughter's hair.

I know about this last wager because I remember the day he came to me with a pair of scissors and said it was time to cut my hair. Two snips and it was done. I cannot forget the way he wept onto the backs of his hands and held the braids together like a broken noose from which a life had suddenly slipped. I was thirteen at the time and my hair had never been cut. It was his pride and joy that I had such hair. But for me it was only a burdensome difference between me and my classmates, so I was glad to be rid of it. What anyone else could have wanted with my long shiny braids is still a mystery to me.

When my father was seventy-three he fell ill and the doctors gave him only a few weeks to live. My father was convinced that his illness had come on him because he'd hit a particularly bad losing streak at cards. He had lost heavily the previous month, and items of value, mostly belonging to my mother, had disappeared from the house. He developed the strange idea that if he could win at cards he could cheat the prediction of the doctors and live at least into his eighties.

By this time I had moved away from home and made a life for myself in an attempt to follow the reasonable dictates of my mother, who had counseled her children severely against all manner of rash ambition and foolhardiness. Her entreaties were leveled especially in my direction since I had shown a suspect enthusiasm for a certain pony at around the age of five. And it is true I felt I had lost a dear friend when my mother saw to it that the neighbors who owned this pony moved it to pasture elsewhere.

But there were other signs that I might wander off into unpredictable pursuits. The most telling of these was that I refused to speak aloud to anyone until the age of eleven. I whispered everything, as if my mind were a repository of secrets which could only be divulged in this intimate manner. If anyone asked me a question, I was always polite about answering, but I had to do it by putting my mouth near the head of my inquisitor and using only my breath and lips to make my reply.

My teachers put my whispering down to shyness and made special accommodations for me. When it came time for recitations I would accompany the teacher into the cloakroom and there whisper to her the memorized verses or the speech I was to have prepared. God knows, I might have continued on like this into the present if my mother hadn't plotted with some neighborhood boys to put burrs into my long hair. She knew by other signs that I had a terrible temper, and she was counting on that to deliver me into the world where people shouted and railed at one another and talked in an audible fashion about things both common and sacred.

When the boys shut me into a shed, according to plan, there was nothing for me to do but to cry out for help and to curse them in a torrent of words I had only heard used by adults. When my mother heard this she rejoiced, thinking that at last she had broken the treacherous hold of the past over me, of my great-grandfather's gypsy blood and the fear that against all her efforts I might be stolen away, as she had been, and as my father had, by some as yet unforeseen predilection. Had I not already experienced the consequences of such a life in our household, I doubt she would have been successful, but the advantages of an ordinary existence among people of a less volatile nature had begun to appeal to me.

It was strange, then, that after all the care my mother had taken for me in this regard, when my father's illness came on him, my mother brought her appeal to me. "Can you do something?" she wrote, in her cramped, left-handed scrawl. "He's been drinking and playing cards for three days and nights. I am at my wit's end. Come home at once."

Somehow I knew this was a message addressed to the very part of me that most baffled and frightened my mother—the part that belonged exclusively to my father and his family's inexplicable manias.

When I arrived home my father was not there.

"He's at the tavern. In the back room," my mother said. "He hasn't eaten for days. And if he's slept, he hasn't done it here."

I made up a strong broth, and as I poured the steaming liquid into a Thermos I heard myself utter syllables and other vestiges of language which I could not reproduce if I wanted to. "What do you mean by that?" my mother demanded, as if a demon had leapt out of me. "What did you say?" I didn't—I couldn't—answer her. But suddenly I felt that an unsuspected network of sympathies and distant connections had begun to reveal itself to me in my father's behalf.

There is a saying that when lovers have need of moonlight, it is there. So it seemed, as I made my way through the deserted town toward the tavern and card room, that all nature had been given notice of my father's predicament, and that the response I was waiting for would not be far off.

But when I arrived at the tavern and had talked my way past the barman and into the card room itself, I saw that my father had an enormous pile of blue chips at his elbow. Several players had fallen out to watch, heavy-lidded and smoking their cigarettes like weary gangsters. Others were slumped on folding chairs near the coffee urn with its empty "Pay Here" styrofoam cup.

My father's cap was pushed to the back of his head so that his forehead shone in the dim light, and he grinned over his cigarette at me with the serious preoccupation of a child who has no intention of obeying anyone. And why should he, I thought as I sat down just behind him and loosened the stopper on the Thermos.

The five or six players still at the table casually appraised my presence to see if it had tipped the scales of their luck in an even more unfavorable direction. Then they tossed their cards aside, drew fresh cards, or folded.

In the center of the table were more blue chips, and poking out from my father's coat pocket I recognized the promissory slips he must have redeemed, for he leaned to me and in a low voice, without taking his eyes from his cards, said, "I'm having a hell of a good time. The time of my life."

He was winning. His face seemed ravaged by the effort, but he was clearly playing on a level that had carried the game far beyond the realm of mere card playing and everyone seemed to know it. The dealer cocked an eyebrow as I poured broth into the plastic Thermos cup and handed it to my father, who slurped from it noisily, then set it down.

"Tell the old kettle she's got to put up with me a few more years," he said, and lit up a fresh cigarette. His eyes as he looked at me, however, seemed over-brilliant, as if doubt, despite all his efforts, had gained a permanent seat at his table. I squeezed his shoulder and kissed him hurriedly on his forehead. The men kept their eyes down, and as I paused at the door, there was a shifting of chairs and a clearing of throats. Just outside the room I nearly collided with the barman, who was carrying in a fresh round of beer. His heavy jowls waggled as he recovered himself and looked hard at me over the icy bottles. Then he disappeared into the card room with his provisions.

I took the long way home, finding pleasure in the fact that at this hour all the stoplights had switched onto a flashing-yellow caution cycle. Even the teenagers who usually cruised the town had gone home or to more secluded spots. *Doubt*, I kept thinking as I drove with my father's face before me, that's the real thief. And I knew my mother had brought me home because of it, because she knew that once again a member of our family was about to be stolen.

Two more days and nights I ministered to my father at the card room. I would never stay long because I had the fear myself that I might spoil his luck. But many unspoken tendernesses passed between us in those brief appearances as he accepted the nourishment I offered, or when he looked up and handed me his beer bottle to take a swig from—a ritual we'd shared since my childhood.

My father continued to win—to the amazement of the local barflies who poked their faces in and out of the card room and gave the dwindling three or four stalwarts who remained at the table a commiserating shake of their heads. There had never been a winning streak like it in the history of the tavern, and indeed, we heard later that the man who owned the card room and tavern had to sell out and open a fruit stand on the edge of town as a result of my father's extraordinary good luck.

Twice during this period my mother urged the doctor to order my father home. She was sure my father would, at some fateful moment, risk the entire winnings in some mad rush toward oblivion. But his doctor spoke of a new "gaming therapy" for the terminally ill, based on my father's surge of energies in the pursuit of his gambling. Little did he know that my father was, by that stage, oblivious to even his winning, he had gone so far into exhaustion.

Luckily for my father, the hour came when, for lack of players, the game folded. Two old friends drove him home and helped him down from the pickup. They paused in the driveway, one on either side of him, letting him steady himself. When the card playing had ended there had been nothing for my father to do but to get drunk.

My mother and I watched from the window as the men steered my father toward the hydrangea bush at the side of the house, where he relieved himself with perfect precision on one mammoth blossom. Then they hoisted him up the stairs and into the entry-way. My mother and I took over from there.

"Give 'em hell, boys," my father shouted after the men, conclud-ing some conversation he was having with himself.

"You betcha," the driver called back, laughing. Then he climbed with his companion into the cab of his truck and roared away.

Tied around my father's waist was a cloth sack full of bills and coins which flapped and jingled against his knees as we bore his weight between us up the next flight of stairs and into the living room. There we deposited him on the couch, where he took up residence, refusing to sleep in his bed—for fear, my mother claimed, that death would know where to find him. But I preferred to think he enjoyed the rhythms of the household; from where he lay at the center of the house, he could overhear all conversations that took place and add his opinions when he felt like it.

My mother was so stricken by the signs of his further decline that she did everything he asked, instead of arguing with him or simply refusing. Instead of taking his winnings straight to the bank so as not to miss a day's interest, she washed an old goldfish bowl and dumped all the money into it, most of it in twenty-dollar bills. Then she placed it on the coffee table near his head so he could run his hand through it at will, or let his visitors do the same.

"Money feels good on your elbow," he would say to them. "I played them under the table for that. Yes sir, take a feel of that!" Then he would lean back on his pillows and tell my mother to bring his guests a shot of whiskey. "Make sure she fills my glass up," he'd say to me so that my mother was certain to overhear. And my mother, who'd never allowed a bottle of whiskey to be brought into her house before now, would look at me as if the two of us were more than any woman should have to bear.

"If you'd only brought him home from that card room," she said again and again. "Maybe it wouldn't have come to this."

This included the fact that my father had radically altered his diet. He lived only on greens. If it was green he would eat it. By my mother's reckoning, the reason for his change of diet was that if he stopped eating what he usually ate, death would think it wasn't him and go look for somebody else.

Another request my father made was asking my mother to sweep the doorway after anyone came in or went out.

"To make sure death wasn't on their heels; to make sure death didn't slip in as they left." This was my mother's reasoning. But my father didn't give any reasons. Nor did he tell us finally why he wanted all the furniture moved out of the room except for the couch where he lay. And the money, they could take that away too.

But soon his strength began to ebb, and more and more family and friends crowded into the vacant room to pass the time with him, to laugh about stories remembered from his childhood or from his nights as a young man at the country dances when he and his older brother would work all day in the cotton fields, hop a freight train to town and dance all night. Then they would have to walk home, getting there just at daybreak in time to go straight to work again in the cotton fields.

"We were like bulls then," my father would say in a burst of the old vigor, then close his eyes suddenly as if he hadn't said anything at all.

As long as he spoke to us, the inevitability of his condition seemed easier to bear. But when, at the last, he simply opened his mouth for food or stared silently toward the far wall, no one knew what to do with themselves.

My own part in that uncertain time came to me accidentally. I found myself in the yard sitting on a stone bench under a little cedar tree my father loved because he liked to sit there and stare at the ocean. The tree whispered, he said. He said it had a way of knowing what your troubles were. Suddenly a craving came over me. I wanted a cigarette, even though I don't smoke, hate smoking, in fact. I was sitting where my father had sat, and to smoke seemed a part of some rightness that had begun to work its way within me. I went into the house and bummed a pack of cigarettes from my brother. For the rest of the morning I sat under the cedar tree and smoked. My thoughts drifted with its shifting and murmurings, and it struck me what a wonderful thing nature is because it knows the value of silence, the innuendos of silence and what they could mean for a word-bound creature such as I was.

I passed the rest of the day in a trance of silences, moving from place to place, revisiting the sites I knew my father loved—the "dragon tree," a hemlock which stood at the far end of the orchard, so named for how the wind tossed its triangular head; the rose arbor where he and my mother had courted; the little marina where I sat in his fishing boat and dutifully smoked the hated cigarettes, flinging them one by one into the brackish water.

I was waiting to know what to do for him, he who would soon be a piece of useless matter of no more consequence than the cigarette butts that floated and washed against the side of his boat. I could feel some action accumulating in me through the steadiness of water raising and lowering the boat, through the sad petal-fall of roses in the arbor and the tossing of the dragon tree.

That night when I walked from the house I was full of purpose. I headed toward the little cedar tree. Without stopping to question the necessity of what I was doing, I began to break off the boughs I could reach and to pile them on the ground.

"What are you doing?" my brother's children wanted to know, crowding around me as if I might be inventing some new game for them.

"What does it look like?" I said.

"Pulling limbs off the tree," the oldest said. Then they dashed away in a pack under the orchard trees, giggling and shrieking.

As I pulled the boughs from the trunk I felt a painful permission, as when two silences, tired of holding back, give over to each other some shared regret. I made my bed on the boughs and resolved to spend the night there in the yard, under the stars, with the hiss of the ocean in my ear, and the maimed cedar tree standing over me like a gift torn out of its wrappings.

My brothers, their wives and my sister had now begun their nightly vigil near my father, taking turns at staying awake. The windows were open for the breeze and I heard my mother trying to answer the question of why I was sleeping outside on the ground—"like a damned fool" I knew they wanted to add.

"She doesn't want to be here when death comes for him" my mother said, with an air of clairvoyance she had developed from a lifetime with my father. "They're too much alike," she said.

The ritual of night games played by the children went on and on past their bedtimes. Inside the house, the kerosene lantern, saved from my father's childhood home, had been lit—another of his strange requests during the time before his silence. He liked the shadows it made and the sweet smell of the kerosene. I watched the darkness as the shapes of my brothers and sister passed near it, gigantic and misshapen where they bent or raised themselves or crossed the room.

Out on the water the wind had come up. In the orchard the children were spinning around in a circle, faster and faster until they were giddy and reeling with speed and darkness. Then they would stop, rest a moment, taking quick ecstatic breaths before plunging again into the opposite direction, swirling round and round in the circle until the excitement could rise no higher, their laughter and cries brimming over, then scattering as they flung one another by the arms or chased each other toward the house as if their lives depended on it.

I lay awake for a long while after their footsteps had died away and the car doors had slammed over the goodbyes of the children being taken home to bed and the last of the others had been bedded down in the house while the adults went on waiting.

It was important to be out there alone and close to the ground. The pungent smell of the cedar boughs was around me, rising up in the crisp night air toward the tree, whose turnings and swayings had altered, as they had to, in order to accompany the changes about to overtake my father and me. I thought of my great-

490

grandfather bathing with his horse in the river, and of my father who had just passed through the longest period in his life without the clean feel of cards falling through his hands as he shuffled or dealt them. He was too weak now even to hold a cigarette; there was a burn mark on the hardwood floor where his last cigarette had fallen. His winnings were safely in the bank and the luck that was to have saved him had gone back to that place luck goes to when it is finished with us.

So this is what it comes to, I thought, and listened to the wind as it mixed gradually with the memory of children's voices which still seemed to rise and fall in the orchard. There was a soft crooning of syllables that was satisfying to my ears, but ultimately useless and absurd. Then it came to me that I was the author of those unwieldy sounds, and that my lips had begun to work of themselves.

In a raw pulsing of language I could not account for, I lay awake through the long night and spoke to my father as one might speak to an ocean or the wind, letting him know by that threadbare accompaniment that the vastness he was about to enter had its rhythms in me also. And that he was not forsaken. And that I was letting him go. That so far I had denied the disreputable world of dancers and drunkards, gamblers and lovers of horses to which I most surely belonged. But from that night forward I vowed to be filled with the first unsavory desire that would have me. To plunge myself into the heart of my life and be ruthlessly lost forever.

nominated by Sara Vogan

from THE PERSON

by LYN HEJINIAN

from SULFUR

Let's get isolated
The temporal is dread
Is there a name
for the imploding series "consciousness
of consciousness"
Realism and depth perception
The audacious science of the thought

of poetry
Person
holding picture of
person holding picture of . . .
Anxiety in space
Can one get by on procrastination
Mortality is a system

of exclusion
I am having a sensation of description
Person holding picture of . . .
Now, you can tell I wish I was a cowgirl
Person having thought
with its capacity to preoccupy
Sound falls

Can one get by on projection
People desire to believe in . . .

Rain falls
Physical reality consists of sympathetic units
Grammar & consciousness
Or if not in the next life
then in the one after that
I'll be a meteorologist
Awaiting the great sequences
of incompleteness
Can one prosper from the impulse to confide
The trees rustle in the wind
and suck in
the rain suppressing sound, and then release it
In discontinuity, distinction
I do not equate goggles with subjectivity
But like a tree that's showing off in the wind

                    *

(a.)

We reproach ourselves for the heroism
of the person in the episode body
Acid-Drop
We are filled with scruples

about beauty and individualism
Spouse, Child, Citizen
A composition
Cheerfulness is indelicate

as a separate body-part
The incriminating contents
of the portrait-bowl
The person is the form

it determines
The limits of the activity
One can shudder without understanding
with chronic ideas

Good—an intuition
But isn't that merely preknowing
—and one can remain
in a state of preknowing indefinitely

Entertainment in poetry
We reproach ourselves for enthusiasm
sniffs on the river
It's unthinkable

that my skull would turn out
to be empty
if it were opened—I feel
my brain

At first I didn't fasten
this feeling to words
Adorable Subject-Object
A moment of intense disorientation as it swings

(b. HABITAT)

its search for a recipient
Musics of the spouse
a simple example: consciousness
sucking on altitudes

currently
your music has an analytically violent sweet sweep
Our house has a porous advantage
over notation

Fire sirens in the rain
that's what I hear
uses of citizenry
in the house

(c.)

One day a certain person—we'll call it
Acid-Drop—since things

periodically seem unreal evidently
to exist

is not . . . no microtones
no bumps . . . the same
as being real—I am happy to have photographs
in which it stands

a moody landscape and a mellow generous drama
Good-Sport, when something new occurs
I will write
Time malfunctions

This form of person is mulish
still I have the impulse
to expect it to phone
in any emergency

and its idleness
The erotic takes its share
of consciousness
The model person has taken

a pose in the shape
of an X or else
it is holding its belly
Melodrama is its laughter

prolonged philosophically
Funny
I do love the poetry
with a certain speed of mind

But funniness!
it is a technical vibration
which enabled them to swallow
at a single gulp

It's also capable of stopping
Do I have time for this?

yes realism, yes time, yes paradise
Under clouds of exterior reality

Study of hearing
yes, I want to study meaning
The cheek that seeks (organ
for apprehension) the breeze

I can't believe it!
Congratulations
to imagine
not being born in fear of solids

                    *

When I get angry I get accessible
Sociable
Waste prose
"Slow down"—there is the musical analogy
Nagging in its social prolongation

Narrative is like insomnia
Life before birth—I'm going to write without saying anything lest
    my behavior contradict my words
Perhaps there is no opposite to creativity
Don't die
The rain jumps
The bird is the real location of the speaker
Do you believe in a Forelife
Patrol—with tree-lined bonds

But number is shameless—expansive sensations!
Cars and calm cups of instruction
My ear, it can jump things
One crams it with incredible justice
The spouse is just such
a role—a mechanism
of associations
Apples that look like clouds
Citizen, sponsor, inhabitant

Life is full of semi-probabilities . . . yes . . . your mouth is like a
   camera
In the trap of fires the rain snapped like a diamond
Science is escapist, a fantasy of instruction
No acoustics
I would find myself on shaky ground, in a dark wood, chewing my
   pencil for nourishment

There is a certain inner after-the-fact continuity
With towerlike still compulsiveness, I repeat
Pretend nothing—closure is misanthropic
Neat nervousness—this was my maternal genius
Eat, who doesn't work
Eat has achieved anti-blankness
Honor among radicals—are we not radicals!
"Buy me a wondrous wonder, a marvelous marvel!"
Let my culture do!

               *

Realism is an unimaginable ballad: direct speech
across the trajectory of nature in its trees
Which word is an object of imitation?
And in returning differ

I have achieved the ability to be pathological
Here I refer to beauty when it forms
and every belief which is a move—
I am a contractor
Hunchbacked grammar to a bridge of the elegy

Into an elegy discontinuity implodes
Taken in . . .
My thoughts take a twist, they are always logical in this direction
The ear opens onto a setting: audience-life
The horse, the drone, the wrong word, and the relief

Red has a rending and yellow a stinging effect
Just as, years later, every attempt
to bring to bear on the objects of any thought

an adamant and relentless intuition jiggled
In correspondence, the sky

Described, the corresponding sky
in circumstantial detail, goes up
as if having yielded . . . as Goethe says, blue seems to yield to
  our gaze . . .
"having as its object something unknown but conscious"
Below the brain are overt gates

NATURE . . .
in the imperfection of the eyes
(an ever-present principle of absent-mindedness and yearning)
really, your ass is like an apple

NATURE

Perceiver at her perception post, strike!
Implosion of the seasons, and cupping
I've seen twin lines of ants come from an oak and a
    skink break off its cobalt tail
Title? Eighty-One Chapters
Plenitude & grace
The grand sanity of the person pushes it
Yeah—and the hardest job of all is made from a dull
    saw and a dry stump
Fact-process and form-process
It's a pleasant duty to perceive

Then nature gave me a direct sensation—
distance, with a sort of shudder
and its undertow, dizziness
rolling the impulse to set in motion
my palpable singe-minded credible intention to cross
from this to the next ridge—all of this in an instant
And I tell you, I almost took off
the decision to fly
interrupted, just there, at a synapse, in the flesh
Collapsing the leap

Intelligence and desire are animal instruments
The person fascinates them with its lethargy
The pulse of the quiet of crickets—the object of science is
    pleasure
Nature takes thornlike comprehension
What is it that has not changed enough?

nominated by Sulfur

PSALM AND LAMENT

by DONALD JUSTICE

from THE NEW CRITERION

in memory of my mother (1897-1974)
Hialeah, Florida

The clocks are sorry, the clocks are very sad.
One stops; one goes on striking the wrong hours.

And the grass burns terribly in the sun;
The grass turns yellow secretly at the roots.

Now suddenly the yard chairs look empty, the sky looks empty,
The sky looks vast and empty.

Out on Red Road the traffic continues. Everything continues.
Nor does memory sleep. It goes on.

Out spring the butterflies of recollection,
And I think that for the first time I understand

The beautiful ordinary light of the patio
And even perhaps the dark rich earth of a heart.

The bedclothes, they say, had been pulled down.
I will not describe it. I do not want it described.

No, but the sheets were drenched and twisted.
They were the very handkerchiefs of grief.

Now summer comes with its schoolboy trumpets and fountains,
But the years are gone. The years are finally over.

And there is only
This long desolation of flower-bordered sidewalks

That runs to the corner, turns and goes on,
That disappears and goes on

Into the black oblivion of a neighborhood and a world
Without billboards or yesterdays.

Sometimes a sad moon comes out and waters the roof tiles.
But the years are gone. There are no more years.

nominated by Arthur Smith

VIEWING THE COAST

by MARK STRAND

from GRAND STREET

I

Sailing a ragged shoreline strewn with rocks
And broken timber silvering in sunlight,
And remembering, not clearly enough, a house
Where roses on the walls have peeled by now,
And ceiling leaks have spread their maps to let
The sky inside, and a Chinese lantern that swung
On the front porch is just a skeleton
Of rusted wire, I wonder at the half-sleep
Of a calling in which I spent so many days
Offshore. The water's phrases break and bubble
Into nothing, long undulating leaves
Of kelp lean one way and in their shade
Small silver herring glide. If I could see
Beneath them to our least beginnings drifting
In the tidal sway and see myself,
What would I know? That what is most remote
Is also best forgotten? This creaking boat
Moves alongside islands that appear
Then slip from sight. Wedge Island, like a shelf,
Slides into view, and the top of Mosher Island.
Then both are gone. The midday spreads a film
Of light over the whole watery scene,
Making it shine but seem less clear; while I,
Drawn from facts of the actual world into

502

A dream where there are no facts, only shapes
Resembling them, find that I desire less.
A deeper music darkens what I see,
And now at noon, parting from this shore,
These islands, I am sure that what was here,
The happiness I had, cannot return.
The land is gone. I have no past to speak of;
The history of this moment is this moment.

II

Now when I said those things about having lost
My happiness, I meant that I couldn't remember
Clearly enough the happiness I had.
I was so far away that nothing was clear,
And I said a few high-sounding things without
Intending to. The fact is that when one wants
To go back, no matter where, the coast is never
Clear. One is bound to see haze or ruins, and that,
As I said, is a little sad. Take the house
I mentioned. What good would it do to be living there now,
Stuck on the shore, watching someone like me
Sail by? And all that stuff about not seeing
Down to our least beginnings, as if anyone could,
And trying to reinforce and even deepen
The longing I felt, was only me trying
To impersonate what one might say in such
A situation. Sometimes when I write,
Things get a little out of hand, which is
What I meant when I said I was drawn
From facts into a dream resembling them.
You see, I am not unhappy, but unhappiness
Must have its say, and a poem is often
The appropriate means for this. Now as to
Desiring less and settling for the dark,
I always say that towards the end of poems
When, having committed myself to a line
Of argument, I see what is no longer
Possible, or rather what is no longer
Possible to speak of. But now that I

Have spoken, all that has changed; the history
Of that moment has lengthened to include this moment
And that makes me happy, as so much does.

*nominated by Sherod Santos,
and David Wojahn*

THE GARDEN
OF EARTHLY DELIGHTS

by CZESLAW MILOSZ

from UNATTAINABLE EARTH (Ecco Press)

1/Summer

In the July sun they were leading me to the Prado,
Straight to the room where *The Garden of Earthly Delights*
Had been prepared for me. So that I run to its waters
And immerse myself in them and recognize myself.

The twentieth century is drawing to its close.
I will be immured in it like a fly in amber.
I was old but my nostrils craved new scents
And through my five senses I received a share in the earth
Of those who led me, our sisters and lovers.

How lightly they walk! Their hips in trousers, not in trailing
   dresses,
Their feet in sandals, not on cothurni,
Their hair not clasped by a tortoiseshell buckle.
Yet constantly the same, renewed by the moon, Luna,
In a chorus that keeps praising Lady Venus.

Their hands touched my hands and they marched, gracious,
As if in the early morning at the outset of the world.

2/A Ball

It is going on inside a transparent ball
Above which God the Father, short, with a trimmed beard,
Sits with a book, enveloped in dark clouds.
He reads an incantation and things are called to being.
As soon as the earth emerges, it bears grasses and trees.
We are those to whom green hills have been offered
And for us this ray descends from opened mists.
Whose hand carries the ball? Probably the Son's.
And the whole Earth is in it, Paradise and Hell.

3/Paradise

Under my sign, Cancer, a pink fountain
Pours out four streams, the sources of four rivers.
But I don't trust it. As I verified myself,
That sign is not lucky. Besides we abhor
The moving jaws of crabs and the calcareous
Cemeteries of the ocean. This, then, is the Fountain
Of Life? Toothed, sharp-edged,
With its innocent, delusive color. And beneath,
Just where the birds alight, glass traps set with glue.
A white elephant, a white giraffe, white unicorns,
Black creatures of the ponds. A lion mauls a deer.
A cat has a mouse. A three-headed lizard,
A three-headed ibis, their meaning unknown.
Or a two-legged dog, no doubt a bad omen.
Adam sits astonished. His feet
Touch the foot of Christ who has brought Eve
And keeps her right hand in his left while lifting
Two fingers of his right like the one who teaches.
Who is she, and who will she be, the beloved
From the Song of Songs? This Wisdom-Sophia,
Seducer, the Mother and Ecclesia?
Thus he created her who will conceive him?
Where then did he get his human form
Before the years and centuries began?
Human, did he exist before the beginning?
And establish a Paradise, though incomplete,

So that she might pluck the fruit, she, the mysterious one,
Whom Adam contemplates, not comprehending?
I am these two, twofold. I ate from the tree
Of knowledge. I was expelled by the archangel's sword.
At night I sensed her pulse. Her mortality.
And we have searched for the real place ever since.

4/Earth

Riding birds, feeling under our thighs the soft feathers
Of goldfinches, orioles, kingfishers,
Or spurring lions into a run, unicorns, leopards,
Whose coats brush against our nakedness,
We circle the vivid and abundant waters,
Mirrors from which emerge a man's and a woman's head,
Or an arm, or the round breasts of the sirens.
Every day is the day of berry harvest here.
The two of us bite into wild strawberries
Bigger than a man, we plunge into cherries,
We are drenched with the juices of their wine,
We celebrate the colors of carmine
And vermillion, as in toys on a Christmas tree.
We are many, a whole tribe swarming,
And so like each other that our lovemaking
Is as sweet and immodest as a game of hide-and-seek.
And we lock ourselves inside the crowns of flowers
Or in transparent, iridescent bubbles.
Meanwhile a flock of lunar signs fills the sky
To prepare the alchemical nuptials of the planets.

5/Earth Again

They are incomprehensible, the things of this earth.
The lure of waters. The lure of fruits.
Lure of the two breasts and long hair of a maiden.
In rouge, in vermillion, in that color of ponds
Found only in the Green Lakes near Wilno.
And ungraspable multitudes swarm, come together
In the crinkles of tree bark, in the telescope's eye,
For an endless wedding,

For the kindling of the eyes, for a sweet dance
In the elements of the air, sea, earth and subterranean caves,
So that for a short moment there is no death
And time does not unreel like a skein of yarn
Thrown into an abyss.

nominated by Ecco Press

OUTSTANDING WRITERS

(The editors also wish to mention the following important works published by small presses last year. Listing is alphabetical by author's last name)

FICTION

The Beauties of Drink—Lee K. Abbott (Iowa Review)
The World of Apples—Lee K. Abbott (Nit & Wit)
Happiness—Walter Abish (New Directions)
The Eyes of Children—Tony Ardizzone (Beloit Fiction Review)
The Psychopathology of Everyday Life—Jonathan Baumbach (Boulevard)
How I Found My Brother—Charles Baxter (Indiana Review)
Depth of Field—Ann Beattie (Shenandoah)
Town Smokes—Pinckney Benedict (Ontario Review)
Stoics—William Blythe (Missouri Review)
The Black Man in the Forest—Cecilia M. Brainard (Amerasia)
All Alices—Pamela Brandt (Minnesota Review)
Recovery—Jessica Brilliant (Chariton Review)
Shame—Jerry Bumpus (Fiction Collective)
Heidi Inside—Richard Burgin (Kansas Quarterly)
The Pilot—James Lee Burke (NER/BLQ)
Gravity—Frederick Busch (Ohio Review)
Max—Ron Carlson (Carolina Quarterly)
Phenomena—Ron Carlson (Writer's Forum)
Astronomy—Jill Ciment (Mississippi Review)
Easy—Christopher Coe (StoryQuarterly)
The Scientific Method—Robert Cohen (Ploughshares)
Billy Ducks Among the Pharaohs—Rick DeMarinis (Cutbank)
The First Suite—Rita Dove (Black American Literature Forum)
Death At Sea—Andre Dubus (Quarterly West)

Mrs. Trom—Rosemary Mahoney (Florida Review)
Homemaker—Donald K. Mangum (Florida Review)
Fathers Overlooking the Water—Charles Marvin (Ascent)
Success—Hilary Masters (Stuart Wright, Publisher)
How Uncle Fox Really Got His Name—Jack Matthews (Western Humanities Review)
The One-Legged Men—Eric McCormack (Interstate)
Life Drawing—Erin McGraw (Georgia Review)
A Man In Louisiana—Thomas McGuane (Shenandoah)
The Cuevas—Kevin McIllvoy (Missouri Review)
There's a Hooker In My House—Daniel Meltzer (Confrontation)
Larceny—Barbara Milton (Apalachee Quarterly)
The Silver Box—Susan Minot (Grand Street)
Reconnaissance—Mary Morris (Agni Review)
The Tenant—Bharati Mukherjee (The Literary Review)
Circle of Prayer—Alice Munro (Paris Review)
Mercury—Yannick D. Murphy (Antioch Review)
In Christ There is No East Or West—Kent Nussey (Black Warrior Review)
A Wild of Sand—Naomi Shihab Nye (Southwest Review)
The Jesuit—Joyce Carol Oates (Missouri Review)
Surf City—Joyce Carol Oates (Partisan Review)
Piers the Imposter—Bette Pesetsky (Paris Review)
The Last Supper—Susan Ponsoldt (Ascent)
Music Story—M.J. Pulaski (NER/BLQ)
What's Left After—Peggy Rambach (Fiction Network)
Fences—Norma Rosen (Orim)
The Fire—Arliss Ryan (Amelia)
Central Avenue Breakdown—Ira Sadoff (Chelsea)
A Night of Music—Marjorie Sandor (Black Warrior Review)
The Subversive Divorce—Lynne Sharon Schwartz (Confrontation)
I Ate Her Heart—Bob Shacochis (New Virginia Review)
Stony Limits—Enid Shomer (Plainswoman)
The Marionette Theatre—Dennis Silk (Conjunctions)
Splinters—Mona Simpson (Southern California Anthology)
Landlady—Roland Sodowsky (Still Point Press)
The Incorrect Hour—Debra Spark (North American Review)
The Sea Fairies—Maura Stanton (Michigan Quarterly)
Hoover—Sharon Sheehe Stark (Boulevard)
Eight Ruins—Michael Stephens (Exquisite Corpse)

NONFICTION

phor—Eric Zencey (North American Review)
"I Brake For Delmore Schwartz": Portrait of the Artist As A Young
   Liar—Maurice Zolotow (Michigan Quarterly Review)
from Departures—Paul Zweig (American Poetry Review)

POETRY

Autobiography, 1952—Yehuda Amichai (Partisan Review)
Emis Esmoor: Passage from India—Ben Belitt (Salmagundi)
Tennyson Under the Yews—Michelle Boisseau (Georgia Review)
Angels—Marianne Boruch (Poetry)
The Ice House—William Carpenter (Northwestern University Press)
The Gift—Raymond Carver (Seneca Review)
On The Nature of the Beast—David Citino (Kansas Quarterly)
Paper House—Norma Cole (Sulfur)
from A Reading—Beverly Dahlen (Ironwood)
His Prayer—Christopher Davis (Denver Quarterly)
Hamtramck: The Polish Women—Toi Derricote (Callaloo)
The Gardener—Stephen Dobyns (Virginia Quarterly Review)
Genie's Prayer, Under the Kitchen Sink—Rita Dove (TriQuarterly)
The Body Opulent—Alice Fulton (Poetry)
To The Republic—James Galvin (American Poetry Review)
Written In My Dream By W.C. Williams—Allen Ginsberg (Poetry)
Floating Mangers—Michele Glazer (Pavement)
Pond—Brooks Haxton (Beloit Poetry Review)
On Nothing—Emily Hiestand (Hudson Review)
Oracles—Richard Howard (Grand Street)
12 Poems From A Work In Progress—Susan Howe (Temblor)
Wag's End—Andrew Hudgins (Reaper)
The Cure, an Anecdote—Mark Jarman (NER/BLQ)
Elegy for Cello and Piano—Donald Justice (Iowa Review)
Pearl—Carolyn Kizer (Poetry)
How To Leave Nothing—Sydney Lea (Crazyhorse)
Always A Rose—Li-Young Lee (BOA Editions)
Winter Words—Philip Levine (Poetry)
Right Now—Robert Lunday (Provincetown Arts)
To An Unborn Child—Cleopatra Mathis (Pacific Review)
Centripetal—Jane Miller (Agni Review)

OUTSTANDING SMALL PRESSES

(These presses made or received nominations for this edition of *The Pushcart Prize*. See the *International Directory of Little Magazines and Small Presses*, Dustbooks, Box 1056, Paradise, CA 95969, for subscription rates, manuscript requirements and a complete international listing of small presses.)

A

Abattoir Editions, see Penumbra Press
Acorns, see Treetop Panorama
Acts, 514 Guerrerro St., San Francisco, CA 94110
Adrift, 239 E. 5th St., #4D, New York, NY 10003
Aegina Press, 4937 Humphrey Rd., Huntington, W.VA 25704
Aerial, P.O. Box 1901, Manassas, VA 22110
Agada, 2020 Essex St., Berkeley, CA 94703
Agincourt Press, 65 Eckerson Rd., Harrington Park, NJ 07640
The Agni Review, P.O. Box 660, Amherst, MA 01004
Albatross, 4014 S.W. 21st Rd., Gainesville, FL 32607
Aldebaran, Roger Williams College, Bristol, RI 02809
Alice James Books, 138 Mt. Auburn St., Cambridge, MA 02138
Alta Napa Press, 1969 Mora Ave., Calistoga, CA 94515
The Altadena Review, P.O. Box 212, Altadena, CA 91001
Amaryllis Review, 535 Parkview Dr., Park City, UT 84060
Amelia, 329 "E" St., Bakersfield, CA 93304
Amerasia Journal, Asian American Studies Center, UCLA, Los Angeles, CA 90024
American Studies Press, Inc., 13511 Palmwood Lane, Tampa, FL 33624

The American Voice, Heyburn Bldg, Ste. 1215, Broadway at 4th
Ave., Louisville, KY 40202
Amicus, Cooper Union, Cooper Square, New York, NY 10003
Another Chicago Magazine, Box 11223, Chicago, IL 60611
Ansuda Publications, P.O. Box 158, Harris, IA 51345
Antaeus, 26 W. 17th St., New York, NY 10011
Antietam Review, 33 W. Washington St., Rm. 215, Hagerstown,
MD 21740
The Antioch Review, P.O. Box 148, Yellow Springs, OH 45387
APAEROS, P.O. Box 759, Veneta, OR 97487
Apalachee Quarterly, P.O. Box 20106, Tallahassee, FL 32304
Appalachian Consortium Press, University Hall, Appalachian St.
Univ., Boone, NC 28608
Applezaba Press, P.O. Box 4134, Long Beach, CA 90804
Arjuna Library Press, 1025 Garner St., Box 18, Colorado Springs,
CO 80905
Arts End Books-Publishers, Box 162, Newton, MA 02168
Ascent, English Dept., 608 S. Wright St., Univ. of Illinois,
Urbana, IL 61801
The Atavist, P.O. Box 5643, Berkeley, CA 94705
Atlantis Editions, P.O. Box 18326, Philadelphia, PA 19120
The Awakener Press, 938 18th St., Hermosa Beach, CA 90254

B

BOA Editions Ltd., 92 Park Ave., Brockport, NY 14420
backspace ink, 372 2nd Ave., San Francisco, CA 94118
Barnwood Press, River House, RR 2, Box 11C, Daleville, IN
47334
Bear & Co., Inc., P.O. Drawer 2860, Santa Fe, NM 87504
The Bellingham Review, see Signpost Press
Bellowing Ark, P.O. Box 45637, Seattle, WA 98145
The Bench Press, 408 Haverford Pl., Swarthmore, PA 19081
Berkeley Poets Workshop & Press, P.O. Box 459, Berkeley, CA
94701
Biblio Press, P.O. Box 22, Fresh Meadows, NY 11365
Bilingual Review Press, Hispanic Research Center, Arizona St.
Univ., Tempe, AZ 85287
BkMk Press, 5216 Rockhill Rd., Univ. of Missouri, Kansas City,
MO 64110

Black American Literature Forum, Parsons Hall 237, Indiana St., Univ., Terre Haute, IN 47809

Black Bear Publications, 1916 Lincon St., Croydon, PA 19020

Black Buzzard Press, 4705 S. 8th Rd., Arlington, VA 22204

The Black Fly Review, Univ. of Maine at Fort Kent, Fort Kent, ME 04743

Black Ice, 6022 Sunnyview Rd., NE, Salem, OR 97305

Black Warrior Review, P.O. Box 2936, University, AL 35486

The Bloomsbury Review, P.O. Box 8928, Denver, CO 80201

The Blue Cloud Quarterly, Blue Cloud Abbey, Marvin, SD 57251

Blue Unicorn, 22 Avon Rd., Kensington, CA 94707

Blueline, Blue Mountain Lake, NY 12812

Bookmakers Guild, Inc., 1430 Florida Ave., Ste. 202, Longmont, CO 80501

Bottom Dog Press, Firelands College, Huron, OH 44839

Bottomfish Magazine, DeAnza College, 21250 Stevens Creek Blvd., Cupertino, CA 95014

Boulevard, 2400 Chestnut St., Philadelphia, PA 14103

Broken Streets, 57 Morningside Dr., E., Bristol, CT 06010

Brunswick Publishing Co., Lawrenceville, VA

Burning Deck, 71 Elmgrove Ave., Providence, RI 02906

C

Caesura, English Dept., Auburn Univ., Auburn University, AL 36849

Cafe Solo, 7975 San Marcos Ave., Atascadero, CA 93422

Callaloo, English Dept., Univ. of Virginia, Charlottesville, VA 22903

Callapooya Collage, 2519 E. Ellendale, Dallas, OR 97338

Calyx, P.O. Box B, Corvallis, OR 97339

Candle, P.O. Box 206, Naselle, WA 98638

Capra Press, P.O. Box 2068, Santa Barbara, CA 93120

Carolina Quarterly, Greenlaw Hall, Univ. of North Carolina, Chapel Hill, NC 27514

Carolina Wren Press, 300 Barclay Rd., Chapel Hill, NC 27514

Celebration, 2707 Lawina Rd., Baltimore, MD 21216

Celestial Otter Press, 28424 Emerald Green Dr., Warrenville, IL 60555

The Celibate Woman Journal, 3306 Ross Pl., NW, Washington, DC 20008

Centennial Review, 110 Morrill Hall, Michigan St. Univ., E. Lansing, MI 48824

Chantry Press, P.O. Box 144, Midland Park, NJ 07432

The Chariton Review, Northeast Missouri St. Univ., Kirksville, MO 63501

The Chattahoochee Review, DeKalb Community College, 2101 Womack Rd., Dunwoody, GA 30338

Chelsea, Box 5880, Grand Central Sta., New York, NY 10163

Cincinnati Poetry Review, English Dept., Univ. of Cincinnati, Cincinnati, OH 45221

Clarity Press, 3277 Roswell Rd., NE, Ste. 469, Atlanta, GA 30305

Cleis Press, P.O. Box 8933, Pittsburgh, PA 15221

Cleveland State University Poetry Center, Rhodes Tower, Rm. 1815, Cleveland, OH 44115

Clinton St. Quarterly, P.O. Box 3588, Portland, OR 97208

Clockwatch Review, 737 Penbrook Way, Hartland, WI 53029

Clothespin Fever Press, 5529 N. Figueroa, Los Angeles, CA 90042

The Clyde Press, 373 Lincoln Parkway, Buffalo, NY 14216

cold-drill, Boise St. University, English Dept., 1910 University Dr., Boise, ID 83725

Cold Knee Mountain Press, P.O. Box 2574, Loop Sta., Minneapolis, MN 55402

Colorado Review, English Dept., Colorado St. Univ., Fort Collins, CO 80523

Confluence Press, Inc., Spalding Hall, LCSC Campus, 8th Ave. at 6th, Lewiston, ID 83501

Confrontation, English Dept., C.W. Post of L.I.U., Greenvale, NY 11548

Conjunctions, 33 W. 9th St., New York, NY 10011

Connecticut Poetry Review, P.O. Box 3783, New Haven, CT 06525

Coordinating Council of Literary Magazines, 666 Broadway, New York, NY 10013

Corona, Box 830688, Univ. of Texas at Dallas, Richardson, TX 75083

Coteau Books, 2337 McIntyre St., Regina, Saskatchewan, CANADA S4P 2S3

Cotton Boll,/Atlanta Review, Sandy Springs P.O. Box 76757, Atlanta, GA 30358

Cotton Lane Press, 2 Cotton Lane, Augusta, GA 30902

Cottonwood, Box J, Kansas Union, Univ. of Kansas, Lawrence, KS 66045

Counter-Propaganda Press, Box 365, Park Forest, IL 60466

Cow in the Road, P.O. Box 90326, San Jose, CA 95109

Coyote Love Press, 294 Spring St., Portland, ME 04102

Crab Creek Review, 806 No. 42nd, Seattle, WA 98103

Crash Magazine, P.O. Box 16074, San Diego, CA 92116

Crawl Out Your Window, 4641 Park Blvd., San Diego, CA 92116

Crazyhorse, English Dept., Univ. of Arkansas, Little Rock, AR 72204

CrazyQuilt Press, 3341 Adams Ave., San Diego, CA 92116

Creative Arts Book Co., 833 Bancroft Way, Berkeley, CA 94710

Creeping Bent, 433 W. Market St., Bethlehem, PA 18018

The Crescent Review, P.O. Box 15065, Ardmore Sta., Winston-Salem, NC 27113

Cross-Canada Writers, Inc., P.O. Box 277, Sta. F, Toronto, Ont. CANADA M4Y 2L7

Cross-Cultural Communications, 239 Wynsum Ave., Merrick, NY 11566

Crosscurrents, 2200 Glastonbury Rd., Westlake Village, CA 91361

Crossroads Communications, P.O. Box 7, Carpentersville, IL 60110

Croton Review, P.O. Box 277, Croton-on-Hudson, NY 10520

Crowdancing Quarterly, 570 W. 10th Ave., Eugene, OR 97401

Cumberland Poetry Review, P.O. Box 120128, Acklen Sta., Nashville, TN 37212

The Cummington Press, 1803 S. 58 St., Omaha, NE 68106

Curbstone Press, 321 Jackson St., Willimantic, CT 06226

CutBank, English Dept., Univ. of Montana, Missoula, MT 59812

D

Dawn Valley Press, P.O. Box 58, New Wilmington, PA 16142

Dawnwood Press, 2 Park Ave., Ste. 2650, New York, NY 10016

Dog River Review, see Trout Creek Press

Dolphin-Moon Press, P.O. Box 22262, Baltimore, MD 21203

Dooryard Press, P.O. Box 221, Story, WY 82842
Druid Books, Ephraim, WI 54211

E

Ecco Press, 26 W. 17th St., New York, NY 10011
Embers, 127 Fort Hale Rd., New Haven, CT 06512
Endeavor Publishing, 30064 Annapolis Circle, Inkster, MI 48144
Epistemology Publishers, P.O. Box 564, Mableton, GA 30059
Erie Street Press, 221 S. Clinton Ave., Oak Park, Il 60302
Evans Publishing, 2500 St. Anthony Blvd., Minneapolis, MN 55418
Event, Douglas College, P.O. Box 2503, New Westminster, B.C., CANADA V3L 5B2
Exile Press, P.O. Box 1768, Novato, CA 94948

F

Fantasy Review, College of Humanities, Florida Atlantic Univ., Boca Raton, FL 33431
Farmer's Market, P.O. Box 1272, Galesburg, IL 61402
The Feminist Press at City Univ. of New York, 311 E. 94th St., New York, NY 10128
Feminist Studies, c/o Women's Studies Program, Univ. of Maryland, College Park, MD 20742
Fessenden Review, P.O. Box 7272, San Diego, CA 92107
Fiction Collective, English Dept., Brooklyn College, Brooklyn, NY 11210
Fiction Network, P.O. Box 5651, San Francisco, CA 94101
Fine Madness, P.O. Box 15176, Seattle, WA 98115
Firebrand Books, 141 The Commons, Ithaca, NY 14850
Five Fingers Review, 100 Valencia St., Ste. 303, San Francisco, CA 94103
The Florida Review, English Dept., Univ. of Central Florida, Orlando, FL 32816
Flume Press, 644 Citrus Ave., Chico, CA 95926
Footwork, Passaic Co. Community College, College Blvd., Paterson, NH 07509

Frontiers, Women Studies Program, Box 325, Univ. of Colorado, Boulder, CO 80309

G

Gandhabba, 622 E. 11th St., New York, NY 10009

Gargoyle Magazine, P.O. Box 30906, Bethesda, MD 20814

Gesture Press, 68 Tyrrel Ave., Toronto, Ont., CANADA M6G 2G4

Granta, 44a Hobson St., Cambridge, CB1 1NL, ENGLAND

Graywolf Press, P.O. Box 75006, St. Paul, MN 55175

Great Point Press, Commercial Wharf, Nantucket, MA 02554

Great River Review, 211 W. 7th, Winona, MN 55987

Green's Magazine, P.O. Box 3236, Regina, Saskatchewan, CANADA S4P 3H1

Greenhouse Review Press, 3965 Bonny Doon Rd., Santa Cruz, CA 95060

Grue Magazine, P.O. Box 370, Times Sq. Mag., New York, NY 10108

Gull Books, Little Westkill Rd., RR#01, Box 273A, Prattsville, NY 12468

H

Hawaii Review, English Dept., Univ. of Hawaii, 1733 Donaghho Rd., Honolulu, HI 96822

Helicon Nine, P.O. Box 22412, Kansas City, MO 64113

Helix Press, 4410 Hickey, Corpus Christi, TX 78413

Henry Printing Co., P.O. Box 68, Greensburg, PA 15601

Hermes House Press, 39 Adare Place, Northampton, MA 01060

Hermitage, P.O. Box 410, Tenafly, NJ 07670

Hiram Poetry Review, P.O. Box 162, Hiram, OH 44234

The Hoboken Terminal, P.O. Box 841, Hoboken, NJ 07030

Howling Dog, 10917 W. Outer Dr., Detroit, MI 48223

The Hudson Review, 684 Park Ave., New York, NY 10021

Hutton Publications, P.O. Box 2377, Coeur d'Alene, ID 83814

Indiana Review, 316 N. Jordan Ave., Bloomington, IN 47405
Indra's Net, 78 Center St., Geneseo, NY 14454
Intertext, 2633 E. 17th Ave., Anchorage, AK 99508
Iowa Review, 308 EPB, Univ. of Iowa, Iowa City, IA 52242
Iowa Woman, P.O. Box 680, Iowa City, IA 52244
Ironwood, P.O. Box 40907, Tucson, AZ 85717

J

Jacar Press, P.O. Box 4, Wendell, NC 27591
The Jackpine Press, 1878 Meadowbrook Dr., Winston-Salem, NC
  27104
Jam Today, 372 Dunstable Rd., Tyngsboro, MA 01879
The James White Review, P.O. Box 3356, Traffic Sta., Minneapo-
  lis, MN 55403
Jewish Currents, 22 E. 17th St., Ste. 601, New York, NY 10003
Jukebox Terrorists with Typewriters, P.O. Box 1220, Belchertown,
  MA 01007

K

Kansas Quarterly, English Dept., Denison Hall, Kansas St. Univ.,
  Manhattan, KS 66506
Katallagete, Box 2307, College Sta., Berea, KY 40404
Kelsey St. Press, P.O. Box 9235, Berkeley, CA 94709
The Kenyon Review, Kenyon College, Gambier, OH 43022
Kick it Over, P.O. Box 5811, Sta. A, Toronto, Ont., CANADA
  M6G 1J2
The Kindred Spirit, Rt. 2, Box 111, St. John, KS 67576
Kinraddie Press, #87, Madrid, NM 87010

L

Lake Street Review Press, Box 7188, Powderhorn Sta., Minneapolis, MN 55407

Landscape, P.O. Box 7107, Berkeley, CA 94707

The Lapis Press, Inc., 1850 Union St., Ste. 466, San Francisco, CA 94123

Late Knocking, P.O. Box 336, Forest Hill, MD 21050

Laughing Waters Press, 1416 Euclid Ave., Boulder, CO 80302

Légèreté, L.I.W.U., P.O. Drawer 1410, Daphne, AL 36526

Liars' Corner Almanac, P.O. Box 657, Athens, OH 45701

Limberlost Press, P.O. Box 1563, Boise, ID 83701

Lips, P.O. Box 1348, Montclair, NJ 07042

The Literary Review, Fairleigh Dickinson Univ., 285 Madison Ave., Madison, NJ 07940

Lobster Tendencies Quarterly, P.O. Box 2555, Stuyvesant Sta., New York, NY 10009

The Lockhart Press, Box 1207, Port Townsend, WA 98368

Long Pond Review, English Dept., Suffolk Co. Community College, Selden, NY 11784

The Long Story, 11 Kingston St., North Andover, MA 01845

Loom Press, Box 1394, Lowell, MA 01853

Lorien House, P.O. Box 1112, Black Mountain, NC 28711

Lost and Found Times, see Luna Bisonte Prods.

Luna Bisonte Prods., 137 Leland Ave., Columbus, OH 43214

M

M.A.F. Press, Box 392, Portlandville, NY 13834

MSS Magazine, Univ. Center, SUNY, Binghamton, NY 13901

The MacGuffin, 18600 Haggerty Rd., Livonia, MI 48152

The Madison Review, English Dept., Univ. of Wisconsin, 600 N. Park St., Madison, WI 53706

The Malahat Review, Univ. of Victoria, P.O. Box 1700, Victoria, B.C. CANADA V8W 2Y2

Man-Root, Box 982, S. San Francisco, CA 94083

Manhattan Review, 304 Third Ave., Ste. 4A, New York, NY 10010

Manna, 4318 Minter School Rd., Sanford, NC 27330

MARK, Grad. Stud. Assoc., Univ. of Toledo, 2801 W. Bancroft ST., Toledo, OH 43606

Massachusetts Review, Memorial Hall, Univ. of Mass., Amherst, MA 01003

Memphis State Review, English Dept., Memphis State Univ., Memphis, TN 38152

Mercury House, 300 Montgomery St., Ste. 700, San Francisco, CA 94104

Metrosphere, English Dept., Box 32, Metropolitan State College, Denver, CO 80204

Mho & Mho Works, P.O. Box 7272, San Diego, CA 94107

Micah Publications, 255 Humphrey St., Marblehead, MA 01945

Michigan Quarterly Review, Univ. of Michigan, 3032 Rackham Bldg., Ann Arbor, MI 48109

Middlewood Press, P.O. Box 11236, Salt Lake City, UT 84147

Midwestern Writer's Showcase, P.O. Box 49, Jerico Springs, MO 64756

Minetta Review: Mandorla, 181 Thompson, #9, New York, NY 10012

The Missouri Review, English Dept., 231 A & S, Univ. of Missouri, Columbia, MO 65211

Modern Haiku, P.O. Box 1752, Madison, WI 53701

MUDFISH, 184 Franklin St., New York, NY 10013

Mystery Time, see Hutton Publications

N

NRG Magazine, 6735 SE 78th, Portland, OR 97206

Naked Man, English Dept., Kansas Univ., Lawrence, KS 66045

National Forum, 216 Petrie Hall, Auburn University, AL 36849

Negative Capability, 6116 Timberly Rd., N, Mobile, AL 36609

New England Review/Breadloaf Quarterly, Middlebury College, Middlebury, VT 05753

New Letters, Univ. of Missouri-K.C., 5100 Rockhill Rd., Kansas City, MO 64110

New Poets Series, Inc., 541 Piccadilly Rd., Baltimore, MD 21204

New Renaissance, 9 Heath Rd., Arlington, MA 02174

Next Exit, 92 Helen St., Kingston, Ont., CANADA K7L 4P3

Night Tree Press, 414 W. Thomas St., Rome, NY 13440

NIMROD, Arts & Humanities Council of Tulsa, 2210 S. Main, Tulsa, OK 74114

Nit & Wit, P.O. Box 627, Geneva, IL 60134

Northern Lit. Quarterly, 10 Murphy Hall, Univ. of Minn., Minneapolis, MN 55455

Northwest Review, 369 PLC, Univ. of Oregon, Eugene, OR 97403

Nostoc Magazine, see Arts End Books-Publishers
Notus, 2420 Walter Dr., Ann Arbor, MI 48103

O

The Ohio Review, Ellis Hall, Ohio Univ., Athens, OH 45701
The Old Red Kimono, Floyd Junior College, P.O. Box 1864, Rome, GA 30163
One-Shot Enterprises, 3379 Morrison Ave., #3, Cincinnati, OH 45220
Ontario Review, 9 Honey Brook Dr., Princeton, NJ 08540
Open Places, Box 2085, Stephens College, Columbia, MO 65215
Osiris, Box 297, Deerfield, MA 01342
Other Voices, 820 Ridge Rd., Highland Park, IL 60035
Outerbridge, College of Staten Island, 715 Ocean Terr., Staten Island, NY 10305
Owl Creek Press, 1620 N. 45th, Seattle, WA 98103
Oxford Magazine, Bachelor Hall, Miami Univ., Oxford, OH 45056
OYEZ Review, Roosevelt Univ., 430 S. Michigan Ave., Chicago, IL 60605

P

Painted Bride Quarterly, 230 Vine St., Philadelphia, PA 19106
The Panhandler, English Dept., Univ. of West Florida, Pensacola, FL 32514
The Paper, 1255 Nuuanu Ave., #1914, Honolulu, HI 96817
Paper Air Magazine, see Singing Horse Press
Parabola, 656 Broadway, New York, NY 10012
The Paris Review, 45-39 171 Pl., Flushing, NY 11358
Park Row Press, 1418 Park Row, LaJolla, CA 92037
Parnassus, P.O. Box 1384, Forest Park, GA 30051
Partisan Review, 141 Bay State Rd., Boston, MA 02215
Passages North, Bonifas Fine Arts Ctr., Escanaba, MI 49829
Paycock Press, P.O. Box 30906, Bethesda, MD 20814
Pencil Press Quarterly, P.O. Box 536177, Orlando, FL 32853
Penumbra Press, Annex 22, Univ. of Nebraska, Omaha, NE 68182
Pergot Press, 1001J Bridgeway, Ste. 227, Sausalito, CA 94965

Permanent Press, Noyac Rd., Sag Harbor, NY 11963

Phoebe, 4400 University Dr., Fairfax, VA 22030

Piedmont Literary Review, P.O. Box 3656, Danville, VA 24543

Pigwidgeon Press, P.O. Box 76, Derby Line, VT 05830

Pikestaff Forum, P.O. Box 127, Normal, IL 61761

Pineapple Press, Inc., P.O. Box 314, Englewood, FL 33533

Plainview Press, 1509 Dexter, Austin, TX 78704

Ploughshares, Box 529, Cambridge, MA 02139

Pocahontas Press, Inc., 2805 Wellesley Court, Blacksburg, VA 24060

Poet & Critic, 203 Ross Hall, Iowa State Univ., Ames, IA 50010

Poet Lore, 4000 Albemarle St., NW, Washington, DC 20016

Poetry Around, 436 Elm, Norman, OK 73069

Poetry East, 404 W. Fond du Lac, Ripon, WI 54971

Poets On, Box 255, Chaplin, CT 06235

Point Riders Press, P.O. Box 2731, Norman, OK 73070

The Post-Apollo Press, 35 Marie St., Sausalito, CA 94965

Prairie Fire, 208-100 Arthur St., Winnipeg, Manitoba, CANADA R3B 1H3

Prairie Journal Press, P.O. Box 6997, Sta "G", Calgary, Alberta, CANADA T3A 3G2

Prairie Schooner, 201 Andrews, Univ. of Nebraska, Lincoln, NE 68588

Press Porcĕpic, 235-560 Johnson St., Victoria, B.C. CANADA V8W 3C6

Primavera, 1212 E. 59th St., Chicago, IL 60637

Processed World, 41 Sutter St., #1829, San Francisco, CA 94104

Proper Tales Press, P.O. Box 789, Sta. F, Toronto, Ont., CANADA M4X 2N7

The Pterodactyl Press, Main Street, Cumberland, IA 50843

Puckerbrush Review, 76 Main St., Orono, ME 04473

Puerto del Sol, College of Arts & Sc., Box 3E, New Mexico St. Univ., Las Cruces, NM 88001

Q

Quarry Press, P.O. Box 1061, Kingston, Ont. CANADA K7L 4Y5

Quarry West, Porter College, Univ. of California, Santa Cruz, CA 95064

Quarterly West, 312 Olpin Union, Univ. of Utah, Salt Lake City, UT 84112

Quarto, 608 Lewisohn Hall, Columbia Univ., New York, NY 10027

Quixote, 1810 Marshall, Houston, TX 77098

R

RFD, Rte. 1, Box 127E, Bakersville, NC 28705

RaJAH, 4024 MLB, Univ. of Michigan, Ann Arbor, MI 48109

Raw Dog Press, 128 Harvey Ave., Doylestown, PA 18901

Readers International, P.O. Box 959, Columbia, LA 71418

Red Bass, P.O. Box 10258, Tallahassee, FL 32302

Reflect, 3306 Argonne Ave., Norfolk, VA 23509

renegade, see Point Riders Press

Rhyme Time, see Hutton Publications

River Styx, 14 S. Euclid, St. Louis, MO 63108

Rocky Top Publications, P.O. Box 33, Stamford, NY 12167

The Round Table, 375 Oakdale Dr., Rochester, NY 14618

Rowan Tree Press, 124 Chestnut St., Boston, MA 02108

The Rydal Press, 960 Camino Santander, Santa Fe, NM 87501

S

SPWAO Showcase, 2926 Wicklow PL., Charlotte, NC 28205

Sagittarius Press, 930 Taylor, Port Townsend, WA 98368

Salthouse, P.O. Box 11537, Milwaukee, WI 53211

Samisdat, Box 129, Richford, VT 05476

Sandscript, Cape Cod Writers Inc., Box 333, Cummaquid, MA 02637

Saturday Press, Inc., P.O. Box 884, Upper Montclair, NJ 07043

Scavenger's Newsletter, 519 Ellinwood, Osage City, KS 66523

Score, 595 Merritt Ave., #2, Oakland, CA 94610

Sea of Amethyst, 55 Revere St., #5, Boston, MA 02114

Second Coming, P.O. Box 31249, San Francisco, CA 94131

Seems, English Dept., P.O. Box 359, Lakeland College, Sheboygan, WI 53211

Seneca Review, Hobart & William Smith Colleges, Geneva, NY 14456

Shadow Press, P.O. Box 8803, Minneapolis, MN 55408

The Sheep Meadow Press, P.O. Box 1345, Riverdale-on-Hudson, NY 10471

Shenandoah, Box 722, Lexington, VA 24450

The Short Story Review, P.O. Box 882108, San Francisco, CA 94188

Sign of the Times, P.O. Box 70672, Seattle, WA 98107

Signpost Press, Inc., 1412 N. State St., Bellingham, WA 98225

Singing Horse Press, P.O. Box 40034, Philadelphia, PA 19106

Skylark, Purdue Univ. Calumet, Hammond, IN 46323

Sonora Review, English Dept., Univ. of Arizona, Tucson, AZ 85721

South Coast Poetry Journal, English Dept., Calif. St. Univ., Fullerton, CA 92634

The South Dakota Review, Univ. of South Dakota, Vermillion, SD 57069

Southern Humanities Review, Auburn Univ., Auburn, AL

Southern Poetry Review, English Dept., Univ. of North Carolina, Charlotte, NC 28223

Southern Review, English Dept., Univ. of Adelaide, GPO Box 498, Adelaide, SOUTH AUSTRALIA 5001

Southwest Review, Box 4374, Southern Methodist Univ., Dallas, TX 75275

Space and Time, 138 W. 70th St., 4B, New York, NY 10023

Spinsters/Aunt Lute, P.O. Box 410687, San Francisco, CA 94141

Spitball, Literary Baseball Magazine, 6224 Collegevue Pl., Cincinnati, OH 45224

St. Andrews Review, St. Andrews Presbyterian College, Laurinburg, NC 28352

St. Louis Journalism Review, 8380 Olive Blvd., St. Louis, MO 63132

Star Line, P.O. Box 1764, Cambridge, MA 02238

Still Point Press, 4222 Willow Grove Rd., Dallas, TX 75220

Stone Country, P.O. Box 132, Menemsha, MA 02552

Stone Drum, P.O. Box 233, Valley View, TX 76272

Stormline Press, Inc., P.O. Box 593, Urbana, IL 61801

Story Quarterly, 175 W. 107th St., #6, New York, NY 10025

Story Time, see Hutton Publications

Studia Mystica, California St., Univ., Sacramento, CA 95819

SUB ROSA, 840 Palisade Ave., #2A, Teaneck, NJ 07666

Sulfur, 852 S. Bedford St., Los Angeles, CA 90035
The Sun, 412 W. Rosemary St., Chapel Hill, NC 27514
SUNRUST, see Dawn Valley Press
Sunstone Press, P.O. Box 2321, Santa Fe, NM 87504
Swallow's Tale Press, P.O. Box 930040, Norcross, GA 30093

T

Talking Leaves Press, 2419 Crabtree Dr., Ft. Collins, CO 80521
The Texas Review, Sam Houston State Univ., Huntsville, TX 77341
Thistledown Press, ltd., 668 East Place, Saskatoon, Saskatchewan, CANADA S7J 2Z5
Thompson & Rutter, Inc., P.O. Box 297, Grantham, NH 03753
The Threepenny Review, P.O. Box 9131, Berkeley, CA 94709
Threshold Books, RD 3, Box 1350, Putney, VT 05346
Tilted Planet Press, P.O. Box 8646, Austin, TX 78713
Tin Wreath, P.O. Box 13401, Albany, NY 12212
Tiptoe Publishing, P.O. Box 206, Naselle, WA 98638
Tissa, Inc., Rte. 1, Box 349A, Culpepper, VA 22701
Tombouctou Books, Box 265, Bolinas, CA 95924
Touchstone, P.O. Box 42331, Houston, TX 77042
Treetop Panorama, RR 1, Box 160, Payson, IL 62360
TriQuarterly, Northwestern Univ., 1735 Benson Ave., Evanston, IL 60201
Trivia, P.O. Box 606, N. Amherst, MA 01059
Trout Creek Press, 5976 Billings Rd., Parkdale, OR 97041
Trouvere Company, Rt. 2, Box 290, Eclectic, AL 36024
Turkey Press, 6746 Sueno Rd., Isla Vista, CA 93117

U

USC Professional Writing Program, DCC 206, Univ. of So. Calif., Los Angeles, CA 90089
Unicorn Press, Inc., P.O. Box 3307, Greensboro, NC 27402
University Editions, 4937 Humphrey Rd., Huntington, W VA 25704

University of Illinois Press, 54 E. Gregory Dr., Champaign, IL 61820

Unknowns, 1900 Century Blvd., NE, Ste. 1, Atlanta, GA 30345

V

Vehicule Press, P.O.B. 125, Place du Parc Sta., Montreal, Que. CANADA H2W 2M9

ViAztlan Magazine, 122 N. Cherry St., San Antonio, TX 79202

W

WARM Journal, 414 First Ave., N. Minneapolis, MN 55401

Washington Book Review, 930 F St., NW, Ste. 707, Washington, DC 20004

Waterfront Press, 52 Maple Ave., Maplewood, NJ 07040

Waves, 79 Denham Dr., Richmond Hill, Ont., CANADA L4C 6H9

Wayland Press, 2640 E. 12th Ave., Box 715, Denver, CO 80206

Webster Review, Webster Univ., Webster Groves, MO 63119

West Branch, English Dept., Bucknell Univ., Lewisburg, PA 17837

West Hills Review, 246 Walt Whitman Rd., Huntington Station, NY 11746

What, Box 338, Sta. J, Toronto, Ont., CANADA M4J 4Y8

The Willow Bee Publishing House, Box 9, Saratoga, WY 82331

Willow Springs, P.U.B. P.O. Box 1063, MS-1, Eastern Washington Univ., Cheney, WA 99004

Wind Magazine, RFD#1, Box 809K, Pikeville, KY 41501

Wind Vein Press, P.O. Box 462, Ketchum, ID 83340

The Windham Phoenix, P.O. Box 752, Willimantic, CT 06226

Wisconsin Academy Review, 1922 University Ave., Madison, WI 53705

The Wise Woman, 2441 Cordova St., Oakland, CA 94602

Without Halos, P.O. Box 1342, Point Pleasant Beach, NJ 08742

The Women's List, see Cold Knee Mountain Press

Woodbine House, 10400 Connecticut Ave., Ste. 512, Kensington, MD 20895

Woods Colt Press, P.O. Box 22524, Kansas City, MO 64113

The Wooster Review, College of Wooster, Wooster, OH 44691

Word Beat Press, P.O. Box 22310, Flagstaff, AZ 86002

The Word Works, Inc., P.O. Box 42164, Washington, DC 20015

World Peace University Publications, 2519 E. Ellendale, Dallas, OR 97338

Wormwood Review, P.O. Box 8840, Stockton, CA 95208

Wright, Stuart (Publisher), Wake Forest Univ., Educ. Dept., Box 7266, Winston-Salem, NC 27109

WRIT Magazine, Two Sussex Ave., Toronto, CANADA M5S 1J5

Writers' Forum, P.O. Box 7150, Univ. of Colorado, Colorado Springs, CO 80933

Writer's Info, see Hutton Publications

Wyoming, The Hub of the Wheel, see Willow Bee Publ. House

Y

The Yale Review, 1902A Yale Sta., New Haven, CT 06520

Yossarian Universal News Service, P.O. Box 236, Millbrae, CA 94030

Z

Zephyr Press, 13 Robinson St., Somerville, MA 02144

ZYZZYVA, 41 Sutter St., Ste. 1400, San Francisco, CA 94104

INDEX

The following is a listing in alphabetical order by author's last name of works reprinted in the first twelve *Pushcart Prize* editions.

CONTRIBUTORS'
NOTES

OPAL PALMER ADISA was born in Kingston, Jamaica. Her books include *Market Woman* and *Pina, the Many-Eyed Fruit,* a children's story. She lives in Oakland, California.

JOHN BERGER is the author of *Ways of Seeing, Pig Earth, Once in Europa* and other books. He lives in France.

MARTHA BERGLAND is completing a collection of stories tentatively called *A Farm Under A Lake*. She lives in Milwaukee.

NORBERT BLEI's novels include *Adventure in An American's Literature* and *The Second Novel*. His work has appeared in *The New Yorker, TriQuarterly* and elsewhere.

PHILIP BOOTH lives in Castine, Maine. His seventh book of poems, *Relations: Selected Poems 1950–1985,* is just out from Viking.

ROSELLEN BROWN's most recent novels, *Civil Wars* and *Tender Mercies* are both available from Penguin. She lives in Houston, Texas.

ROBERT COHEN's first novel will be published by Harper and Row in 1988. He lives in New York.

STEPHEN DOBYNS' latest book is *Cemetery Nights,* published by Viking.

CAROL EMSHWILLER has published in *Croton Review, New Directions, 13th Moon,* and *TriQuarterly*. She lives in California.

TESS GALLAGHER's *New And Selected Poems* is just out from Graywolf Press. She lives in Pt. Angeles, Washington.

WILLIAM H. GASS is the author of seven books. His *Habitations of the Word* won the National Book Critics Circle Award in 1986.

ALBERT GOLDBARTH's most recent book is *Arts and Sciences*. He teaches at Wichita State University.

ALLEN GROSSMAN teaches at Brandheis University and is the author of six collections of poetry.

THOM GUNN is author of *Passages of Joy, Jack Straw's Castle* and numerous books of poetry. He lives in San Francisco.

DONALD HALL's most recent poetry collection is *The Happy Man* (Random House). He lives in New Hampshire.

DAN HALPERN is editor of Ecco Press and *Antaeus*. He lives in New York.

O. B. HARDISON, Jr's books include *Entering the Maze: Identity and Change in Modern Culture* (Oxford University Press). He is former director of the Folger Shakespeare Library in Washington and currently teaches at Georgetown University.

SEAMUS HEANEY divides his time between Dublin and Harvard. His new book of poems, *The Haw Lantern*, is just out.

LYN HEJINIAN's work previously appeared in *Pushcart Prize VI*. She lives in Berkeley, California and is the publisher of Tuumba Press.

PATRICIA HENLEY is the author of *Learning to Die*, a poetry chapbook, and *Friday Night at Silver Star* (Graywolf Press). She teaches at Purdue University.

SUSAN HOWE lives in Guilford, Connecticut and is the author of *My Emily Dickinson* (North Atlantic Books).

RICHARD JACKSON's most recent poetry gathering is *Worlds Apart* (University of Alabama Press). He teaches at the University of Tennessee.

HAROLD JAFFE is co-editor of *Fiction International* and lives in San Diego. He is the author of two novels; *Dos Indios* (1983) and *Mole's Pity* (1979) and is at work on a new group of fictions.

ELIZABETH JOLLEY lives near Perth, Australia. Her most recent book was just published by Persea Books, New York.

DONALD JUSTICE's most recent collection of poetry, *The Sunset Maker*, has just been published by Atheneum.

GORDON LISH is an editor at Knopf and editor of *The Quarterly*. He is the author of two novels and teaches at New York University and Columbia.

PHILLIP LOPATE's latest novel is *The Rag Merchant* (Viking). He teaches at the University of Houston.

DEVORAH MAJOR is director of California's Poets in the Schools. Her work has appeared in *Y'Bird, River Styx, Black Scholar* and elsewhere.

JEAN MCGARRY has published *Airs of Providence*, a collection of short fiction (Johns Hopkins University Press). Her new book, *The Very Rich Hours*, is just out from the same publisher.

THOMAS McGRATH's *New and Selected Poems* is forthcoming from Copper Canyon Press. He lives in Minneapolis.

SANDRA McPHERSON is the author of poetry collections from Ecco Press, Owl Creek Press and Trace Editions. She teaches at the University of California, Davis.

CZESLAW MILOSZ was awarded the Nobel Prize for Literature in 1980. He lives in Berkeley, California.

FAE MYENNE NG has published in *The Crescent Review* and *City Lights Review*. She is a Bunting Fellow at Radcliffe.

JOYCE CAROL OATES teaches at Princeton University. She is the author of many books and has appeared in Pushcart Prizes I, VII and VIII.

MICHAEL PALMER's books include *Without Music, The Circular Gates,* and *Notes for Echo Lake.* He is a choreographer with the Margaret Jenkins Dance Company, and lives in San Francisco.

ROBERT PINSKY's most recent book, *History of My Heart,* was awarded the William Carlos Williams Prize by the Poetry Society of America.

C. E. POVERMAN lives and works in Tucson. His latest novel, *Solomon's Daughter* (Viking) is included in the Penguin Contemporary American Fiction series.

IRINA RATUSHINSKAIA was sentenced in 1983 to 12 years in a labor camp in the Soviet Union but was released in 1986. She is a highly regarded poet. (See references to her in William Gass' essay in this edition, page 165.)

DAVID REID is a contributor to *Vanity Fair* and is editor of *University Publishing.* He lives in San Diego.

LESLIE SCALAPINO has published two books with North Point Press and a third is set for 1988. She lives in Oakland, California.

LLOYD SCHWARTZ is classical music critic for the *Boston Phoenix.* He teaches at the *University of Massachusetts,* Boston.

LOUIS SIMPSON was awarded the Pulitzer Prize for his poetry. He lives on Long Island, New York.

ELIZABETH SPENCER is the author of *The Sale Line* (Doubleday) and many other books and stories. She teaches at the University of North Carolina, Chapel Hill.

GEORGE STARBUCK received the Lenore Marshall/Nation prize in 1983. His next book is *The Book of Rows.*

GERALD STERN's new poetry gathering, *Lovesick,* is just out from Harper and Row. He teaches at the University of Iowa.

MARK STRAND is the author of six volumes of poetry, most recently *Selected Poems* (Atheneum). He lives in Salt Lake City.

SUSAN TICHY's next book is *A Smell of Burning Starts the Day* (Wesleyan University Press). She teaches at Ohio University.

BILL TREMBLAY's poems have appeared in *Chicago Review, Tar River Poetry, Minnesota Review, Ironwood* and elsewhere. He is an editor of *Colorado Review*.

LEE UPTON's poems have appeared in *American Poetry Review, Yale Review, Poetry, Field* and elsewhere.

ELIOT WEINBERGER is the author of *Works on Paper* and the translator of *The Collected Poems of Octavio Paz*, both from New Directions. His *19 Ways of Looking at Wang Wei* is just out from Moyer-Bell.

PAUL WEST's most recent book is *Sheer Fiction*, a selection of his essays (McPherson & Co.). He lives in Ithaca, New York.

C. K. WILLIAMS lives in Paris and is the author of the poetry collections *I Am The Better Name, With Ignorance,* and *TAR*.

For a complete list of books available from Penguin in the United States, write to Dept. DG, Penguin Books, 299 Murray Hill Parkway, East Rutherford, New Jersey 07073.

For a complete list of books available from Penguin in Canada, write to Penguin Books Canada Limited, 2801 John Street, Markham, Ontario L3R 1B4.